D1710318

MAKING OF THE AMERICAN WEST

Selected titles in the Perspectives in American Social History series

PERSPECTIVES IN
AMERICAN SOCIAL HISTORY

Making of the American West

People and Perspectives

Benjamin H. Johnson, Editor
Peter C. Mancall, Series Editor

Santa Barbara, California · Denver, Colorado · Oxford, England

Library of Congress Cataloging-in-Publication Data

Making of the American West / edited by Benjamin H. Johnson.
 p. cm. — (Perspectives in American social history series)
 Includes bibliographical references and index.
 ISBN 978-1-85109-763-0 (hard copy : alk. paper) — ISBN 978-1-85109-768-5 (ebook)   1. West (U.S.)—History.   2. West (U.S.)—Social conditions.   3. Frontier and pioneer life—West (U.S.)   4. West (U.S.)—Ethnic relations.   5. West (U.S.)—Economic conditions.

 F591.M28 2007
 978—dc22

                                                                                    2007004384

09 08 07   10 9 8 7 6 5 4 3 2 1

This book is also available on the World Wide Web as an eBook. Visit abc-clio.com for details.

ABC-CLIO, Inc.
130 Cremona Drive, P.O. Box 1911
Santa Barbara, California 93116-1911

Production Editor: Vicki Moran
Editorial Assistant: Sara Springer
Production Manager: Don Schmidt
Media Editor: Julie Dunbar
Media Manager: Caroline Price
File Management Coordinator: Paula Gerard

for Michelle, of course

Contents

Series Introduction

Social history is, simply put, the study of past societies. More specifically, social historians attempt to describe societies in their totality, and hence often eschew analysis of politics and ideas. Though many social historians argue that it is impossible to understand how societies functioned without some consideration of the ways that politics works on a daily basis or what ideas could be found circulating at any given time, they tend to pay little attention to the formal arenas of electoral politics or intellectual currents. In the United States, social historians have been engaged in describing components of the population which had earlier often escaped formal analysis, notably women, members of ethnic or cultural minorities, or those who had fewer economic opportunities than the elite.

Social history became a vibrant discipline in the United States after it had already gained enormous influence in Western Europe. In France, social history in its modern form emerged with the rising prominence of a group of scholars associated with the journal *Annales Economie, Societé, Civilisation* (or *Annales ESC* as it is known). In its pages and in a series of books from historians affiliated with the École des Hautes Études en Sciences Sociale in Paris, brilliant historians such as Marc Bloch, Jacques Le Goff, and Emanuel LeRoy Ladurie described seemingly every aspect of French society. Among the masterpieces of this historical reconstruction was Fernand Braudel's monumental study, *The Mediterranean and the Mediterranean World in the Age of Philip II*, published first in Paris in 1946 and in a revised edition in English in 1972. In this work Braudel argued that the only way to understand a place in its totality was to describe its environment, its social and economic structures, and its political systems. In Britain the emphasis of social historians has been less on questions of environment, per se, than in a description of human communities in all their complexities. For example, social historians there have taken advantage of that nation's remarkable local archives to reconstruct the history of the family and details of its rural past. Works such as Peter Laslett's *The World We Have Lost*, first printed in 1966, and the multi-authored *Agrarian History of England and Wales*, which began to appear in print in 1967, revealed that painstaking work could reveal the lives and habits of individuals who never previously attracted the interest of biographers, demographers, or most historians.

Social history in the United States gained a large following in the second half of the twentieth century, especially during the 1960s and 1970s. Its development sprang from political, technical, and intellectual impulses deeply embedded in the culture of the modern university. The politics of civil rights and social reform fueled the passions of historians who strove to tell the stories of the underclass. They benefited from the adoption by historians of statistical analysis, which allowed scholars to trace where individuals lived, how often they moved, what kinds of jobs they took, and whether their economic status declined, stagnated, or improved over time. As history departments expanded, many who emerged from graduate schools focused their attention on groups previously ignored or marginalized. Women's history became a central concern among American historians, as did the history of African Americans, Native Americans, Latinos and others. These historians pushed historical study in the United States farther away from the study of formal politics and intellectual trends. Though few Americanists could achieve the technical brilliance of some social historians in Europe, collectively they have been engaged in a vast act of description, with the goal of describing seemingly every facet of life from 1492 to the present.

The sixteen volumes in this series together represent the continuing efforts of historians to describe American society. Most of the volumes focus on chronological areas, from the broad sweep of the colonial era to the more narrowly defined collections of essays on the eras of the Cold War, the Baby Boom, and America in the age of the Vietnam War. The series also includes entire volumes on the epochs that defined the nation, the American Revolution and the Civil War, as well as volumes dedicated to the process of westward expansion, women's rights, and African-American history.

This social history series derives its strength from the talented editors of individual volumes. Each editor is an expert in his or her own field who selected and organized the contents of his or her volume. Editors solicited other experienced historians to write individual essays. Every volume contains first-rate analysis complemented by lively anecdotes designed to reveal the complex contours of specific historical moments. The many illustrations to be found in these volumes testify too to the recognition that any society can be understood not only by the texts that its participants produce but also by the images that they craft. Primary source documents in each volume will allow interested readers to pursue some specific topics in greater depth, and each volume contains a chronology to provide guidance to the flow of events over time. These tools—anecdotes, images, texts, and timelines—allow readers to gauge the inner workings of America in particular periods and yet also to glimpse connections between eras.

The articles in these volumes testify to the abundant strengths of historical scholarship in the United States in the early years of the twenty-first century. Despite the occasional academic contest that flares into public notice, or the self-serving cant of politicians who want to manipulate the nation's past for partisan ends—for example, in debates over the second amendment to the United States Constitution and what it means about potential limits to the rights of gun ownership—the articles here all reveal the vast increase in knowledge of the American past that has taken place over the last half century. Social historians do not dominate history faculties in American colleges and universities, but no one could deny them a seat at the intellectual table. Without their efforts, intellectual, cultural, and political historians would be hard pressed to understand why certain ideas circulated when they did, why some religious movements prospered or foundered, how developments in fields such as medicine and engineering reflected larger concerns, and what shaped the world we inhabit.

Fernand Braudel and his colleagues envisioned entire laboratories of historians in which scholars working together would be able to produce *histoire totale:* total history. Historians today seek more humble goals for our collective enterprise. But as the richly textured essays in these volumes reveal, scholarly collaboration has in fact brought us much closer to that dream. These volumes do not and cannot include every aspect of American history. However, every page reveals something interesting or valuable about how American society functioned. Together, these books suggest the crucial necessity of stepping back to view the grand complexities of the past rather than pursuing narrower prospects and lesser goals.

Peter C. Mancall

Series Editor

Introduction

Americans know a great deal about the West, or at least they think they do. It is a place of wide open spaces, where fiercely independent people—ranchers, cowboys, and Indians, among others—live in direct contact with some of the most splendid natural areas on the planet. Many think of it as somehow the most quintessentially American region—where national self-conceptions of ruggedness and an egalitarian ethos are at their strongest. Just ask the Marlboro Man, John Wayne, or Clint Eastwood.

This book offers a ground-level view into that historical and mythic terrain. It explores the settlement, conquest, and incorporation of the American West from the viewpoints of the diverse groups that lived through these processes. At the start of the nineteenth century, North America west of the Mississippi river was the domain of Spanish settlers and a plethora of Indian peoples, but well beyond the control of any one people or nation. The United States, still in its infancy, and the vast empires of Spain, England, and France all claimed or aspired to hold portions of this territory, but none had extensively explored its landscape or come to know its many native groups. Within decades, however, the expansionistic United States had effectively asserted its control over the region, boldly seizing Texas and the rest of the southwest from Mexico, risking war with England to press its claims in the Pacific Northwest, and militarily defeating powerful native groups. The continent's map took on its modern form. Americans flocked to these territories—ancestral homelands for many of those already there, but new to those heading west by wagon trail, foot, and later, rail.

By the early twentieth century, the West had grown so much and so fast that the United States was unthinkable in its absence. Gold from California, Nevada, and Colorado created vast new fortunes. Pacific ports like San Francisco and Seattle were key nodes of trade with Asia. Western iron, coal, and oil fueled the United States' rise as the globe's preeminent industrial producer. Wheat from the prairie states and fruits and vegetables from California fed a rapidly-growing and increasingly urban nation. American soldiers and officers went from fighting Indian wars, to combating rebels against American rule in the Philippines, to fighting on the western front in the First World War. Cities like Denver and Los Angeles dominated vast hinterlands. In the realm of culture, westerns were among the most popular dime novels and motion pictures of the early twentieth century. Scenic parts of the West preserved as National Parks and Forests embodied Americans' newfound appreciation for wilderness and belief in the sustainable use of natural resources.

Although the process of conquering and settling the West involved high-level politics, diplomacy, and wars, it was also driven by the ordinary women and men who are the focus of this book. Western history was made by such people as the traders and trappers who often served as bridges between American society and Indian peoples, by the tens of thousands of eastern farm families who packed their belongings into wagons and headed west on the Oregon trail, and by the Lakota and Hispanic farmers of New Mexico who resisted the American onslaught. Migrants from south China and Chile to the gold fields of California, and from the slums of England to the Mormon promised land of Desert, made the settlement of the West a story of global proportions.

This book tells the larger story of Western history through the stories of these and other peoples, from the early nineteenth century through the region's full incorporation into national political, economic, and cultural life by the 1910s. Each stand-alone chapter profiles a specific group, beginning with a discussion of the Indian peoples who lived in the region long before there was such a thing as the United States, and ending with a look at some of the artists and boosters who did so much to fix certain images of the West in the modern American mind. Within each chapter, a sidebar tells the story of a representative or particularly fascinating individual or family from the group in question. Following the chapters is a small set of primary source documents from the time that allow further explorations into this fascinating history.

Some of these groups and individuals are familiar staples of the Western past. In these chapters, cowboys ride the range. Indians and settlers come into conflict. Custer leads the 7th Cavalry to the worse defeat in U.S. military history. Miners pan for gold in streams of the Sierra. Chinese workers lay track for the transcontinental railroad. The Wells Fargo company runs stagecoach deliveries. Mormons flee persecution to found their own homeland in the Great Basin. Outlaws and bad men wreak violence on Western communities.

Even these familiar characters, however, act in what may be surprising ways. Cowboys go on strike. Indians move to cities in search of work that reservations can't offer, use the programs meant to destroy their cultures to learn new ways of standing up for their people, and organize political pressure groups. Soldiers find boredom more often than the thrill of combat and loathe their own officers as intensely as their likely antagonists on the battlefield. Miners find themselves the disgruntled employees of distant, impersonal corporations.

The book also includes other individuals and groups who are not necessarily thought of as "Western," but who play key roles in making this history. African Americans flee the South after the end of Reconstruction, hoping to find their own freedom in the West. Savvy business tycoons rely on the federal government as much as their own ingenuity and hard work. Different groups of women find new demands but sometimes new freedoms in different parts of the West. Mexican migrants in search of work maintain the region's traditional ties to the Meso-American heartland. And humans are not the only actors here: Animals play key roles in the lives of different westerners, and become the subjects of stories and legends that people tell.

The documents similarly blend the familiar and the surprising. The Ghost Dance movement, which helped provoke the infamous 1890 massacre at Wounded Knee, is discussed here, but in a document in which Indians speak of Jesus coming to them after being crucified by whites. Men labor underground in trying and shocking conditions. An old man looks back on his life, emphasizing faith, family, and community, even as he offers frank appraisals of his father's multiple wives. The Constitution and Declaration of Independence are invoked to protest ill treatment, but by a Hispanic rebel. The story of crossing the continent is told, but by a woman as preoccupied with the onerous demands of childcare and cooking as with the larger triumph of moving west.

The West has always been an idea as much as a place. This is as true of Western historians as the people whom they study. How historians study the west—what they mean by the "West," who qualifies as a "Westerner," and what relationship western history has to the wider histories of North America, Indian peoples, and the United States—has changed dramatically over the last century.

The work of Frederick Jackson Turner, one of the most important intellectuals and historians of U.S. history, shaped Western history for many decades. Turner first came to prominence by giving a talk entitled "The Significance of the Frontier in American History," at a conference in Chicago in 1893, held at the World Fair commemorating the 400th anniversary of Columbus' voyage. He was prompted by the declaration of the federal census bureau that the continent was now so populated that the frontier had "closed." With the frontier now officially at an end, Turner tried to state as clearly as possible what its influences had been. In the process, he articulated one of the most influential and controversial ways of understanding not just Western history, but all of American history.

"Up to our own day," he told his audience, "American history has been in a large degree the history of the colonization of the Great West. The existence of an area of free land, its continuous recession, and the advance of American settlement westward, explain American development" (Turner in Faragher 1994, p. 31). The frontier, which he called "the meeting point between savagery and civilization," not only shaped American culture, but did so in extraordinarily positive ways: "American social development has been continually beginning over again on the frontier. This perennial rebirth, this fluidity of American life, this expansion westward with its new opportunities, its continuous touch with the simplicity of primitive society, furnish the forces dominating the American character" (ibid., p. 32). Now that the frontier was over, the United States had entered a new phase in its history.

Turner's essay has accurately been called the "single most influential piece of writing in the history of American history" (Faragher 1994, p. 1). By crystallizing themes already in circulation in popular culture—many members of his audience in Chicago attended Buffalo Bill's Wild West Show that week, where they would have seen a celebration of the frontier that paralleled Turner's academic arguments—Turner secured an influence far beyond a narrow range of historical specialists. Theodore Roosevelt praised his essay, western films enacted many of his ideas, and Turner's thesis was a dominant way of understanding the American past through the 1960s.

More than a century after his address, however, historians are deeply divided over the validity of the Turner thesis. Most scholars of the American past would now question his assumption that the United States is so distinct from other countries, a nation fundamentally more egalitarian or democratic than other western industrial nations. At the very least, they would add slavery and its legacies and the industrial revolution—forces that Turner only mentioned in passing—to the major factors accounting for American development.

Even within the community of Western historians, the Turner thesis has been met with skepticism and even outright hostility, particularly since the 1980s, when a group of scholars loosely known as "New Western Historians" emerged. As a group these scholars told a much more sobering story about the Western past. There were losers as well as winners in the making of the West, they insisted, pointing in particular to Indians and Hispanics subjected to violent conquest and a rule by outsiders that they had not requested. What was "free land" to Turner and the white pioneers he celebrated was in fact, they argued, somebody else's home, taken by violence. For these people, the making of the West was all about defeat and subjugation, not freedom and democracy. Even the archetypal figures of the older story—ranchers, yeoman farmers, and miners—were often overcome by the challenges of the region's harsh environment and the transient nature of its human communities. To meet these challenges they were as likely to rely on the structures of larger communities as individual fortitude—consider the remarkable success of the close-knit Mormons. And if anything, they were more dependent on the concentrated power of corporations like the railroads than were other Americans.

Moreover, these scholars argued, white westerners, far from being more in touch with "primitive" conditions, were more likely than most Americans to live in cities, and the federal government played a larger role in their region than elsewhere. After all, at the start of the twenty-first century, it still owns nearly half of the lands of the eleven westernmost states. Turner's focus on the supposed "closing" of the frontier struck many of these authors as particularly dangerous, for it artificially cut off the modern, twentieth century West from its origins in the nineteenth century, falsely suggesting that Western history did not need to include the twentieth century. As with the popular imagination and the older scholarship, this new body of literature placed the west at the center of American history, but in a more sober and less celebratory way. A racially diverse nation with an advanced corporate economy and a powerful central state could still look to the Western past for much of its origins. Western history still speaks to the present.

The recent contentious debates over the Western past make it all the more interesting to study and teach. The authors in this volume adopt no single position on these matters, either individually or collectively. Instead, these essays and documents (along with their own, sometimes differing arguments and interpretations) give readers the materials with which to construct their own understandings of Western history. They do so by focusing on the experiences of a wide range of people involved in the making of this history. Although the volume is organized by different groups, there is extensive overlap between the chapters. There were, for example, black soldiers, Latino entrepreneurs, Asian workers, Indian artists, and women outlaws. And of course not all members of a particular group experienced this history in similar ways, or agreed with one another. Consider that Mormons were subjected to savage violence by their fellow white Americans, that soldiers were deeply divided by race and class, and that workers had very different ideas about the ways they should organize to protect their interests.

While each chapter retains its focus on a discrete group of people, several large themes link these essays and their subject together. One underlying assumption is that people make their own history—that the past is not the unfolding of any kind of pre-ordained plan or the product of mechanistic social forces, but rather the outcome of the different needs, desires, visions, and aspirations of human beings. This is not to say that people got what they wanted, or that there weren't victims in this history. The essay on Indian peoples, for example, discusses the terrible losses that came with the conquest of the West, and the chapters on women, Asians, and Latinos all discuss the daunting obstacles and suffering that many of their subjects faced. But there is also considerable triumph here, even for those, like Indians, who faced the longest odds. People make their own history, even if not under circumstances of their choosing.

A second theme is that the historical actors discussed here attached their own explanations and meanings to the circumstances of their lives. They too, in a sense, were Western historians, seeking to interpret the past to understand their own present. And like contemporary historians, they held different and sometimes conflicting understandings of their past and present. Consider the very term "West." Americans moving to Oregon, Colorado, or the Plains states thought of their new home as the "West," but to Chinese migrants it would have made more sense to call these very same places the "East." For migrants from Mexico and elsewhere in Latin America, "North" would have been a better term. Mormons may have gotten to the Salt Lake Valley by heading west, but they understood their new home in religious terms, as the re-birth of Zion. Indeed, these essays repeatedly show how active and creative a mental life even ordinary, uneducated women and men had. This theme is the clearest in the essay on artists and boosters, which discusses the use of images to offer very specific ideas about what the West was and wasn't and who was and wasn't a westerner, but it also emerges in the discussion of others—the stories hunters told about their animals, the eloquent aspirations of backwoods trappers for creativity and renewal, and the hopes that workers held for a world where their labor would earn not just more money but more respect.

One major way people understood the world around them was by re-sorting to race, a third major theme in these essays. By the time that Euro-Americans moved into the West in the nineteenth century, most believed that humanity could be divided into distinct races—people from distinct backgrounds and with distinct physical and mental attributes that would be passed on to their descendants. Race in fact has no real basis in biol-ogy—people from one supposed "race" differ from one another as much as they differ from those of another "race"—and many people had ances-tors from multiple "races." Nevertheless, race shaped peoples' experiences in fundamental ways. Thus the experiences of white pioneers, supported by the 1862 Homestead Act and other federal measures in their search for independence and prosperity in the West, sharply contrasted with the deep hostility and suspicion with which white authorities responded to African-American movements to Kansas. While almost all white Americans were recent migrants to the West, they felt perfectly entitled to attempt to exclude those from places like China and Mexico. And racial animosity was used as a justification for horrific violence, particularly directed against Indians.

Economic forces, a fourth major theme, also profoundly shaped the experiences of different people living in the West. The booming market economy of the United States was arguably as much a factor in its eventual absorption of this territory as were its armies, political system, or rapidly expanding population. American goods flooded into New Mexico, for exam-ple, decades before American armies, and the conversion of animals such as beavers and horses into valuable commodities helped to transform many still-independent Indian peoples. Increasing land prices and the integra-tion of cattle raising into fluctuating national markets helped to strip most Latinos in the southwest of their land in the decades following the U.S.-Mexican War. The rise of a more industrial and corporate economy in the later nineteenth century had far-flung impacts on social life, whether to make a much greater portion of society dependent on wage labor for survival or to encourage people to see animals, no longer as needed for productive labor, in sentimental terms. Demand for labor by agribusiness and railroad companies helped draw hundreds of thousands of Mexicans to cross the border in the early twentieth century.

Larger racial and economic dynamics played themselves out differently in different places. Place mattered—a fifth major theme. In a sense, the West was not one place, but many. Race relations could be strikingly different from place to place. In the late nineteenth century, for example, in areas near the border where Latinos remained a majority, Anglo-Americans quite often married Latino women, learned Spanish, and even converted to Ca-tholicism. Where Latinos were a smaller minority, and a much more heavily migrant population, however, they experienced exploitation and ostracism nearly as severe as did African Americans. The social life of the countryside and cities could be similarly divergent, one reason why so many western Af-rican Americans were drawn to the greater freedoms that urban life offered them. Gender role and relationships between men and women also differed enormously across the expanse of the West. White society was much more accepting of marriage and long-term liaisons across racial lines in places like fur trading posts where white women were in short supply. Polygamy was practiced by numerous Plains Indian peoples and encouraged by the Mormon Church in Utah until the 1890s, but abhorred elsewhere.

The West and its many regions also changed substantially over time, the sixth and final major theme. In the broadest sense, over the course of the nineteenth century the region was transformed from a borderland of many peoples and nations—the United States, England, Spain and then Mexico, and numerous Indian peoples—to a region of the United States whose people were now more tightly linked to national economic, racial, and political systems. This incorporation was often a violent process, as witnessed by vigorous Indian military resistance, Latino rebels, outlaws embodying deep discontent, de facto warfare between the Mormon Church and the federal government, and labor strife. It also had its cultural side, with images of the West coming to exert a major role on wider notions of American-ness. These essays as a whole focus on this period of incorporation, and thus concern themselves mostly with the period of the early nineteenth century through about World War I. But this emphasis doesn't mean that there was a sharp break in Western history, or that the peoples and conflicts of the West somehow disappeared in the early twentieth century. As the chapters on Indians, women, and animals in particular emphasize, people are still making the history of the West. All the more reason, then, to learn something from it.

About the Editor and Contributors

Benjamin Heber Johnson is associate professor of history at Southern Methodist University. A native of Houston, he holds a Ph.D. from Yale University. His research and teaching focus on the U.S.–Mexico borderlands and the American encounter with the natural world. In 2003 he published *Revolution in Texas: How a Forgotten Rebellion and Its Bloody Suppression Turned Mexicans into Americans* (Yale University Press), a study of racial violence and Mexican-American civil rights politics that has received national media attention. With photographer Jeffrey Gusky, he is completing a work entitled *An American Place: The Odyssey of a Border Town*, which uses one town to tell the larger history of the role of the border in American life. He is also under contract with Yale University Press for *Escaping the Dark, Gray City: How Conservation Re-Made City, Suburb, and Countryside in the Progressive Era*. He has received awards and fellowships from the Forest History Society, the American Council of Learned Societies, the National Endowment for the Humanities, the Huntington Library, and the Dallas Institute for Humanities and Culture.

Kevin Adams is an assistant professor of history at Kent State University, where he teaches graduate and undergraduate courses on War and Society in the United States, as well as the lower-division post-Civil War survey. He is currently finishing a book with the University of Oklahoma Press on the post-Civil War frontier Army, a work that is a revision of his dissertation, which was completed at the University of California, Berkeley in 2004.

Jimmy L. Bryan Jr. received his Ph.D. from Southern Methodist University. He has taught at Western Washington University, the University of Nevada-Reno, and at the University of Texas at Dallas. He is the author and editor of several books and articles on the American West, including the forthcoming *Romantic Warrior: Walter P. Lane and Adventurous Manhood, 1817–1892*.

Flannery Burke is an assistant professor in the Department of History at California State University, Northridge. Her book, *Longing and Belonging: Mabel Dodge Luhan and Greenwich Village's Avant-Garde in Taos* is forthcoming from the University Press of Kansas.

Ryan J. Carey received his Ph.D. in history from the University of Texas at Austin and teaches western and environmental history at Simon's Rock College of Bard. Currently, he is working on a manuscript entitled *Building a Better Oregon: Cartography, Corporations, and the State, 1846–1905*. His work demonstrates how maps created an important link between industrial corporations and the U.S. government in integrating the resources, subjects, and markets of the Pacific Northwest into the nation's economic and political core. He has been a fellow at the Henry E. Huntington Library, the Harvard Business School, and the American Heritage Center at the University of Wyoming.

D. Anthony Tyeeme Clark is a citizen of the Sac and Fox Tribe of the Mississippi in Iowa and a veteran of the United States Marine Corps. He is assistant professor of American Indian Studies at the University of Illinois at Urbana-Champaign, as well as co-editor of the Indigenous Futures Series at the University of Nebraska Press and book review editor for the *Indigenous Studies Journal*. His current book projects include: *Roots of Red Power: American Indian Protest and Resistance, From Wounded Knee to Chicago*; and, with Cornel Pewewardy, *Indian Like Me? Looking Forward to the History of "Indian" Mascots*.

Jon T. Coleman is an assistant history professor at the University of Notre Dame. He is the author of *Vicious: Wolves and Men in America* (Yale, 2004).

Jessie L. Embry is the Associate Director of the Charles Redd Center for Western Studies and an associate research professor at Brigham Young University. She is the author of seven books and over 100 articles on Western American, Mormon, and Utah women, and oral history topics.

Lisa Hsia is a Ph.D. student in U.S. history at UCLA. Her research interests are Asian American history and food history. She received her B.A. in History from UC Berkeley in 2004.

Greg Hall earned his Ph.D. in history at Washington State University. He is an assistant professor in the Department of History at Western Illinois University. His research interests focus primarily on the labor history of the U.S. West. He is the author of *Harvest Wobblies: The Industrial Workers of the World and Agricultural Laborers in the American West, 1905–1930* (Oregon State University Press, 2001). He is currently working on a second monograph that will examine the twentieth-century history of fruit and vegetable cannery workers in California, Oregon, and Washington.

Dwayne A. Mack is an assistant professor of history and Carter G. Woodson Chair in African American History at Berea College in Berea, Kentucky. He has written on Blacks in the West and the civil rights movement. Some of his articles include: "Hazel Scott: A Career Curtailed," *Journal of African American History*, spring 2006; "Ain't Gonna Let Nobody Turn Me Around: Berea College's Participation in the Selma to Montgomery March," *Ohio Valley History*, fall 2005; "Crusade for Equality: The Civil Rights Struggle in Spokane during the Early 1960s," *Pacific Northwest Quarterly*, volume 95 #1, winter 2003/2004; and "May the Work I've Done Speak for Me": African American

Civilian Conservation Corps Enrollees in Libby and Troy, Montana, 1933–34," *The Western Journal of Black Studies,* volume 27 #4, winter 2003.

Helen McLure earned her B.A. and M.A. from the University of Texas at Arlington and is currently a Ph.D. candidate at Southern Methodist University. She has published articles in the *Southwestern Historical Quarterly* and the *Western Historical Quarterly,* and won the Bert M. Fireman Award from the Western History Association in 2001 for "The Wild, Wild Web: The Mythic American West and the Electronic Frontier." In 2005, she received the Irene Ledesma Prize from the Coalition for Western Women's History.

Martin Padget teaches American Studies at the University of Wales, Aberystwyth, in the United Kingdom. He is the author of two monographs, *Indian Country: Travels in the American Southwest, 1840–1935* (Albuquerque: University of New Mexico Press, 2004) and *Photographers of the Western Isles* (Edinburgh: Birlinn, 2007), and the co-author of *Beginning Ethnic American Literatures* (Manchester: Manchester University Press, 2001). His current book project examines travel writing and the Southwest from the Spanish colonial era to the present day.

Omar Valerio-Jiménez is an Assistant Professor in the History Department at the University of Iowa. His study of the Lower Rio Grande region, *Rio Grande Crossings: Identity and Nation in the Mexico-Texas Borderlands, 1740–1890,* is under contract with Duke University Press. He teaches courses in Latina/o, American West, borderlands, and immigration history.

Chronology

10,000 B.C. "Clovis Points" developed; enable more effective hunting

ca. A.D. 1300 Navajos arrive in the Southwest

1492 Christopher Columbus finds land in the Bahamas, connecting Europe and the Americas

1528 Alvar Nuñez Cabeza de Vaca is shipwrecked on Texas coast and begins eight-year journey through the West

1540–1542 Francisco Vázquez de Coronado leads Spanish expedition through present-day Southwest and Great Plains

1598 Juan de Oñate leads establishment of Spanish settlements in northern New Mexico among Pueblo Indian peoples

1607 English founding of Jamestown

1608 French founding of Quebec

1680 Pueblo Revolt expels Spanish from New Mexico for twelve years

1707 Evidence of trading for horses on Great Plains

1718 Spanish found the Presidio of San Antonio de Béxar, which later grows into the city of San Antonio

1770s Comanche, Lakota, and other Indian peoples start wholesale incorporation of the horse into their societies

1781 Spanish found El Pueblo de Nuestra Señora de la Reina de los Angeles (later known to Americans as Los Angeles) in the province of Alta California

1799 Daniel Boone heads west from Kentucky into Spanish territory west of the Mississippi

1803 Lewis and Clark expedition sent by the U.S. government to explore route to the Pacific

1803 Louisiana Purchase transfers title of the Louisiana Territory from France to the United States; Indian peoples still inhabit and control most of this territory

1808 John Jacob Astor establishes the American Fur Company

1809 Manuel Lisa founds Missouri Fur Company

1821 Mexico wins independence from Spain after a decade of struggle

1821 Santa Fé Trail opened, connects U.S. and New Mexican markets

Secularization of most missions transfers considerable land and livestock from Indian to Hispanic hands

1824 Mexican government gives final approval to Stephen F. Austin for a colonization plan to bring Anglo-American settlers into Texas

1832 Sac and Fox leader Black Sparrow Hawk defeated by U.S. forces and forced to cede more territory in present-day Iowa

1833 Bent's Fort established on the Santa Fe Trail

1834 Protestants open mission in present-day Oregon

1836 Texas Revolution results in Texas's independence from Mexico

1837 Epidemic diseases hit some Great Plains Indian peoples

1842 Juan Seguin, partisan of the Texas Revolution, forced out of San Antonio and Texas by Anglo-Texans

1844 Murder of Joseph Smith in Illinois leads Mormons to look farther west for a place free from persecution

1846 U.S.-Mexican War begins after the annexation of Texas and clash near present-day Brownsville, Texas

1847 Mormons begin arriving in Salt Lake Valley of present-day Utah

1848 Treaty of Guadalupe-Hidalgo settles U.S.-Mexican War, giving the United States possession of the present-day Southwest

1848 Well-publicized discovery of Gold in California inaugurates Gold Rush

1850s Drought, harsh winters, environmental degradation, and increased human predation diminish Southern Plains bison herd

1850 California's Foreign Miners' Tax effectively excludes Mexicans, Mexican Americans, Chileans, and Chinese miners from much of the Gold Rush's prosperity

1850 Compromise of 1850, designed to reconcile sectional tension over slavery's westward expansion, admits California as a free state and created the territories of New Mexico and Utah

1892   Violent mining strike near Coeur d'Alene, Idaho

1893   Western Federation of Miners founded

1905   Industrial Workers of the World founded

1907   "Gentleman's Agreement" drastically curtails Japanese migration

1908   Japanese Association of America founded

1911   Start of Mexican Revolution, during which more than a million Mexicans migrate to the United States

1911   Society of American Indians founded

1912   Founding of National Association for the Advancement of Colored People, which soon boasts numerous Western chapters

1917   Immigration Act ends almost all Asian immigration

1917   Large timber-workers strike in the Northwest

1917   United States enters World War I

1924   Rin-Tin-Tin appears in first movie

Indian New Deal

1944   National Congress of American Indians founded

1952   Start of Relocation Services Program, Bureau of Indian Affairs initiative to move Indians to cities

1953   Congress votes for "termination" policy, designed to end existence of autonomous tribal governments and tribal identities

Give Me Your Home: Animals and the American West

1

Jon T. Coleman

With his rough hands, worn chaps, and sky-blue eyes, the cowboy exuded sex. Admirers fancied his hat, his blond hair, and the way he filled his jeans, but his secret weapons were his lips. Unlike so many Western heroes, this hunk could communicate. Lovers treasured his conversational skills, which was something of a surprise, for he did not speak to them. He talked to horses.

The cowboy was Tom Booker, the lead character in Nicholas Evans's 1995 novel *The Horse Whisperer*. An amalgam of John Wayne, Deepak Chopra, and Dr. Dolittle, Booker's rugged sensitivity disarmed female humans, including Annie Graves, the hard-charging New York magazine editor who traveled to his Montana ranch to cure her daughter's injured horse. He repaired the stallion, conducted an affair with Annie, and patched up the daughter's wrecked psyche. A therapeutic cowpoke, Booker slung empathy instead of six guns. His ability to communicate across species boundaries softened him, while his frontier machismo kept him from appearing weak. It is no wonder that Robert Redford played Booker in the movie version of the book. The character blends the sentimentality and conservative values that define Redford's muscular liberalism, and the horse, that iconic Western animal, which is the glue that keeps left and right clasped harmoniously together. Booker can express emotions, care deeply, and feel the pain of others without seeming feminine, radical, or French, because he directs his New Age energies at horses rather than people.

Evans's novel borrows from several pop culture caches. The love story mimics Robert James Waller's best-selling novel *Bridges of Madison County*, while the subplot about the broken daughter and her damaged horse recalls a host of melodramas featuring adolescent girls and their steeds. The book's take on human psychology can be traced to the self-help movement and New Age spirituality, while its cowboy masculinity and rural ethics hark back to countless Western films and television programs. The derivativeness of the novel is striking and raises a quandary: if the book represents a collage of pilfered elements, where did Evans get the notion of cowboys talking to horses?

According to interviews, he modeled Booker on numerous horse healers and trainers in Britain and the United States, all of them famous for their nonviolent techniques (Adams 1995). They do not "break" animals; they use ethological observations to see the world from the animals' point of view. Rather than force their horses to submit to their control, riders elicit the desired response by imagining how the horse perceives the order. If the command makes sense to the horse, then she will follow it gladly. Most horse trouble comes from people sending mixed signals. Humans ask mounts to do something that appears irrational to them, and then they punish the animals for acting sanely. A horse whisperer spends most of his time instructing owners on how to get out of their horse's way.

Booker "talks" to beasts by taking an anthropomorphic plunge into their heads. But why must he perform that feat in a cowboy hat and boots? A handsome, nonviolent trainer could ply his trade in a Kentucky barn, a racetrack in Saratoga, or the stables of wealthy clients in England or Saudi Arabia. What compelled the British Evans to set his tale in the West, on a ranch in Montana? And why does this setting seem right? When did westerners become the special friends of nonhuman creatures?

In a region of vast distances, the expanse separating the lives of real Western animals from their fictional counterparts is truly monumental. Eighteen-wheelers haul cattle toward slaughterhouses, while Timmy calls Lassie home. Coyotes swallow strychnine baits as Roy Rogers yodels atop Trigger. Vacuum trucks suck prairie dogs from their holes, and Kevin Costner dances with wolves. The residents of the geographical area known today as the American West have at turns loathed, loved, rode, traded, slaughtered, ingested, and mythologized nonhuman creatures for thousands of years.

A line drawn at the European conquest of the region used to help make sense of this garbled record. Prior to colonization, animals were considered "people"—or members of trans-species "republics" (Worster 1993, p. 55; White 1994, p. 237). Humans hunted, ate, and, in the cases of dogs and turkeys, lived with animals, but spirituality, rather than instrumentality, guided their relationships. Native Americans treated nonhumans as potential allies and potent adversaries. Indeed, the species divide separating buffalo, salmon, beavers, and grizzly bears from humans often dissolved. Creation myths featured animal heroes such as Coyote, Rabbit, and Buffalo Woman. In stories, animals married and had sexual intercourse with humans. People decorated their homes, their tools and weapons, and their bodies with animal drawings, skins, claws, feathers, and skulls. Hunters and fishers performed rituals and conducted ceremonies to placate the spirits of their quarry. Affronts such as hoarding game or letting a dog gnaw on a deer carcass warranted supernatural reprisals. Humans treated animals seriously; if not, they invited violence, starvation, and chaos into their lives.

This world of awe and reciprocity contrasted sharply with the European vision of animals as soul-less commodities. Capitalism wreaked havoc on animal bodies and spirits. Stripped of their religious portent, animals became

Rath & Wright's buffalo hide yard in 1878, showing 40,000 buffalo hides, Dodge City, Kansas. (*National Archives and Records Administration*)

trade items—pelts, skins, tallow, and hamburger. Beginning in the sixteenth century, Native groups traded buffalo robes and beaver pelts with Spanish, French, British, and American traders. During the 1830s competing fur companies nearly wiped out the West's beaver population, and in the next decades, human and animal relations reached an all-time low on the Great Plains. Under military and economic pressure, Native Americans killed more bison to acquire guns, horses, and trade goods, and, after the Civil War, U.S. hunters joined the slaughter. As the railroads advanced onto the Plains, white crews armed with high-powered rifles fanned out into the grasslands. They destroyed entire herds, stripping their hides and leaving the carcasses to rot. Turned to leather, and trimmed and sewn into giant belts, the skins drove the East's industrial machines.

Following the destruction of the bison, fertilizer companies paid bone-hunters to gather the animals' remains and stack them in piles. These pyramids of ribs, femurs, and craniums stand as counter monuments to the cowboy—or the Indian—seated on his pony. The dry sockets and bleached smiles mock the belief that a benevolent partnership ever existed between humans and animals in the West.

Yet the horse whisperer abides. In legions of images and storylines, Western humans continue to bond with animals. Colonization was supposed to end this intimacy, spoiling any chance for nonutilitarian relationships across species boundaries. Several reasons for the cliche's survival come to mind. The horse whisperer, Lassie, Rin-Tin-Tin, Trigger, Seabiscuit, even John Wayne's dog in *Hondo* represent the spread of sentimental pet-keeping in the twentieth-century United States. Industrialization freed some creatures— dogs and horses especially—from work. They became animals of leisure, creatures purchased for enjoyment and companionship. Modern Americans want to feel close to these companion species, and the culture industry feeds that longing by offering them stories about crime-fighting dogs or horsemen reading equine minds.

Hollywood contributed to the Western-ness of these animal fantasies by filming them on location near Los Angeles. Had the movie industry stayed on the East Coast, its original home, then cops, not cowboys, might have become the icons of mounted American virility. "Hi-Yo! Silver!" might have been "Yo! Silver!" The accidents of movie-making (the need for sunshine and cheap land) and anachronism (projecting modern attitudes back onto the past) explain the ubiquity and longevity of the idea that westerners possessed a special connection with animals.

It may seem hard to overestimate the allure of Hollywood's cowboy fictions in an era in which the president of the United States signals his resolve by wearing pointy-toed boots and uttering phrases like "Wanted dead or alive" and "We'll smoke 'em out," but people imagined fanciful relationships with animals long before film makers and television producers invaded Los Angeles. Indeed, the horse whisperer belongs to a regional tradition of trans-species partnerships and amalgamations that extends across the colonization divide. Before, during, and after the European conquest of the West, human beings singled out certain Western animals as kin, allies, guides, and inspiration. These claims of affinity often obscured harsher realities. Humans befriended and brutalized Western fauna—sometimes at one and the same time. Animals stirred mixed emotions and contradictory behavior, producing a thicket of lies, sins, and delusions but also experiments in cooperation and mimicry. Organizing the past into epochs with dominant viewpoints— whether reciprocity or instrumentality, empathy or detachment—makes Western history seem more coherent than it actually was. A continuous muddle, the region's animal past offers lingering mysteries rather than clear demarcations.

Native Americans and the Mixed Blessings of Animal Wealth

Apart from vegans, cat ladies, and PETA activists, Western animals could ask for no more stalwart allies than Native Americans. Indigenous peoples devoured them, of course, but they also observed, copied, and worshiped them. Animals and Indians coexisted for thousands of years in the microregions that would become the American West. In two of those areas, the Pacific Northwest and the Great Plains, Native groups established partnerships with individual species that dramatically enhanced their material wealth and political might. Salmon and horses empowered their human allies. The people with the closest ties to these beasts became rich, but they also became increasingly vulnerable and nervous. They confronted the dilemma of abundance, a predicament that the late rapper Notorious B.I.G. once reduced to a simple equation: more money, more problems. The Natives who bet their societies on a single species prospered for a time, but in the end they found little peace.

Anxiety traveled with the enormous fish that returned annually to their spawning grounds along the rivers of the Pacific Northwest. Anadromous salmon began their lives in the freshwater streams that fed the ocean, and after spending their adulthood in the sea, they returned to the rivers to reproduce and die. Most years, seemingly uncountable numbers of pinks, sockeyes, cohos, and steelheads fought currents and leapt waterfalls to complete their life cycles, giving the Indian fishers a steady supply with which to fill their weirs, sieves, and gillnets. But El Ninos, droughts, floods, fires, and epizootic diseases often disrupted the runs, and the low number of fish in some years disappointed and alarmed the humans. Those living near the coast risked the most. They depended on the salmon for almost all of their sustenance, and when the fish failed to appear in strength, groups like the Chinooks, Clatsops, Tillamooks, and Alseas went hungry.

The stories they told about the fish reflected this dependence. One Clatsop myth featured a comic dialog between Coyote and his scat. Coyote wanted to catch the salmon near a Clatsop village, but he did not know the local fishing and cooking taboos. Every time he tried for a fish, he broke a law, ensuring his failure. Coyote turned to his poop for advice. The scat poked fun at Coyote's ignorance, and this mockery underscored the tale's moral: only fools try to fish without knowing the local customs. Taboos and rituals kept the salmon swimming upstream every year; greed, ignorance, and disrespect made them hard to catch or worse, caused them to disappear altogether.

The capriciousness of the salmon runs interjected a strain of ambivalence into Native stories and rituals. "The myths," writes one historian, "projected a complex understanding of salmon: revered and cursed, immortal and rotting, avenging and merciful, killer and victim" (Taylor 1999, p. 24). The Native fishers respected their prey. They saw them as spiritual beings, not as blank commodities. But the emotions underlying this soulful understanding were neither warm nor charitable. The salmon solicited respect and moderation by putting their human partners on notice: behave correctly or we will abandon you. Fear cemented their trans-species alliance.

The humans stayed in the relationship for the calories. When the salmon ran in great numbers, the people with the choice fishing spots wallowed in pink flesh. One of the best fisheries was at The Dalles on the Columbia River. A series of rapids and waterfalls, The Dalles was a fine place to corral and harvest salmon, but the site's inland location made it truly prime real estate. Salmon stop eating when they begin their journey to their spawning grounds. Energy stores fuel them for a while, but eventually the fish burn all their fat and begin to consume their own muscles. The Dalles stood at this metabolic crossroads. The fish entered the rapids in perfect shape, lean and meaty, ripe for preservation. (The fatter salmon downstream were harder to dry, while the emaciated salmon upstream were not worth the labor of curing their flesh.)

The Indians at The Dalles turned most of their catch into pemmican, a mixture of pulverized, dried salmon and berries. Pemmican kept for years, and the Wasco and Wishram Indians that controlled The Dalles traded the jerky with tribes in California and the Northern Great Plains. Pemmican bought furs, slaves, bison meat, copper, and hemp. It cemented alliances and soothed conflicts. Suitors needed baskets of it to offer as gifts to the families of their betrothed. The not-too-fat, not-too-skinny salmon at The Dalles transformed the thousand or so humans living along the fifteen-mile stretch of rough water into regional players. The fish not only fed their population but also furnished a surplus of 1,000 pounds of pemmican each year for each household. The humans used that abundance to build the relationships of trade, marriage, and alliance that supported their prestige and power. The salmon gave them bountiful lives, and the Indian fishers acknowledged the gift with their anxiety.

Salmon wealth tempted humans to stay in place. Tribes erected permanent villages, and families controlled fishing sites, passing the right to use sections of river down through the generations. On the Great Plains, another animal asset uprooted entire societies. Spanish horses entered the Plains in the seventeenth century and stirred up the region's human population. Groups shifted locales, occupations, and outlooks. Farmers abandoned their fields, mountain peoples left the hills, and Plains outliers built empires in the grasslands' center. The Lakota Sioux, an agricultural people living in the Upper Mississippi Valley prior to acquiring horses in the 1780s, provided the most spectacular example of the beasts' transformational powers. The Lakota rode their equine partners to fame, fortune, and two stunning victories against the equally expansive United States, in 1868 and 1876. Historians have studied the Lakota's brand of mounted nomadism extensively and have used the group's success to depict the Plains Indians' partnership with horses as both revolutionary and largely positive. But recently, that view has darkened and grown more complicated. Outside the Lakota, most human and horse alliances on the Plains ended badly. Instead of enhancing Native lives, horses ruined them.

The Comanche, not the Lakota, owned the most horses on the Plains. Crossing from pedestrianism into equestrianism in the early eighteenth century, they built their herds from wild Spanish "Barbs" turned loose during the 1680 Pueblo revolt and mounts stolen from Apaches and Jumanos. Once horsed, the Comanches abandoned their home in the Rocky Mountains to hunt bison and raise horses on the Southern Plains. The new location also put them within striking distance of the Indian Pueblos and Spanish settlements in New Mexico, which they at turns traded with and raided. By 1775, the Comanches possessed a bustling horse empire. Being ideal breeding grounds, the Southern Plains spurred reproduction, and the herds expanded further as the Comanches plundered their neighbors. By the nineteenth century, reports one historian, "the average . . . Comanche or Kiowa family owned thirty-five horses and mules, five to six times more than basic hunting and transportation needs would have required" (Hämäläinen 2003, p. 849). This abundance of horses actually changed the Comanches' occupation. They became pastoralists, horse breeders, and traders who also hunted bison on occasion.

The Comanches' animal wealth was both astounding and combustible. The large herds attracted raiders, and Comanche men protected their assets through aggressive retaliation. While they were raiding in Texas and New

Hide depicting a Shoshone buffalo hunt, ca. 1875. (*Werner Forman/Corbis*)

Mexico, their wives and captive slaves tended the horses and mules, a job that grew more difficult as the number of livestock increased. On the Plains, grass and weather pushed horses and humans around. They moved in constant search of fresh pasture, and in the winters they huddled in river bottoms where the horses could feed on cottonwood bark. These herding practices strained an ecosystem upon which many Plains mammals depended. Bison wintered in the river bottoms as well. The Comanches fed their horses the calories that energized their principal food supply, and by the 1850s, drought, harsh winters, environmental degradation, and increased human predation had destroyed the Southern Plains bison herds. The Comanches started eating their horses.

Equestrianism launched the Comanches toward economic and military prominence, but too much equestrianism dragged them toward poverty. Indian groups throughout the Plains endeavored to find solutions to equally vexing horse problems. In the North, hard winters kept the Blackfeet, the Gros Ventres, the Crees, and the Assinboines from building large herds. Forced to replace weather casualties each spring, they invited European traders into the region and raided each other incessantly. On the Missouri River, the Mandans, Hidatsas, and Arikaras adopted horses, but only a couple per household. They continued to farm the river's flood plain and reside in permanent villages along its banks. To protect their crops and stay in place, they forfeited their chance at equestrian wealth and power, a costly decision that put them at the mercy of more committed nomads. Farther south, the Pawnees, Poncas, Kansas, Wichitas, and Otoes tried a more vigorous form of seminomadism. Like the Mandans and Arikaras, they planted corn and other crops in river bottoms, but instead of living in permanent villages, they migrated to the Plains en masse twice a year for extended bison hunts. This strategy required more horses and guaranteed the tribes a vegetable fallback if the hunting expeditions fell short. Yet the seminomads too paid for their halfway adaptive strategy. The Lakota harassed them in small war parties, killing Pawnees and then escaping before they could organize a counterattack. To access bison meat and robes, groups like the Pawnees ran a gauntlet manned by fully nomadic people.

Yet, if the Lakota were such hardcore equestrians, how did they escape the misery of the equally dedicated Comanche? The answer involves location and timing. The Lakota's herds lived far enough north to experience tough winters. Horses died in the snow and cold, preventing the humans from accumulating large surpluses. The Lakotas averaged twenty horses per household: plenty for enjoying the pleasures of nomadism and few enough to forgo the sorrows of pastorialism. They also adopted horses later than most groups. Relative newcomers to the Plains, they had yet to endure the deleterious social and ecological effects of equestrianism when the Americans invaded the region.

The United States conquered Native peoples already laid flat by their encounters with horses. The animals had bucked the Comanches and driven groups like the Crow and Pawnee in search of military partners with whom to fend off the Lakotas and their Cheyenne and Arapohoe allies. Intertribal conflict and interspecies competition during winters in river bottoms crippled the nomads' primary resource: the bison herds. The equestrian societies were teetering before the Americans arrived with their buffalo guns and railroads.

The U.S. Army, the spearhead of an industrialized nation emerging from one of the world's first modern wars, met an array of extraordinary adaptive peoples whose animal partnerships had, in most instances, come unraveled. The soldiers considered their Indian opponents primitives. They called them savages and saw bison hunting nomadism as a weakness to exploit. Educated by "total war" in suppressing a rebellion within their own nation, the Americans attacked women and children in winter camps, hoping to disrupt society as much as destroy warriors. Yet, if riding horses and shooting buffalo signaled the Indians' frailty and incivility, then the behavior of the white soldiers warrants an explanation. Instead of shunning the lifestyle they hoped to destroy, they eagerly sought out opportunities to hunt bison on horseback. The Americans styled themselves as horsemen and hunters. They declared their equestrianism to be a "sport," an activity done for excitement not subsistence. Still, while they did not require buffalo meat and hides to survive on the Plains, Americans wanted to imagine themselves charging down massive beasts on horseback. Like the Indians, they needed animal partners in taking possession of the West. They simply needed them for different reasons.

Western Animals and the American Conquest

George Custer accidentally brained his mount while hunting buffalo for fun in the middle of General Winfield Scott Hancock's military campaign against the Cheyenne in 1867. The episode reeked of stupidity, and Custer acknowledged as much, calling his actions "rashly imprudent" (Custer 1966, p. 79).

A rumor had brought Custer to the "magnificent game country" along the Arkansas River (p. 79). Hancock and 1,400 men rode out onto the Plains to investigate reports that the Cheyenne planned to attack white Kansans. The expedition met several Cheyenne leaders at Fort Larned, and Hancock warned them to keep their people south of the Arkansas. Afterward, the general moved his force to a position from which they could observe the Cheyenne camp. Once under watch, however, the Indians promptly disappeared. Splitting into smaller groups, they abandoned their village and drifted unseen into the night. Hancock ordered Custer, his ranking cavalry officer, after them, and it was during this pursuit that he shot his horse.

For Custer, the whole campaign resembled a hunt. To find the Cheyenne, he sent out his well-trained "pointers or setters" to range and beat "the ground in search of coveted game" (p. 72). Turning his human scouts (among them Wild Bill Hickok, "one of the most perfect types of physical manhood" that Custer "ever saw") into beasts took some imaginative effort, but depicting the Cheyenne as "game" required none (p. 69). Custer already conceived of his Indian adversaries as animals. Contrary to the soft-hearted reformers and army-bashing newspapermen in the East, he knew that their "cruel and ferocious natures" made them worse than "any wild beast of the desert" (p. 22).

Custer's metaphors confused the difference between military campaigns and animal hunts. So did his luggage. Along with his tent, guns, maps, uniforms, and rations, he brought two English greyhounds with him on the expedition. He transported the hounds to chase antelope, and on the morning of April 16 he spotted some. He rode out to them with the dogs and his chief bugler. When the hounds spotted the herd, he unleashed them and followed. The "exciting chase" lasted several minutes, but it soon became clear that the "antelope were in no danger of being caught by the dogs" and he called them off (p. 80). After collecting the "blown" canines, Custer had turned his thoughts to the bugler he had left behind, plodding on a slow "common-bred" horse, and the marching column that they both needed to rejoin, when he saw "a dark-looking animal grazing nearly a mile distant" (p. 80).

A wild buffalo! Custer had never seen a wild buffalo, and he very much wanted to kill one. The bison, however, spotted him and bolted. Custer spurred his horse and soon caught up. The bull was enormous: "Of the hundreds of thousand of buffaloes which I have since seen, none have corresponded with him in size and grandeur." He yelled with "wild excitement and delight" alongside the charging beast (pp. 80–81). He might have shot him with his revolver, but the chase was too thrilling. They ran for miles to extend his "enjoyment." Finally the bull tired, and Custer aimed for the kill. The buffalo, however, ruined the climactic moment by swerving to gore the horse, and the horse veered to escape. Custer grabbed for the reins with both hands, his finger still on the trigger. The gun went off, extinguishing the horse midstride.

In his memoir *My Life on the Plains*, Custer's dismounted body hovers over the Plains for two sentences encompassing forty-nine words. As a writer, the lieutenant colonel luxuriated in subordinate clauses, and he burdened his description of being tossed with so many qualifying phrases that gravity dissolved into contemplation: "Quick as thought I disengaged myself from the stirrups and found myself whirling through the air over and beyond the head of my horse. My only thought, as I was describing this trajectory, and my first thought on reaching terra firma, was: 'What will the buffalo do with me?'" (p. 82). Custer uses the word "thought" three times to dramatize an unthinkable experience. The horse fell, and Custer flew too quickly for his brain waves to coalesce into ideas. And the scene ends on an even more cerebral note. The collision frightened the buffalo away, leaving Custer alone with his "bitter reflections" (p. 82).

Of course, midair ruminations are a literary contrivance, a verbal form of slow-motion photography. Writing years after the fact, Custer stretched time to heighten the impact of his fall. The two sentences reflected his artistic choices, not his lived reality, which makes them even more baffling. The in-flight musings stand out as odd, because Custer lets no thoughts enter his head prior to his levitation. Until that moment, he ran on emotion and lust. He had left his troops to chase antelopes for sport, and his desire to "taste" the exhilaration of buffalo hunting drove him further from his responsibilities (p. 79). The sprint alongside the bull is nearly erotic, with Custer bellowing in "delight" as he prolongs his "excitement" (p. 81). Enraptured, his intellect overwhelmed by sensation, he crashes to earth after running to death the animal companion that had carried him into battle during the Civil War.

A spectacle of poor judgment, the accident seemed to forecast Custer's doom: on June 25, 1876, another rash decision would kill him and 210 subordinates at the Battle of the Little Bighorn. Yet, while we know that his impetuousness and arrogance will lead him and others to a stupendous fall, Custer never hid these personality traits from his contemporaries. He flaunted his brashness, even when it made him look foolish. For Custer, leaving his command to charge after a trophy animal was a justifiable, if not an altogether wise, maneuver. He felt confident enough about the incident to publish an account of it in a national magazine (the *Galaxy* magazine serialized Custer's Plains memoir between 1872 and 1874). He assumed that his readers would not only understand but also appreciate his behavior.

Custer publicized his hunting adventures to further his transformation from a cavalier into a Plainsman. He had built his cavalier reputation as an officer during the Civil War. He charged enemy lines, enthralled newspaper reporters with his tales of daring, and stole the show with his horsemanship and flowing locks during the Army of the Potomac's victory parade in Washington, D.C. Custer the cavalier was flashy, young, romantic, violent, and pretty. But, to the chagrin of the human behind the image, he was also perishable. On the Great Plains, the cavalier persona faded like a sun-bleached daguerreotype. In the West, Custer lost rank. A temporary brevet major-general during the war, he became a lieutenant colonel at the conclusion of hostilities. Then he lost his writers. Many Eastern newspapers depicted the frontier army as cruel and corrupt and their battles with Native tribes as despicable massacres. Finally, he just got lost. Warfare on the Plains proved frustrating and bewildering. Custer struggled to locate his enemies and to find his bearings in a deceptive environment.

Mirages epitomized the trickery of the grasslands. The phenomenon interested Custer, and he mentions mirages often in his memoir. A young officer told him about the time that his command charged a dozen buffalo carcasses, mistaking them for Indians. The mirage multiplied and animated the skeletons. From a distance, they looked like mounted warriors lining up for a fight. The Plains struck Custer as oceanic. Hillocks and depressions resembled wave crests and troughs. The immense, shifting landscape distorted scale and distance. Conestoga wagons became "large sailing vessels under sail" after a mirage had elevated "the wagons to treble their height and magnif[ied] the size of the covers" (p. 17). These false perceptions could kill. White emigrants and their livestock perished traveling to water that always appeared five to ten miles ahead. Custer's outfit nearly massacred itself on account of a mirage. Still searching for the Cheyenne, Custer ordered a night-time reconnaissance mission. The scouting party, led by an officer with "professed experience on and knowledge of the Plains," lost their way and rode through the dark in a giant circle (p. 91). At dawn, they approached an encampment filled with structures that rose from the grass like pale tepees. Eager to fight they attacked the village, halting only when the rising sun revealed their comrades eating breakfast in front of their white canvas Sibley tents.

The U.S. Army needed scouts to see straight. Custer called the white men who performed this service plainsmen (he labeled the Indians who did as "friendly"). The plainsmen's vitality grew from their relationship with the Western landscape. The plainsmen felt at home in expanses of grass. Mirages never fooled them, and they rarely lost their way. Indeed, they penetrated the oceanlike surface of the Plains to locate hidden resources and adversaries. They found water, cottonwood groves (in winter, both Indians and cavalry horses subsisted on tree bark), animal game, and "hostile" Native Americans. The plainsmen signaled their superior Western-ness with their clothing. Wild Bill Hickok's attire combined the "immaculate neatness of the dandy with the extravagant taste and style of the frontiersmen" (pp. 68–69). The costume indicated inward character. With their attention to presentation and manners, the plainsmen were, at least in Custer's eyes, "gentlemen by instinct" (p. 112).

Custer quickly adopted the plainsmen's style. He wore buckskin, experimented with his facial hair (he grew a beard during the 1868–1869 Washita Campaign), and never missed an opportunity to display and advertise his hunting prowess. Hunting, more than Indian-fighting, helped turn him into a "white scout." Custer needed guides, most of them Indian, to help him find human enemies on the Plains. Chasing antelope and bison gave him the chance to locate prey, offer advice, and play frontiersmen before an appreciative audience. Wealthy tourists traveled by rail to Kansas to kill buffalo with him. In the summers of 1869 and 1870, Custer's regiment camped near Fort Hays, and "English noblemen, eastern industrialists, and eminent

"Our first grizzly," killed
by General Custer
and Colonel Ludlow.
By Illingworth, 1874,
during the Black Hills
expedition. (*National
Archives and Records
Administration*)

political leaders" visited to hunt and cavort with "the buckskinned celebrity" (Utley 1988, pp. 105–106). Custer vaunted his hunting adventures in letters to the outdoor sporting magazine *Turf, Field, and Farm*, and in 1871 he reached the apex of his guiding career: he accompanied Russia's Grand Duke Alexis on a bison hunt with the West's ultimate "white scout," Buffalo Bill Cody.

Custer wrote about his hunting to claim a Western identity. Killing animals signaled his mastery over a bewildering environment. He belonged on the Plains with those other examples of perfect manhood, Wild Bill Hickok and Buffalo Bill. At home in a landscape that confused and frightened most white Americans, these men embodied the exotic blending of East and West. Violent yet refined, primitive yet gentlemanly, buckskinned yet dapper, the plainsmen stood between, and above, savagery and civilization. But if hunting offered Custer a pathway to exalted manliness, why did he admit to shooting his own horse? Why not lie, or simply bypass the episode in favor of another buffalo hunt that ended in triumph rather than ignominy?

Perhaps he offered the episode as a lesson, a morality tale about following orders and forestalling gratification. His accident could teach young Americans to value and care for their animal property. "Do not gamble other creatures' lives," Custer might have cautioned, "especially in the reckless pursuit of sport." But he issued no such warning, for he did not view shooting his horse as a mistake. After the mishap, he encouraged his men to chase after buffalo with their pistols drawn. Custer knew of "no better drill for perfecting men in the use of firearms on horseback . . . than buffalo-hunting over moderately rough country" (Custer 1966, p. 111). Killing bison at point-blank range from horseback gave recruits "confidence and security in the saddle" (ibid.).

Buffalo hunting was a training exercise for soldiers, and buffalo hunting stories were training exercises for the readers of the *Galaxy* or *My Life on the Plains*. Custer informed Americans about the West, and he instructed them in the attitudes and actions necessary for taking possession of the region. Hunting exposed men and animals to danger. A poorly timed swerve could unseat the most accomplished equestrian. The possibility of accidents fueled Custer's glee. Risking his life excited him. Custer did not drink, but he enjoyed gambling. As a hunter and a cavalry officer, however, he never risked only his own life. Subordinates, be they animals or corporals, always tempted death with him. Hunting buffalo with pistols taught soldiers more than horsemanship; it offered enlisted men a glimpse of the awesome power that officers like Custer held over them. When ordered to charge, they were expected to behave like their courageous and obedient mounts. Custer adored his horses and no doubt he liked some of his men, but he built his reputation as a cavalry commander on a series of brash decisions that placed his life and the lives of his underlings in tremendous peril. Hunting and warfare were endeavors of chance offering titillation and adventure. *My Life on the Plains* sold that excitement, yet it did so with an implicit promise: the hunts and wars would be dangerous, but ultimately they would end well. A plainsman held the reins.

Rin-Tin-Tin: A Wolf in a Wolf-less West

Moving from an accidental shooting depicted in an army colonel's reminiscences to a 1924 silent film starring a German shepherd may seem like a bizarre and imprudent leap in subject matter, but the movie *Clash of the Wolves* and the memoir *My Life on the Plains* actually help illuminate each other. Custer chose to write about his embarrassing dismount, and Rin-Tin-Tin's owners decided to cast him as a wolf, for many of the same reasons. Crowds purchased tickets to see Rin-Tin-Tin play a role, and they purchased magazines and books to watch Custer change costumes and audition personae—horseman, hunter, guide, and cavalry officer. While on a campaign to destroy bison hunting equestrians, he became one. He appropriated the Indian hunter's seat on horseback and retailored the role. Instead of the savage warrior, he offered his audience the buckskinned plainsmen, the deadly gentleman who felt at ease in the untamed West yet remained civilized and white. At first glance the six-gun was the prop that signaled the plainsman's Western-ness, but the horse pulled off the role. Both Indians and plainsmen rode; they shared an animal partner. The horse shouldered Custer's claim to nativity. It rooted him in place.

As Lobo in *Clash of the Wolves*, Rin-Tin-Tin played both the animal partner and the identity-shifting non-Westerner. On screen, he teamed up with the greenhorn prospector Dave Weston to thwart William "Borax" Horton's claim-jumping plans and win the love of May Barstowe, the rancher's

John Hill

On Sunday, August 30, 1863, in Utah's Cache Valley, John Hill died trying to prevent bears from devouring his vegetables. The local newspaper described Hill's death as "tragic," but "ironic" suits the scene better. No animal bit or mauled Hill. He died like a bear, perforated with hunters' bullets. Hill's last words: "Boys! You have riddled me now," capped a series of unlucky turns that transformed a human farmer itching for a shot at an animal nemesis into a target.

The bears had been at the corn and carrots. Hill and his nephew Robert decided to ambush the thieves. They crept into the cornfield, searching for tracks and listening for grunts. Halfway through, they heard some rustling on the opposite edge of the field and moved toward the sound. The noisemakers, however, were humans—five young men from Hyrum, a small neighboring town, out that night seeking their own revenge against ursine thieves. Dark shapes moved

inside the patch. The "Hyrum boys" aimed their rifles and watched the forms step out of the corn. They shot the lead figure, and John Hill collapsed in the dim moonlight.

A case of bad timing and poor visibility, Hill's death was an unfortunate, but not that unusual, an accident. Throughout American history, excited hunters, out for payback, food, or sport, often mistook each other for fauna. But the Hill episode was more than a factual description of a lethal blunder; it also belonged to a storytelling tradition: the American bear legend. Bear tales followed Euro-Americans, their corn, and their livestock across the continent. Americans told stories about bears invading communal corn-husking parties, hunters killing onrushing boars with musket ramrods, and farm wives slaughtering monster bruins at their doorstep. Often, these stories appeared years after the fact in local histories, county almanacs, and family reminiscences.

---

daughter. Lobo, a half-breed wolf-dog, helps to season Weston, an innocent unfamiliar with the region's code of cruelty. In the West, "the first sign of weakness means death" (Logue 2004, DVD). Lobo's pack would destroy him the instant he falters, and in a pivotal scene, Weston saves the canine by removing a cactus spike from his paw. Together man and animal find love, family, and a home. Lobo and his pack dispatch the villain, Weston marries Barstowe, and everyone goes on a picnic. In the last scene, Lobo and his mate Nanette (and their pups) enjoy a romantic boat ride with their human counterparts. Together, the trans-species pack rewrites the code of the West. Instead of "weakness means death," a new motto flashes across the screen: "wolf heart and human heart are ever the same when love rules" (ibid.).

Clash of the Wolves premiered at the height of Rin-Tin-Tin's career. Born in Lorraine, France, in 1918, "Rinty" entered into his principal human partnership at the end of World War I. Lee Duncan, a corporal in the U.S. Army, found the pup in an abandoned German Dog Corp station in Lorraine and rescued him. After naming him Rin-Tin-Tin for the small good-luck dolls the French sold to the U.S. soldiers, Duncan took the dog home to Santa Monica. The corporal had some low-level Hollywood connections, the actor Eugene Pallette was an army buddy, and he began entering the dog in jumping competitions and shopping him around to studios. In 1922, Rinty leapt eleven feet at a dog show. Newsreel footage transmitted the feat to movie-

The compilers of these texts included the legends to signal the distance between their lives and those of their progenitors. Contemporary westerners luxuriated in the staid prosperity that the blood of their forbearers purchased. In these narrative formulations, bears prowled the line separating civilization from savagery, peace from violence, modernity from antiquity. The animals marked the line between a wild past and a settled present.

Yet, even as the bear stories erected some boundaries, they eroded others. In the tales, hunters and bears frequently switched roles and identities. Trackers stepped into forgotten traps. Guns jammed or misfired, turning human predators into bears' quarry. Many bear stories featured the sudden overturning of natural hierarchies and gender orders. Hunters lost their power and virulence, their impotence frequently symbolized by a missing or dysfunctional firearm. Made vulnerable, the men resembled the people, animals, or vegetables they sought to protect. They became victims and foodstuff. Or, they became like bears, targets of human aggression.

John Hill, therefore, pacified an agricultural landscape. He fell to friendly fire during the campaign to make the West safe for marketable plants and animals. He was a vegetable martyr, a casualty of conquest. He was also a stock character in a storytelling genre that interpreted and justified the alteration of the Western environment. In their animal legends, Americans often placed themselves in the roles of the creatures they sought to destroy. They imagined themselves as powerless animals at the moment they exerted their dominion most forcefully. These stories eased the colonization of the West through a double act of appropriation. Americans took the bears' territory; then they borrowed the animals' viewpoint to narrate the acquisition.

goers across the nation. That same year, the German shepherd won his first acting gig in *The Man from Hell's River*. The French-born Alsatian supposedly replaced an actual wolf that refused to hit his mark. By the end of his career (and his life) in 1932, Rinty had starred in twenty-six films. He kept Warner Bros. studios solvent during some tough times, earning $6,000 a month for his efforts. Rinty's offspring continued in show business. They performed in movies and on television, most famously the 1950s children's television program *The Adventures of Rin Tin Tin*.

Adults, however, bought tickets to see *Clash of the Wolves*, and the film's drawing power raises a quandary. Why would Americans pay money to watch a German shepherd play a sympathetic wolf? In the 1920s, the government of the United States had exterminated wolves. The Predator, Animal, and Rodent Control Division of the Department of Agriculture waged a popular war against the varmints across the West. Livestock associations and state governments contributed funds to the predator control campaigns, paying professional hunters to track down and annihilate wolves. By 1950, only a few small packs remained in the continental United States. Outside of the upper Midwest (northern Minnesota, Wisconsin, and Michigan), the country was a lupine wasteland. To drive wolves from agricultural landscapes, the hunters sometimes resorted to vicious techniques. They shotgunned wolf pups and fed strychnine to their parents. They dragged the animals to death behind horses and wired the muzzles (and sometimes the penises) of captive wolves shut. Given the violence and sadism on display in the West, it is hard to imagine a movie producer marching into the offices of a studio boss in the 1920s to declare that he wanted to make a film about love bringing human and wolf hearts together.

But someone pitched the idea, and *Clash of the Wolves* got made and successfully toured the country. The movie worked for two reasons. First, Rin-Tin-Tin movies showcased a performance not a role. The audience came to see a dog pretend to be an actor as well as a wolf. The tricks that Rin-Tin-Tin executed thrilled the crowd as much as the storyline. Indeed, the movie's plot served the animal's stunts, rather than the other way around. Rin-Tin-Tin could jump, fight, carry stuffed animals in his mouth, play dead, and hop around on three paws. The writers worked all of these tricks into the story. He also displayed a deep reservoir of patience for silly costumes. For much of the film, Lobo wore a beard and moccasins to mask his wolf-ness. In one of the most exciting scenes, he unlaced his booties to climb up a slick ramp and attack the claim jumper "Borax" Horton. The bootie-untying scene added nothing to the plot. It was an excuse for spotlighting Rin-Tin-Tin's ability to take off his moccasins with his front teeth. The audience cheered for an animal to perform the human task of unlacing shoes as much as they cheered for Lobo to catch Borax.

Rin-Tin-Tin's primary role was "an animal feigning humanness." Viewers projected their thoughts and emotions onto him, and those fantasies turned him into a movie star. The mystery of *Clash of the Wolves* arises from Rin-Tin-Tin's secondary role—"German shepherd pretending to be a wolf." If behaving like a person humanized the canine, why didn't acting like a wolf demonize him?

Rin-Tin-Tin needed the goodwill of his audience; he "acted" through their imaginative empathy. Reviled creatures, wolves seem unlikely conduits of trans-species understanding. Yet, in the 1920s, they were. They facilitated human and animal togetherness, and they helped Western Americans to express a fondness for wild carnivores even as they exterminated them.

The name of Rin-Tin-Tin's character, Lobo, linked him to a tradition of American storytelling that featured sympathetic wolves. Ernest Thompson Seton wrote the genre's defining tale in 1894. In *Lobo, King of the Currumpaw*, Seton told the story of a doomed-yet-heroic outlaw. Lobo devoured livestock in the Currumpaw region of New Mexico. Like Rin-Tin-Tin in *Clash of the Wolves*, he commanded a lethal pack. (His gang, however, probably looked more dangerously wolfish. In the movie, the director surrounds Rin-Tin-Tin with German shepherds, huskies, and two canines that appear to be scrawny coyotes.) A savant as well as a prodigious killer, Lobo outwitted all the hunters sent against him until Seton finally snared him. Seton succeeded where all others had failed because he had discovered the "King's" fatal weakness—his love for his mate, Blanca. Seton captured Blanca, and after two cowboys lassoed and stretched her between their horses "until the blood burst from her mouth, her eyes glazed, her limbs stiffened and then fell limp," he staked out her carcass and ringed it with steal traps (Seton 2000, p. 36). Lobo walked into the ambush, his grief for his "darling" overwhelming his sagacity. Seton carried him to camp, and he died later that night; not from injuries, but from "a broken heart" (ibid., p. 43).

While a killer and a molester of property, Seton's Lobo remained an object of sentimentality. Seton and his readers understood him: Lobo was a wild animal possessing the engrained urge to devour livestock. He belonged in a countryside dotted with ranches as little as a buffalo, or the way an Indian belonged in a conquered West. Their savagery and lawlessness marked all three for extinction. Standing over Lobo's body, Seton announced the inevitability of this ending: "Grand old outlaw, hero of a thousand raids, in a few minutes you will be a great load of carrion. It cannot be otherwise" (p. 41). The conviction that time only moves forward and that history must churn certain humans and animals beneath its wheels triggered an outpouring of fondness and regret from the people seated in the driver's seat. Seton admired Lobo and was sad to see him die. Bill Caywood, the hunter hero of several last wolf stories written in the 1920s by Stanley Young and Arthur Carhart, saw his victims as "kindred spirits" (Carhart and Young 1929, pp. 288–289). Looking down at the remains of the Greenhorn wolf, his final and toughest foe, he pondered the shared fate of Western wolves, Indians, bison, mail carriers, stage coaches, longhorns, and himself:

> Here lay a big symbol. The West of the old days was passing. A new day was coming. In it there would be no naked red men riding in warring parties toward white settlements. There would be no big herds of bison that spread for acres over the open prairies. The Pony Express was but a memory, a tradition. The old stage coach was now crowded out by high-powered gas wagons. The longhorn cow had given way to grade and purebred whitefaces. Even the old type of man that trod the open spaces was giving way to a business man of the New West. (Ibid., p. 289)

The New West had no room for master killers, human or canid.

Rin-Tin-Tin resurrected a "big symbol" in *Clash of the Wolves*. He reached back across an extinction divide to enliven an icon: Lobo, the king wolf, victim of history. By playing this part, the German shepherd revised Western history. Instead of dying, Rin-Tin-Tin's Lobo adapts. An act of kindness civilizes him, and he enters into a partnership with the tenderfoot Dave Weston. Lobo saves Weston's life and facilitates his romance with Mary. The animal helps the outsider stake his claim to the West. Weston is definitely a "New West" type. In the final picnic scene, instead of chaps and a cowboy hat, he wears a sweater. His and Lobo's ascendancy banishes a different set of Old West figures: the claim-jumper Borax, the rancher and his wolf-hunting posse, and Lobo's old pack mates. These victims of history share a common trait: they are violent and pitiless. The New West belongs to the lovers—husbands and wives, dogs and bitches, and, most especially, men and wolves.

Conclusion

Americans could conquer the West; they could disrupt older human and animal bonds, extinguishing partnerships built on respect and anxiety. But they could not possess the region without their own beastly allies. The need for animal acceptance, reassurance, and exaltation explains why Nicholas Evans and then Robert Redford set *The Horse Whisperer* in Montana, why George Custer labored to claim the identity of a mounted warrior, and why Rin-Tin-Tin played a wolf. The history of animals in the American West is in many respects a wretched, bloody mess. Custer shooting his companion in the head while trying to kill another creature for fun (and to boost his already distended self-esteem) comes too close to representing normative historical behavior for comfort. And this enduring uneasiness keeps Western novelists, artists, and film makers coming back to animals. Americans want Western beasts to understand them, to see their goodness and forgive their transgressions. They want a menagerie of "human whisperers" to empathize with them and remove the thorns of violence and remorse that keep them from feeling at home in a stolen land.

References and Further Reading

Adams, Noah. "British Novelist Sells First Book for $6 Million." Nicholas Evans interview, *All Things Considered*, NPR, August 31, 1995.

Carhart, Arthur, and Stanley Paul Young. *The Last Stand of the Pack.* New York: Sears, 1929.

Clash of the Wolves, DVD, directed by Charles A. Logue. In *More Treasures of the American Film Archives, 1894–1931, Program Two,* 1925. San Francisco: National Film Preservation Foundation, 2004.

Custer, George A. *My Life on the Plains*, ed. Milo Milton Quaife. Lincoln: University of Nebraska Press, 1966.

Hämäläinen, Pekka. "The Rise and Fall of the Plains Indians Horse Cultures." *Journal of American History* 90 (December 2003): 833–862.

Richards, Daniel B. Hill. *The Hill Family History.* Salt Lake City, UT: Magazine Printing Company, 1927.

Seton, Ernest Thompson. *Wild Animals I Have Known* [1898]. Mineola, NY: Dover, 2000.

Taylor, Joseph E. *Making Salmon: An Environmental History of the Northwest Fisheries Crisis.* Seattle: University of Washington Press, 1999.

Utley, Robert. *Cavalier in Buckskin: George Armstrong Custer and the Western Military Frontier.* Norman: University of Oklahoma Press, 1988.

White, Richard. "Animals and Enterprise." In Clyde A. Milner II, et al., eds., *The Oxford History of the American West.* New York: Oxford University Press, 1994, 237–274.

Worster, Donald. *An Unsettled Country: Changing Landscapes of the American West.* Albuquerque: University of New Mexico Press, 1993, 55–90.

American Indian Peoples | 2

D. Anthony Tyeeme Clark

Facing East from the Mississippi River

The encroachment of European peoples into the fertile lands of the upper Mississippi River valley devastated the lives and ways of the indigenous peoples they displaced. In 1831, as a consequence of diplomatic intimidation and army muscle, a sa ki wa i na i me skwa ki a were escorted west of me di si bo wa ne ko to si ke we ki into the "single backbone country" (Iowa). When they returned east during the annual planting cycle to Illinois, U.S. troops responded with brute force. Chased by the settlers-colonizers' military, Muk ka ta mish a ka kaik (in translation, Black Sparrow Hawk) led the families who followed him north toward Madison, then through Sauk and Crawford counties into southern Vernon County on his way back west to the Mississippi River. The chase ended in August on so-called Battle Island, now part of Blackhawk Park located three miles north of De Soto, Wisconsin, where in August of 1832 the militia and their Sioux military allies butchered children, mothers, and respected Elders. Survivors were taken into military custody. Black Sparrow Hawk's experiences were typical of those of many Indian peoples on half the continent over the next fifty years.

The longer-term results of the 1832 massacre were similarly devastating. At Fort Armstrong, at Rock Island, Illinois, in September of 1832, Sac and Meskwaki diplomats led by the controversial leader Keokuk surrendered "all the lands to which the said tribes have title, or claim" except for 400 square miles of gently rolling prairie on each side of the Iowa River from the point in the north where the Red Cedar River joined with the Iowa to the northern boundary of the state of Missouri (Kappler 1904, p. 349). They agreed to take into their villages surviving family members who earlier that year had followed Black Sparrow Hawk into Illinois and Michigan Territory. As reparation for the "husbands, fathers and brothers" massacred on the upper Mississippi, as "a striking evidence of their mercy and liberality," the United States promised the surviving women and children "thirty-five beef cattle,

White artist Robert M. Sully's visual representation of Black Sparrow Hawk's transformation from "merciless Indian savage" to "domesticated gentleman." Painted in 1833 at Fort Monroe, Virginia, while Black Sparrow Hawk was a prisoner of war in the custody of the U.S. military, Sully's painting implied that Black Sparrow Hawk willingly abandoned his family and people to become a civilized man and deliberately emphasized the fall of the Sac Nation. (*Wisconsin Historical Society/WHi-11706*)

twelve bushels of salt, thirty barrels of pork, fifty barrels of flour, and . . . six thousand bushels of maize (ibid., p. 350).

Reflecting on his captivity through a U.S. government translator and his Sac wife (and later embellished by a local publisher), Black Sparrow Hawk described what he witnessed in the days following the massacre as he faced east from a boat traveling downstream (south) on the Mississippi River:

> On our way down, I surveyed the country that had cost us so much trouble, anxiety, and blood, and that now caused me to be a prisoner of war. I reflected on the ingratitude of the whites, when I saw their fine houses, rich harvests, and everything desirable around them; and recollected that all this land had been ours, for which me and my people had never received a dollar, and that the whites were not satisfied until they took our village and our grave-yards from us, and removed us across the Mississippi River. (Nichols 1999, p. 79)

Signified in Black Sparrow Hawk's translated words are insufferably painful and heartbreaking losses. The Sac military leader was not alone in expressing sorrow and anger as means of coping with the destruction of the world in which he lived. Catastrophic trauma (what amounts to intergenerational post-traumatic stress) is a prevailing theme in the histories and contemporary lived experiences of Indian peoples. Through their government and its coercive instruments, U.S. citizens enthusiastically relocated Indians in order to occupy their homes, farmlands, and cemeteries. They appropriated indigenous voices, visions, and symbols and claimed them as their own. These aggressive people from the East labored to replace indigenous ways of governing with their ways of administration and legislation. They replaced indigenous ways of reconciliation and rehabilitation with alien laws and punishments. They criminalized indigenous sacred ways. They compelled parents to send children far away to distant schools. Indigenous ways of expression spoken for tens of thousands of years were replaced with a foreign language. Through assorted forms of coercion, they used their military, churches, courts, legislatures, and schools to exchange indigenous ways of becoming and being with unfamiliar and bewildering identities.

As a consequence of the lingering residue of nineteenth-century colonization, Indian nations today still have real problems, and they need genuine solutions and culturally relevant approaches to deal effectively with them. Remarkably, given contemporary conditions and the histories that produced them, Indian peoples are still here. Notwithstanding passionate efforts to destroy them, or wishing them gone, they hold on to lifelines of tribal identities, cherishing them and passing them on to subsequent generations. Some tribal peoples, such as the citizens of the Navajo Nation, do so living on the same lands they have occupied for thousands of years. Others, like the Ojibwa and Tohono O'odham (pronounced *tah-hoe-na aut-um*) peoples, do so in ancestral homelands disrupted by international boundaries that separate the United States from Canada and Mexico. Still others, such as the Delaware and Osage peoples, like the Meskwaki and Sac, do so having been forcibly removed to new territories several times over many decades.

A word of warning must be introduced here. Along with the concern to give voice to—or represent—"Indian," one is obliged to be selective. Terms like "American Indian" or "Native American" are historical and linguistic constructs with meanings that change over time and in different contexts. Another qualification concerns the very term "Indians," which makes a specified grouping of human beings seem allied and homogeneous—essentially one people, with one view about other cultures and one way of thinking about them. Of course, that is not the case. Indian peoples always have had many internal differences—between different nations, between regions of what has become the United States, between those peoples colonized by Spanish-speaking and English-speaking colonizers, and so on. Attitudes toward visitors, sojourners, settlers, and colonizers among Indian peoples varied greatly, as they still do.

Despite the worst poverty rates among all population groups in the twenty-first century and staggering statistics that reveal how poor health, unresponsive schools, inadequate employment options, and brutality devastate Indian country, Indians still enthusiastically prefer their own diverse ways, languages, and values. Indigenous cultures always have offered and continue to provide strength and guidance in virtually all aspects of indigenous societies. Indians have maintained the will to continue living as separate and sovereign peoples and to insist on negotiating relationships with non-Indians on their terms, rather than on the conditions dictated by the colonizers' government. Yes, many Indian people enjoy the trappings of consumer and pop-culture society. But many Indians manage to return to their place—their identity, which is rooted in tribal, traditional ways of becoming and being in this world. In the twenty-first century, what non-Indians imagine still as "their" West nonetheless remains Indian country.

Fast Forward: Grim Realities in Indian Country Today

In the opening decades of the twentieth century, with their "West" conquered and the map filled in, many Euro-Americans believed that Indians—as a race and as many different nations of people—would vanish from the geographical and political landscape of "their" country. Thus, they resolved independently to memorialize the "Indians" of their imaginations while simultaneously coercing actual Indian peoples into accepting as normal alien and destructive ways of living. With Sac and Meskwaki peoples long ago removed to Iowa, Kansas, and Oklahoma, the scene of the 1832 slaughter in Wisconsin today is associated with the so-called Battle of the Bad Axe and is surrounded by place names such as Victory, Battle Creek, Battle Island, and Battle Slough. Blackhawk County Park, located between De Soto and Genoa, is a two-acre site that includes a public boat launch and concession stand. South of the county property is Blackhawk Park, operated by the U.S. Army Corp of Engineers, complete with 150 campsites and water-based outdoor recreation.

The excesses of American colonization, like those inscribed in names that venerate a massacre as a "battle," are apparent everywhere in Indian country—on the landscape, in symbolism, and in the lives of Indian peoples. Understood sociologically, colonization is the large-scale migration of settler populations into already-occupied territories. Such migrations are closely followed by expansions of settler cultures—politics and laws, social institutions, and religions—and the displacement, subjugation, division, and ideological domination of indigenous peoples. In the context of U.S. history, colonization continues to be a means of impeding the freedom and self-government of Indian nations for the unequivocal purpose of transferring material wealth and emotional well-being from the colonized to the colonizer.

There is no partisan-free upside to the ominous particulars of ongoing colonization. It is a form of concentrated, pervasive brutality that manifests in a variety of ways. In the contemporary United States, Indians endure high rates of poverty and unemployment. According to the Bureau of Indian Affairs, a colonial bureaucracy since 1824 tasked with administering the decisions of Congress and the Department of the Interior, Indian peoples "experience an extreme lack of economic opportunities and lower than average quality of life when measured against the dominant society" (quoted in

"Sexual Assault in Indian Country," p. 3). Average unemployment across all Indian reservations in 1999 was 43 percent; on some rural reservations it ranged into the 80 percent range and higher. Urban Indian populations fare little better. In Minneapolis, nearly one-fourth of all Indian men were officially unemployed at the time that the census was taken in 1990, four times the unemployment rate for white men. Based on a three-year average, 24.3 percent of all American Indians and Alaska Natives lived in poverty from 2003 through 2004, more than twice the poverty rate of whites (10.5 percent). Related to poverty and unemployment, the rates of food insecurity and hunger among Indians are twice the rates for all non-Indians and three times higher than the rates for white families.

Violence, disease, and suicide are also major problems in Indian country. The reported rate of violent crime is well above that of all other groups and more than twice the national average. Nearly a third of all Indian victims of violence are between the ages of eighteen and twenty-four. During a four-year period between 1992 and 1996, that group of Indians experienced the highest per capita rate of violence of any racial group considered by age—about one violent crime for every four persons. Indians are 2.2 times more likely than non-Hispanic whites of similar age to die from complications of diabetes and diabetes-related illnesses. According to the U.S. Census Bureau in 2005, American Indians and Alaska Natives (29 percent) are almost twice as likely not to have health insurance as white families (14.6 percent). Indian children are twice as likely to attempt suicide as any other race or ethnic group. Of all women, Indian women between the ages of twenty-five and forty-four had the highest suicide rate in 2000.

Indian women are raped, abused, stalked, and murdered more than any other group in the country. In a study by the American Indian Women's Chemical Health Project, 75 percent of the Indian women surveyed reported having experienced some type of sexual assault in their lives. Distressing research gathered by the Bureau of Justice Statistics between 1993 and 1998 revealed that twenty-three of every thousand American Indian females are victims of intimate violence or rape. In their lifetimes, one in three Indian women will be raped. Six in 10 will be physically assaulted. Indian women experience 66 percent of the violent crimes committed against Indian peoples. This reported rate of victimization is nearly double that for African Americans, triple that for whites, and twelve times the victimization rate for Asian Americans. (Non-Indian men overwhelmingly are the offenders in these cases.) In 2001 the U.S. Department of Justice found that violent crime was "primarily interracial" for American Indian victims. Some nine in ten Indian victims of rape or sexual assault reported assailants who were white or black.

Other issues complicate the matter of violence in the lives of Indian women. Mistrust for white-dominated agencies, widespread fear of and cynicism regarding law enforcement, dread of rejection, memories of forced sterilization and other violent "treatment" procedures, and a reluctance by state and tribal agencies to prosecute crimes all intersect in the lives of Indian women.

Because of a Supreme Court ruling in 1978, Indian courts have the authority to prosecute at most one in every ten offenders who victimize Indian women.

When tribal police are called to a home for a domestic violence incident, they are able to intervene at that moment. If the offender is non-Indian, however, the tribal police cannot arrest him, nor can the tribal prosecutor bring charges. For crimes committed by non-Indian offenders, the tribal government's only recourse is to refer the matter to a U.S. Attorney, who represents the U.S. federal government in United States district court and United States court of appeals, and who often declines to prosecute. In cases of domestic violence, according to one study, the statutory hurdle is so high that even breaking the victim's nose is insufficient grounds to secure a felony conviction for assault under the federal definition, which requires serious bodily injury. Thus, violence directed at Indian peoples by non-Indians and the limited abilities of Indian governments to respond effectively are as much a part of the present as they were of a past marred by colonization.

Grassroots leaders like Karen Artichoker, director of the Sacred Circle National Resource Center to End Violence Against Native Women and co-author of *Domestic Violence Is Not Lakota/Dakota Tradition*, have led anti-violence efforts on behalf of indigenous women for decades. Grass-roots groups such as Sacred Circle and larger bodies such as the National Congress of American Indians succeeded in bringing Indian women's need for protection before congressional lawmakers. In October of 2005, Congress approved the Violence Against Women Act's Title IX—Safety for Indian Women—increasing the authority of tribal governments to protect women. In the optimistic words of Mandan and Hidatsa journalist and *Missoulian* columnist Jodi Rave, "The new law brings anti-domestic violence advocates closer to realizing a vision that transforms indigenous communities: where respect is restored to women, where change can infuse law enforcement practices, where healing can find its place among families."

Rewind: The Menacing Face of Nineteenth-Century Conquest

The August 1832 massacre of women and children at Bad Axe and the coerced removal of the survivors were not isolated incidents. They were indicative of a systematic pattern that continued into the early decades of the twentieth century. Before March 1803, when Congress admitted Ohio as the seventeenth state, Indian nations were seen by the U.S. as sovereign throughout the territory west of the original thirteen states. If Euro-Americans were to expand and take control of the continent, however, Indian peoples would have to be driven out, which they were as the U.S. and state governments collaborated to forcibly remove Indian peoples from states such as Indiana and Illinois. During the American Civil War and afterward, the U.S. government used its army to bring a final solution to the so-called "Indian question." Indian women and children, in particular, were targeted for wholesale slaughter in order to destroy Indian nations.

The founding fathers were themselves advocates of indiscriminately slaying indigenous peoples. As if looking in a mirror when creating the

"Facts . . . submitted to a candid world" used to explain the 1776 declaration of independence from their homeland, the founders asserted that the king of England had brought on "the inhabitants of our frontiers . . . the merciless Indian Savages" and their "undistinguished destruction of all ages, sexes, and conditions." George Washington, in 1779, instructed one of his generals to attack the Haudenosaunee and "lay waste all settlements around . . . that the country may not be merely overrun but destroyed," pressing the general not to "listen to any overture of peace before the total ruin of their settlements is effected" (quoted in Stannard 1992, p. 119). Andrew Jackson, the first president to come from a territory west of the Appalachian Mountains and architect of the earliest forced removals of Indian peoples to locations west of the Mississippi River, still was recommending after his presidency that soldiers systematically seek out and slaughter Indian women and children. To do otherwise, he wrote, was analogous to trailing "a wolf in the hammocks without knowing first where the den and whelps were" (ibid., p. 122). Jackson was not alone.

From the Michigan Territory and Illinois to the Great Plains and Colorado, to Nevada and Utah and Idaho, to Montana, all the way to California—from the Mississippi River to the Pacific Ocean—the United States waged an all-out war of conquest that targeted women and children, on the one hand, and relied upon various forms of violence and intimidation, on the other. The perpetrators were not always the military. On February 26, 1860, Hank Larrabee and a band of non-Indian thugs invaded what the Wiyot people in their language called Tuluwat—the center of their world in present-day California. Larrabee and his coconspirators killed as many as 100 Eel River/Wiyot people. Wiyot oral tradition tells that Larrabee's victims included every child in the tribe but one.

While doing so may not have been official policy, it does appear that state militias and the federal military systematically targeted women and children. On January 29, 1863, Patrick Edward Connor and about 200 troopers of the California Volunteer Regiment attacked a Northwestern Shoshoni winter village located at the convergence of Beaver Creek and Bear River, what was at the time claimed by the United States as Washington Territory (a short distance north of the present Utah-Idaho border). "Very quickly, the lopsided battle became a wholesale slaughter," in the words of historian and biographer Scott Christiansen, relying on the account of Sergeant William L. Beach of Company K, 2nd Cavalry Regiment, California Volunteers:

> The soldiers massacred Shoshone men, women, and children, and held infants by their heels while they "beat their brains out on any hard substance they could find." . . . The soldiers pulled their pistols and shot many of them directly in the face from arm's length. Soldiers [burned] the wickiups and tepees and [killed] any who they found still living. . . . The soldiers [used] bayonets to determine whether the fallen Indians had died, shooting others, or using axes to split open the heads of those yet alive. (Christiansen 1999, pp. 52, 53, 54)

Mae Timbimboo Parry, a Shoshone descendant of the victims at Bear River, characterizes the slaughter this way: "No butcher could have murdered any better than Colonel Connor and his vicious California volunteers. . . . To the Northwestern Shoshone Indians he was an unjust man and a coward" (quoted in Madsen 1985, pp. 233, 238).

The massacre at Bear River during the Civil War was not a solitary episode. After a Denver newspaper printed a front-page editorial in 1864 advocating the "extermination of the red devils" and urging its readers to "take a few months off and dedicate that time to wiping out the Indians," Methodist minister Colonel John M. Chivington told a cheering crowd in August that the Colorado militia would "kill and scalp all little and big" because "nits make lice" (quoted in Smith 2005, p. 80). He later dismissed the possibility of peaceful negotiations: "It simply is not possible for Indians to obey or even understand any treaty. I am fully satisfied, gentlemen, that to kill them is the only way we will ever have peace and quiet in Colorado" (quoted in Melmer 2002).

Chivington made good on his promise. During the early morning hours of November 29, 1864, he led a regiment of Colorado Volunteers against Cheyenne peoples camped at Sand Creek. Federal army officers earlier had promised these people safety, but Chivington ordered an attack nonetheless. The Colorado militia lost nine men in the process of slaying between 200 and 400, most of them women and children. They scalped and sexually mutilated many of the bodies, later exhibiting their trophies to cheering crowds in Denver.

The carnage continued well into the closing decades of the nineteenth century. On January 23, 1870, four cavalry companies, fifty-five mounted infantrymen, and a company of foot soldiers commanded by Lieutenant Colonel Eugene Baker slaughtered 173 Piegan women, children, and old men while they slept in their camp at the extreme upper end of present Lake Elwell, 20 miles northeast of Conrad, Montana. At dawn, within easy range of the lodges grouped near the Marias River, 200 soldiers opened fire with their 50-caliber rifles. Less than three hours later, 53 women and children and 120 men had been slaughtered. The cavalry suffered one fatality. Responding to a question regarding his support of killing defenseless women and children and explicitly "endors[ing] the conduct of Colonel Baker," Montana member of Congress James T. Cavanaugh quoted General William Selby Harney, suggesting that the Piegan children "are nits, and will become lice" (quoted in Welch 1994, p. 36).

The close of the commonly referred to "Indian wars" often is marked with the massacre of the Hohwoju Lakota of the Spotted Elk band at Wounded Knee on December 29, 1890. The bloodbath that resulted in the deaths of at least 350 women, children, and men lasted less than an hour. One soldier later reminisced that "women and children fell like hickory nuts after heavy frost" (U.S. Senate Select Committee on Indian Affairs 1990, p. 96). Hugh McGinnis, another soldier, recalled that "the first volley from the Hotchkiss guns mowed down scores of women and children. . . . Children as well as women with babes in their arms were brought down as far [away] as two miles" (ibid., p. 97). The gun to which McGinnis referred was a 1.65-inch light mountain gun mounted on a carriage that fired exploding shells and grapeshot (which, when fired, separated into pieces, taking out anything in its pathway). It was designed to be light enough to travel with cavalry and had an effective range beyond that of rifled small arms. One female survivor received fifteen wounds from the four Hotchkiss guns deployed on Wounded Knee.

More Army Medals of Honor—the highest award for bravery that can be given to any individual in the U.S. Army—were conferred for the massacre at Wounded Knee than were awarded for any other military action in U.S. history. Congress earlier had empowered the president to present the medal "to such non-commissioned officers and privates as shall most distinguish themselves by their gallantry in action" (quoted in Coy 2003, p. 19).

Moving Forward? Assimilating Indian Country

The westward expansion of Euro-Americans at the expense of Indian nations is widely remembered in American popular culture both as a series of military events and as peaceful and inevitable. The military collapse of American Indian peoples who fought back to protect their homelands did come at an astonishing pace, despite major defeats such as the U.S. Army Seventh Cavalry's embarrassing thrashing at Peji Sla Wakapa in 1876.

Many Euro-Americans continue to believe that in winning the West, aggressive "savages" were conquered by superior military technology, and that unrivaled "civilized" intelligences and exceptionally well-endowed white men overcame inferior indigenous cultures, mentalities, and peoples. The focus on American European greatness enabled the settlers-colonizers to envision the aftermath of the "Indian wars" as a time ripe for remaking "the Indian" and "the West" over into their superior, more civilized image, and, conveniently, to assume control of indigenous land, resources, and human beings. Indian peoples were left to deal with the tremendous costs of ongoing colonization and heal the considerable wounds that accompanied its grisly consequences.

In the closing decades of the nineteenth century, it was clear to Indian diplomats and soldiers that using military force to defend their homelands and their citizens was no longer a reasonable strategy. A fresh approach—a new line of attack—was necessary. Increasingly during those years and well into the early years of the twentieth century, armed resistance changed course as writing and political activism, strategies used throughout the nineteenth century, surged in its closing decades to replace armed combat. Dr. Charles Alexander Eastman, to mention one example of a new generation of what he called "pioneers in a new line of defense" (Eastman 1977, p. 188), trained as a teenager after 1862 in Canada to return one day and reclaim his homeland in Minnesota from the U.S. citizens who had stolen it. He believed that U.S. soldiers had murdered his father, and his life took a dramatic turn when his father arrived and took him south, back into the United States.

On January 1, 1891, the thirty-two-year-old Eastman led a team of 100 rescuers, mostly Indians, northeast from White Clay Creek into the Badlands of South Dakota. It was a belated effort three days after the massacre on the snowy banks of Wounded Knee Creek and the morning after a frighteningly cold two-day blizzard. The doctor and his team's mission were recounted a quarter-century later in his ninth book, *From the Deep Woods to Civilization*. Writing from his home on Granite Lake near Munsonville, New Hampshire, in 1916, Eastman described the grim situation:

> Fully three miles from the scene of the massacre we found the body of a woman completely covered with a blanket of snow, and from this point on we found them scattered along as they had been relentlessly hunted down and slaughtered while fleeing for their lives. Some of our people discovered relatives or friends among the dead, and there was much wailing and mourning. When we reached the spot where the Indian camp had stood, among the fragments of burned tents and other belongings we saw the frozen bodies lying close together or piled upon another. I counted eighty bodies of men who had been in council and who were almost as helpless as the women and babes when the deadly fire began, for nearly all their guns had been taken from them. . . . It took all of my nerve to keep my composure in the face of this spectacle. (Ibid., pp. 111–112)

Eastman was born in 1858 to a Dakota-dialect speaking family living in what today is upstate Minnesota. Their lives, like those of their Lakota relatives in 1890, fundamentally changed after December of 1862. With more than 3,000 spectators observing, by order of Abraham Lincoln on December 26, the military killed thirty-eight Dakota men in the largest single-day mass execution in U.S. history. The chain of events leading up to these hangings was complicated but are suggestive of a broader pattern of forced relocations and subsequent diaspora—a cycle of invasion, conquest, removal, and colonization—that marked the experiences of the citizens of many different Indian nations throughout the nineteenth and into the twentieth century. For dozens of Dakota families—including women and children and the elderly—the connection to homeland was finally shattered after several decades of assaults on their land, spirituality, educational system, and physical well-being (and resulting in the lack of unity necessary for effective resistance) in 1862 when settlers used the U.S.-Dakota War of 1862 as a rationale to seize all remaining Dakota lands. With the enthusiastic support of the local settlers in November of 1862, the U.S. military moved the Dakota peoples in two groups from the Lower Sioux Agency and incarcerated them in concentration camps at Fort Snelling and Mankato, Minnesota, before forcibly removing more than 1,600 people after the mass-hanging to a reservation in Crow Creek, Dakota Territory. Hundreds of men, including Charles Eastman's father, were sent to a prison in Davenport, Iowa, where they remained for three years. Others, including Eastman and his uncle, escaped the madness by fleeing north into Canada.

Separated at age four from his father, who was imprisoned at Davenport, Iowa, in 1863, Eastman lived with his maternal uncle in what is now Manitoba. Nine years later, in 1872, he returned south to reside with his bilingual father and paternal grandmother, who lived near Flandreau, in Dakota Territory, on 160 acres obtained through the Homestead Act of 1862 and a provision negotiated as part of a treaty between the Sioux and Arapaho governments and the United States. Over the next eighteen years Eastman attended English-language schools in Dakota Territory, Wisconsin, Illinois,

Santee educator, author, performer, lecturer and public speaker, boy and girl scout leader, and medical doctor Charles Alexander Eastman in 1887, the year he graduated from Dartmouth College in Hanover, New Hampshire. In May 1890 at the age of 32, Eastman took his medical degree from Boston University and was appointed U.S. government physician at the Pine Ridge Reservation where, on New Year's Day in 1891, he led a 100-member response team to assist survivors of the massacre at Wounded Knee. (*Courtesy of Dartmouth College Library*)

New Hampshire, and Massachusetts. He graduated from the Boston University School of Medicine in June 1890. Returning to South Dakota in November, Eastman assumed the duties of government physician at the Pine Ridge reservation, home of the Oglala Lakota.

When scholars refer to "Indian education," they usually mean the education of Indian children in American European schools like the mission school that Eastman attended in Dakota Territory. The education of Indian peoples by others—by missionaries, federal employees, or public school teachers—was formulated through policies and curricula largely uninfluenced by Indian people themselves. During the era of Indian education in which support for a system of government Indian schools emerged, the education division of the Department of Interior's Indian Office was professionalized, and national Indian policy turned from military conquest and legislative relocation to bureaucratic control. By the late nineteenth century, in the wake of its military success, the United States intended to annihilate the cultures of Indian peoples through this "education," which targeted young people. The so-called humanitarians—the white people who called themselves "Friends of the Indian"—were instrumental in this effort.

The U.S. Indian Training and Industrial School at Carlisle, Pennsylvania, the model for early government Indian education, was a military-style institution that housed students as young as five years old brought from as far away as the other side of the continent. Governmental officials found the Carlisle model an appealing alternative to costly military campaigns. By the end of the century, there were 24 off-reservation boarding schools like Carlisle, as well as 81 boarding schools and 147 day schools on the reservations themselves.

Indian children sent to boarding schools were separated from their families for most of the year, and even for years at a time, without a single family visit. Not only did large numbers of students in these schools suffer from loneliness but many died from starvation and disease because of inadequate food and medical care. Physical hardship was part of a systematic assault that included sexual and physical abuse that continued well into the twentieth century. In 1987, for example, the FBI found evidence that a teacher at the government-run Hopi day school in Arizona had sexually abused as many as 142 boys between 1979 and the time of his arrest in 1987.

Congressional appropriations inaugurated in 1891 and expanded in 1906 relocated the responsibility for educating Indian children away from the off-reservation government Indian schools to locally managed non-Indian public schools, where federal government appropriations for Indian students typically disappeared into general operating budgets. After 1906 not only did the government education of Indian children shift away from off-reservation boarding schools but, in addition, the curricular content was transferred to solely vocational education aimed at providing minimal job skills. The Indian services attached employment bureaus to most schools. These bureaus contracted locally with private citizens to provide cheap labor for their businesses.

Simultaneously, because non-Indian public schools also were in the midst of changing curricular concepts—"tracking" students according to contrived notions of intellectual abilities and providing vocational educations to students identified as academically weak—supporters of the gradual assimilation of Indian peoples into American European society seized the opportunity to send Indian children to local non-Indian schools and terminate federal supervision of Indian education. In 1908 only twenty-four Indian children attended public schools. After 1910, Indian service functionaries were instructed to transfer Indian children to schools that surrounded reservations. By 1928 there were approximately 79,000 Indian young people identified as school-age children. More than 10,000 were not in school. Another 6,000 attended church mission schools. More than 5,000 children were enrolled in day schools on their reservations. Some 21,000 attended boarding schools, and the remaining 36,000 children were enrolled in non-Indian public schools near their reservations. The vast majority of the public school students were tracked into vocational education.

By 1900, these three major forms of American European education were solidly established. A fourth form that should be mentioned is the mission school like the one at Flandreau in Dakota Territory that Charles Eastman attended. In 1819, Congress approved an appropriation, in the words of the legitimating legislation, to "put into the hands of their [Indian] children the primer and the hoe [so that] they will grow up in the habits of morality and industry" (Peyer 1997, p. 59). Just twenty-three years later that appropriation for mission schools had grown from $10,000 to $214,000. Churches also accessed congressional appropriations through a competitive contract system well into the twentieth century. Using these federal funds, as well as donations from parishioners, evangelistic churches throughout the intervening years supported proselytizing activity among receptive citizens of Indian nations for over a century.

In addition to providing schools in which Indian children were taught how to be non-Indians, the U.S. government dismantled the legal authority of Indian governments and extended federal, state, and local laws to all Indian peoples. In its deliberate efforts to colonize Indian nations internally, Congress ended all future treaty negotiations with political representatives of Indian governments and extended criminal jurisdiction into territories and among populations over which Indian nations long had claimed sovereignty. The same year in which Richard Henry Pratt opened the school for Indian children at Carlisle Barracks in Pennsylvania, Ezra Hayt, commissioner of Indian Affairs, reported to Congress that

> a civilized community could not exist . . . without law, and a semi-civilized and barbarous people are in a hopeless state of anarchy without its protection and sanctions. It is true that the various tribes have regulations and customs of their own, which, however, are founded on superstition and ignorance of the usages of civilized communities, and generally tend to perpetuate feuds and keep alive animosities. (Olson and Wilson 1984, p. 62)

Influenced by miseducated assumptions (such as those represented by Hayt), congressional efforts to replace the authority of Indian governments with their own began in 1871 with an amendment to the annual Indian appropriations bill. Prior to 1871, Euro-Americans had concluded that the treaty system had to end. Although the U.S. government did not recognize fee-simple title to land claimed by Indian nations, these officials nonetheless still negotiated treaties and agreements with Indian political leaders and in some ways continued to deal with Indian nations as members of an international community of nation-states. For a variety of reasons, those practices ended in 1871 with a rider added to a small appropriation for removing families and their personal property from the Yanktonais bands of the Dakota-dialect-speaking peoples to a reservation in what became the southeastern portion of South Dakota. With its annual appropriations, Congress announced that

> Hereafter no Indian nation or tribe within the territory of the United States shall be acknowledged or recognized as an independent nation, tribe, or power with whom the United States may contract by treaty: Provided further, That nothing herein contained shall be construed to invalidate or impair the obligation of any treaty heretofore lawfully made and ratified with any such Indian nation or tribe. (Prucha 2000, p. 135)

Instead of sending representatives to negotiate with the political leaders of Indian nations, Congress after 1871 stood in to legislate for them, sometimes soliciting and at other times slighting their advice, but mostly delegating its legislative authority to the Department of Interior's Indian services—the Bureau of Indian Affairs.

Moving Out and Moving On?
Industrialization and Wage Labor

Few American Indian families completely escaped the immediate and longer-term consequences of coerced education. Most Indian people, like their immigrant neighbors, also experienced the consequences of industrialization and wage labor. That was the case for those persons working farms in the valley of the Big Blue River on the Otoe-Missouria reservation in Nebraska, the sawmills operating in the Apukshunnubbee district of the Choctaw Nation in Indian Territory, and the deerskin glove–producing industry on the Duck Valley reservation straddling the Idaho and Nevada borders.

Wherever Indians lived, the tentacles of industrialization and wage labor wound their way through their lives. An Anishinaabeg family farming hard-red spring wheat in the western portion of the White Earth reservation on the Minnesota side of the Red River Valley in 1900 found the price of their crop influenced not just by federal government representatives located at White Earth Village but also by operators of the grain elevator in Mahnomen, functionaries of the Great Northern Railway located in St. Paul, and owners of the flour mills in Minneapolis, the nation's leading flour-producing center. Keres-speaking men from the Pueblo of Laguna working rail lines after 1880 often found themselves far from their homes in growing cities like Albuquerque to the east and Richmond, California, to the west.

The Anishinnabe and Laguna Pueblo families were connected in many ways with the emerging global marketplace, and individuals from both purchased the products of an increasingly industrialized economy. When not at work, they might have contemplated paying for ready-made clothing, a Shepard's Blizzard ice cream freezer, or a general purpose plow from the Sears, Roebuck and Company's "mammoth catalogue." The railroad corporations that delivered their packages from Chicago also took away bushels of their wheat, their manufactured goods, and even their daughters and sons.

Everywhere Indians joined each other and others in cities. The son of a wheat-farming family near Mahnomen, for instance, might board a railroad car bound for Minneapolis to look for work there in the mills. The total population of Minneapolis, including at least 600 Natives in 1920, mushroomed from 13,066 in 1870 to 380,582 by 1920. After 1879 a sister might continue from Minneapolis through Chicago to eastern Pennsylvania and the government Indian school at Carlisle. During the summer, rather than return to White Earth reservation, she might work as a clerk at the Wanamaker department store in Philadelphia, a city with an overall population that ballooned from 847,170 in 1880 to 1,823,779 in 1920. The son of a Keres-speaking family from Laguna Pueblo might hop a train operated by the Santa Fe Railway (which took over the Atlantic and Pacific Railway Company in 1893) on its way to the waste-cleaning building in Richmond, California, just a ferry-ride from San Francisco—a sprawling metropolis swollen by population growth from 298,997 to 506,676 in only thirty years. Through the reservation at White Earth and the pueblo at Laguna, as well as down the middle of Minneapolis and Richmond, steel tracks cut a tremendous gash. These tracks reminded everyone that while railroads gave, they also took away.

Railroads did not take people away only to large cities. Urbanization was not limited to metropolitan areas. As the Indian population increased after 1900, American Indian peoples migrated from rural, reservation areas to off-reservation farming communities and commercial centers, small industrial towns, and larger cities. Everywhere, the Indian "urban" population grew from at least 0.4 percent of 237,196 persons in 1900 to 6.1 percent of 244,437 in 1920—from about 949 individuals to approximately 14,911.

Migrations from rural reservations and off-reservation areas after 1900 clearly were toward small industrial towns and cities, and in greater percentages and numbers over time. In the Puget Sound watershed of Washington State, for instance, 22 percent of 4,000 Indians lived in cities and mill towns in 1900. Twenty years later that percentage had grown to 32 percent. Natives living along the downtown Seattle waterfront and outside the downtown core in mainly white, working-class neighborhoods in 1920 came from fourteen different states.

Thus, although more research is needed on the pre-1920 urbanization of Indian peoples, we can nonetheless conclude that Indians, along with everyone else, were experiencing dislocations through urbanization, migration, and changing economic circumstances resulting from industrialization. Just like their middle-class, white, and English-speaking counterparts, Indians were seeking avenues in which to respond to these changes and alleviate the problems associated with them. Furthermore, industrialization, urbanization, and government-sponsored child removal policies combined to create a mobile class of Indians who had unprecedented opportunities to form webs of relationships between widely separated Indian communities and individuals that joined them in new and interesting ways.

Early Twentieth-Century Political Mobilization: A Society and a Brotherhood

Webs of relationship that generated new means of political organization and activism were one unintended consequence of coerced education in foreign-language schools. Growing out of the U.S. heartland—Oklahoma, Kansas, Nebraska, and the Dakotas—organizations such as the Society of American Indians and the Brotherhood of North American Indians were among the earliest collaborative efforts by the citizens of Indian nations in the twentieth century to influence political decision-making in Washington, D.C. The experiences of Luther Standing Bear and Richard C. Adams offer powerful examples of this modern organized resistance, the ways in which individual

Fifth annual meeting of the Society of American Indians, taken outside of the Engineering Building on the campus of Haskell Institute in Lawrence, Kansas, on October 1, 1915. In a context when Indian peoples were not represented in federal, state, or local governments as citizens of Indian nations, the Society was an early effort by Indian peoples in the twentieth century to lobby Congress and the media to more effectively represent Indian nations and their needs. (Quarterly Journal of the Society of American Indians *3, no. 4 (October–December 1915), Plate 14*)

Indians used the English language and writing to strike back at the colonizer, and the emergence of political activism in the opening years of the twentieth century that through webs of relationship joined displaced Indian individuals together with tribally connected citizens of Indian nations.

Contemplating the meaning of an overland journey east in 1879 from South Dakota to the government Indian school in Carlisle, Pennsylvania, Standing Bear remembered one stop in Sioux City, Iowa:

> The white people were yelling at us and making a great noise. When the train stopped, we raised the windows to look out. Soon they started to throw money at us. . . . We threw the money all back at them. At this, the white people laughed and threw more money. . . . Many of the little Indian boys and girls were afraid of the white people. I really did not blame them, because the whites acted so wild at seeing us. They tried to give the war-whoop and mimic the Indian and in other ways got us all wrought up and excited, and we did not like this sort of treatment. (Standing Bear 1975, pp. 129–130)

When he was sixty years old, more than simply documenting a memory in his second of four books, Standing Bear wrested the meaning of "Indian" away from "the whites that acted so wild at seeing us," away from the "Wild West" shows and Hollywood motion pictures in which he was an actor, away from certain historians and anthropologists with whom he disagreed.

Luther Standing Bear, the brother of Henry Standing Bear—one of the six original Indian organizers of the first Indian-organized national conference in the twentieth century—joined the Society of American Indians from the Pine Ridge reservation in South Dakota in 1912 at the age of forty-four.

An actor in the Wild West shows produced by William F. Cody until the serious injuries he suffered in a train wreck just outside Chicago almost ended his life in 1904, Standing Bear later moved to Los Angeles, where he became an actor in the genre of Hollywood westerns. While living in California he wrote four books.

As an activist and author, Standing Bear wrote to correct injustices—to explain "things [done by the Indian] that are more often than not erroneous" (Standing Bear 1978, p. 42). He maneuvered symbols and metaphors to make Indian nations present and powerful outside of indigenous contexts. In the language of the destroyers of indigenous worlds, he fought back against declarations of Indian demise, destructive government policies, and the contagious diseases that slaughtered their extended families. He located the cause of their problems outside of indigenous cultures: "The Lakotas were blessed with good health . . . [a]nd as far as I can remember there was no such thing as a contagious disease," he wrote in his third book, *Land of the Spotted Eagle*.

> But when our mode of life changed and we began to eat "spotted buffalo" and learned to eat bread, sugar, candy, and canned goods, we then realized the meaning of disease, particularly so when students returning from school came weakened and undermined in health, many of them to die in young manhood and womanhood. . . . Had the Indian been as completely subdued in spirit as he was in body he would have perished within the century of his subjection. But it is the unquenchable spirit that has saved him—his clinging to Indian ways, Indian thought, and tradition, that has kept him and is keeping him today. The white man's ways were not his ways and many of the things that he has tried to adopt have proven disastrous and to his utter shame. (Ibid., pp. 60–61, 190)

Through his command of the colonizer's language, Standing Bear resurrected out of an earlier existence not corrupted by "contagious disease" Lakota ways of doing and thinking in the world and their interdependent relationships, which enabled (and enable) them to be Lakota. His disease-free past countered the actual presence of those war-whooping "white people" playing Indian at a railroad depot in Sioux City, Iowa. It substituted something potent—but not wild or savage—to represent the ways of living in the world that could defend Lakotas and other Indian nations against both contagious disease and the savagery of government Indian administration.

In 1891, just months after the massacre at Wounded Knee and twelve years after they left home to attend the first class at the government Indian school in Carlisle, Luther Standing Bear and Clarence Three Stars clandestinely joined with others to form a group of government Indian school graduates in the Allen Issue Station District of the Pine Ridge Agency. As Standing Bear recalled their efforts in his second book, their earliest efforts led to the formation of an issues-oriented body, the Oglala Council, which labored to counter unwanted aspects of government Indian administration, provided for less advantaged persons in their communities, and located their authority in the diplomacy of their predecessors. Earlier, in 1874 on the Yankton reservation, Philip Joseph Deloria and other leaders at Standing Rock had formed the Planting Society, renamed the Brotherhood of

Laura Miriam Cornelius Kellogg (Oneida)

Remembered for her work as an activist and organizer, author, playwright, and linguist, Laura Miriam Cornelius Kellogg was one of the most widely known Indian women during the period between the two world wars. She was brilliant, creative, and controversial. According to historian Laurence Hauptman, citing interviews with respected elders Norbert Hill, Sr., Ruth Baird, Frank Danforth, and others, Oneidas credit her with being the best Indian speaker of her generation, male or female.

Born in September 1880, Cornelius Kellogg was a descendant of Tekawyatron, a nineteenth-century Oneida leader in New York and Wisconsin, and Elijah Skenandoah, the pine tree chief, Turtle Clan leader, and holder of the Oneida tribal belt and accompanying treaties struck in New York. After attending Grafton Hall, an Episcopalian boarding school in Fond du Lac, Wisconsin, Cornelius Kellogg attended but did not graduate from Stanford University, Barnard College, the New York School of Philanthropy (later the Columbia University School of Social Work), Cornell University, and the University of Wisconsin. She was among the founders of the Society of American Indians in 1911 and, before 1915, the only woman elected to a leadership position in that all-Indian national organization.

In many ways the young woman was a popular educator who countered negative portrayals of Indian character and ability. Readers of the *New York Times* in 1910 read about a fiery twenty-nine-year-old Oneida woman who immodestly defied William Cody, the performer and scriptwriter for the popular "Wild West" shows. According to the journalist who related the exchange, the performer asked the young woman what tribe she belonged to. Her response was that she did not belong to a tribe: "I am of the Six Nations of New York. We weren't tribes." She offered *New York Times* readers something else to consider, too. "What about Sequoia, the Cherokee who invented the alphabet?"

> What about the Iroquois whose constitution suggested the idea of a separate States Government to your statesman Benjamin Franklin for the Constitution of the United States? Was it not Oronhiatekha who gave to the world the best system of insurance discovered yet? These men gave inventions and creations to the world. They were doing things which the white man has done since, and wherever they have had half a chance they have always done them. The trouble is that the white man has judged all Indians by those of the plains. (Quoted in "Refutes Buffalo Bill," p. 9)

Thus she argued that Indians, and in particular her Haudenosaunee relatives, shaped non-Indian cultures and societies in crucial ways.

Cornelius Kellogg was fiercely concerned

Christian Unity in 1893, an organization of prominent men able to perform charitable work who also were first-responders to emergencies and family tragedies. What Deloria and others discovered as Christian men was not that they had to abandon all of the beliefs of the past. They used the tools offered by functionaries of the colonizer's church and remained Lakota at the same time. All four—the Standing Bear brothers, Three Stars, and Deloria—later participated in the Society of American Indians.

The making of the Society of American Indians emerged over a period of twenty years from extensive webs of relationship and from prior efforts at organization that joined tribally connected American Indian women and men. From the "inaugural national Indian conference," as organizers adver-

about responding to what she termed "the health question of the race." Between 1908 and 1912, social science surveys confirmed what she and other Indians had known for some time: Indians on reservations and in government Indian schools experienced infectious disease disproportionately to other populations, including urban ones. Two diseases in particular—trachoma and tuberculosis—had reached near-epidemic proportions.

Cornelius Kellogg was concerned about and had a personal stake in the well-being of Indian peoples. She attacked government Indian schools as agents of violence in which "[t]he Government has tried to tell the Indian child everything Indian was to be despised . . . instead of being told to respect the things that are respectable in his own culture" (U.S. Senate Committee on Indian Affairs 1917, p. 512). She characterized federal supervision as "a reign of terror" (p. 510). Her solution was not to withdraw summarily the institutions of U.S. government from Indian nations. Instead, she explained, "change must only be gradual" (p. 519).

What she advocated was a transition from government paternalism—from Indians being government wards—to self-government for Indian nations. Her plan for self-government had four crucial elements: the development of

industries connected to viable markets, the use of labor rather than currency as the principal means of exchange, planned communities, and democratic, consensus-building governments. She identified three guiding principles essential to the well-being of self-governing Indian nations: "the influence of human ties" and "the ties of home," "the original laws of health" and "our own ways of living," and the long-term interests in allotments and inheritances from allotments on Indian reservations.

Thus, during the opening decades of the twentieth century, Cornelius Kellogg offered a territorial and culturally sensitive solution to the devastation of ongoing colonization. She stood against the further loss of reservation land—the key element in keeping Indian nations all together in one place and the most important factor in securing economic security and political independence. Her model for self-government acknowledged a common wish among Indians to remain with their people.

References

"Refutes Buffalo Bill: Indian Maiden Tells Him His Views of the Red Man Are Wrong." *New York Times*, May 13, 1910.
U.S. Senate Committee on Indian Affairs. *Indian Appropriation Bill: Hearings on H.R. 18453*, 64th Cong., 2d sess., 1917.

tised the October 1911 meeting in Columbus, Ohio, through its final meeting in Chicago in 1923, the Society for twelve years provided a meeting ground for Indian advocates of race progress, developing leadership and the autonomy of Indian nations. At its twelve annual meetings in places with opportunities for media attention, Indians from reservation communities, rural locations, small towns and growing cities, and government service gathered to discuss solutions to their shared concerns. The diversity of participants, open debates, unguarded yearly election of officers, and locations for annual meetings combined to offer opportunities for Indians to develop already emerging political strategies for negotiating with representatives of an occupation government.

Among the organizers of the Brotherhood of North American Indians in 1911 were persons, such as Richard C. Adams, devoted to political strategies that returned self-government to Indian nations. In his published work and in his correspondence, Adams often added to his signature the words "Representing the Delaware Indians." He represented the Delaware tribe and individuals in many ways. For twenty-four years after 1897 he did so legally and legislatively in Washington, D.C. He also did so as the author of five books, as an archivist of documents important to Delaware political history, as knowledge keeper and poet, and as a political activist. He was born in Wyandotte County, Kansas, in 1864, thirty-five years after a forced removal into what would become Kansas Territory and three years before what Delaware peoples today refer to as their "last removal." His family reluctantly moved to Cherokee Nation, Indian Territory, in 1869, where they lived near Alluwe among the center of Delaware political activity in what became Nowata and Washington counties, Oklahoma.

Adams introduced the Brotherhood of North American Indians—and the more general idea of Indian representatives of Indian nations in Congress—in a 1912 memorial demanding the "right to have Indian delegates on the floor of the Congress of the United States" and the "right to ratify or reject by vote of the tribe or tribes affected, after 60 days notice, any legislation of the Congress of the United States . . . in all cases where there has not been an agreement with the Indians" (Senate Committee on Indian Affairs 1912, p. 6).

Adams's proposal was in the political tradition of his Cherokee neighbors and relatives living in Indian Territory who earlier in the nineteenth century had been forced from their homelands east of the Mississippi River. In the English-language translation of the treaty negotiated in November 1785 between representatives of the governments of the Cherokee Nation and the United States at Hopewell, South Carolina, both parties agreed that Cherokee political leaders "shall have the right to send a deputy of their choice, whenever they think fit, to Congress" (Kappler 1904, p. 10). This provision of the 1785 treaty was reiterated in the treaty struck at New Echota in 1835. However, fifty years after Hopewell, representatives of the Cherokee Nation surrendered this authority. Under staggering pressure, they also transferred to the federal government of the United States those Cherokee Nation lands located east of the Mississippi.

In addition to calling for Indian congressional representatives, thus reinstating political power to Indian nations, Adams also championed ten "Indian rights" and detailed a legislative agenda. He further recommended appropriations for the government administration of Indian services, as well as the creation of advisory boards of Indians "for each Indian school or agency" and "greater cooperation between the Federal Government and State governments in matters of education for all Indian youth" (Senate Committee on Indian Affairs 1912, p. 6).

He called on Congress to grant Indians "the right of petition and assembly without restriction or restraint, and the right to come and go at will without the permission of any superintendent or agent." He argued for what would become a policy of "Indian preference," asking that "Indians by blood

. . . be given preference in the Indian Service as superintendents, financial clerks, teachers, farmers, and mechanics" (ibid.). Finally, he called on Congress to grant "[p]rotection as persons under the Constitution of the United States, for all Indians, whether as tribes or individuals, of life, liberty, and property, and the right to enforce such protection in the courts." Further, he pleaded that

> [s]urely our interests are vast enough, our people intelligent enough and our personal training of more than 100 years under Government control and tutorship good enough to entitle us now to have a voice in the making and administering of the laws that affect our people and control our property. . . . If after 100 years of Government wardship, we are not in a position to attend to our own affairs and our own business, then there must be something wrong with the training and civilization administered to us by the government. (Ibid., pp. 6–7)

Thus Adams offered a vision for possible futures among Indian and non-Indian peoples with Indian nations as active participants in the politics and policies that affect them.

The Middle of the Twentieth Century: A Time of Liquidation and Relocation, and Television and Fighting Back

As a recent study concerned with the rise of modern Indian nations suggests, Indian peoples still faced at least four persistent problems in the middle of the twentieth century. First, the citizens of Indian nations were mired in dreadful economic and social conditions—the worst among all of the racial and ethnic groups in the United States. Second, political oppression remained relentless. Third, the Bureau of Indian Affairs and many churches continued their efforts to suppress the sacred ways of Indian peoples, including efforts to compel people to use the English language and to dress and act in all ways as non-Indians. And fourth, Congress in 1953 announced the termination policy in the form of House Concurrent Resolution 108, a "final solution" that in theory would lead to selling off all remaining tribal lands, withdrawal of all treaty-guaranteed federal support, and the forcing of the rapid assimilation of Indian peoples into the majority, English-language-speaking society.

In addition to terrible living conditions, ruthless and ongoing colonization, and termination, the Bureau of Indian Affairs turned an option of choice—personal decisions about moving into U.S. cities—into a coercive policy called "relocation." Relocation was a mid-twentieth-century version of nineteenth-century removals, except that a century later the government decided that cities, not some destination outside of the United States, would be the new dumping ground for otherwise unwanted human beings. During the 1930s, Congress had promised to build up reservations as vibrant centers of Indian life and then failed to allocate sufficient funds to reach those lofty goals. Having played a major role in making reservations unsustainable, Congress and the mainstream press then identified the reservation system made by non-Indians as the problem and offered as a solution the idea of integrating Indian people into cities.

The decades-long consequences were dramatic. In 1948 the Bureau of Indian Affairs established the Branch of Relocation to promote urban "resettlement" among the citizens of the Navajo Nation and the Hopi people surrounded by the state of Arizona. In 1952 the BIA created the Relocation Services Program, and the relocation policy gained momentum. The BIA relocated at least 30,000 individual Indians during the decade after 1950, and 38,000 more between 1960 and 1968. The growth of the Indian urban population during the two decades after 1950 is striking. In 1950, just 16.3 percent of the total Indian population lived in U.S. cities. Twenty years later, 44.6 percent of the total Indian population was urban. By 1970, as a result of this dramatic urban migration, at least eight U.S. cities—all in the West—had larger Indian populations than any land-based Indian nation except that of the Navajos. And this demographic shift from reservations to Western cities created real problems. Living off of their reservations, away from their communities and extended families—no longer under the jurisdiction of the Bureau of Indian Affairs—Indian peoples lost access to the educational and community services that earlier had been negotiated by shrewd and forward-looking diplomats representing their nations.

Despite tremendous pressures to leave their nations, most Indian peoples, however, remained at home. Many of those people who left did so only temporarily, or frequently returned to maintain close connections and to support family members left behind. In the end, and once again, the colonizer's desire to destroy Indian nations and cultures failed.

Newspaper articles and television reports of this period—the years at midcentury—mark a growing and increasingly savoir-faire politicization among Indian peoples and, in some ways, an increasing thoughtfulness among non-Indians about their responsibilities to the people whose ancestors they had displaced. This dual politicization—among the citizens of Indian nations and among the mainstream "public"—was the consequence, in part, once again, of Indian people appropriating the colonizer's tools to counter colonization and preserve, even expand, cultural autonomy and political self-determination. Two of the most powerful tools that Indians and their allies used—and continue to use—were U.S. jurisprudence, through which they fought for treaty-based justice on legal grounds; and the mainstream journalistic media, through which they struggled for changes in public policy such as termination—also called "liquidation"—and relocation on technological grounds.

One of the most far-reaching political organizations after 1950 was the National Congress of American Indians, a group founded in 1944 whose members included Indian nations and not only individual Indians like the earlier Society of American Indians and Brotherhood of North American Indians. Through its public relations arm and a national network of 183,000 citizens of Indian nations who provided political letter writing and local community activism, the NCAI influenced media coverage of Indian political issues. The mass media, particularly local newspapers and the new medium of television, shaped the course of discussions at both the policy-making level and around kitchen tables.

A local broadcast in Iowa in 1952 offers insight into the potential for television at the time to allow Indian people to be heard beyond their homelands, outside of their nations. That year an Iowa television station broadcast *The Whole Town's Talking*, which focused on the Sac and Fox Tribe of the Mississippi in Iowa (who call themselves the Meskwaki Nation), one of ten Indian nations that Congress would mark for "liquidation" with HCR 108 the following year. It featured live coverage of a tribal council meeting, chaired by George Young Bear, a graduate of the Indian Industrial School in Lawrence, Kansas. On television, the council discussed a range of issues important to Meskwaki citizens, from the future of their school, to the failure of the U.S. government to honor treaties and agreements with them adequately, to the ambiguous status and problems of land ownership and taxation on the Meskwaki Settlement. During the broadcast, one elder offered a long and heartfelt, emotional speech in Meskwaki. Another faced the camera and, in English, suggested that the nineteenth-century treaties "must have ripped somewhere along the line . . . because if the government had done what they started out to do, today's Indians under sixty years of age would be self-supporting" (quoted in Wilson 1998, p. 45). Another elder in the gathered crowd stood and addressed the television audience directly. "My dear friends," he said. "This is indeed an honor and a pleasure to appear before you this evening, because this is the first time we have appeared before you, in public" (quoted in ibid.).

Futures: Not the End of the Stories, Not the End of the Songs

As in 1952, the citizens of Indian nations are still today not represented in Congress or the White House, or in state legislatures, or in county and city governments. Indian nations are represented in state and other place names, in athletic traditions and symbols, and in schools and motion pictures, but largely on the colonizer's—not the colonized's—terms. Therefore, access to mass media technologies is crucial.

At first glance, politics practiced in the twenty-first century among Indian peoples seems curiously consistent with the sort of politics exercised fifty years ago, and earlier. Since the opening decades of the twentieth century, when the Society of American Indians and the Brotherhood of North American Indians emerged as political vehicles for citizens of Indian nations otherwise unrepresented in Congress and state legislatures—as the example of the live broadcast on an Iowa television station in 1952 suggests—there have been a proliferation of arenas through which Indians have joined culture and government to debate and negotiate matters of a political nature. And they continue to do so.

In the 1970s, when the governments of Indian nations assumed more powers and responsibilities—in no small way a result of changes in U.S.

government relations with Indian nations, generally, and the end of the termination policy in particular—the authority of the Bureau of Indian Affairs and the churches faded. This released a surge of cultural pride, as well as providing an opportunity for Indian nations to reclaim through the courts rights to land and hunting and fishing, the right to be heard in tribal rather than state courts, and the right to charter and regulate schools and colleges. And, ironically, nineteenth- and twentieth-century policies that resulted in what might be the most massive land transfer in global history eventually provided a context for resistance. Accompanied by the creation of isolated reservations, these earlier policies unraveled in the closing decades of the twentieth century as reservations became cherished homelands and the foundation from which a modern sovereignty movement has swept, and continues to seize, Indian country across the West.

Although Indian peoples have their private ways that are not available for wider consumption, there is a formal government dimension to the post-1970s cultural revival that competes as well as works with the authority of federal, state, and local governments. Today, for instance, the Indian nations of the Great Plains and the Intertribal Bison Cooperative work to bring back the buffalo, a move that is fundamental to the well-being of these Indian peoples. The Tohono O'odham Community Action, another contemporary example of joining culture and politics, is a community-based organization dedicated to creating cultural revitalization through community health and sustainable development on the Tohono O'odham Nation. Its efforts to combat diabetes and revitalize the consumption of traditional foods were featured on the CBS program *60 Minutes* in July 2005. Larger than the state of Connecticut, the Tohono O'odham Nation sits in the heart of the Sonoran Desert, 60 miles west of Tucson, Arizona. More than 50 percent of all Tohono O'odham adults have adult-onset diabetes, the highest rate in the world. Until 1960, diabetes was unknown among the Tohono O'odham people.

In the twenty-first century, the joining of culture and politics surges through mass media communications—in particular over the airwaves and through cyberspace, as well as through the reproducible languages of music and performance. On the internet, Indian peoples can—and do—disseminate territorially based and culturally informed perspectives on a wide range of issues from the debates over intelligent design to global warming, from recovering and protecting indigenous languages to covering Indians in professional baseball. Thus understood, many of the "issues" that non-Indians identify as their own, many Indian people likely see as their issues as well, but with an "Indian" perspective.

Resistance to colonization continues, too. From grounded locations in Wisconsin, Nebraska, South Dakota, Arizona, and Washington State—indeed, throughout the contemporary West—the internet and mass-produced media produce a discourse of culturally specific resistance. Technologies such as the internet and mass-produced media make possible virtual migrations of this sort of information to locations where it is received in ways that nourish a global network of relationships fundamentally concerned with decolonization, with reversing the residue of earlier wounds aggravated by ongoing colonization. From efforts in Arizona to save the sacred San Francisco Peaks

Twenty-eight-year-old media activist, musical artist, citizen of the Diné Nation, and volunteer for the Save the Peaks Coalition, Klee Benally (center) during a press conference outside of Flagstaff City Hall in February 2004. Members of the Coalition address environmental and human rights concerns with the Arizona Snowbowl Ski Resort's proposed expansion of their 777-acre U.S. Forest Service–issued Special Use Permit on the San Francisco Peaks. The conflict over the Peaks dates back to the 1930s when ski enthusiasts built a small lodge on the southwestern side of the mountain. Reaching up to 12,000 feet, just north of the reservation border-town of Flagstaff, Arizona, the three volcanic mountains are a sacred, spiritual place for healing and ceremony. Thus, recreational development causes the Peaks to lose their healing power and impairs the ability of Indian peoples to pray and conduct ceremonies. "I hope people realize this is not just about one mountain, but about healing our communities," Benally told an *Indian Country Today* reporter in September 2006. (*Jill Torrance/ Arizona Daily Sun*)

from the negative effects of a winter sport industry to efforts in New York to draw attention to the destructive consequences of anti-Indian politics—a 2005 Supreme Court decision that elevated the right of a county government to tax and even confiscate property from the citizens of an Indian nation—Indian peoples use media and the courts to fight back. They join culture and politics to stay alive.

Thus understood in a contemporary context, territorially situated indigenous language-based knowledge and politics always have circulated through available technologies and with the movement of people. It has not vanished. Neither have the peoples who pass it along from one generation to the next. At its point of reception, such knowledge blends with others. It changes. It grows from diverse communities of origin to connect Indian peoples otherwise separated by geographic distance, language, occupation and employment status, and other sources for individual and group identification. The consequence is survival.

References and Further Reading

Christiansen, Scott R. *Sagwitch: Shoshone Chieftain, Mormon Elder, 1822–1887.* Logan: Utah State University Press, 1999.

Coy, Jimmie Dean. *Valor: A Gathering of Eagles.* Theodore, AL: Evergreen Press, 2003.

Eastman, Charles A. (Ohiyesa). *From the Deep Woods to Civilization: Chapters in the Autobiography of an Indian.* Lincoln: University of Nebraska Press, 1977.

Kappler, Charles J., ed. *Indian Affairs: Laws and Treaties.* Vol. 2: *Treaties.* Washington, DC: Government Printing Office, 1904.

Madsen, Brigham D. *The Shoshoni Frontier and the Bear River Massacre.* Salt Lake City: University of Utah Press, 1985.

Melmer, David. "Sand Creek Returned to Rightful Owners." *Indian Country Today*, May 6, 2002.

Nichols, Roger, ed. *Black Hawk's Autobiography.* Ames: Iowa State University Press, 1999.

Olson, James S., and Raymond Wilson. *Native Americans in the Twentieth Century.* Urbana: University of Illinois Press, 1984.

Peyer, Bernd C. *The Tutor'd Mind: Indian Missionary-Writers in Antebellum America.* Amherst: University of Massachusetts Press, 1997.

Prucha, Francis Paul, ed. *Documents of United States Indian Policy.* 3d ed. Lincoln: University of Nebraska Press, 2000.

Rave, Jodi. "Domestic Violence: Tribal Leaders Making Strides to Protect Women." *Missoulian.* 1 October 2001.

"Sexual Assault in Indian Country: Confronting Sexual Violence." Enola, PA: National Sexual Violence Resource Center, 2000.

Smith, Andrea. *Conquest: Sexual Violence and American Indian Genocide.* Boston: South End Press, 2005.

Standing Bear, Luther. *My People the Sioux.* Lincoln: University of Nebraska Press, 1975.

Standing Bear, Luther. *Land of the Spotted Eagle.* Lincoln: University of Nebraska Press, 1978.

Stannard, David E. *American Holocaust: The Conquest of the New World.* New York: Oxford University Press, 1992.

U.S. Senate Committee on Indian Affairs. *Memorial of the Brotherhood of North American Indians*, 62d Cong., 2d sess., S. Doc. 489, 1912.

U.S. Senate Select Committee on Indian Affairs. *Wounded Knee Memorial and Historic Site: Hearings on S. 2869 and H.R. 4660*, 101st Cong., 2d sess., 1990.

Welch, James. *Killing Custer: The Battle of the Little Bighorn and the Fate of the Plains Indians.* New York: Penguin Books, 1994.

Wilson, Pamela. "Confronting the 'Indian Problem': Media Discourses of Race, Ethnicity, Nation, and Empire in 1950s America." In Sasha Torres, ed., *Living Color: Race and Television in the United States.* Durham, NC: Duke University Press, 1998.

Wilson, Waziyatawin Angela. "Decolonizing the 1862 Death Marches." In Waziyatawin Angela Wilson, ed., *In the Footsteps of Our Ancestors: The Dakota Commemorative Marches of the 21st Century.* St. Paul, MN: Living Justice Press, 2006.

Latinos 3

Omar Valerio-Jiménez

Before the American West became a destination for westward-moving Americans, it had been Mexico's Far North for Spanish colonists moving northward from central New Spain. The Spanish colonists, however, did not arrive in an uninhabited area; rather, they entered a region that had long been an American Indian homeland. This indigenous homeland had witnessed various internal migrations of semisedentary and nomadic American Indians who moved in search of food, trade, and seasonal shelter. Before the region became an indigenous homeland, their ancestors had migrated southward into the region after crossing eastward across the Bering Strait. So the American West has long been a destination for eastward-, southward-, northward-, and—ultimately, and only recently—westward-moving peoples. For Spanish-speaking people, the "American West" became a place for settlement beginning in the sixteenth century.

From bases in the Caribbean and central Mexico, Spanish explorers made excursions along the Gulf of Mexico, throughout the Southwest, and up the Pacific coast in search of precious minerals, Indian slaves, and a passage to the Orient. Juan Ponce de León and Alvar Núñez Cabeza de Vaca led expeditions into Florida and Tejas, while Francisco Vázquez de Coronado and Juan Rodríguez Cabrillo explored Arizona, Nuevo México, and California, giving Spanish place names to rivers, mountains, and towns. Among the first European settlements that these men established were St. Augustine, Florida

NOTE: The terms "Hispanics" and "Latinos" refer to the same group of people, those with ancestry in Latin America. I have chosen to use "Latinos" because it is a term chosen by many of the people to whom it refers, whereas "Hispanic" was chosen by non-Latino government officials. The use of these terms, however, varies with a person's region, class, immigration experience, and educational background. Moreover, there is no historically appropriate term that has been used throughout the history of the United States.

(1565), and San Juan, Nuevo México (1598). These expeditions also led cartographers to create maps of the region and some of the first European-authored written records. No mineral wealth or passages to Asia were found in these initial explorations, but the Spaniards did make contact with various indigenous groups. Through that initial contact, the Europeans introduced deadly diseases to which Native Americans had no antibodies. Soon indigenous nations throughout the Southeast and Southwest began witnessing a dramatic population decline. In addition to coping with the exposure to new pathogens, Indians also began to resist European efforts to enslave them.

The Spaniards established more settlements in the seventeenth and eighteenth centuries in order to stake a territorial claim and to obtain more subjects for the Spanish Crown. Competition with France, England, and Russia over territory in North America led Spain to promote settlements as a defensive measure. A colony of French Huegenots in Florida alarmed the Spanish, motivating them to send a military expedition to expel the Protestants and to construct a series of presidios (forts) along the peninsula's coasts. In addition to territory Spain sought more subjects, so its expeditions included Catholic missionaries who were responsible for converting indigenous nations. The Jesuit order established missions in northern Florida that were soon abandoned because of conflicts with indigenous nations. Meanwhile, Franciscan clergy began ministering to Nuevo México's Pueblo Indians in the 1590s (three decades before the English colonies of Jamestown and Plymouth Plantation), while Jesuit priests established missions among Arizona's Pima Indians a century later. Responding to French colonization along the Mississippi River and in Louisiana, Spanish officials sent colonists to establish presidios and Franciscan missions throughout Texas in the decade following 1710. From that defensive colonization emerged Arizona's Tubac and Tucson as well as Nacogdoches and San Antonio in Tejas. By the eighteenth century, a rumored Russian invasion of the Pacific Northwest spurred the establishment of a string of protective Spanish settlements in California.

The defensive colonization of New Spain's northern borderlands depended on missions, presidios, and pueblos (towns). The incorporation of Indians into Catholic missions was the result of an approach that could be described as a "frontier of inclusion" policy. The Spaniards believed that Indians who converted to Catholicism could become part of Spanish society. By contrast, the British followed a policy best described as a "frontier of exclusion," which provided little, if any, room for Indians within British, and later Anglo-American, society. In Spanish society, Indians were expected to become loyal subjects, willing laborers, and potential mates, in return for the "salvation" of their souls. To carry out this policy each mission was a combination of a church, workplace, and cultural center. The missionaries prohibited Indians from practicing Native religions. Instead, the priest expected Indians to practice Catholicism, learn the Spanish language, and acculturate to European norms. Accompanying the missionaries were soldiers who provided protection from imperial rivals and hostile Indians. Based in the presidios, the soldiers were also needed to quell uprisings of Indians who rebelled against the imposition of Spanish religion and culture. Among the colonists were civilians who founded Spanish towns while pursuing agricul-

Depiction of nineteenth-century life around Mission Santa Clara de Asis in California painted in the early twentieth century. (*Lake County Museum/Corbis*)

tural and livestock production. These *pobladores* (settlers) established such civilian communities as Los Angeles, San José, Albuquerque, and Laredo (Weber 1992, pp. 1–270).

Unlike U.S. expansion, in which American colonists eagerly moved westward, New Spain's northern expansion was difficult because of a lack of interest among Spanish colonists. New Spain's northern frontier was unappealing because it was remote from Spanish population centers and dangerous because of the threat of Indian attacks. The high cost of transportation to northern settlements, combined with Spain's mercantilist policy (requiring all trade to pass through official ports), created shortages of goods and raised their value. Straining under such a strict trade policy, northern colonists smuggled goods bought from American merchants. In order to attract colonists northward, Spanish officials made them promises of land, tax exemptions, transportation subsidies, and monetary stipends. Despite such benefits, however, conflicts soon developed among the missionaries, soldiers, and pobladores over control of Indians. The missionaries complained that soldiers stationed in the presidios were abducting and sexually assaulting Indian women, and stealing Indian children to sell as slaves. The soldiers, meanwhile, were selling Indians as slaves to the pobladores, who used the indigenous captives as domestic servants and agricultural workers. The income from the sale of Indian captives was critical for the soldiers, who were rarely paid or supplied with provisions by colonial authorities. Pobladores complained not only that the missions had obtained the best arable lands but also that the missionaries had exclusive control over the Indians' labor. The relationship among the three groups was further complicated by the dependence of the pobladores and missionaries on the soldiers for military protection. To protect Spanish settlements in the northern borderlands, Spanish officials alternated between a "velvet glove" policy of providing indigenous nations with gifts to buy the peace, and the "iron fist" policy of punishing Indians with military force.

The nineteenth century would usher in dramatic changes for colonists in New Spain's northern borderlands. In 1810 insurgents in New Spain launched an independence movement that would last eleven years, resulting in the creation of the independent nation of México. The long independence struggle left the nation's infrastructure in shambles, the economy devastated, the population decimated, and the treasury bankrupt. Few colonists in the northern borderlands witnessed or participated in the independence insurgency, but they experienced the dramatic effects of the nation's devastation as Mexico lost any control of its northern borderlands. No longer able to pay its soldiers in the north or to send money to the missions and civilian governments, Mexico's central government abandoned its velvet glove and iron fist policies. The northern colonists were left to fend for themselves. The lack of military protection emboldened indigenous nations like the Comanches and Apaches to increase their attacks on Spanish settlements throughout the northern borderlands. Ironically, Spanish colonialism had introduced the horses that had made these indigenous nations highly mobile in the American West. The Apaches and Comanches became excellent equestrians, and they used their mobility to raid for additional horses and livestock and traded those products with Spanish and Anglo-American colonists. The threat of Indian attacks further isolated Mexicans in the northern borderlands from Mexico's central government and led them to develop additional commercial ties with Anglo Americans. As more and more Anglo Americans moved into Mexico's Far North, their presence upset the tenuous balance previously established between Mexican settlements and indigenous nations. Anglo-American settlements forced Indians off Native lands and raised the level of competition over territory. Indians took advantage of the presence of Americans by establishing trade ties and decreasing their dependence on Mexican colonists for manufactured goods. Indian raids on American and Mexican settlements increased as indigenous nations traded with one group of colonists to raid another group. The increase in trade with American merchants and decrease in communications with the newly independent Mexican nation created ambiguous loyalties for the Spanish-speaking residents of Mexico's Far North (Weber 1982, pp. 83–146).

Mexico's independence transformed Spanish subjects into Mexican citizens but failed to promote national unity. Political struggles between centralists and federalists in Mexico led to more instability. The centralists favored a strong central government, while the federalists sought a more diversified system of power-sharing among the states. Most residents of the northern borderlands favored increased regional autonomy, which meant support for the federalists. In place of an attachment to the nation, Mexican citizens in the Far North felt a stronger attachment to their region. But that regionalism was localized. Few residents shared a sense of belonging to California or to New Mexico. Instead, residents expressed an attachment to a town or a series of towns. Residents of southern California became known as *los abajeños,* while those in northern California were *los arribeños.* Similar divisions developed across Mexico's Far North. Because colonists in each region interacted with different groups of indigenous nations, each region created distinct treaties and trade arrangements. In the aftermath of Mexican independence, a mixture of policies toward indigenous nations in Mexico's Far North emerged as the central government failed to promote a singular policy. The main factors uniting colonists separated by thousands of miles were a shared religious linguistic background (Gonzales 1999, pp. 58–65).

One of the most dramatic developments resulting from Mexico's independence was the secularization of the missions, or the transfer of control over the missions from missionaries to secular (or parish-supported) clergy. California serves as a good example of the effects of this policy's implementation. The long independence struggle cut off financial support for the missions and introduced economic pressures to secularize the missions. Colonists in the northern borderlands advocated secularization because they wanted to obtain control of the missions' land and indigenous labor force. In theory, secularization was designed to return the missions' land to their Native inhabitants. The reality that materialized was quite different as politically connected military officials and elite Californios expanded their landholdings. Secularization enhanced the existing class divisions by enlarging the elite's wealth. The missionaries lost control of Indian labor, while the Indians lost the land they were promised. More than 90 percent of the mission land ended up in the hands of wealthy rancheros. Without the missionaries nominally looking out for the Indians' interests, elite rancheros had more freedom to punish Indian laborers. Consequently, the rancheros imposed harsher treatment on indigenous laborers than had the missionaries.

Mexico's independence liberalized commerce in the northern borderlands, as illustrated by New Mexico's burgeoning new trade. Shortly after independence, U.S. traders from Missouri and other nearby states arrived in New Mexico and established a lucrative commercial enterprise. The increase in trade with U.S. cities led to the creation of the Santa Fe Trail. Nuevomexicanos preferred commerce with Americans than with Chihuahua merchants (who had previously supplied most of their goods), because American merchants could provide less expensive items and a greater variety of merchandise. In exchange for blankets, furs, and livestock, Nuevomexicanos acquired manufactured clothes, furniture, and weapons. This lucrative trade attracted still more Americans and created a wealthy class of middlemen among Nuevomexicanos. Wealthy landowners took advantage of their access to capital to compete with U.S. merchants and the Chihuahua traders in Mexico. Soon families such as the Armijos and Chávezes became the most prominent merchants along the Santa Fe Trail and the Chihuahua Trail. A new trade route, the Pacific Trail, through Utah and across California to the Pacific coast soon opened (Weber 1982, pp. 147–241).

With the nation's independence, Mexican officials seized on a colonization plan as the way to solve the scarcity of Spanish settlements in Texas. The colonization plan (officially enacted in 1824) followed the policy of Spanish colonial officials who had allowed Americans to settle in East Texas. Spanish officials had planned to make Texas a buffer zone for settlements in the Mexican interior. Moses Austin secured an agreement to bring 300 Catholic families from Louisiana to settle in Texas. After his death, his son Stephen F. Austin led the settlement of U.S. immigrants in central Texas. Mexico's officials wanted to increase the population of non-Indian settlers in Texas to protect old settlements from Indian attacks and to guard against the encroachment of foreign powers (principally the United States). The colonization plan offered settlers land, security, and tax exemptions. Mexican officials targeted Europeans and Americans with this plan, but Americans became the main colonists. Mexican officials allowed American settlers to enter Texas with their slaves, even though Mexico had outlawed slavery in 1829. In exchange, the colonists were to become Mexican citizens and obey the nation's laws. In order to be allowed to immigrate into Texas, colonists needed to ask Mexican officials for permission. American immigrants from Louisiana and other Southern states quickly flooded into the state, bringing their slaves with them. The colonization plan was so successful in attracting American immigrants to Texas that soon the first "illegal immigrants" entered the state, without bothering to secure permission. By 1830 the more than 7,000 Americans easily outnumbered some 3,000 Tejanos (Texas Mexicans) residing in Texas (De León 1999, pp. 7–34).

In addition to their numerical superiority, Americans' practices worried Mexican officials. Americans neglected to become Mexican citizens, failed to learn the Spanish language, and ignored many of the nation's laws. Alarmed by this development the Mexican government restricted further immigration, outlawed slavery in the territory, and imposed some taxes. These restrictions antagonized Americans, who lobbied to reverse them. Several prominent Tejanos, including Lorenzo de Zavala and Juan N. Seguín, successfully urged Mexico to rescind the immigration restrictions. In the meantime, however, the flood of immigrants continued unabated. By 1834, Texas was home to close to 21,000 Americans and their slaves. The following year, approximately 1,000 Americans were entering Texas every month. With such overwhelming numbers, Americans were soon plotting to launch a separatist revolt. When the centralists assumed power of Mexico's national government, they took steps to gain greater control by eliminating the autonomy previously enjoyed by the states. Americans in Texas seized on this attempt to reduce their autonomy as the opportunity to launch their separatist revolt. Joined by Tejanos, the Texas separatists lost the infamous battle at the Alamo but later obtained retribution with the defeat of the Mexican Army and capture of Santa Anna at San Jacinto. The separatists forced Santa Anna to sign the Treaty of Velasco, recognizing the independence of Texas. Mexico never accepted the legitimacy of this treaty, and it would attempt to recapture Texas on several occasions throughout the nine-year existence of the breakaway republic (Acuña 1988, pp. 25–53; Meier and Ribera 1993, pp. 53–68).

In the aftermath of the Texas revolt, race relations between Anglo Texans and Tejanos deteriorated. The political alliance with Tejanos disintegrated as Anglo Texans sought revenge for their defeats at the Alamo and Goliad during the Texas revolt. Not willing to distinguish Tejanos from Mexicans, Anglo Texans turned their anger at Mexican officials into violence against Tejano civilians. Throughout central Texas, vigilantes attacked Mexicans, stole their cattle, and appropriated their land. Because their settlements were close to the American colonies, Tejanos living along the San Antonio and Guadalupe rivers experienced the worst retributions. Angry Americans destroyed Goliad, while chasing Tejanos from Victoria and Refugio. The violence extended into East Texas, where vigilantes forced more than 100 Tejano families to abandon their homes and lands. Many elite landowners, like the family of Martin De León in Victoria, fled to New Orleans for safety. However, most escaped toward the heavily Tejano region between the Nueces and Rio Grande rivers or continued into Mexico. Even prominent Tejanos who had allied with Anglo Texans were not immune from the violence. As the mayor of San Antonio, Juan Seguín attempted to help fellow Tejanos who asked for protection from Anglo Texan vigilantes. "At every hour of the day and night," wrote Seguín, "my countrymen ran to me for protection against the assaults or exactions of those adventurers." For defending Tejanos, Seguín earned the enmity of Anglo Texans. Ruminating about his decision, Seguín asked, "Were not the victims my own countrymen, friends, and associates? Could I leave them defenseless, exposed to the assaults of foreigners who, on the pretext that they were Mexicans, treated them worse than brutes?" The vigilantes quickly forgot Seguín's heroic feats during the Texas revolt and issued death threats against him. To protect his family, Seguín resigned as mayor and left for Mexico.

Tensions between the Republic of Texas and Mexico remained high during its nine-year existence. Mexico's refusal to recognize the independent republic contributed to the bad relations, but so did the expansionist designs of Texas leaders. In an attempt to gain control of the Santa Fe Trail trade and obtain much needed income, Texas sent an expedition into New Mexico that suffered a humiliating defeat at the hands of the Mexican Army. In retaliation, Mexico's troops attacked San Antonio, raised the Mexican flag, and retreated to the Rio Grande after holding the city for a few days. Several months later the Mexican Army again captured San Antonio but was forced to retreat under pressure from Texan troops. Furious at what they considered an invasion of Texas soil, the Texas government sent an expedition to the Rio Grande. After seizing the river towns of Laredo and Guerrero, some Texans attempted to capture Mier. The Mexican Army defeated the Texans at Mier, executed several prisoners, and forced the remainder to travel to Mexico City. The attacks on San Antonio and the so-called Mier Expedition became the subject of lurid accounts, describing Mexicans' supposed brutality and hatred. Most Tejanos attempted to remain neutral during these attacks and counterattacks, but some were forced to take sides. One of those was Seguín, the former Texas patriot and San Antonio mayor, who had fled to Mexico and then was forced to join the Mexican Army or face imprisonment. As a member of the Mexican Army, Seguín took part in the capture of San Antonio in 1842. The diplomatic tensions exacerbated the racial animosity that Tejanos experienced in the aftermath of the Texas revolt. Tensions would escalate into military conflict again when the United States annexed Texas in 1845. Considering that action a prelude to war, Mexico broke off diplomatic relations with the United States. The war began the following year after the

United States sent its troops into the Nueces Strip (land between the Nueces and Rio Grande rivers), which was claimed by Mexico, and provoked a skirmish with Mexican troops (De la Teja 1991, pp. 1–70).

Conquerors Become the Conquered

The U.S. victory in the Mexican-American War (known in Mexico as the War of North American Aggression) transformed the United States into a continental nation by absorbing the territory known today as the "American West" into the nation. With the end of the war in 1848 and the signing of the Treaty of Guadalupe Hidalgo, the Mexicans living in the annexed territories had to make a choice about their citizenship. They could retain their Mexican citizenship by moving south into Mexico, or they could become U.S. citizens by remaining on their lands. Only 2,000 Mexicans moved south, while close to 100,000 stayed put and became U.S. citizens. In addition to guaranteeing all rights accorded to other U.S. citizens, the Treaty of Guadalupe Hidalgo also promised annexed Mexicans that the United States would respect their property rights. Those promises, however, were unfulfilled. During the second half of the nineteenth century, Mexican Americans lost political power, social standing, and economic control as their citizenship rights were repeatedly denied. While westward-moving Americans viewed this period as one involving rugged "pioneers" following wagon trails in search of the nation's "Manifest Destiny," American Indians and Mexicans viewed the same period as one of conquest and dispossession.

The introduction of a new system of government was partly responsible for the loss of political power, because aspiring officeholders needed to be knowledgeable of U.S. laws and increasingly fluent in the English language. But a more significant cause was the outright denial of the right to vote. Throughout the American West, Mexican Americans encountered harassment and intimidation when they attempted to vote. In Texas, newspapers and Anglo vigilantes threatened ranch owners who encouraged Mexican-American workers to exercise the franchise. Violence was also responsible for their loss of property as vigilantes and squatters drove landowners off their land. Some Mexican Americans lost land after neglecting to pay property taxes (a new legal requirement unknown in the Mexican legal system). Others attempted to obtain legal title to their lands through U.S. courts but lost property to their lawyers, who demanded payment in land for their services. Juan Cortina, a south Texas land grant descendant, described the process in a proclamation: "These [vile men], as we have said, form, with a multitude of lawyers, a secret conclave, with all its ramifications, for the sole purpose of despoiling the Mexicans of their lands."

As their political and economic influence decreased, the social standing of Mexican Americans diminished. Some returned to Mexico "as strangers to the old country to beg for an asylum," in Cortina's words, while others became increasingly marginalized in the new society and soon realized that the promises of the Treaty of Guadalupe Hidalgo were "but the baseless fabric of a dream." The loss of political power made Mexican Americans and

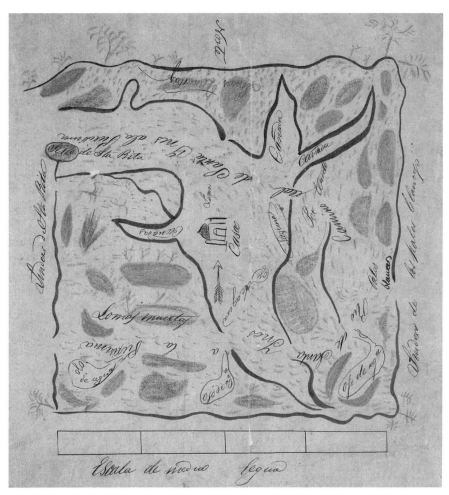

Diseño of Rancho Santa Rosa in Santa Barbara, California, around 1842. A *diseño* is an informal map that was used in Alta California to demarcate land claims. Under the Land Law Act of 1851, California rancheros were required to appear before a commission to prove rightful land ownership. Many land-owners were unable to afford the costly litigation and lost their land. (*Landcase Maps Collection, Land Case Map D-1342, The Bancroft Library, University of California, Berkeley*)

other Latin Americans more vulnerable to discriminatory laws. One such law was enacted during California's Gold Rush, which brought immigrants from all over the world to the Golden State. Joining Americans were French, Chinese, Chilean, and Mexican miners. Competition for precious gold diggings degenerated into violence against people of color. Because law enforcement was minimal in makeshift towns and mining camps, vigilantes preyed on miners who looked "foreign." Self-appointed vigilante committees of Anglo-American miners targeted Mexicans and Chileans suspected of petty crimes for hangings and whippings. Nativism, an antiforeigner sentiment, became widespread among U.S. miners, who successfully lobbied the state's legislators to pass the Foreign Miners' License Tax in 1850. This law required foreign miners to pay a prohibitive fee, twenty dollars a month, for the "privilege" of mining for gold in California. Targeted by this new tax were Latin American and Asian miners, and to a lesser extent French immigrants. The state legislature repealed the law within a year of its passage, but the damage had been done. The law had a devastating effect in Calaveras, Tuolumne, and Mariposa counties, where more than two-thirds of the 15,000 Mexicans left the area. Most returned to urban centers in southern California or crossed the border into Mexico. The Foreign Miners' Tax and a subsequent law passed in 1852 are examples of Anglo-American efforts to use the government to eliminate economic competition from nonwhite and immigrant populations.

In response to the ethnic tensions in the postwar period, some Mexican Americans resisted their displacement by engaging in banditry. The most famous bandit during California's Gold Rush was Joaquín Murrieta. Drawn from Sonora, Mexico, to California's southern mines, Murrieta and his family left productive mining claims because Anglos violently evicted them. Anglo vigilantes raped Murrieta's wife, Rosa Felíz de Murrieta, lynched his brother, Jésus Carrillo Murrieta, and whipped Joaquín. After leaving the mines, the Murrietas survived by running a gambling table until they encountered more persecution from the Anglos. Eventually, Murrieta and his friends turned on their enemies. They began stealing gold and livestock; some accounts claim that Murrieta targeted only his persecutors, while others argue that he attacked indiscriminately. Soon reports of attacks by Joaquín Murrieta and his gang spread throughout the Southern Mines, and newspapers reported that Anglos were under siege. Murrieta sightings were so widespread that some wondered if more than one gang was responsible for the attacks. The state governor offered a reward for Murrieta's capture, and eventually a team of rangers killed several Mexican suspects. The rangers beheaded several of the men, one of whom they maintained was Murrieta, and claimed the reward. Officials placed one of the severed heads in a jar and exhibited the "head of the renowned bandit Joaquín" throughout the state. Murrieta's death was also controversial, because his friends and descendants claimed that he died of natural causes (Johnson 2000, pp. 28–53).

At around the same time, Tiburcio Vásquez and his friends became the main suspects in the death of a constable at a fandango in Monterey in northern California. When a vigilante committee caught and hanged one of the Mexican suspects, Vásquez fled and joined a band of cattle rustlers. Over the next two decades, Vásquez committed various robberies and landed in several jails. Ultimately, the state legislature offered a reward for his capture, which occurred in Los Angeles. After being found guilty of various crimes, Tiburcio Vásquez met his end in the noose of the state's hangman. While outlaws of various ethnic backgrounds operated throughout the state, most Anglos claimed that the bandits were predominantly Mexican Americans. Murrieta and Vásquez gained widespread notoriety for their attacks against Anglos, but they also became heroes to the dispossessed Californios who believed that such violent resistance was justified (Gonzales 1999, pp. 89–90; Rosenbaum 1981).

Mexican Americans' loss of political and economic power varied by region and depended on their ability to remain a majority of the population.

A sharp increase in Anglo-American migration overwhelmed the native Californio residents of Los Angeles by the 1860s. With less than a fifth of the city's population, Mexican Americans quickly lost most political offices. Californios' political fortunes were much different farther north in Santa Barbara, where they maintained a numerical majority throughout most of the nineteenth century. In addition to their majority status, the practice of bloc voting helped Mexican Americans secure city and county offices. With the strong support of the Mexican-American electorate, Californio elite politicians, such as Pablo de la Guerra and Nicholas Covarrubias, repeatedly defeated Anglo-American politicians. The Californio political machine continuously battled Anglo-American political aspirants and successfully drove the *Gazette*, an anti-Californio newspaper, out of town by orchestrating a boycott. De la Guerra was such a strong political powerbroker that he was able to lead Mexican Americans to switch from the Democratic to the Republican party to prevent an Anglo American from winning elected office. Mexican Americans' control of politics in Santa Barbara began to decrease in the 1870s as the Anglo-American population rose and they established coalitions to defeat Californio politicians (Camarillo 1979, pp. 53–78).

In Arizona, Mexican Americans held onto some key political positions even as they lost some elected offices to Anglo newcomers. Estévan Ochoa, a prominent businessman, served as an Arizona territorial legislator, city councilman, and Tucson mayor. Ochoa supported the public school system, lobbied the legislature to remove language restrictions from jury service, and sought to have all laws published in English and Spanish. Hispanos in New Mexico had even greater political success. They managed to hold on to more elected offices than in any other region because of their numerical majority. Nuevomexicanos, such as Donaciano Vigil and Miguel Otero, captured local offices and elected fellow Hispanos to both houses of the territorial legislature (Sheridan 1986, pp. 41–54).

While Mexican Americans throughout the American West had difficulty maintaining control of their land after U.S. annexation, the loss of land occurred unevenly. In areas with a large influx of Anglo Americans, like northern California and central Texas, landowners suffered a rapid loss of property to speculators and squatters. However, in areas such as southern Arizona and southern Texas, Mexican Americans remained a majority of the population, and some managed to maintain control of their property throughout the nineteenth century. The rancheros of Hidalgo county, in southern Texas, are illustrative of Tejano landowners in the region. The state of Texas certified the majority of Spanish and Mexican land grant titles of those landowners. In subsequent years the rancheros took an active part in the commercial ranching operations, including the sale of wool from sheep and trade in cattle, horses, and mules. Unlike the large landowners of neighboring Webb and Cameron counties, most rancheros in Hidalgo held smaller plots of land. The majority of these rancheros owned less than 200 head of cattle. These landowners eventually experienced a gradual loss of land through a combination of social and economic factors. As ranching became increasingly commercialized and dominated by corporate concerns, rancheros who owned smaller plots of land as a result of partible inheritance practices lost ground.

Latinos, Marriage, and Divorce in the American West

Before westward moving white settlers viewed the American West as a land of opportunities, Spanish colonists and later Mexican citizens traveled northward into the same area for new social and economic possibilities. Once Mexico's Far North became the American West, Mexicans continued to see the area as one that offered certain advantages. In the nineteenth century, the liberal divorce laws of Western states attracted many Americans trapped in bad marriages. The practice of moving west to obtain a divorce was so popular (Western states routinely topped the list of states granting the highest number of divorces), that it became known as the "interstate divorce trade." Soon after American annexation, Mexican Americans throughout the American West also took advantage of these laws. For Mexican-American women the liberal marriage and divorce laws of Western states provided new opportunities not available under the Spanish and Mexican legal system. Among Mexican Americans, the practice of securing divorces acquired international dimensions as some couples who had married in Mexico, later divorced in the United States.

Four years after U.S. annexation, a Mexican-American couple who lived in Carrizo, Texas, crossed the Rio Grande to be married in Guerrero, Tamaulipas. Antonia Díaz married Felipe Cuellar in the Mexican border town because it was the site of the nearest Catholic Church and the home of their relatives. Only four years had passed since this area of South Texas had been annexed to the United States at the conclusion of the Mexican-American War (1846 1848), and no Catholic Church existed in their community on the U.S. side of the border. Once married, the couple returned to Texas to establish a home. Felipe and Antonia lived in Carrizo for the next seven years. The marriage fell apart in 1859, when Felipe abandoned Antonia and

In addition to the increased competition, rancheros had limited access to the credit that was needed to weather periods of drought and environmental devastation. By the end of the nineteenth century, many displaced rancheros had migrated into the cities or accepted jobs with larger ranching operations (Alonzo 1998, pp. 161–181).

In New Mexico, Mexican Americans also remained the majority of the population and managed to maintain control of the territory throughout the nineteenth century. When the United States annexed Mexico's northern territories, there were some 60,000 Spanish-speaking residents living in New Mexico, more than lived in California and Texas combined. Before the U.S. takeover, Hispanos (the name preferred by New Mexicans) had developed close trade ties with Americans. The Santa Fe trade (which had begun with Mexico's independence in 1821) funneled U.S.-manufactured goods from Missouri through New Mexico into Mexico's northern provinces. In exchange, U.S. traders obtained mules, wool, and other livestock products. This lucrative trade led to sharp class divisions among Hispanos, with a few elite merchants profiting from the trade while the poor were excluded. Among the most successful in exploiting the new merchant capitalism was Gertrudis Barceló, a widow who ran a very profitable gambling hall. Originally from Sonora, Barcelo had received an education, married into an established Hispano family, and become business savvy when the American

returned to Mexico. Had she lived in Mexico, Antonia would have had little recourse but to turn to relatives for assistance because a legal separation was all but impossible. However, since Antonia lived in the United States, she immediately filed for divorce in a district court. Their marriage had been troubled for some time, according to Antonia, because Felipe "was guilty of excesses, cruel treatment, and outrages toward her of such a character as to render their living together insupportable" (*The Ranchero* [Corpus Christi, Texas], May 12, 1860, p. 2).

Abandonment and cruel treatment were common reasons for obtaining a divorce in the American West. Many men (and a few women) left their spouses to find work but never returned. Recognizing this common practice, Western legislators passed laws with liberal divorce rules based on abandonment. In Texas, a wife could file for divorce based on abandon-

ment even if the initial separation had begun while the couple lived outside of the state. But the abandoned wife had to wait three years before filing for divorce. During this time, the woman and her children might sink into poverty because her husband continued to control their property even while absent from the home. By filing for divorce based on cruel treatment, however, Antonia could initiate the proceedings immediately. Texas law was vague about what constituted "cruel treatment," so judges could interpret this provision liberally. Most divorce petitions based on cruel treatment were quickly granted, including in Antonia's case (Valerio-Jiménez 2001, pp. 306–384).

Reference and Further Reading

Valerio-Jiménez, Omar S. "Indios Bárbaros, Divorcées, and Flocks of Vampires: Identity and Nation on the Rio Grande, 1749–1894." Ph.D. diss., University of California, Los Angeles, 2001.

merchants began arriving in New Mexico. Her gambling hall served to familiarize the new arrivals with the Spanish language, Mexican customs, and music. Employing her business acumen, Barcelo invested her earnings in the U.S. trade and before her death became one of the wealthiest residents of New Mexico (González 1999, pp. 39–78).

Negotiating Social Changes

U.S. annexation did not lead only to negative changes. It also brought some unexpected opportunities for Mexican-American women throughout the West. The change in jurisdiction from Mexican to U.S. courts allowed women greater freedom in marital relations. In the former Mexican territories, U.S. civil authorities gained control over marital concerns from Mexican religious officials. Couples wishing to marry enjoyed more options than they had in Mexico, where the only avenue was the Catholic Church. Under U.S. jurisdiction, couples could marry through a variety of Protestant churches, the Catholic Church, or a Jewish synagogue. They could also avoid a religious ceremony altogether by marrying in a civil ceremony before a justice of the peace or a county judge. This development helped interfaith couples who wished to marry without forcing one of the parties to convert. The option to

Mexican adobe house near Las Vegas, New Mexico, ca. 1875. (*Denver Public Library, Western History Collection, Z 8832*)

marry outside of the Catholic Church also led to an increase in the number of interethnic marriages, because non-Catholics could now marry Mexicans (who were predominantly Catholic at the time).

Furthermore, if women faced domestic disputes, they could appeal to the courts to punish abusive husbands. U.S. tribunals were more willing to punish husbands for mistreating their wives than were Mexican courts. The primary goal of courts in Mexico was to reconcile the couple and preserve the marriage. U.S. courts also permitted women to obtain divorces more easily than Mexican tribunals. Throughout the American West, states passed liberal divorce laws in an effort to attract westward-moving migrants. The number of divorces in the United States rose sharply in the second half of the nineteenth century, and the American West continued to be a magnet for couples wishing to get an easy legal separation. Under Mexican jurisdiction women who faced troubled marriages had attempted to secure a divorce, but religious authorities made the process long and difficult. Once U.S. courts began operating, Mexican-American women took advantage of liberal divorce laws to gain a legal separation from abusive or neglectful husbands. By securing a divorce, women could regain control of their property, custody of their children, and use of their maiden name. Most important, a divorce allowed women to remarry in the civil courts. The possibility of remarriage was significant, because life on the frontier was much easier for a married couple than for a single parent. Ultimately, the changes in legal jurisdiction over marriage gave Mexican-American women more independence from the control of the Catholic Church and from male partners (Valerio-Jiménez 2001, pp. 306–384).

Although Mexican-American women gained some legal advantages in negotiating marriage and divorce, they faced considerable new obstacles in their attempts to hold on to their property. Under Spanish and Mexican laws, women had specific property rights that gave some significant independence. Adult women could own their own property and could retain ownership even after marriage, in order to safeguard their economic status if their husbands died or encountered financial difficulties. Spanish and Mexican courts did not hold wives accountable for their husbands' debts. Inheritance laws stipulated that widows receive a portion of their spouse's estate, and also required that daughters receive the same amount of property as sons. After the U.S. takeover in 1848, several Southwestern states adopted portions of Spanish and Mexican laws that gave specific, but limited, rights to women. In California and Texas, for example, women could retain ownership of separate property when married, and they gained an equal interest in community property amassed during the marriage. A few widows used these specific rights to maintain control of their property into the late nineteenth century, and some women married to Anglos used their husbands' legal knowledge and connections to retain control of their property. But the majority of Mexican-American women lost their real estate and personal property throughout the second half of the nineteenth century to lawyers, land speculators, and local governments. The U.S. conquest took its toll disproportionately on Mexican-American women as they fell into deeper poverty than their male counterparts (González 1999, pp. 10, 79–106; Chávez-García 2004, pp. 123–150; York Enstam 1999).

Hispanos in New Mexico also accommodated to the U.S. takeover, but they used trade ties with U.S. merchants in addition to exploiting family links. As the Santa Fe trade brought more Americans into New Mexico, it facilitated intermarriages between American men and elite New Mexican women. While the percentage of Hispano women who married the newcomers was small, these unions helped to establish intercultural ties and allowed American men to adapt to Hispano society. Conversely, these marriages also gave elite Hispanos familial links with U.S. merchants. The U.S. takeover led to changes in the patterns of inheritance. Under Mexican rule, parents distributed property equally among sons and daughters. After 1848, Mexican-American women increasingly left their property to their sons, in an effort to keep the land within the family. Although weary of the U.S. takeover, residents quickly adapted—especially the elite merchants whose trading opportunities expanded. Unlike Texas, where Anglo-American migration overwhelmed the Tejanos, New Mexico was not a popular destination for American migrants for the first two decades after U.S. rule. With few Americans vying for political office, New Mexicans easily captured local offices, and they consistently elected Mexican Americans to the territorial government. Miguel Otero won three consecutive elections to the U.S. House of Representatives beginning in the 1850s. After leaving politics, Otero established several business ventures and became director of the Maxwell Land Company and vice president of the Santa Fe Railroad. His family's political influence remained strong into the late nineteenth century, as evidenced by the appointment of his son, Miguel II, as the territorial governor (González 1999, pp. 79–106; Griswold del Castillo and De León 1996, pp. 50–51).

The Civil War, Land Struggles, and Armed Rebellions

The Civil War split the Mexican-American community into opposing camps, much as it did the rest of the nation. Most of the 9,900 Mexican-American soldiers, principally troops from California and New Mexico, fought for the Union. Led by Salvador Vallejo, some 450 Californios in the Native California Cavalry patrolled the Mexican border and lent assistance to New Mexico's Union Army. Approximately 5,000 Hispanos volunteered in New Mexico to keep Texas's Confederate troops from taking over the state. Although Confederate forces occupied Albuquerque and Santa Fe for a time, Union troops under the command of Manuel Chávez forced their withdrawal to Texas. A Confederate draft in Texas ensured that the majority of Tejano soldiers (2,550) fought for the Southern cause. Several Tejano Confederates, like Santos Benavides from Laredo, had actively supported slave owners by capturing runaway slaves in Mexico and returning them to Texas. Other Tejanos had sought to weaken the "peculiar institution" by helping runaway slaves escape across the Rio Grande to obtain freedom in Mexico. When the Civil War erupted, some 960 Tejanos joined the Union Army. Led by Octaviano Zapata, Juan Cortina, and Cecilio Valerio, most Tejano Unionists enlisted in the South Texas border region along the Rio Grande. That region played a critical role in the war because both sides fought to control the border, over which the Confederacy transported cotton across the Rio Grande for shipment to foreign markets through Matamoros (Thompson 1977, p. 26; Thompson 1986, p. 43).

Competition over land in New Mexico increased as American immigration to the region rose. An increasing number of Americans began arriving after the Civil War and the completion of the railroad. Among the arrivals were former Civil War soldiers, miners, and land prospectors. This migration would hasten the demise of Hispano ownership as some 80 percent of land grantees lost their property. One infamous example of how political corruption led to dispossession was the Santa Fe Ring, a Republican political machine consisting of Anglo lawyers and businessmen allied with elite Hispano families. Using their political connections and legal expertise, members of this corrupt ring acquired land inexpensively at forced auctions. Officials auctioned property at sheriff sales to pay for outstanding debts or back taxes. By influencing legislation and winning favorable court decisions, ring members obtained millions of acres of land, including the Tierra Amarilla Grant (some 600,000 acres). In addition to enriching themselves, the Santa Fe Ring allied themselves with other land companies whose property acquisitions would generate intense turmoil among Hispano villagers.

The dispossession of Hispanos created enough discontent to fuel several rebellions. One uprising began after the Maxwell Land Grant and Railway Company of England acquired some 2 million acres of land in northern New Mexico and southern Colorado. Several Anglo miners and ranchers as well as Hispano settlers had claimed a right to live on what they considered public domain land as homesteaders and squatters. When the company attempted to remove the Hispano and Anglo settlers in the 1880s, both groups fought

back to defend their way of life. They began to attack law-enforcement officers, steal the Maxwell Company's livestock, and destroy its property. After
company agents offered compensation to the settlers for their improvements
on the land, most of the Anglo ranchers gradually accepted the company's
offers. Hispano villagers, however, continued to harass company agents,
destroy fences, and ignore eviction notices. The company eventually secured
agreements from the Hispano settlers by allowing them to lease the land for
a share of their agricultural production. As the Maxwell Land Grant Company was obtaining the agreements from settlers, several disputes over land
erupted in Lincoln and San Miguel counties.

In southern Lincoln County, a similar dispute focused on land use and
water rights among Hispano sheep raisers, Anglo land speculators allied with
the Santa Fe Ring, and newly arrived Texas livestock producers. Violent
attacks left scores dead on both sides, but eventually the Hispanos lost control to a land company and a coalition of Texas ranchers and livestock companies. A more organized resistance movement developed in San Miguel
County among Hispanos fighting land companies over rights to grazing lands
considered community property. Under cover of darkness, a secret organization of Hispano settlers carried out fence-cutting expeditions while conceal-
ing their identities behind white masks (from which the movement obtained
its name, Las Gorras Blancas). In addition to cutting fences around land
they considered community property, Las Gorras Blancas attacked railroad
lines, destroyed crops, and threatened railroad employees. They expanded
their targets to include timber companies, and they allied with the Knights
of Labor to demand an end to the unequal pay scale for Anglo and Hispano
workers. Led by former Knights of Labor members, Juan José Herrera and his
brothers, the group won support from *La Voz del Pueblo*, a Spanish-language
newspaper based in Las Vegas, New Mexico. Members of Las Gorras Blancas
also enjoyed widespread community support, as witnesses refused to testify
and juries failed to convict several groups of men arrested for fence cutting.
Members of the group organized a political party known as El Partido del
Pueblo (the People's Party), which won several elected offices throughout
the 1890s (Rosenbaum 1981; Montoya 2002, pp. 78–156).

Immigration in the Twentieth Century

Economic developments throughout the American West during the last
two decades of the nineteenth century drew immigrants to the region as
decreasing opportunities in Mexico encouraged Mexicans to head north.
With the assistance of federally funded irrigation projects, large-scale agribusiness concerns gradually replaced subsistence agriculture. Commercial
farming operations became "factories in the fields," producing large quantities of citrus, nuts, grains, and vegetables. Mining operations shifted from
silver and gold production to coal and copper to supply the demand from
industrial markets in the eastern United States. Using modern technology,
mining companies were able to extract minerals from previously untapped
natural deposits in Arizona, Colorado, and New Mexico. Railroad companies

also profited from the largess of the federal government via tax breaks, loans, and deeds of land. Both agribusiness and mining production benefited from the completion of the continental railroad, which enabled them to transport their products to markets in the eastern United States and to ports for export to world markets. Technological improvements affected agribusiness as well, because the advent of refrigerated railroad boxcars made it possible for agricultural companies to ship perishable produce to distant markets.

Mexico continued to exert an influence in the American West, as its rapid economic development was fueled by the labor of Mexican Americans and recent Mexican immigrants. Mexicans became the main source of labor as the supply of Asian laborers decreased with the passage of the Chinese Exclusion Act (1882) and the Gentlemen's Agreement (1907). As land developers forced small Mexican-American property holders off their ancestral lands, the displaced workers migrated to urban centers or became wage workers for agribusiness, mining operators, or railroad companies. Joining them were Mexican immigrant workers attracted to the United States by the abundance of jobs, long-standing ties of family and friends in the region, and the existence of Mexican settlements. Mexican immigrants not only added to the native-born population of Mexican Americans but also reinforced Mexican cultural traditions. Railroads throughout the American West made transportation inexpensive and convenient for these immigrants. The most popular destinations were California and Texas, but Arizona mining operations and railroad construction throughout the region also attracted recent immigrants. Mexican immigrants offered industrial concerns a steady supply of inexpensive and convenient labor, since their journey to the United States was relatively short. American labor recruiters even traveled into Mexico to attract additional workers for expanding Western industries.

The great demand for laborers in the American West coincided with several economic and political developments in Mexico that forced many laborers to leave for the United States. During the last third of the nineteenth century, Mexico also experienced a rapid modernization under the leadership of dictator Porfirio Díaz. His administration sought foreign investors to "modernize" the nation, promoted the consolidation of large landed estates, and eliminated many communal landholdings. Díaz's policies left many Indians and poor peasants landless at the same time that the nation was experiencing a population boom. The mechanization of agriculture and industry further displaced workers. In addition to unfavorable economic policies, workers faced repression from a dictator intent on quashing dissent. Ultimately, widespread unemployment and the lack of land pushed many Mexicans into the United States, where jobs were plentiful. Díaz promoted an ambitious railroad construction plan that ultimately connected major Mexican cities to the United States and its extensive railway network. These railway lines facilitated the importation of U.S. manufactured goods and the exportation of raw materials and produce. They also helped displaced workers move to the United States. While U.S. investments and technology transformed Mexico during this period, Mexico also exerted significant influence on the United States by sending its raw materials and many immigrants to shape the American West (Gutiérrez 1995, pp. 39–68; Sánchez 1993, pp. 17–37).

Mexican laborers picking cotton in a Texas field in 1919. Mexican labor was essential to the boom in western agriculture in the late nineteenth and early twentieth centuries. (*Bettmann/Corbis*)

The influx of Mexican immigrants led to significant changes within the Mexican-American community. Recent arrivals helped to reinforce Mexican culture in urban neighborhoods and rural settlements by increasing the number of Spanish-speakers and of the practitioners of Mexican customs. The immigrants commemorated the traditional *fiestas patrias* (September 16 and Cinco de Mayo), established Spanish-speaking literary and theatrical organizations, and added to the number of fraternal societies. The large number of recent immigrants also generated tensions with native-born Mexican Americans. The native-born and recent arrivals competed for jobs and housing. This competition led some Mexican Americans to resent the recent arrivals and to begin distinguishing themselves from recent immigrants by claiming a "Spanish" ancestry and downplaying their Mexican heritage.

While immigrants reinforced Native traditions, Americanization efforts and consumer culture continued to transform Mexican culture. Mexican-American children absorbed American customs and learned the English language in public schools. In addition, Catholic and Protestant schools sought to instill American values and traditions in the children. The spread of U.S. manufactured goods helped to change Mexican-American adults as they adopted new appliances, clothing, and machinery. Mexican-American families began accepting American food and holidays as the English language seeped into their everyday conversations.

During the late nineteenth and early twentieth centuries, Anglo tourism boosters in the American West promoted the region's "Spanish" past of quaint adobes and romantic missions, while denying the region's Mexican heritage. Encouraged by Helen Hunt Jackson's *Ramona* novel, Californians enthusiastically staged elaborate mission plays celebrating the state's constructed Spanish "fantasy heritage." Throughout the U.S. Southwest, tourism officials emphasized this "fantasy heritage" by celebrating a romantic Spanish colonial past while neglecting the region's Mexican heritage. At the same time, the *Los Angeles Times* sponsored a competition in which it invited readers to submit "Spanish" recipes, which would eventually be published in a cookbook. City leaders also organized the Fiesta de Los Angeles to showcase the region's "Spanish" past. Ironically, these celebrations coincided with the increasing marginalization and repression of Mexican Americans. Unlike the celebrated Spanish settlers of the region, who were accepted posthumously by Anglo society, Mexican Americans struggled with residential segregation, political exclusion, and low-paying jobs. Throughout the American Southwest, tourism officials promoted monuments to a "Spanish fantasy past" as they simultaneously whitewashed the Mexican present (McWilliams 1948, pp. 43–53; Deverell 2004, pp. 1–10; Chávez 1984, pp. 85–106).

To meet the challenges facing the community, Mexican Americans created new social and cultural organizations. The large number of Mexican immigrants spawned the creation of *mutualistas* (mutual-aid societies) and a surge in the number of Spanish-language newspapers. Mutual-aid societies were fraternal lodges that immigrants established to help them adjust to life in a new country without family networks. Named after Mexico's national heroes like Benito Juárez and Ignacio Zaragoza, the mutualistas provided poor immigrants with health insurance, death benefits, and other social services. Although many mutualistas catered to recent immigrants, several included Mexican-American members. Some mutual-aid societies, such as the Alianza Hispano-Americana, included businessmen as well as laborers and strove to defend the civil rights of its members. Mutualistas also sponsored schools and Spanish-language newspapers. While most newspapers focused on reporting local events and society activities, others promoted a spirited defense of the Mexican community's civil rights. Among the most famous newspapers were Tucson's *El Fronterizo,* published by Carlos I. Velasco, which criticized the land dispossession and violent persecution suffered by the local community. Velasco and the editors of *Las Dos Repúblicas* found common cause in promoting cultural pride and denouncing negative characterizations of Mexicans that appeared in the English-language press. Both the Spanish-language press and the mutualistas became precursors for the various civil rights organizations that would emerge at the beginning of the next century (Gonzales 1999, pp. 82–112; Griswold del Castillo and De León 1996, pp. 39–58).

Mexican immigration accelerated with the start of the Mexican Revolution. After ousting Díaz, the insurgents engaged in a long civil war that devastated the nation and sent many northward. Some moved to the United States to escape the violence, while others fled the increasing joblessness in Mexico caused by the revolution. From 1890 to the late 1920s, from one to one-and-a-half million Mexicans, about a tenth of Mexico's population, immigrated to the United States. Such a massive influx transformed many Mexican-American communities and further exacerbated preexisting tensions as many Mexican immigrants competed with Mexican Americans for jobs, housing, and political influence. As nativist sentiment grew during the 1920s, the press and politicians accused Mexican immigrants of contributing to an increase in crime, a drop in educational achievement, and the decay of cities. Despite the anti-immigrant sentiment, agricultural employers lobbied for exemptions in the Quota Acts (1921 and 1924), to allow continued entry for immigrants from Latin America and to ensure a steady supply of labor. Jobs continued to pull Mexican immigrants to the U.S. Southwest until the Great Depression, when a reverse migration began (Gutiérrez 1995, pp. 39–68).

In the 1930s, the Department of Labor, in cooperation with state and local government agencies, subjected Mexicans to a repatriation and deportation campaign. Employing the Immigration Act of 1929, federal officials imprisoned and fined undocumented Mexican immigrants. As jobs decreased during the Great Depression, state and local officials joined federal authorities in targeting Mexicans for forcible repatriation. Government officials were concerned that Mexican immigrants competed with native-born workers over scarce jobs, and that Mexicans were allegedly over-represented among the unemployed and among those seeking aid with relief programs. Accompanying the immigrants who "voluntarily" repatriated were those who were encouraged to leave the country because of increasing hostility against immigrants and by officials who denied immigrants access to relief agencies. More than 400,000 Mexicans left the United States for Mexico during the 1930s, including the immigrants' Mexican-American children, who had never been in Mexico. These children experienced culture shock when they were uprooted from their schools and friends in the United States and sent to a country that was familiar to their parents but strange for them (Gonzales 1999, pp. 146–150).

In the 1940s, Mexican immigrants once again entered the United States as the nation faced labor shortages caused by World War II. Agribusiness interests persuaded Congress to institute the Bracero Program in 1942 to import temporary guest workers from Mexico. An overwhelmingly male labor force participated in this program, which provided a three- to six-month contract to work mainly in agriculture (although some laborers worked in railroad construction). The Bracero Program prohibited the contract workers from organizing unions, obtaining citizenship, or bringing their families. Despite these setbacks, approximately 4.8 million Mexicans participated in the program during its twenty-two-year existence. Mexican workers became braceros because wages in the United States were still higher than those they could obtain in Mexico. Most braceros worked in Texas, California, the Pacific Northwest, and the Midwest.

One of the unintended consequences of the Bracero Program was the growth of undocumented immigration, as some Mexican workers circumvented the limitations of the guest-worker program. Armed with knowledge of U.S. labor market conditions from former braceros, many undocumented workers relied on social networks of friends and family to gain employment. As the number of apprehensions of undocumented workers by the Border Patrol increased throughout the late 1940s and early 1950s, xenophobia increased, as did pressure on Congress. Responding to this pressure, the Immigration and Naturalization Service launched "Operation Wetback" in

1954 to deport undocumented workers. Within several months, the INS had deported more than 1 million undocumented Mexican workers. The need for agricultural workers continued unabated, however, so the Bracero Program was extended. Although the Bracero Program was originally intended to fill World War II labor shortages, its importance for agricultural concerns led to pressure to renew the program several times until it finally ended in 1964. With the end of the Bracero Program, undocumented immigration once again grew as the transnational social networks and labor recruitment continued attracting Mexican laborers (Gutiérrez 1996, pp. 45–85).

Cubans, Puerto Ricans, and Central Americans joined Mexicans as immigrants in the second half of the twentieth century, increasing the Latino population and adding to its diversity. Although Cuban exiles immigrated to the United States as early as the late nineteenth century, most Cuban immigrants arrived after the 1959 Cuban revolution. The first large wave of immigration was composed of middle- and upper-class Cubans opposed to Fidel Castro's government and attracted by the economic opportunities in the United States. Subsequent waves in the 1970s and 1980s included many political refugees, but also some immigrants motivated by the attraction of greater employment opportunities. Because of its political opposition to Castro's government, the U.S. government has considered most Cuban immigrants as political refugees. The refugee designation has given Cuban immigrants many advantages (such as access to government aid) not available to immigrants from other parts of Latin America. Although most Cuban immigrants settled in Florida and the East Coast, some migrated to Los Angeles and other West Coast cities.

Puerto Ricans began moving to the United States in large numbers after they obtained U.S. citizenship in 1917. Large-scale migration from Puerto Rico began in the 1940s, encouraged by the loss of agricultural jobs and U.S. labor recruiters. In the 1960s, the island's economic restructuring spurred more outmigration as capital-intensive industries replaced labor-intensive ones and led to steep drops in employment. Puerto Ricans have long participated in circular migration that shuttles them between the U.S. mainland and Puerto Rico. Among the western destinations for Puerto Ricans are Hawaii and Los Angeles. Immigration from Central America began increasing in the 1960s as the region experienced agricultural modernization that displaced peasants. This immigrant flow increased substantially in the 1970s as right-wing dictatorships in El Salvador, Guatemala, and Nicaragua began systematically repressing dissent. The friendly relations between these dictatorships and the U.S. government prevented U.S. officials from identifying most Central American immigrants as political refugees. The lone exception was the wave of Nicaraguan immigrants during the 1980s, who were considered political refugees when the leftist Sandinista government held power. Central American immigrants settled throughout the United States, but a sizable portion made their new homes in Western cities such as San Francisco, Los Angeles, Houston, and Dallas (Romero, Hondagneu-Sotelo, and Ortiz 1997, pp. 81–114, 135–153).

The American West continues to be a destination for Latinos in the twenty-first century. Once predominantly Mexican, the region today includes

Latin American immigrants from the Caribbean, Central America, and South America. These new arrivals have not only increased the ethnic diversity of the nation's population but also helped to highlight the internal diversity within Latino communities. Although politicians and advertisers describe a homogenous Latino (or Hispanic) community, the Latino population is extremely heterogeneous. From musical tastes to preferences for sports, and from religious identification to political affiliations, Latinos exhibit a wide variety of opinions. Educational levels among Latinos also vary according to the population's socioeconomic status. They are increasingly gaining political influence because more immigrants are registering to vote and becoming involved in local and national political contests. As more Latino students enter college, join the professional ranks, and become involved in politics, they will not only continue to shape the future of the American West but will also increasingly influence the direction of the nation as a whole.

References and Further Reading

Acuña, Rodolfo. *Occupied America: A History of Chicanos.* New York: Harper and Row, 1988.

Alonzo, Armando C. *Tejano Legacy: Rancheros and Settlers in South Texas, 1734–1900.* Albuquerque: University of New Mexico Press, 1998.

Camarillo, Albert. *Chicanos in a Changing Society: From Mexican Pueblos to American Barrios in Santa Barbara and Southern California, 1848–1930.* Cambridge: Harvard University Press, 1979.

Chávez, John R. *The Lost Land: The Chicano Image of the Southwest.* Albuquerque: University of New Mexico Press, 1984.

Chávez-García, Miroslava. *Negotiating Conquest: Gender and Power in California, 1770s to 1880s.* Tucson: University of Arizona Press, 2004.

De la Teja, Jesús F., ed. *A Revolution Remembered: The Memoirs and Selected Correspondence of Juan N. Seguín.* Austin, TX: State House Press, 1991.

De León, Arnoldo. *Mexican Americans in Texas: A Brief History.* 2d ed. Wheeling, IL: Harlan Davidson, 1993, 1999).

Deverell, William. *Whitewashed Adobe: The Rise of Los Angeles and the Remaking of Its Mexican Past.* Berkeley: University of California Press, 2004.

Enstam, Elizabeth York. "Women and the Law." Handbook of Texas Online, 1999. http://www.tsha.utexas.edu/handbook/online/articles/WW/jsw2 .html (accessed April 3, 2006).

González, Deena J. *Refusing the Favor: The Spanish-Mexican Women of Santa Fe, 1820–1880.* New York: Oxford University Press, 1999.

González, Juan. *Harvest of Empire: A History of Latinos in America.* New York: Penguin Books, 2000.

Gonzales, Manuel G. *Mexicanos: A History of Mexicans in the United States.* Bloomington: Indiana University Press, 1999.

Griswold del Castillo, Richard, and Arnoldo De León. *North to Aztlán: A History of Mexican Americans in the United States.* New York: Twayne Publishers, 1996.

Gutiérrez, David G. *Walls and Mirrors: Mexican Americans, Mexican Immigrants, and the Politics of Ethnicity.* Berkeley: University of California Press, 1995.

Gutiérrez, David G. *Between Two Worlds: Mexican Immigrants in the United States.* Wilmington, DE: Scholarly Resources, 1996.

Johnson, Susan Lee. *Roaring Camp: The Social World of the California Gold Rush.* New York: W. W. Norton, 2000.

Meier, Matt S., and Feliciano Ribera. *Mexican Americans/American Mexicans: From Conquistadors to Chicanos.* New York: Hill and Wang, 1993.

McWilliams, Carey. *North From Mexico: The Spanish-Speaking People of the United States.* New York: Monthly Press, 1948.

Montoya, Maria E. *Translating Property: The Maxwell Land Grant and the Conflict over Land in the American West, 1840–1900.* Berkeley: University of California Press, 2002.

Romero, Mary, Pierrette Hondagneu-Sotelo, and Vilma Ortiz, eds. *Challenging Fronteras: Structuring Latina and Latino Lives in the U.S.* New York: Routledge, 1997.

Rosenbaum, Robert J. *Mexicano Resistance in the Southwest: The Sacred Right of Self-Preservation.* Austin: University of Texas Press, 1981.

Sánchez, George J. *Becoming Mexican American: Ethnicity, Culture and Identity in Chicano Los Angeles, 1900–1945.* New York: Oxford University Press, 1993.

Sheridan, Thomas E. *Los Tucsonenses: The Mexican Community in Tucson, 1854–1941.* Tucson: University of Arizona Press, 1986.

Thompson, Jerry D. *Vaqueros in Blue and Gray.* Austin: Presidial Press, 1977.

Thompson, Jerry D. *Mexican Texans in the Union Army.* El Paso: Texas Western Press, 1986.

Valerio-Jiménez, Omar S. "Indios Bárbaros, Divorcées, and Flocks of Vampires: Identity and Nation on the Rio Grande, 1749–1894." Ph.D. diss., University of California, Los Angeles, 2001.

Weber, David J. *The Mexican Frontier, 1821–1846: The American Southwest under Mexico.* Albuquerque: University of New Mexico Press, 1982.

Weber, David J. *The Spanish Frontier in North America.* New Haven: Yale University Press, 1992.

Commerce of the Elsewhere: Trappers and Traders in the Antebellum West

4

Jimmy L. Bryan, Jr.

The reclusive mountain man penetrating the snowy recesses of the Rockies and the resolute Santa Fe trader wrestling caravans across the high Cimarron represent popular images that have contributed to the lore of the American West. Scholars, however, have spent the last forty years deflating the myths that surround these trappers and traders. They point out that the frontier was neither an empty nor a separate space. Instead, frontiers were regions in which a variety of cultures encountered one another and where the marketplace established intricate networks of trade. Many historians also dismiss the notion that trappers and traders were rugged individualists who quelled the wilderness with little or no aid from their community or nation. Not only did these adventurers operate within corporate organizations, scholars argue, but they also benefited from the active support of the U.S. government.

Trappers and traders of the early nineteenth century, however, did not perceive these tensions. To them, frontiers represented adventurous expanses—the elsewhere—in which they sought their fortunes. To them the elsewhere lay apart from the metropolis and from the domestic spaces in the East, but trappers and traders also recognized and exploited the connections with the marketplace. They embraced corporate action and led the vanguard of expansion, drawing a reactionary government in their wake.

Mountain men and Santa Fe overlanders, furthermore, believed that they significantly contributed to the territorial ambitions of the United States. Their experiences helped to define new ideas of nationhood, manliness, and whiteness. In creating these self-images, trappers and traders often denigrated the achievements and contributions of other groups. To them, Indians, *mexicanos*, and the French lacked ambition, ingenuity, and enterprise; as a result, they were not worthy of the land's bounty. Despite this ethnocentric view, many diverse groups participated in the commerce of the elsewhere, arriving from every region of the continent and influencing each other in a variety of beneficial and sometimes devastating ways.

Trapping furs was one of the oldest industries in the Western Hemi-sphere. Since the 1530s, when French explorer Jacques Cartier stumbled upon the Native fur trade on the St. Lawrence River, the traffic in beaver had become one of the most important commercial activities in North America. New France dominated the trade, expanding its trapping ventures into the Great Lakes and eventually down the Mississippi River. In 1763, after the Seven Years' War, France ceded Canada to Great Britain and Louisiana to Spain. In Canada, British capitalists took control of the fur trade and incorporated two organizations—the Hudson's Bay and the North West companies. In 1805 the first agents of these British concerns pressed into the Fraser and Columbia valleys on the Pacific coast.

The British colonies along the Atlantic coast also engaged in local fur trapping economies, yet their efforts never attained the scope achieved by the Canadian companies. In 1783, when the United States achieved its independence from Great Britain, the peace terms designated the Mississippi River as the western boundary. Even in the more remote regions of the newly defined nation, centuries of trapping had depleted the population of fur-bearing animals. In 1803, the United States purchased Louisiana from the French. The acquisition brought expansive resources under the nominal control of the United States and incorporated regions already participating in the world economy. The territory was vast and ill-defined, and U.S. policy-makers took advantage of its vague dimensions by pressing their territorial claims to the Columbia River on the Pacific—a region populated by numerous Indian groups and exploited by the British-Canadian fur companies.

In order to strengthen U.S. claims to the Columbia, to find a route across the Rockies, and to investigate the natural resources of the region, U.S. president Thomas Jefferson dispatched an expedition under the command of Meriwether Lewis and William Clark. In May 1804 the party started up the Missouri, crossed the Continental Divide into the Columbia River valley, and reached the Pacific a year and a half later. In September 1806, Lewis and Clark returned to St. Louis brimming with wonderful tales of their journey. The explorers reported an abundance of resources, including fur-bearing animals.

Manuel Lisa of St. Louis was one of the first merchants to use the intelligence obtained by Lewis and Clark. He was a native of New Orleans or Cuba, the son of a minor Spanish official. When Spain assumed control over Louisiana, Lisa had relocated to St. Louis and established a profitable merchant, land-speculating, and slave-trading business. At the time, St. Louis served as the trading center of French and Spanish fur trappers who continued to cull the upper Mississippi and the western Great Lakes. When Lewis and Clark arrived in St. Louis after their long journey to the Pacific, Lisa decided to take advantage of the information that they brought from the upper Missouri, and in 1807 he organized and led the first of thirteen expeditions.

Lisa planned his expeditions carefully, and in 1809, after he had proved their profitability, nine of his fellow merchants joined him and created the St. Louis Missouri Fur Company—later reorganized as the Missouri Fur Company. These enterprising individuals banded together and supplied the capital and goods that they shipped to the company's posts along the Mis-

Manuel Lisa, St. Louis merchant and founder of the Missouri Fur Company (1772–1820). (*Denver Public Library, Western History Collection, Z 8832*)

souri. There, company agents traded with a variety of Indian groups who performed the actual trapping.

Competition, however, would arrive from the East. German-born John Jacob Astor epitomized those visionaries who coupled enterprise with nationhood. In 1784, at the age of twenty, he had arrived in the United States and opened a shop in New York City where he dealt, among other items, in furs that he purchased from the British-Canadian companies. Astor soon formulated a plan to gain direct access to fur sources by establishing a series of his own trading posts that would connect New York with the Columbia. Recognizing that he would directly compete with the British in Canada, he sought the support of the federal government by casting his venture in terms of expanding the American empire. He secured an interview with Jefferson, who could pledge only his enthusiasm for the project. When Astor failed in securing the backing of the United States, he tried to gain the cooperation of the Canadian companies as well as the Russians, who were already trapping in the southern reaches of Alaska. The British companies rejected his proposals, and the Russians promised only nominal support. Astor continued to use nationalist rhetoric in his correspondence with U.S. officials in order to win their support, but, as his negotiations with the Canadians and the Russians suggest, he sought assistance from any quarter he could find.

Like Lisa, Astor fashioned a well-organized corporation that would execute his plans. In 1808 he established the Pacific Fur Company, drawing associates from St. Louis, Montreal, and New York. Astor's plan called for the erection of a post at the mouth of the Columbia, but unlike Lisa, Astor would not make the trip himself. He commissioned a vessel, the *Tonquin*, to sail around Cape Horn and rendezvous with an overland expedition commanded by Astor's partner in St. Louis, Wilson Price Hunt.

In March 1811, Hunt and his British-Canadian guides set out across the continent. After a year's toilsome journey, they arrived at Astoria, the post established by the crew of the *Tonquin* at the mouth of the Columbia. Through his agents, Astor endeavored to secure trading arrangements with the British, the Russians, and the Chinese. He continued to petition government officials to remind them that the outpost was the spearhead of U.S. expansion, but the war that erupted between the United States and Great Britain occupied their attention. Not only did the War of 1812 complicate relations between the Astorians and the British fur companies in the Northwest, it also disrupted the crucial trade routes with Europe and Asia.

Astor sold his Columbian post in 1813 and continued to suffer setbacks. He refocused his efforts on the Missouri interior, directly competing with Lisa's and other ventures. Both Lisa and Astor experienced modest successes, but the system required significant investments. Employing the old French and British model, they purchased goods to trade with Indians for their furs, but after the Panic of 1819 capital became scarce and merchants were less likely to risk their livelihoods. That year Astor became despondent, turned over the day-to-day operations to his son, and traveled through Europe for the next fifteen years. In 1820, on his last expedition up the Missouri, Lisa died, deeply in debt before he could recover his fortune.

The demand for furs—especially beaver—continued to surge in Europe and Asia, and another St. Louis merchant, William H. Ashley, innovated a new way to obtain fur in order to take advantage of those markets. Instead of investing in large amounts of supplies and incurring the expense of shipping them to trading posts, Ashley developed a rendezvous system. He joined interests with fellow merchant William Henry and established the Rocky Mountain Fur Company. On February 13, 1822, they placed advertisements in the St. Louis newspapers, calling to "Enterprising Young Men" who would "ascend the river Missouri to its source" (Clokey 1980, p. 67) and perform the trapping themselves. Ashley wanted 100 men to live in the mountains for up to two years, gathering furs and bringing them to a predetermined rendezvous for transport back to the East. The rendezvous system that Ashley implemented evolved into the much celebrated mountain man culture. Young, idealistic Anglo-American men—so the story goes—challenged the Rocky Mountains and emerged from their experience endowed with a rough-hewn manliness. Others followed Ashley's model and expanded the fur trapping territory into the Columbia valley and into Mexico.

Jedediah Smith best represented both the actual and imaginary mountain man. Born to modest New York farmers, Smith wandered from job to job through the Ohio valley before he answered Ashley's call for "Enterprising Young Men." In his early twenties, Smith quickly proved his usefulness and became one of Ashley's most productive partners. He was instrumental in the expansion of the company's interests beyond the Rockies, relocated the South Pass, and led the first Anglo-American expedition across the Great Basin into Mexican California. In 1825 he brought a caravan to St. Louis laden with 9,000 pounds of beaver pelts. That year, he and two other partners bought out Ashley's share in the company. Five years later Smith sold his interests in the company and invested in another enterprise—trade with New Mexico. In 1831, scouting ahead of his train of goods, he encountered a group of Comanches who attacked and killed the mountain man turned Santa Fe trader.

As Smith's experience demonstrated, the overland trade with Santa Fe was another celebrated example of the commerce of the elsewhere. For more than two centuries Spaniards, Pueblos, and their Mexican progeny eked out a livelihood in the distant Río Grande valley of north-central New Mexico. Santa Fe, the capital of the province, represented the edge of New Spain's northern frontier—266 miles north of El Paso, 550 miles north of its principal supplier, Chihuahua. In 1792, during the interlude in which Spain administered Louisiana, Pedro Vial explored a route between Santa Fe and St. Louis. But in 1800, before merchants could take advantage of the road, Spanish authorities returned the costly province to the French, who in turned sold it to the United States three years later. Inhabitants of New Mexico once again found themselves seemingly separated from the rest of the world. Spanish mercantile law restricted exports from foreign nations to only a handful of ports, a thousand miles away from Santa Fe, and the distance to St. Louis was too prohibitive to support smuggling. In 1821, however, Mexico secured its independence from Spain and removed these restrictions.

Late that year, at least three small groups of Missouri traders appeared in Santa Fe to test this new market. The first was William Becknell, a native of Virginia who moved to St. Charles, Missouri, around 1810. He had engaged in several occupations, including drawing salt from Boon's Lick, volunteering during the War of 1812, and operating a ferry. He suffered heavily during the Panic of 1819, and when he heard that Mexico had declared its independence from Spain, he correctly surmised that the new nation would also lift the old regime's trade restrictions. When he returned to St. Louis from Santa Fe, he brought mules and pouches full of silver—both scarce commodities after the panic. On his second journey to Santa Fe, in 1822, Becknell carried goods over the trail with a train of wagons, inaugurating a profitable exchange that endured until the arrival of the railroad sixty years later.

Between 1821 and 1880, caravans large and small crossed the plains between Santa Fe and St. Louis. They carried manufactured goods from Europe and the East Coast of the United States, silver mined in central Mexico, woolens and other local Santa Fe wares, beaver pelts, and mules. Between 1822 and 1843, the traders from Missouri hauled an average of $130,000 in goods annually, but profits varied widely. In 1833, St. Louis businessmen Ceran St. Vrain and the brothers William and Charles Bent established Bent's Fort on the Santa Fe Trail. Situated on the Arkansas River

Illustration of Bent's Fort on the Santa Fe Trail, ca. 1845. (*Library of Congress*)

of present-day southeastern Colorado, the post served not only as a way station for traders but also as an important center of commerce between Bent,
St. Vrain Company, and a variety of Native groups. In 1826, Missouri traders
pressed beyond Santa Fe, taking their goods into the interior of Mexico—to
Chihuahua, Durango, Sonora, and Zacatecas—closer to the silver mines
and mints.

The Santa Fe trade, however, was not one-sided. Many Nuevomexicano
merchants also took advantage of the opportunities found in the commerce
of the elsewhere. By the 1840s they dominated the trade between Santa
Fe and Chihuahua. In 1838 sheep rancher José Chávez and other wealthy
Nuevomexicanos traveled to St. Louis with a five-wagon train reportedly
capitalized with $60,000 in specie to purchase U.S. merchandise. Three years
later, Chávez took part in a caravan of twenty-two wagons carrying almost
$200,000 in silver and returned to New Mexico with 72 tons of goods. Some
Mexican companies sent agents to the eastern United States and Europe to
secure direct access to wholesale manufacturers, bypassing the merchants in
St. Louis. Mexican traders represented a significant portion of the trade that
followed the Santa Fe Trail.

Despite the popular images of solitary men bracing against the privations
of the wilderness, trappers and traders led very social lives. Fur hunters rarely
traveled alone when they plumbed the waterways of the Rocky Mountains.
Unforeseen accidents, the wildlife, and unfriendly Indians made operating
within a group necessary. During the day, they performed the routine of
setting and checking traps. At night they ate a meal over a fire, mended
their clothes, repaired their equipment, swapped stories, and sang songs.
Typically, these mountain men would gather their pelts and carry them to
an annual rendezvous, where they exchanged their caches for wages and
supplies. The place of meeting varied each year, but the activities followed

predictable patterns. When a group arrived, storytelling served as the mode of introduction. In 1833 at the Bear River rendezvous, for example, trapper Zenas Leonard recalled that he and his companions would discuss "the many scenes encountered by each of us, and the many hair-breadth 'scapes that such-and-such a one had made" (Leonard 1839, p. 71). Over the course of several days, the men partook in games of skill, endurance, and chance. They danced, sang, and told more stories. Whiskey flowed liberally and added to the hilarity and violence of the rendezvous. As Leonard noted, "[T]he men get a little mellow and have a real jubilee" (ibid., p. 72).

In order to gain an advantage on their competitors, many trappers established winter camps in the Rockies. Some built cabins of logs, while others drew lessons from Native groups and constructed buffalo-skin huts. They divided daily chores between camp tenders and hunters. The tenders maintained the structures, fires, and stores while the hunters provided food, and, when the opportunity permitted, trapped beaver from the frozen streams. Many mountain men wintered at more permanent posts, such as Fort Union and Fort Laramie. At those locations some trappers maintained families, and communities emerged that endured for decades.

Overland expeditions to Santa Fe were equally social affairs. Caravans that crossed the plains often numbered into the hundreds and followed a general routine, with most men serving as teamsters, or driving teams of oxen or mules. As the train wound its way through the prairie, outriders would scout ahead, heedful of Indians as well as hunting for food. Often they would encounter the massive bison herd of the Southern Plains, and hunter, teamster, and boss alike would promptly abandon their duties and rush off into the chase. Veteran trader Josiah Gregg recalled one such scene: "No sooner were the movements of our mounted men perceived, than the whole extent of country, as far as the eye could reach, became perfectly animate with living objects, fleeing and scampering in every direction" (Gregg 1844, vol. 2, p. 24). The routine at night consisted of cooking a meal over a fire—often over burning buffalo dung, because wood was so scarce on the prairie. Like fur trappers, they played games and told stories, and each member of the expedition had to take a turn on the watch. For many, standing alone in the dark, swallowed by the expanse of the plains, was a humbling experience. Matthew Field, former St. Louis stage actor turned Santa Fe trader, recalled those scenes in poetry: "Night on the Prairie! Lone and solemn night./Night on the desert waste, where howling strays/The hungered wolf, baying the silver light" (Field 1960, p. 287).

Santa Fe and other towns of New Mexico, such as Taos and Las Vegas, served not only as commercial destinations but also as welcome oases for trail-weary traders. Upon their arrival, the traders made arrangements with their local agents and paid the Mexican duties—unless they had connections or otherwise devised ways to avoid them. In the later decades of the trade, many merchants found the New Mexican market saturated with American goods and sought arrangements to travel farther south, resolved to remain until the market improved, or sold their goods at a depressed price. While the market fluctuated, traders could count upon the constancy of the diversions that Nuevomexicanos devised to separate traders from their money. Several establishments provided alcohol, gambling, and prostitution, while the village often held public dances, or fandangos, during which Anglo-American traders socialized with the townsfolk.

While the commerce of the elsewhere promised profit and frivolity, it also promised risk and privation. Culling mountain streams for fur and driving caravans across the plains required daily toil. The less prepared or less fortunate trapper or trader might endure thirst and starvation that occasionally resulted in death. Crossing swollen rivers or snow-bound passes—treacherous landscapes of various kinds—sometimes proved fatal. Every trapper and trader had to face and come to terms with his own or his companions' death.

Violence was yet another condition that trappers and traders confronted and often embraced. Misunderstandings on the trail, contests for leadership, or rivalries with competing groups often resulted in bruises and broken bones and occasionally death. Alcohol certainly contributed to the disquiet between men of the fur and Santa Fe trade. "I have known of disorders and serious brawls in fandangos," recalled trader James J. Webb, "but it was almost invariably where Americans and whiskey were found in profusion" (Webb 1931, p. 97).

Conflict also occurred between trappers and traders and Native Americans. The Blackfeet and Gros Ventres obtained a reputation for their hostility toward American fur trappers. In 1832 they clashed with mountain men at Pierre's Hole in present-day Wyoming. On the Southern Plains, Comanches occasionally attacked the caravans of the Santa Fe Trail, including an 1831 raid that killed Jedediah Smith. These skirmishes contributed to the belief that Indians represented a mindless savagery bent on the destruction of civilized enterprise, but the conflicts actually occurred as a result of the shifting trade relationships wrought by the commerce of the elsewhere. The Blackfeet and Gros Ventres had long enjoyed a beneficial trade with the British-Canadian companies, but with the arrival of the American fur companies, which found eager allies among their enemies, the Blackfeet and Gros Ventres found themselves removed from their once favorable position. The Comanches also reacted against these shifting relationships. During the late eighteenth century, they controlled a vast trade network on the Southern Plains, but the emergence of the Santa Fe trade, and especially the establishment of Bent's Fort on the Arkansas River, threatened their hegemony. As many nations do—European and American alike—the Blackfeet, Gros Ventres, and the Comanches resorted to violence to defend or to regain their place within the global economy.

As the experiences of both trappers and traders illustrate, the marketplace penetrated even the most remote sections of the North American frontier, dispelling the myth that frontiers lay disconnected from the world. Santa Fe was not the end of the trail for Missouri or Mexican merchants. While it provided an important market, the city also served as an exchange point between U.S.-manufactured goods and Mexican-mined silver. Improvements in transportation within the United States—the Erie Canal, the National Road, steam boats—contributed to keeping U.S. prices down and providing better quality goods for mexicano consumers. Merchants drew not only upon manufacturers on the East Coast but also those from Europe. The

British also assisted in advancing Mexican mining technologies and financed improvements, demonstrating the global connections of the trade.

This global economy worked in both directions. Mountain men, for example, trapped beaver in the streams of the Rockies, gathered them at a predetermined rendezvous, and transported them overland by wagon to distant river ports, from which rafts or steamboats carried them to St. Louis. From those Mississippi wharves, the fur corporations sent their pelts across the continent and across the Atlantic, and, in the case of Astor, across the Pacific to China. Before the Civil War, U.S. fur companies sent the bulk of their beaver directly to Great Britain, bypassing U.S. middlemen on the Atlantic coast.

Despite the popular image of the rugged individualist, trappers and traders understood the necessity of corporate action. Indeed, they dared the elsewhere for personal gain, but they rarely attempted it alone. Mountain men traveled in groups for mutual protection, and Santa Fe traders crossed the plains in large caravans, numbering as many as 200 traders. Well-organized businesses dominated the earliest U.S. ventures in the fur trade with associations like Lisa's Missouri Fur Company, Astor's Pacific Fur Company, or Ashley's Rocky Mountain Fur Company. These organizations not only represented local cooperatives that pooled capital but also served as importers of goods from the eastern United States and Europe. Ashley's mountain men worked more individually and with more freedom of action than their counterparts employed by Lisa and Astor, but they nonetheless operated as contract labor, bound to a business-oriented system. They formed copartnerships with formal contracts and found financial backing with merchants at St. Louis and further east. Ashley's rendezvous system—much romanticized in the lore of the West—was an innovation that made the gathering and transporting of commodities much more efficient than before.

Santa Fe traders also relied upon cooperative organizations. When they first left stations like Independence, Missouri, they often traveled in separate groups, but upon reaching Council Grove in present-day Kansas, the traders would connect themselves to a larger group, elect a captain, and agree upon bylaws of conduct. By the 1840s, highly organized business associations dominated the Santa Fe trade, just as they had the fur industry. They brought a more professional approach to the trade, operating more wagons, hiring wage labor, studying the market, making advance arrangements, and representing wholesalers.

While trappers and traders actively petitioned U.S. authorities to support their enterprises, the federal government played only a minor role in developing the trans-Mississippi West during the antebellum period. They asked for assistance but rarely received it, although frontier entrepreneurs forged ahead, drawing the U.S. government in their wake. John Jacob Astor used his connections to gain access to the president, vice president, senators, and cabinet members in order to convince them to support his Columbian venture; when they refused, the New York millionaire risked his fortune and established Astoria—the first U.S. settlement on the Pacific coast.

In other cases, the U.S. government used traders and trappers when they could not employ their own resources in the West. In 1814, William Clark, acting as Indian agent for the United States in the region, turned to Manuel

Lisa for help. Acting in the dual role of government subagent and private fur trading entrepreneur, Lisa helped quell the discontent among Native groups in the region. The United States also established forts along the Missouri but not until the late 1840s—four decades after Lisa began his ventures and two decades after Ashley issued his call for "enterprizing young men." In the case of Fort Laramie, the federal government purchased an existing post that fur traders had established fifteen years before.

This pattern continued on the Santa Fe Trail. When William Becknell crossed the international boundary, he did so without the sanction of the United States or Mexico; those governments, however, recognized the benefits of trade. New Mexico raised revenues by assessing duties on imports, and in 1825 the U.S. Congress sought to facilitate that commerce by appropriating $30,000 to survey the route between St. Louis and the Mexican border. The trail, however, was already decades old, and for at least four years numerous merchants had cut well-defined ruts into the prairie. Veteran caravans, furthermore, largely ignored the government's road. In the estimation of one such veteran, Josiah Gregg, the route "seems to have been of but little service to travellers, who continued to follow the trail previously made by the wagons" (Gregg 1844, vol. 2, p. 44). In the 1830s the U.S. Army dispatched several patrols down the Santa Fe and up the fur trails in an effort to awe the Natives into quiescence, but they experienced little success. Trappers and traders asked for and welcomed any assistance they could receive, but the federal government would not have a major role in the West until the United States acquired the Mexican northwest in 1848 and until it dramatically expanded its powers during the Civil War.

Indeed, many trappers and traders recognized and celebrated their role in expanding the influence of the United States over the continent. They often expressed themselves in nationalistic terms. In 1826, for example, Jedediah Smith had crossed the Rocky Mountains to California, where he met fellow American William H. Cunningham, captain of the ship *Courier*. Smith remarked on the adventurous spirit that they both represented. "Meeting in a distant country by routes so different gave an instance of that restless enterprise that has led and is now leading our countrymen to all parts of the world that has made them travellers on every ocean until it can now be said there is not a breeze of heaven but spreads an american [*sic*] flag" (Smith 1826, p. 75). While on the Santa Fe Trail, Gregg and his companions celebrated the Fourth of July. He believed that the rigors of the frontier created a more pure form of patriotism. "This anniversary is always hailed with heart-felt joy by the wayfarer in the remote desert," he explained, "for here the strifes and intrigues of party-spirit are unknown: nothing intrudes, in these wild solitudes, to mar that harmony of feeling . . . which every true-hearted American experiences on this great day" (Gregg 1844, vol. 2, p. 89). Smith and Gregg exemplified the notions that many of their fellow traders espoused. Not only did they serve as the vanguard of American destiny into regions claimed by other groups but they also personified the ideal, unblemished American patriot.

In the same way that trappers and traders contributed to the American idea of nation, they also contributed to an emerging idea of manliness—the

frontier hero. According to this new belief, Anglo-American men could rede-
fine themselves in the crucible of the elsewhere. At the 1837 Green River
rendezvous, freshman trapper David L. Brown encountered men who represented this new archetype. Writing about veteran mountain man James
Bridger, Brown described his impressive vitality: "The physical conformation
of the man was in admirable keeping with his character," Brown insisted.
"Tall—six feet at least—muscular, without an ounce of superfluous flesh to
impede its force or exhaust its elasticity. . . . [He] might have served as a
model for a sculptor or painter, by which to express the perfection of graceful
strength and easy activity" (quoted in White 1996, vol. 1, p. 392).

For many Americans who espoused the spirit of enterprise as an important national characteristic, adventurism—the quest for excitement through
manly risk-taking—lay at the core of that identification. In 1823, in an introduction to the publication of William Becknell's account of his first expedition
to Santa Fe, the editor of the *Missouri Intelligencer* expressed how intertwined
those two concepts are, suggesting that "new scenes of adventure will appear
and new sources of wealth be opened beyond the promise of these little beginnings" (ibid., vol. 2, p. 60). The writer perceived little difference between
the lure of excitement and the lure of riches. Furthermore, the Becknell
expedition revealed the exceptional nature of American adventurism. "The
adventurous enterprise and hardy habits of this frontier people [traders] will
soon penetrate beyond the mountains, compete for trade on the shores of
the Pacific, and investigate the advantages of that immense country, which
extends to the South" (ibid.). The phrase "adventurous enterprise" captures
the notion that the economic ventures on the North American frontiers represented the efforts of a people, a "frontier people," that were unique and
uncommon—that they represented a people who served as the vanguard of
their nation's economic and cultural expansion.

Courage, vitality, ambition, fortitude, and ingenuity were all important
markers of masculine identity for men of enterprise—virtues, they believed,
that only Anglo-Americans possessed. Indians were too uncivilized, Mexicans too lazy and too unintelligent, and the French too uncouth for enterprise. As these attitudes reveal, trappers and traders not only perceived their
experience in terms of nationhood and manliness; they also believed that
they demonstrated the superiority of the white race.

Native America, according to this argument, lacked the civilization to
properly exploit the bounty of the elsewhere. As a member of an 1842

Manliness was a precious commodity among men of enterprise. Courage gave them the ability to meet the perils of frontier commerce, and youth
granted them the vitality necessary to undertake visionary enterprise. They
embraced ambition as a driving force behind their decisions to enter the
elsewhere, but the higher they aspired, the lower they fell. Many trappers
and traders would lament the travails in which their impulses had trapped
them. The regularity of disaster compelled adventurers to rely upon their
faith in the elsewhere to instill within themselves the fortitude to endure
and eventually succeed in their ventures. Enterprisers believed that they
could call upon their ingenuity and devise measures to mitigate the impact
of misfortune.

Benjamin Franklin Coons

Benjamin F. "Frank" Coons was born in St. Louis in the 1820s. His father operated a dry goods and grocery business and prospered enough to send Frank and his siblings to college in the East. By the time the junior Coons returned to the city of his birth, he was ready to make his mark on the world. He could have remained in St. Louis, followed his father's example, and established his own store, but like many romantics of his generation, Coons daydreamed of risk and renown. Having spent his childhood of the 1830s and 1840s upon the threshold of the West, in a community of venturesome fur trappers and Santa Fe traders, he looked to the commerce of the elsewhere for his fortune.

The aspiring merchant-adventurer began his journey in his native St. Louis. In the summer of 1846, he and a group of overlanders organized a caravan and followed the invasion force under U.S. Gen. Stephen W. Kearney to New Mexico. Meeting only marginal success, Coons would not let his misfortunes deter him, and he led more trains from St. Louis in 1847 and 1848, venturing farther south into Chihuahua. In late 1848 he rented a rancho on the Río Grande, opposite the Mexican town of El Paso del Norte, and constructed a variety of buildings to house a merchant establishment and to serve as a post for the U.S. Army. In 1850 he attempted to bring goods to his store from a more direct route across southern Texas, but the venture proved too costly. Lack of water, incompetent drivers, and an attack by Apaches destroyed Coons's chances for successes. He lost his government contract and defaulted on his lease. Ever sustained by his romantic resilience, Coons sought to correct his misfortunes in California, where, as he claimed, "by bold

adventures and much endurance" he accumulated some $80,000. After ten years spent suffering the vicissitudes of the adventurous merchant, he returned to St. Louis, married, and established a sheep ranch.

Superficially, Coons's motivation for trekking about the Southwest was economic, yet a romantic impulse determined the choices he made to achieve his goals. He was the archetypical man of adventurous enterprise. He did not seek his fortune in the more settled regions of the West such as St. Louis, Chicago, Cincinnati, or New Orleans. Instead, visions of the elsewhere haunted him, lured him into spaces like New Mexico, Chihuahua, Texas, and California. He embraced the opportunities for risk-taking, not only for the chance of realizing profits but also for the opportunity to discover the vital male within himself.

Like many of his fellow romantics, Coons was acutely aware of his condition. In his letters home, he used metaphorical narratives that explored the mentality of adventurism. For example, during his 1850 trek across southwest Texas, he paused at the Devil's River to permit his pack animals and teamsters to rest. He took the opportunity to write a lengthy and reflective letter to his sister in which he compared his life as a man of enterprise to that of fishing in the river. "We pull and pull and bait and bait and watch and watch—get bite after bite—but all mere nibbles." Such a life, Coons explained, required a stout dose of manly fortitude. "Again we try our luck and will continue to try—till rod and tackle all are gone and the very rock slips from our feet—letting us fall full into the pond from wherever we seek our game." Such misfortunes certainly demoralized Coons, but

expedition designed to attack the caravans on the Santa Fe Trail, Steward A. Miller argued that Anglo-American enterprise would triumph over savages. "That such a country, so well adopted to the purposes of civilized life, should have remained so long in the occupancy of the savage Indians . . . is a matter

he relied on his faith in the elsewhere—faith that the next venture in a new place and a new time would restore his prospects. "My life has been estranged and broken," he lamented, "my rod severly [sic] bent—but still, cold and chilled—midst the stones of misfortune and trouble—I sit watching that cork—expecting every moment to see it snatched under and the golden fish of wealth follow the next pull from the water."

Coons also recognized the centrality of risk-taking in the commerce of the elsewhere. In an account of his crossing the boulder-strewn Devil's River, he captured his daring disposition. In the middle of the river, he stood upon a rock and looked to another to continue his crossing. In between lay a smaller rock that would have given him easier access to his next target, but he was a risk-taker. "I scorned the idea of making two leaps to gain only six feet so acting under the impulse of the moment I leaped and barely touched the farthest stone." Unfortunately, he failed to consider that slippery moss covered the next boulder, and he slipped and fell into the river. "Had I been contented to step first to the small rock . . . I should have accomplished the feat without exertion or danger." Coons was not particularly pleased that he often made such decisions, but well understood the lesson. "If we seek to gain fortune too speedily and scorn the small and unimportant chances thrown our way—we must look well to it, else our calculations may fail and we fall short of our aim and thus be engulfed in troubled waters." Yet Coons appeared to have been susceptible to making such rash choices. The trek across Texas seemed to have been such an ill-considered leap.

Indeed, in describing his decision-making as an "impulse" Coons suggested that he was helpless against his urge to take the more daring approach, but it also defined an important aspect of his masculine self. Risk-taking, enduring failure, and accomplishing feats of enterprise forged a potent masculine vitality. "[My] resolutions to cut my way through the heavy and dark forest into which i [sic] have unfortunately entered, grows with my growth," Coons wrote from Durango, Mexico. "[My] energies as yet are wholesome and from constant use their sinews have enlarged, their muscles swolen [sic] in size." The commerce of the elsewhere created ordeals by which Coons and his kind could invigorate their mental and physical manliness. He drew pride from his ability to withstand and overcome the trials and privations with which adventure tested him. "Mine is not a mind that can quickly sink and decay from the effects of disappointment's cold and chilly blasts."

Coons was a latecomer to the commerce of the elsewhere, but his romantic outlook, his compulsion toward risk-taking, and his views on manliness very much characterized the way in which his fellow trappers and traders viewed themselves.

References

Handbook of Texas Online, s.v. "Coons, Benjamin Franklin." http://www.tsha.utexas. edu/handbook/online/articles/CC/fcodb.html (accessed September 24, 2005).

Ben E. Pingenot, ed. "Journal of a Wagon Train Expedition from Fort Inge to El Paso del Norte in 1850." *Military History of the West* 25 (1995): p. 72.

Coons's letters dated July 16 and December 5, 1850; May 31, 1853; and January 23, 1852 (typescripts). Coons Family Papers. St. Louis: Missouri Historical Society.

of surprise." Miller noted that, until recently, the "civilized world" had not been aware of the wealth found in the West. He insisted: "It can not be that the Deity ever intended such a bountiful country to remain in the possession of a few wandering Tribes" (Miller 1843, April 27 entry). Because they wandered, Native Americans exhibited the lack of manly fortitude to remain in one place and the lack of the enterprise to make that place productive.

Mexicans, as viewed by Anglo-American adventurers, were especially lacking in the virtues of enterprise. After his first trip to Santa Fe, Becknell found the inhabitants living there "in a state of extreme indolence and ignorance. Their mechanical improvements are very limited, and they appear to know little of the benefit of industry, or the advantage of the arts" (White 1996, vol. 2, p. 65). Traders often used to describe their Mexican neighbors as suffering a lack of ambition and ingenuity.

The French in the United States did not escape the derision of trappers and traders. Even as late as 1837, U.S. Army officer and would-be Santa Fe trader William Gilpin could discern the French influence in St. Louis: "The french language & a *French air* predominate, tho' signs present themselves every where how rapidly the Anglo Saxon . . . is pushing aside the Frenchman, & eating him up." The French gave way to Anglo-American enterprise: "The big steamers that bring the sinews of commerce are Anglo-Saxon, the huge stone warehouses into which they are piled, have an Anglo-Saxon look, and an Anglo-saxon ship bears them hence" (Gilpin 1837, February 27 letter). The French apparently did not deserve credit for having established St. Louis as a remote fur-trading outpost and nursing its survival for almost forty years before the United States assumed control of the region.

The experiences of Manuel Lisa and José Chávez not only disproved these misconceptions, they also revealed the true diversity of the commerce of the elsewhere. The camps and settlements of trappers and traders dramatically illustrated this multiethnic environment. Astoria was one of the most cosmopolitan towns in all of North America. A handful of Anglo-Americans—U.S. citizens and British Canadians—lived among a variety of Native groups, French Canadians, Russians, Chinese, and Hawaiians. In his painting "Interior of Fort Laramie," Alfred Jacob Miller captured the diversity of the Rocky Mountain fur trade. The people inside, he explained, "gather here from all quarters. From the Gila at the South, the Red River at the North, and the Columbia River West, each has its quota and representatives." The artist lists no fewer than nine Indian groups, and added: "As a contrast, there are Canadian Trappers, free and otherwise, Half breeds, Kentuckians, Missourians, and Down Easters" (Miller 1968, plate 150).

Nuevomexicanos, as Chávez demonstrated, played a significant role in the overland trade between Mexico and the United States, and they also participated in the Southwestern fur trade centered about Taos. Lisa illustrated how the descendants of Native, French, and Spanish Americans dominated the early St. Louis–based fur trade. Pierre Chouteau, for example, was a native of St. Louis, a grandson of the city's founder. Using the powerful connections of his family, he entered the fur trade, participating in both Lisa's and rival John Jacob Astor's operations.

The métis—the children of French trappers and Native women—might not have had the advantages of the Chouteaus, but many parlayed their expertise into jobs as guides for a variety of U.S.-backed expeditions. Métis voyageurs performed crucial services to the Lewis and Clark Expedition, and would later engage in the American fur trade—filling the rolls of Lisa's,

Interior of Fort Laramie, by Alfred Jacob Miller, ca. 1837. (*Francis G. Mayer/Corbis*)

Astor's, and Ashley's companies. Antoine Clement, for example, was the son of a French-Canadian father and an Indian mother. As a hunter and guide, he attained renown among those who ventured onto the plains and mountains. Inventors of Western lore like artist Alfred Jacob Miller and author Matthew Field used Clement as an example of the frontier's exotic allure.

Fewer in number, African Americans also participated in the commerce of the elsewhere. Some served as servants like York, who accompanied William Clark to the Pacific. Fur trader accounts often mention the presence of black and mulatto trappers, but only one, James P. Beckwourth, left an account of his life. He was born in Virginia to his slave-owning father and slave mother. Sometime in the decade following 1810 his father moved to Missouri, where he granted his son freedom. In 1824, Beckwourth joined William H. Ashley's group and trapped in the Rocky Mountains. For more than a decade he worked for Ashley's company and at times lived among the Crows. He served during the Florida Seminole War before entering the commerce along the Santa Fe Trail. Beckwourth traded with Anglo-Americans, Nuevomexicanos, Cheyennes, and Comanches. During the U.S.-Mexican War he operated a hotel in Santa Fe, and he rushed off to California in a search for gold.

Multiethnic peoples like Beckwourth and Clement might have found a measure of freedom in the world of trappers and traders, but they rarely found acceptance. Anglo-Americans who feared the specter of racial miscegenation condemned peoples of mixed ancestry. Certainly some observers wrote about the admirable qualities found in Beckwourth and Clement, but these writers still cast them as people apart from the rest of humanity. They were exotic and non-American, according to this argument—people who were tragically unsuccessful at bridging the gap between American civilization and the savage frontier.

Whether beneficial or detrimental, the commerce of the elsewhere wrought significant changes in Native and Latin American cultures. North American Indians had long histories of trading and hunting, for centuries—if not millennia—before the arrival of Europeans, but the values that they assigned to those activities differed. Traditionally, trade played a ceremonial function, steeped in ritual and spiritual meaning. The act of reciprocity created avenues of interaction between groups that enabled Indians to receive supplies from disparate corners of the continent. When Europeans arrived, they brought with them new ideas of trade. They transformed beaver and buffalo peltry into commodities to exchange for profit. Hunting still continued to provide food for, and served the spiritual needs of, Native Americans, but after they had established relations with European-Americans, hunting developed into a commercial function. The appearance of new trading partners disrupted existing relationships between Native groups.

Trappers and traders certainly contributed to the changes in Indian society, but they were not responsible for the creation of its social inequities. Reciprocity might appear like a less crass form of trade, but it nonetheless represented a power arrangement between "haves" and "have-nots," forging bonds of obligation that perpetuated hierarchical social structures within and between Native groups. Furthermore, most Indians willingly entered into these new trading relationships with European-Americans, deliberately making decisions for themselves based upon their own self-interests—often with unforeseen and devastating results.

Such was the case of the Mandans. They enjoyed a preeminent position among Native groups in their dealings with American fur traders. Lewis and Clark wintered at their villages in present-day North Dakota. In 1809, Manuel Lisa established a post among them. While historians may have overemphasized Mandan dependence upon European technology and goods, these Natives nonetheless took advantage of their position by dealing with the fur traders. In some cases their cooperation created resentment among and conflict with neighboring groups of Indians, and their interaction with trappers came at a devastating cost. Mandans, like most Native groups, lacked sufficient immunities from the diseases that European Americans carried, and in 1837 smallpox decimated their towns. Within six months, only about 100 of 1,800 Mandans had survived the epidemic.

Although many Nuevomexicanos were familiar with the Western European traditions of commerce, the Santa Fe trade also changed their world. Wealthy mexicanos like José Chávez took advantage of their position to exploit the new markets that opened for them. Unencumbered by import duties, they seized control of the traffic between Santa Fe and the interior of Mexico and by the 1840s threatened to do the same with the Missouri trade. In 1845, however, the United States annexed the Republic of Texas, which claimed the Río Grande as its boundary, including Santa Fe. The Mexican government refused to recognize the union. The next year, in part to make good on its claim, the United States invaded Mexico and sent Gen. Stephen W. Kearney into New Mexico. He immediately organized an occupying government that stripped away many of the laws that protected local merchants. The treaty of Guadalupe Hidalgo, which brought the war to an end, obligated the United States to protect the rights of mexicanos, but U.S. authorities rarely enforced those guarantees. An influx of Anglo-American merchants and capital blocked access to opportunities for many merchants of New Mexico.

This commerce also affected the lives of Native women, who performed a crucial function as trading partners, wives, lovers, and liaisons between Indians and trappers. Many Anglo-Americans condemned the Native practice of polygamy as well as arranged and bartered marriages, but when faced with the necessity of forging good relations with a group, many trappers set aside such qualms. Observers romanticized these transactions as part of a process to rescue Indian maids from the clutches of their unscrupulous male kin. Alfred Jacob Miller offered this explanation in his most celebrated watercolor, "The Trapper's Bride." In this scene, the young, slender bride tentatively offers her hand to the dashing, buckskin-clad trapper. Her father and the leader of her group received $600 in firearms, blankets, red flannel, alcohol, and tobacco. This arrangement, according to Miller, was a desirable one for the girl. Marrying the trapper represented a step up on the social ladder. He believed that Anglo-American men treated their wives better than Native men, regarding them "as a companion and faithful friend of man" (ibid., plate 12), but he contradicts himself in a painting of veteran mountain man Joseph R. Walker and his Indian wife. The couple ride horseback through the mountains—Walker in the center and foreground. In the misty background follows his wife. "The sketch exhibits a certain etiquette," Miller explained. "The Squaw's station in travelling [*sic*] is at a considerable distance in the rear of her liege lord, and never at the side of him" (ibid., plate 78). While not a scene that depicts abject servitude, the wife certainly represented subordination. According to George Catlin, Miller's artist contemporary, Indian wives were disposable. As he visited the Mandans, he witnessed marriages that served as little more than business transactions. He believed that they created loveless relationships that couples rarely consummated with sex. So callous were the trappers whom Catlin encountered that they would cast aside their Indian brides once those marriages outlived their usefulness. "[U]nceremoniously do they annul and abolish this connexion [*sic*] when they wish to leave the country, or change their positions from one tribe to another" (Catlin 1844, vol. 1, p. 120).

In some ways, however, marriage to Anglo-American trappers benefited Native women—especially those among plains Indians who found their roles diminished after the adoption of horse culture. Marriage with trappers forged economic opportunities for the group that generated value and prestige for some women. While many of these unions served as temporary contingencies, as many others survived as permanent relationships. Indian wives could remain with their own kin while their husbands spent most of the year trapping, but many moved to trading posts like Fort Union, creating new homes and communities. Even casual encounters could prove beneficial. Many Native American cultures practiced a more permissive sexuality than Anglo-America. Sexual contact with trappers could create bonds of obligation with little or no stigma attached to the women. Indeed, such encounters could heighten women's spiritual prestige within their community.

The commerce of the elsewhere also affected the women of Santa Fe. Unlike Anglo-American women, mexicanas could own property and enter contracts. A rare few made the best of the new opportunities that the trade with the United States created. María Gertrudis Barceló, for example, was the daughter of a wealthy Sonoran family who in the early 1820s moved to New Mexico. In 1825, Barceló opened a gambling parlor in Santa Fe and catered to the Missouri traders who traveled down the trail. She used her position to forge business relationships with both U.S. and New Mexican merchants. During the U.S.-Mexican War, Barceló managed to maintain her status by cooperating with U.S. occupation authorities. In 1852, she died a woman of property.

Barceló, however, was the exception. Like Native women, some Nuevomexicanos married Anglo-American traders and obtained some measure of security within the shifting fortunes of Santa Fe, but for most, the introduction of an aggressive market economy disrupted their traditional societies. After the arrival of St. Louis traders, most women of Santa Fe found themselves in a perpetual cycle of poverty, finding employment in the most menial and lowest paying jobs.

The commerce of the elsewhere served as the far-reaching extension of a global economy. Trappers in the Rocky Mountains shipped their furs to the Atlantic coast, Europe, and Asia. Missouri traders carried British manufactures overland to Santa Fe and farther into the interior of Mexico. Trappers and traders embraced the necessity of corporate action, traveling in groups for protection and operating within well-organized business associations. They petitioned the U.S. authorities to support their ventures in the West, but for much of the early nineteenth century the federal government offered little assistance and their contributions often misfired—such as the survey of the Santa Fe Trail, which few caravans followed.

Anglo-American trappers and traders congratulated themselves on their contribution to the expansion of the United States. They established posts in remote regions and mapped trails that later immigrants would follow into territories over which their nation had little or no title. Their experiences helped to define the frontier hero as a new archetype of American manliness and whiteness. Many believed in the superiority of Anglo-American institutions and enterprise over Native ignorance, Mexican indolence, and French indulgence.

The actual experience of the elsewhere, however, demonstrated that it was a diverse place. Nuevomexicanos demonstrated their capacity for enterprise as they began to take control of the transcontinental trade between Mexico and Missouri, but they lost their advantage after the United States invaded and blocked their opportunities for success. Relying upon generations of experience, métis voyageurs served as invaluable guides, teaching novice Anglo-American trappers how to survive in the elsewhere, but trappers and traders also exacted unintended devastation among the groups that they encountered. Many Native peoples reorientated their traditional ways of trade and incorporated the commodity-driven commerce of Anglo-Americans. That contact occasionally resulted in disastrous epidemics that swept away entire cultures.

Despite their professed qualms about Native American marriage practices, many trappers and traders purchased or otherwise arranged for Indian brides in order to facilitate trade with their people. A few of these marriages endured, but many were loveless business transactions that ended when they had outlived their usefulness. Some Santa Fe women also sought marriage with Anglo-American traders but were just as often disappointed. The dynamic new economy that surrounded their town in the early nineteenth century offered them few opportunities and often compelled them to take the lowest paying jobs.

The commerce of the elsewhere drew the North American frontiers into a global economy and wrought dramatic changes among the people it touched. A diverse range of individuals cooperated or resisted based on an equally diverse range of needs, desires, and meanings. It opened the way for the United States to wrest a transcontinental empire from Mexico and Native America, and provided some groups with grand opportunities for prosperity while it devastated and impoverished others.

References and Further Reading

Anderson, Dean L. "The Flow of European Trade Goods into the Western Great Lakes Region, 1715–1760." In Jennifer H. Brown et al., eds., *The Fur Trade Revisited: Selected Papers of the Sixth North American Fur Trade Conference.* East Lansing: Michigan State University Press, 1994, 93–115.

Anfinson, John Ogden. "Transitions in the Fur Trade, Continuity in Mandan Economy and Society to 1837." Ph.D. diss., University of Minnesota, Minneapolis-St. Paul, 1987.

Atherton, Lewis E. "The Santa Fe Trader as Mercantile Capitalist." *Missouri Historical Review* 77 (1982): 1–12.

Barbour, Barton H. *Fort Union and the Upper Missouri Fur Trade.* Norman: University of Oklahoma Press, 2001.

Boyle, Susan Calafate. *Los Capitalistas: Hispano Merchants and the Santa Fe Trade.* Albuquerque: University of New Mexico Press, 1997.

Catlin, George. *Letters and Notes on the Manners, Customs, and Conditions of North American Indians* [1844]. 2 vols. New York: Dover Publications, 1973.

Clokey, Richard M. *William H. Ashley: Enterprise and Politics in the Trans-Mississippi West.* Norman: University of Oklahoma Press, 1980.

DeVoto, Bernard. *Across the Wide Missouri.* New York: Houghton Mifflin Company, 1947.

Dunwidde, Peter W. "The Nature of the Relationship between the Blackfeet Indians and the Men of the Fur Trade." *Annals of Wyoming* 46 (1974): 123–133.

Field, Matthew. *Matt Field on the Santa Fe Trail.* Compiled by Clyde and Mae Reed Porter. Norman: University of Oklahoma Press, 1960.

Gilman, Rhoda R., ed. *Aspects of the Fur Trade: Selected Papers of the 1965 North American Fur Trade Conference.* St. Paul: Minnesota Historical Society, 1967.

Gilpin, William. *Letters* [1837]. St. Louis: Missouri Historical Society.

Goetzmann, William H. *Exploration and Empire: The Explorer and the Scientist in the Winning of the American West.* New York: W. W. Norton and Company, 1966.

González, Deena J. *Refusing the Favor: The Spanish-Mexican Women of Santa Fe, 1820–1880.* New York: Oxford University Press, 1999.

Gregg, Josiah. *Commerce of the Prairies* [1844]. 2 vols. Ann Arbor, MI: University Microfilms, 1966.

Hämäläinen, Pekka. "The Western Comanche Trade Center: Rethinking the Plains Indian Trade System." *Western Historical Quarterly* 29 (1998): 485–513.

Hyslop, Stephen G. *Bound for Santa Fe: The Road to New Mexico and the American Conquest, 1806–1848.* Norman: University of Oklahoma Press, 2002.

Isenberg, Andrew C. "The Market Revolution in the Borderlands: George Champlin Silbey in Missouri and New Mexico, 1808–1826." *Journal of the Early Republic* 21 (2001): 445–466.

Lansing, Michael. "Plains Indian Women and Interracial Marriage in the Upper Missouri Trade, 1804–1868." *Western Historical Quarterly* 31 (2000): 413–433.

Leonard, Zenas. *Narrative of the Adventures of Zenas Leonard* [1839]. Ann Arbor, MI: University Microfilms, 1966.

Miller, Alfred Jacob. *The West of Alfred Jacob Miller.* Norman: University of Oklahoma Press, 1968.

Miller, Steward Alexander. *Papers* [1843]. Austin: Center for American History, University of Texas at Austin.

Milner, Clyde A. II, Carol A. O'Connor, and Martha A. Sandweiss, eds. *The Oxford History of the American West.* New York: Oxford University Press, 1994.

Oglesby, Richard Edward. *Manuel Lisa and the Opening of the Missouri Fur Trade.* Norman: University of Oklahoma Press, 1963.

Oman, Kerry R. "Winter in the Rockies: Winter Quarters of the Mountain Man." *Montana: The Magazine of Western History* 52 (2002): 34–47

Phillips, Paul Chrisler. *The Fur Trade.* 2 vols. Norman: University of Oklahoma Press, 1961.

Ronda, James P. *Astoria and Empire.* Lincoln: University of Nebraska Press, 1990.

Schitz, Thomas F. "The Gros Ventres and the Upper Missouri Fur Trade, 1806–1835." *Annals of Wyoming* 56 (1984): 21–28.

Smith, Jedediah Strong. *Papers* [1826]. St. Louis: Missouri Historical Society.

Taylor, Quintard. *In Search of the Racial Frontier: African Americans in the West, 1528–1900.* New York: W. W. Norton and Company, 1998.

Utley, Robert M. *A Life Wild and Perilous: Mountain Men and the Paths to the Pacific.* New York: Henry Holt and Company, 1997.

Webb, James Josiah. *Adventures in the Santa Fé Trade, 1844–1847.* Edited by Ralph P. Bieber. Glendale, CA: Arthur H. Clark Company, 1931.

Weber, David J. *New Spain's Far Northern Frontier: Essays on Spain in the American West, 1540–1821.* Dallas, TX: Southern Methodist University Press, 1979.

Weber, David J. *The Mexican Frontier, 1821–1846: The American Southwest under Mexico.* Albuquerque: University of New Mexico Press, 1982.

White, Bruce M. "A Skilled Game of Exchange: Ojibway Fur Trade Protocol." *Minnesota History* 50 (1987): 229–240.

White, Bruce M. "The Woman Who Married a Beaver: Trade Patterns and Gender Roles in the Ojibwa Fur Trade." *Ethnohistory* 46 (1999): 109–147.

White, David A., comp. *News of the Plains and Rockies, 1803–1865.* 2 vols. Spokane, WA: Arthur H. Clark Company, 1996.

Soldiers in the American West | 5

Kevin Adams

A study of the U.S. Army's place in the history of the American West is essentially the history of the region, for the army has been inextricably connected to the process of Western expansion from the first days of the United States of America. Its disastrous performance in several campaigns against Native Americans caused George Washington no shortage of headaches in the 1790s, and absorbed nearly 40 percent of the federal budget in the middle of that decade. From those inauspicious beginnings, the army played a central role in the geographical expansion of the United States beyond the Mississippi River. Contemporary Americans might be surprised to learn that such pacific and cosmopolitan metropolises as San Francisco, Minneapolis, Salt Lake City, and Omaha harbored significant military garrisons in earlier generations, with some of those cities maintaining their military significance until the budget cuts of the 1990s.

This chapter will capture the army's significance in the process of Western expansion by capturing the experiences of federal soldiers, who were an important component of the diverse population of the West. Who were these soldiers? What social and cultural worlds did they create while stationed in the West? What do their lives tells us about this period of American culture and society?

Institutional Contexts and Constraints

There is no avoiding the raison d'etre for the army's presence on the Western frontier; like all armies, the U.S. Army from the early national period to the dawn of the twentieth century was an institution dedicated to the organized, efficient, and overwhelming application of lethal, state-sponsored force. Although the army was never large, sometimes poorly led and organized, and rarely able to accumulate overwhelming force at the proper time and place against its foes, it represented the point of the spear for federal military action against a wide array of indigenous peoples from the Old Northwest to the Pacific coast. From the earliest days of the republic, this operational role defined the army. From the early unsuccessful campaigns of Generals Josiah Harmer and Arthur St. Clair into the Ohio backcountry (1790–1791) to Wounded Knee (1890), the army served as a fulcrum of an Indian policy derided by reformer Helen Hunt Jackson as *A Century of Dishonor* (1881).

Jackson's critique both captured an important component of the army's frontier history, and totally ignored its arguably more substantial contributions to the defeats of Mexico in the 1840s and Spain in the 1890s. Although in those two wars the United States relied heavily upon volunteer regiments raised by states, regular army forces provided the most readily deployed and reliable combat forces—some 27,000 soldiers in the Mexican War alone (Foos 2002, p. 85). Many civilians who flocked to the colors during these wars found themselves serving as rear-area garrison and occupation forces, relegated to "second-team" status in the face of the regulars' skills and discipline. On the frontier one might trace the army's campaigns against Indians throughout most of the territory west of the Mississippi River, yet from the perspective of the murderous twentieth century, those campaigns were usually low-intensity conflicts. A surprising number of them also proved to be fruitless or outright failures. For most soldiers, frontier service entailed a deadening routine of tedious labor details; the army was, to use the description of a West Point graduate in the 1890s, akin to "a well trained fire department with no fires, and the firemen sitting out in front of the fire house playing checkers" (Coffman 1986, p. 404). Occasionally (and for many bored soldiers thankfully), this tedium was broken by formal campaigns against various tribes and hastily planned "scouts" and rescue missions.

Interested readers may trace these expeditions, large and small, through the works of Robert Utley and Durwood Ball listed in the *References* below; in general, the army spent much of the pre–Civil War era engaged with tribes just beyond the Mississippi River, in places like central Texas, the Dakota Territory, and Kansas. Antebellum conflicts also occurred in the Pacific Northwest—where thousands of American settlers flocked in the 1840s and 1850s—and surrounded outposts found deep in the interior. These garrisons, such as Wyoming's Fort Laramie, were often relics left behind by earlier fur traders. After the Civil War, there were intermittent bursts of military activity that largely bypassed the Northwest, California, and the inhospitable landscape of the Great Basin. The early post–Civil War campaigns were initiated after treaties negotiated by the U.S. Indian Peace commissioners in 1867 (for the Southern Plains tribes) and 1868 (for Northern Plains tribes, culminating in the Treaty of Fort Laramie with the Sioux in November of that year) failed to secure a lasting peace. These campaigns faced more than a few setbacks, but were largely finished on the Southern Plains by the early 1870s, and on the Northern Plains by the late 1870s. Smaller and unrelated "outbreaks" by the Utes (1879), the Nez Perce (1877), California's Modocs (1872–1873), and the Bannocks (1877–1878) also occupied the army's attention. Its other theater of operations would be the Southwest, where the relatively late arrival of American settlers postponed conflict with the powerful Apaches.

These campaigns, which persisted for most of the 1880s, were launched in some of the continent's most inhospitable territory. They pushed the army to its limit and possessed an intensity more reminiscent of some of the army's antebellum encounters.

Despite the indispensable role played by the army in the western expansion of the United States, it was a small and poorly organized bureaucracy. It was never very big; on the eve of the Mexican War, Congress mandated a force of just under 10,000 commissioned officers and enlisted men, some of whom served in urban centers nowhere near the frontier. In 1860 the legal strength of the army, as distinct from its actual strength—as frequent desertions, illnesses, and resignations meant that far fewer men were actually in arms at any given time—stood at 18,615 officers and men, a force laughably inadequate to the challenges presented by the expanding federal domain (Ball 2001, p. *xx*). A temporary boost created by the demands of the Civil War did not last long; Congress soon shrank the force from a strength of 54,000 (the size dictated by an act signed by President Johnson in July 1866) to a force of 25,000 enlisted men and 2,000 commissioned officers. Again, its actual strength was far lower, with one scholar observing that only rarely "did the regimental roles bear the names of more than 19,000 soldiers" (Utley 1973, p. 19). Out of this total a good percentage served in the South, particularly during the Reconstruction era, or in the nation's urban centers. For the rest of the Indian Wars period, the army remained at this strength, producing a series of fuming commanding generals who agreed with General George Crook's 1880 complaint: "I don't believe that any force in the world has ever been called upon to do so much in the ratio of its effective strength as has the little handful of men on frontier, we call the Regular Army" (*Annual Report* 1880, p. 80).

Small as it was, the army was also poorly trained. Enlisted recruits did not undergo systematic basic training; instead, they were shipped to a series of recruit depots, where they learned a few rudiments of military life, and were then forwarded to their units, perhaps to end up in combat with nary an idea how to load and aim their weapons. Once they were stationed on the frontier, things rarely improved. Confronted with a series of congressional opponents, a wary army practiced strict fiscal economy during the course of the nineteenth century. This often meant, for instance, that the army could not afford to support a program of target practice more robust than a few rounds a month per man. Large-scale maneuvers were unheard of until the 1880s, while army culture emphasized the importance of obedience on the part of enlisted men—a fact that did not improve its performance in the confused circumstances of Indian Wars combat, which tended to reward individual judgment and tactical flexibility.

Many of the army's failings were not entirely of its own doing, however, but were created by vague congressional mandates and statutes, along with aggressive restrictions placed upon the army in the cost-cutting aftermath of Reconstruction. Moreover, as studies of federal military policy toward the Indians have shown, the army frequently bore the burdens imposed by policy flux and strategic uncertainty. Profound disagreements about the command structure and the chain of command (in particular, the exact duties of the general-in-chief and the secretary of war, and their relationship to each other) plagued the army from the Jacksonian era to the very end of the frontier period. The frequent changes in presidential administration and cabinet personnel also bedeviled professional soldiers, whose careers transcended the electoral cycle, while hot-button issues such as the expansion of slavery, the Mexican War, and Reconstruction produced a series of operational limitations on the army. Most notably that occurred in the aftermath of the Civil War, when Democrats opposed to congressional Reconstruction gradually pushed through measures shrinking the army, while sometimes withholding the army's pay—in one case in 1877 for nearly an entire year (Utley 1973). Another stipulation came in the form of an amendment to the 1878 Army Appropriation Bill, which strictly limited the ability of the army to engage in domestic policing duties, a direct attack on the army's duties during Reconstruction (Tate, 1999). (Interestingly, this very nineteenth-century issue has re-entered the policy spectrum in the aftermath of the terrorist attacks of 2001 and Hurricane Katrina in 2005, with some policy-makers advocating the modification of the army's *posse comitatus* powers.)

All too often, however, soldiers in the West did not rise to the challenges presented by the above factors; left holding the bag of Indian policy, the army displayed a marked tendency promptly to drop it. Personal rivalries and petty disputes among ranking officers could—and did—paralyze army operations at times. Moreover, officers displayed little interest in professional study when their only opponents were so-called savages. General John Schofield exemplified this line of thinking when he wrote General of the Army William T. Sherman in October of 1876, and postulated: "The small demands of our indian [sic] frontier are ephemeral in character and of secondary importance in our permanent military establishment. The main purpose of our military peace establishment is to provide the defense for our sea-board against invasion" (Andrews 1968, p. 166). This dismissive view of frontier conflict weakened the army immeasurably, especially when its effect was enhanced by the tendency of well-heeled officers to consider themselves as gentlemanly men of leisure, a seniority-based promotion system that failed to reward professional study, and a shortage of professional schools that army leaders began to address only at the tail end of the frontier period.

Soldiers' Lives

The general lack of consensus that attended discussions of federal Indian policy and the army's role in western expansion should not come as a surprise, for soldiers were a diverse group of men who were always internally divided along lines of rank and social class. Some fairly clear patterns manifested themselves in the demographics of the U.S. Army during the nineteenth century. Commissioned officers, in general, came from prosperous middle-class backgrounds. Outside of those men who gained commissions during the Civil War, commissioned officers throughout the nineteenth century were very often college graduates in a century in which only about 1 in 100 white persons graduated from college. For example, some 76 percent of officers who joined the army after 1867 had graduated from West Point, with an unknown number of other officers having graduated from or attended other institutions of higher learning (Coffman 1986). In short, as one historian of the post–Civil War period phrased it, the typical West Point graduate's "socioeconomic background differed little from [those of] the men who ran the economic and political institutions of the nation" (Cooper 1980, p. 30).

This is not to suggest that the army was exclusively a bastion of WASP elitism. A good number of West Point graduates did not enter the university as favored members of the elite but as representatives of the broad and expanding middle class of the United States. Nor were commissions in the frontier army for native-born Americans only; in the post–Civil War frontier army, at least, foreigners earned commissions roughly in proportion to their percentage in the population (approximately 10 percent of the officers serving between 1870 and 1890 were foreign born). The main difference between native- and foreign-born officers seems to have rested in the fact that native-born officers earned commissions from the ranks at a much lower rate than foreign-born officers, at least between 1870 and 1890 (24 percent versus 62.5 percent) (Adams forthcoming).

Nineteenth-century enlisted men rarely entered the army with the same ideals of duty and service that motivated officers. They enlisted to meet more pressing and immediate needs: employment, food, and shelter, items often left in short supply for working-class Americans by the frequent depressions and dislocations of the burgeoning U.S. economy. Civilians may have complained about the character of recruits, but the army was—and could afford to be—fairly selective in accepting prospective recruits. There were simply too many applicants and too small of a force structure for it to have been otherwise. Between 1880 and 1891, for instance, some 309,060 men applied for enlistment in the U.S. Army; only 81,605 (26.4 percent) were accepted, figures that work out to 25,755 applicants per year with just over 6,800 being accepted (ibid.).

These men were young. The average age of enlistees in the 1840s and the mid-1850s fluctuated between twenty-four and twenty-five years (Ball 2001). Less work has been done on the post–Civil War army, but an analysis of more than 1,000 soldiers serving in the trans-Mississippi West in 1880 revealed an average age of 29.17 years, a figure skewed by the small minority of career soldiers in their late thirties, forties, and early fifties, and perhaps a small sample size (ibid.). They were noticeably unskilled: 21.4 percent of first-time recruits in 1878 listed no other occupation than "laborer," while many others worked in industries that were undergoing de-skilling (for example, shoemaker, cigar-maker), were highly susceptible to the natural variations of the business cycle (puddler or roller in a steel mill), or were caught in the intense spasms of labor unrest endemic to the nineteenth century (ibid.). The enlistment register for 1878, for example, contains many men from Ohio, West Virginia, Pennsylvania, and Maryland who had worked in the railroad industry but were now locked out, or blacklisted (ibid.). The words of Private Ami Mulford might stand in for thousands of enlisted men when he introduced his autobiographical account, *Fighting Indians in the Seventh U.S. Cavalry, Custer's Favorite Regiment* (a book, incidentally, that is

Troop C, Fifth Cavalry, which arrested boomers and squatters prior to the opening of Oklahoma, ca. 1888. (*National Archives and Records Administration*)

remarkably short on Indian fighting and remarkably long concerning imperious officers), by writing: "Money was tight and hard to get, and although there was plenty of work, there were a great many out of employment, and to make it still worse, also were out of money—which was the case with one man I will make you acquainted with before we are through with this history" (Mulford 1972, p. 5).

Enlisted men also fit a fairly specific geographic profile. Few were born west of the Mississippi, since many of those states and territories had a negligible Anglo-American population before the early 1870s, when the last of the Indian Wars' recruits were born. Even California, which leapt from a backwater Mexican province to a thriving U.S. state virtually overnight, saw only sixteen of its native sons enlist in 1878, a minuscule 0.3 percent of the total first-time enlistees for that year. Only ten men who enlisted that year were born in Alaska, Colorado, Kansas, and Oregon; none hailed from the other territories composing the Pacific Northwest, the Southwest, or the Rocky Mountain West (Adams forthcoming). Nor were white Southerners much interested in joining the U.S. Army, particularly in the aftermath of the Civil War. In 1880, only 3 percent of recruits had been born in the "Deep South" states of Alabama, Arkansas, Florida, Georgia, Louisiana, Mississippi, and South Carolina, a figure that includes African-American enlistees (Coffman 1986). Two years earlier there had been more first-time white enlistees born at sea—four—than white recruits born in Arkansas, Mississippi, and Florida—three (Adams forthcoming).

This left the Northeast as the main source of white enlisted recruits, a trend that persisted in the nineteenth century. Some 27.3 percent of all recruits who signed on in 1880 did so in either New York or Boston (Coffman 1986). Massachusetts and New York were joined by Pennsylvania and Ohio as the most common birthplaces of native-born white soldiers. The representation of these four states in the pool of native-born white soldiers, at least in the few samples undertaken to date, suggests a remarkable degree of demographic consistency: a nearly complete survey of both new enlistments and re-enlistments for white soldiers in 1872 reveals that 61.8 percent were born in New York, Pennsylvania, Ohio, and Massachusetts, while a comparable analysis of new white recruits in 1878 returned a percentage of 61.5, and a sample of 1,040 enlisted men based on the 1880 census generated a nearly identical percentage (61.3) (Adams forthcoming). After the creation of permanent black regiments in 1866 (many of whose soldiers initially came from all points of the North and South, having transferred directly from the U.S. Colored Troops), African-American soldiers tended to come disproportionately from the upper South, where army recruiters set up stations with them in mind; Tennessee, Kentucky, Virginia, Maryland, and the District of Columbia were particularly fruitful grounds for black recruits (Dobak and Phillips 2001).

Observers in the antebellum period noticed early on that immigrants predominated within the ranks. During the 1840s, some 40 percent of recruits were foreign born according to the records of the General Recruiting Service (Foos 2002). The surge of immigration after Ireland's potato famine and the upheavals of 1848 affected the army as well: by the early 1850s, immigrants had shifted from a large minority to an overwhelming majority of recruits as foreigners outnumbered native-born recruits by slightly more than 2 to 1 in the early 1850s (Utley 1967). As in civil society, Irish and German immigrants constituted more than two-thirds of the immigrant stream: 70.9 percent of immigrants to the United States in the 1840s were Irish or German; 71.8 percent were so in the 1850s (Tindall and Shi 2004).

This basic pattern was replicated in the post–Civil War years, though in some ways it grew more extreme. Of the 7.7 million immigrants who entered the United States between 1851 and 1880, 54.9 percent were born in Ireland or Germany; unlike the antebellum period, the Irish and Germans entered the army at a rate disproportionate to their percentage in the population (ibid.). An in-progress analysis of 1872's enlistment register reveals that 65.97 percent of all foreign-born enlistees (including soldiers who re-enlisted) were German or Irish. In 1878, 68.2 percent of all new immigrant enlistees hailed from Germany and Ireland, while a sampling of enlisted men taken from the 1880 census suggested that 71.8 percent of foreign-born enlisted men came from those two countries (Adams forthcoming). Overall, despite the drop in immigration after the Civil War, European immigrants continued to flock to the army for the rest of the nineteenth century, a fact confirmed by a variety of sources. Some 147 of the 409 enlisted Indian Wars' Medal of Honor winners were foreign born (35.9 percent), for example, while a compilation of recruiting statistics between 1880 and 1891 shows that more than 30,000 of the 75,500 white enlistees (including those who re-enlisted) were foreign born (40.0 percent) (ibid.).

Immigrants enlisted for a number of reasons. For some, the army provided a familiar environment in an unfamiliar country. The periodic levees raised by European nation-states had exposed many immigrants to military service in their homelands, a factor that increased with importance as compulsory military service spread throughout Europe. For individuals whose skills may not have enabled them to climb the occupational ladder, knowledge of the military profession helped them to gain a secure, though poorly paying, refuge in a tumultuous economic environment. Similarly, the presence of other countrymen—particularly for the Irish and German—might have encouraged immigrants to try soldiering for a spell. Others joined for reasons familiar to native-born recruits: contemporary labor markets funneled unskilled and rural laborers into a variety of low-paying, poorly esteemed, and transient jobs, one of which was service in the U.S. Army. Often lacking possession of English, immigrants were especially prone to end up in these jobs, at least initially (and since soldiers were young men, by and large, one can surmise that most immigrants signed on within a few years of having arrived in the United States).

In sum, any study of enlisted men will uncover a fairly definite profile: new arrivals from abroad, along with unemployed, de-skilled, and transient workers, especially from the urban Northeast and the rural portions of Pennsylvania and Ohio, dominated in the ranks, while their commanders, especially if native-born, rarely came from the ranks and were typically college-educated. Demographically, army outfits were much more similar to the cosmopolitan and expanding Eastern urban centers than to the surrounding frontier landscape. In retrospect, it seems like a combustible mix. A sergeant who served in the late 1840s and early 1850s, though admitting that his peers had flaws, described them as "a remarkably good set of men," who perhaps only lacked "the strong will and judgment to act independently—to blaze the way and decide their own destiny" (Utley 1967, pp. 35–36).

Fault Lines

Soldiers provoked tension and controversy, both within society as a whole and within the military. To a citizenry steeped in the traditional praise of the volunteer militia and dismissive of dependent persons (be they unemployed laborers, women, children, or slaves), the notion of enlisting for a fixed term of service in the U.S. Army as a common soldier was anathema. Soldiers—as well as officers—received an amount of ridicule disproportionate to their place in American society. When young subaltern Ulysses S. Grant paraded down the streets of Cincinnati in dress uniform, "imagining that every one was looking at me, with a feeling akin to mine when I first saw General Scott," he was met by "a little urchin, bareheaded, barefooted, with dirty and ragged pants . . . and a shirt that had not seen a wash-tub for weeks" who turned toward Grant and yelled, "Soldcr! Will you work? No, sir-ee; I'll sell my shirt first!!" This incident, Grant recalled in his *Memoirs*, "gave me a distaste for military uniform that I never recovered from" (Grant 1992, p. 30). Little had changed after the Civil War; a young enlistee in the early 1870s took pains to avoid being seen in uniform in his Ohio hometown, because "at that time, any young man wearing the uniform of a United Sates soldier was looked upon as an idler—too lazy to work." In that endeavor he failed; not having apprised his mother of his plan to enlist, she fainted dead away upon seeing him in uniform in a chance encounter in public (Brininstool 1926, pp. 19–20).

These beliefs were not confined to civil society, but were sometimes repeated with official sanction by the highest levels of the army hierarchy.

"The material offered in time of peace, is not of the most desirable character, consisting principally of newly arrived immigrants, of those broken down by bad habits and dissipation, the idle and the improvident," an official antebellum report on the demographics of the army concluded. Virtually the same language appeared in the post–Civil War era. Praising the development of a much-improved rifle for the army, General Edward Ord gloomily opined that "I rather think we have a much less intelligent soldier to handle it" (Utley 1973, p. 22). To frustrated commissioned officers who regarded the tale of their professional careers as one of declension after serving in the grand campaigns of the Civil War, the assertion of the *New York Sun* that "the Regular Army is composed of bummers, loafers, and foreign paupers" struck a chord (ibid.).

As these dismissals of enlisted men illustrate, the common opprobrium of their civilian peers may have united soldiers of all pay grades throughout the nineteenth century, but nothing divided this disparate group of men so much as rank. The gulf between enlisted man and officer was so vast in the late nineteenth century as to forestall nearly all contact outside of official business. A soldier desiring to speak to any officer, for example, had to secure permission from his first sergeant before doing so. Officers, for their own part, were, by declaration of Congress, "gentlemen," and sought to live up to that role. In many ways, official army culture after the Civil War bore a closer resemblance to that of George Washington's Continental Army than it did to the U.S. Army in 1910.

Army culture was heavily mediated by period conceptions of class relations. As befitting a society that many contemporaries feared was becoming indelibly stratified thanks to the growing pains of economic expansion, industrialization, and urbanization, soldiers and officers understood the class system and social relations of the United States in completely different ways. One vision of frontier military life can be summarized by Lieutenant Charles King, who became one of the late nineteenth century's most profitable novelists by taking the frontier romance to a new level of realism and description. In one of his nonfiction descriptions of life in the frontier army, he captured the dominant conception of military life when he described Fort Hayes, Kansas:

> The band, in the their neat summer dress, were grouped around the flagstaff, while the strains of "*Soldaten Lieder*" thrilled through the soft evening air, and, fairly carried away by the cadence of the sweet music, a party of young ladies and officers had dropped their croquet mallets and were waltzing upon the green carpet of the parade. Seated upon the verandas, other ladies and older officers were smilingly watching the pretty scene, and on the western side of the quadrangle the men in their white stable frocks were just breaking ranks after marching up from the never neglected care of their horses. (King 1890, pp. 4–5)

Here King painted a portrait of army life familiar to commissioned officers, one of untrammeled and pleasant leisure, in which common soldiers, like their horses, served as dutiful background figures. Well-compensated for their services (a second lieutenant after the Civil War earned a salary of

Brigadier General Eli Lundy Huggins

In an army filled with interesting characters, few illustrate the potential utility of its soldiers for American historians better than Eli Lundy Huggins. His varied career exemplifies the centrality of the U.S. Army to the history of the nineteenth-century United States as a whole, while the details of his personal life illuminate contemporary life in the officer corps. Huggins was born in 1842 in Illinois, and his family moved to Minnesota when Huggins was young, where they served as Presbyterian missionaries to the Sioux. When war broke out between the North and the South in 1861, Huggins enlisted in the 2nd Minnesota Infantry as a private at the age of eighteen—leaving the Gopher State just before his family, along with thousands of other settlers, fled the uprising of Little Crow and the Eastern Sioux in 1862. In this often-forgotten episode in U.S. history, the corruption of Indian agents in conjunction with endemic poverty and overcrowding on their reservation prompted the Eastern Sioux to launch an offensive against nearby settlers, killing more than 700 whites, including Huggins's younger brother Rufus.

By the time news of Rufus's death reached Huggins, he was already a combat soldier in the strategically crucial Kentucky-Tennessee theater. War's end would find him a decorated veteran (wounded three times at Chickamauga), with a commission as a volunteer lieutenant of artillery. Military service apparently appealed to Huggins, and with the help of a congressman from Minnesota who knew his family, he received a regular army commission as a second lieutenant in the 2nd Artillery Regiment in February 1866.

It was at this point that Huggins, a longtime bachelor, began a faithful and lifelong correspondence with his sisters. His letters convey in a vivid and honest manner, the trials and tribulations of a young officer stationed on the forlorn frontier, along with insightful snapshots of the sociocultural world of Gilded Age frontier officers. They also speak to his generous nature, for one can track the thousands of dollars of cumulative financial aid he gave to his sisters in his lifetime, assistance that continued in spite of perpetual money woes—an 1878 missive, for instance, found him writing: "In 1866 I had just entered the regular army as 2nd Lieut. I don't seem to have made much headway in the world since then in any way, except that I am more than 11 years nearer the 'Jumping Off place' I suppose."

His early army career found him on the Pacific Coast, where much of the army's artillery force served in coastal casements. Orders sending him and the battery he commanded from San Francisco Bay's Alcatraz to Fort Kodiak in the newly acquired territory of Alaska in 1868 saved Huggins from the dull lethargy of service in the artillery, and introduced this intelligent and curious man to a unique and exciting environment. Almost as soon as he landed he commenced agricultural experiments, recording the surprisingly mild weather. He learned to read and speak Russian from the local mixed-race population and vainly hoped for an appointment as military attaché to Moscow. And Huggins undertook a series of ethnographic studies of Alaska's natives, and their sociocultural adjustment to the arrival of civilization in the form of Russian colonizers. So detailed and prized were these perspectives that they would be reprinted in several journals during World War II and ultimately collected into *Kodiak and Afognak Life, 1868–1870*, which was published in 1981.

His return to the continental United States in 1870 soon led him to a variety of politically charged assignments. Service in Reconstruction South Carolina and North Carolina led him to ponder the fluid nature of race relations after abolition, and the prevalence of what he called "amalgamation": "I think more than half the people here are colored," he wrote from Summerville, South Carolina, in September of 1875,

Eli Lundy Huggins, U.S. Army officer (1842–1929). (*Library of Congress*)

"but not very many are black." Two years later, while stationed in Washington, D.C., Huggins's battery was quickly moved to Cumberland, Maryland, during the General Strike of 1877. He credited the army's discipline with averting a great slaughter: "We could have had a fight most any time since we left Washington," he wrote, "if we had cared to fire upon men who were *armed* only with sticks and stones." The dispersal of the mobs did not alleviate the widespread distress among workers, a point that eluded Huggins as it did the majority of his politically conservative professional peers. Transferred to command of Carlisle Barracks, Pennsylvania, he witnessed—and heatedly berated—unemployed refugees from the labor wars of 1877 begging for food at the post.

Dissatisfied with the pace of promotion in the artillery, a branch especially stagnant in that regard, he transferred to the 2nd Cavalry Regiment in the spring of 1879 because, as he put it, "I could not hope for a Captaincy for several years in the Artillery."

Twelve days later he had his captaincy and command of Troop E of that regiment. As soon as he joined his unit, he found himself in the field against the Sioux in Montana.

Both combat and garrison service suited Huggins; he easily fell into a routine of summer campaigns, and leisurely living (with servants) in a "one high story with a high mansard roof" home complete with "three large down stairs rooms, besides a large kitchen," and bedroom in the attic, important details for a man who considered a civilian with a personal carriage and two servants to be living in "plain comfortable style." His letters describe in good detail the leisure activities, personal beliefs, and consumption practices of period officers. From always having "a soldier follow me at a short distance when I ride out," to a promise to wear his swallow tails "next chance," Huggins lived out a declaration made shortly after his arrival on the Northern Plains: "Oh, I tell you a Capt. Of Cavalry puts on lots of style, especially a new one."

Captain Eli Huggins was no sated staff officer, however. He learned the Sioux language, if an 1880 order directing him to report to General George Crook—because "it is understood that Capt. Huggins is conversant with the language of the Sioux Indians"—is accurate. On the recommendation of General Nelson Miles, he won the Medal of Honor for gallantry displayed in battle against the Oglala Sioux along the Milk River in 1880.

His fine service caught the eye of Miles, an officer whose star was ascending in that same period, and Huggins soon found himself detailed to various headquarters on the frontier

(*continued on following page*)

Brigadier General Eli Lundy Huggins (continued)

and as an acting assistant inspector-general in the Department of the Columbia, positions that provided plenty of leisure time to write, a vocation that brought public notice when G.P. Putnam's Sons published a volume of his poetry in 1890. In the volume's namesake poem, "Winona: A Dakota Legend," Huggins struck a theme common to army officers—namely, the romantic inevitability of the Indian's decline: "Save a few stately names, the vanished race/ Whose dust we daily trample leave no trace/Or monument. . . . the white man's breath,/To him a besom of consuming death,/Sweeps him like ashes from his natal hearth,/E'en as one day some race of stronger birth/Will sweep our children's children from the earth."

Ultimately, Huggins would become aide-de-camp to Miles, a position that he filled from June 1890 to April 1895. Mostly based in Chicago, Huggins continually reiterated his weariness with ostentatious Chicago society ("I am heartily tired of Chicago, and my detail here, and feel tempted to ask for as long a leave as I can get and to join my regiment at the end of it," read one representative complaint); heated army disputes (such as the Battle of Wounded Knee, which Miles—and by extension, Huggins—found himself in the midst of); and the prospect of Gilded Age class warfare. Not even the proximity of Fort Sheridan, constructed in the late 1880s for the express purpose of suppressing workers' rebellions, alleviated this concern. Return to line duty at Fort Riley, Kansas, came as a relief to the new major, who did manage to secure a long leave, which he used to tour Europe.

Service in the Spanish American War as a volunteer colonel commanding the 8th U.S. Volunteer Infantry Regiment introduced Huggins to familiar duties along new frontiers. The summer and fall of 1900 saw Huggins serving in China with his regiment, which was sent to China to help suppress the Boxer Rebellion, with his letters providing a valuable window into this little studied episode in U.S. history. In 1901, Huggins became governor-general of several Philippine provinces, a duty that once again demonstrated his facility with foreign languages, as the hundreds of Spanish-language documents in his papers attest. (By this point in his career, he claimed to be familiar with four languages: Russian, Spanish, Portuguese, and French). He finally left Asia for the United States on the day before Christmas in 1901; he soon gained command of his old regiment, the Second Cavalry, stationed at Fort Meyer, Virginia. There he served until retirement in February of 1903, and it was there that he was finally promoted to brigadier-general the day before he ended his more than forty years of military service.

Upon retirement Huggins lived in Muskogee, Oklahoma, for a few years, just one of the many places he had invested in real estate throughout his footloose military career. He then moved in with a sister in Berkeley, where, from his Durant Avenue residence, he continued an active life, taking an especial interest in railing against the intellectual tomfoolery of soft-headed University of California professors whom he heard at public lectures. Brigadier General Eli Lundy Huggins arrived at his final "Jumping Off place" in San Diego at the age of eighty-seven in 1929; he was buried in Oakland's Mountain View Cemetery. For posterity he left behind a voluminous and rich collection of personal correspondence, military records, poetry, and amateur scholarship, sources that his descendants have contextualized with their own memories. In these latter-day recollections, it is revealed that Huggins's frequent financial assistance to his siblings—the purpose of which went unspoken in letters to his sisters—actually paid for the upkeep of his son, the illegitimate (and unacknowledged) product of a union with a native woman in Alaska. All of these documents can be viewed at the University of California's Bancroft Library.

$1,400 at a time when more than 90 percent of U.S. families brought home less than $1,200 per year, while Custer's salary as a lieutenant-colonel in 1876 exceeded the median household income of the United States in 1950), officers cultivated a world centered upon leisure and sociability (Adams forthcoming). Dances, dinners, and conspicuous consumption dominated their lives, with even remote and forlorn posts presenting surprising comforts. Enlisted men existed on the margins of this world; the aloof dignity prized by officers prevented much interaction between the ranks, while the frequent diatribes that appeared in the major military periodical, *The Army and Navy Journal*, concerning the necessity of absolute obedience on the part of enlisted men, hammered home the point to any officers unclear on the proper relationship between the ranks.

Enlisted men, on the other hand, often burned with resentment over the conditions of military life. Particularly onerous were the manual labor duties known as fatigue duty, which occupied a good portion of the frontier soldier's day. As one enlisted man wrote in a letter to a loved one: "[T]he soldiers in the Department of the Platte know better how to handle pick & shovel than they do a gun" (Rickey 1963, p. 93). Things had changed little since the antebellum period, when an enlisted recruit griped that upon enlisting: "I never was told that I would be called on to make roads, build bridges, quarry stone, burn brick and lime, carry the hod, cut wood, hew timber, construct it into rafts and float it to the garrison . . . etc., etc., etc." (Foos 2002, p. 24). Believing that "soldier" was an occupation worthy of respect, nineteenth-century soldiers reacted fiercely to the domination of time by nonmilitary tasks, especially when those tasks revolved around performing personal services for officers: "I had often heard of nigers [*sic*] standing outside and holding the horses," Private William Earl Smith wrote in his diary on one occasion in the 1870s, "but I never node how it went before"—a point that others made less crudely (Smith 1989, p. 30). William Bladen Jett, a self-described "reluctant corporal," recalled that his first day as a soldier left him wishing "I was well out of the Army. I may say here that I never got over that wish during the five years I was a slave in Uncle Sam's service"; he always rued his decision "to put myself in virtual slavery for five years at thirteen dollars a month" (Walker 1971, pp. 5, 14).

Above all, there was a clash of work cultures; like their civilian peers, enlisted men reserved the one inalienable right of labor in the nineteenth century: the freedom to leave a job the worker did not like, and to contract for a better bargain somewhere else as an economic free agent. Enlisted men saw the army no differently. When the terms of the service did not please enlisted men, they simply left, a decision that they usually made quite quickly—numerous Gilded Age surveys conducted by the army showed that the vast majority of deserters were recruits in their first year of service. They failed to perceive, or chose to ignore, that they had volunteered for an entirely different sort of job, one in which leaving the job site was a federal crime. Little, however, seemed to stem the extraordinarily high rates of desertion found in the nineteenth century, even though the army's civilian and military leadership spent a lot of time pondering the problem. For the decades preceding the Civil War, up to a third of the enlisted personnel deserted

in particularly bad years (little wonder that the army found it impracti-
cable to restrict foreign citizens from enlisting—they needed the bodies!).
Desertion rates dropped after the Civil War, but the cumulative toll on the
post–Civil War army was staggering: a third of the men who had enlisted
in the U.S. Army between 1867 and 1891 deserted, and only about a fifth
of that total were ever arrested and tried by a military court (Rickey 1963;
Annual Report 1889).

Views of the "Other": Race and Ethnicity

Importantly, though class tensions smoldered in the army, antebellum
nativism, post–Civil War xenophobia over increasing immigration, and
turn-of-the-century doubts concerning the "whiteness" of immigrants had
shallow roots in the army, if any at all. Desperate to recruit men, the army
officially began to accept non-naturalized recruits in 1847, a move that only
confirmed the earlier practice of disregarding the standing prohibition against
enlisting foreign citizens. Few native-born soldiers seem to have occupied
themselves with the protoracist ravings that preoccupied elements of civil
U.S. society in the 1850s and late nineteenth century; some dwelt upon the
"national characters" of different nationalities, but given the complicated
tangle of ideas undergirding such words as "blood," "race," and "national-
ity" in the nineteenth century, to label such musings as racist dramatically
misreads a pre-Mendelian age in which Darwinian theory had not yet demonstrated the mechanism by which natural selection operates. Even as
the xenophobia that reasserted itself in the late nineteenth century (and
which did racialize immigrants after the turn of the century) grew in popularity, the army remained relatively immune to its claims—not until 1894 did
recruits have to pass a literacy test and be a citizen or declare their intention
to naturalize. Significantly, these "reforms" were initiated by Congress, not
the army.

Instead, immigrants were treated remarkably well, though they often
experienced quaint condescension concerning their accents and customs.
Charles King, who transformed the casual prejudices of Gilded Age army
officers into a modern-day version of nobility, also captured the prevailing
acceptance of immigrants in the army when he detailed the composition of
the U.S. Army:

> Ours is a mixed array of nationalities—Mulligan and Mesiwinkel, Crapaud
> and John Bull, stand shoulder to shoulder with Yanks from every portion
> of the country. In four regiments only is exclusiveness as to race permitted
> by law. Only darkies can join their ranks. Otherwise there is a promiscuous
> arrangement which, oddly enough, has many a recommendation. They
> balance one another as it were—the phlegmatic Teuton and the fiery Celt,
> mercurial Gaul and stolid Anglo-Saxon. Dashed and strongly tinctured with
> the clear headed individuality of the American, they make up a company
> which for *personnel* is admirably adapted to the needs of our democratic service.
> (King 1890, p. 7)

King's vision of a "democratic service" would be echoed by Corporal E. A. Bode, a German immigrant who served in the post–Civil War era. Describing his peers around the camp fire, Bode wrote:

> We found men without the least knowledge of the English language who had enlisted after unsuccessful attempts to obtain work. [One] said he wanted to join "soldier boys," a very dubious honor, another had to leave on account of a girl. We found men of intellect and stupidity, sons of congressmen and sons of farmers, rich and poor, men who are willing to work and can not find it in civil life, men who are looking for work and hope they never find any: gamblers, thieves, cutthroats, drunkards, men who were formally commissioned officers. There was a combination and variety of stock which, under careful training, had produced some of the best soldiers on the frontier. (Smith 1989, 124)

Collectively, Bode and King speak to the army's general tolerance of ethnic diversity in the nineteenth century. Just as some have considered the post-1950 military to have been the most fully integrated portion of U.S. society, the nineteenth-century army proved to be remarkably progressive on this issue, a development that is even more surprising when one considers that the native-born enlisted men came from backgrounds very similar to those of working and lower-middle-class xenophobes. While not all soldiers were saints, and some were so low as to be "formally commissioned officers" (pointedly lumped with society's blackguards by Bode), ethnic divisions did not affect the frontier army to any significant degree.

The army thus provides an important corrective to the views previously entertained by historians about the interplay of class and ethnicity. With a demographic profile that produced strong tensions elsewhere, the army largely avoided those disputes, at least among persons of Euro-American heritage. Perhaps the judgment that ethnic conflict was endemic and unavoidable in the nineteenth century needs to be re-evaluated in favor of an approach that does regional complexity and diversity more justice. Perhaps it will turn out that the urban centers of the Northeast represent the exceptional behavior, not the normative one.

It must be stressed that the army's tolerance of diversity extended only to persons of European descent. The four regiments of African-American soldiers serving after the Civil War (the 9th and 10th Cavalry, and 24th and 25th Infantry) faced challenges that exceeded the difficulties and harsh material circumstances experienced by all frontier soldiers. For soldiers who served in the post–Civil War army, race served as a divisive force as powerful as the forces of rank and class. Racism manifested itself in individual and institutional ways. Not until the latter years of the frontier period were any of the black regiments transferred out of the isolated desert Southwest to more comfortable assignments in Western urban centers, or Great Plains forts. White officers who served with the black regiments, especially in the early years, were disproportionately drawn from the bottom tiers of U.S. Military Academy graduates and volunteer forces, as a number of competent white officers declined assignment to the black units—including George Custer and General Wesley Merritt (Kenner, 1999). Some of these officers mistreated their men in appalling ways, as scholars have traced through the trial records of courts-martial. Meanwhile, there were only a handful of black officers who served in the Gilded Age army, and most were chaplains. Those men who earned commissions in the line faced a lonely life of social ostracism that paralleled the isolation of West Point. One, Henry Flipper, found himself dismissed from the army after a court-martial returned a verdict harsher than that given to white officers in similar circumstances. Despite these travails, black soldiers demonstrated their commitment and fidelity by maintaining desertion and alcoholism rates far below those of their white peers, and they proved their worth in several campaigns in New Mexico, Texas, and Arizona.

The Army and Indian Policy

The army's role in conquering the Indian peoples of the West made it the subject of sustained controversy in the nineteenth century. From the 1830s on, the army bore the brunt of vociferous criticism from Eastern reformers, self-styled "friends of the Indian," and budget-paring congressmen eagerly casting about for savings. Their criticism revolved around two interrelated propositions: (1.) federal Indian policy toward Native Americans was unjust; and (2.) in carrying out these dubious policies, the army's treatment of Indians provided a shameful and lengthy list of viciousness, barbarism, and cruelty. "I only know the names of three savages upon the Plains," Wendell Phillips declared in the aftermath of one controversial battle, "Colonel Baker, General Custer, and at the head of all, General Sheridan" (Hutton 1985, p. 196).

Although sometimes self-interested, the critics of the army did not have to dream up tragedies and atrocities (though they sometimes did, or fancifully misrepresented what had occurred on the frontier). General William Harney, who believed in the words of one scholar that "the only way to impress Indians was to kill a lot of them," earned the nickname "Squaw Killer" in the 1850s after soldiers under his command fired into caves in which Sioux women and children were hiding (Ball 2001, pp. 46–47). Campaigns against the tribes and bands in the Pacific Northwest were particularly bloody, and trained an entire generation of frontier commanders in a mode of "total war" that surpassed in ferocity anything found on the larger killing fields of the American Civil War. George Custer's brutally effective assault against the accommodationist Southern Cheyenne chief Black Kettle and his village, located on the Washita River (in present-day Oklahoma) in 1868, also initiated a wave of angry denunciations of the army. These denunciations were fueled by the account of an anonymous officer that alluded to the slaughter of women and children, and the "sadistic pleasure" that Custer enjoyed as the tribe's dogs and ponies were killed (Hutton 1985, p. 96).

The reality on the ground was generally more complicated than these charges allowed. Black Kettle's village did contain combatants who were fully aware that they were engaged in a campaign, and Custer seems to have prevented the killing of some noncombatants; also, he did take a number of prisoners. But so powerful was the backlash against the army, that the transfer of Indian affairs to the War Department, which had seemed secure as a rider to 1868's army appropriation bill, was suddenly expunged from the bill at the insistence of its sponsors (ibid.).

It would be both factually incorrect and morally dubious to relegate such episodes as Sand Creek to the footnotes of history, or, worse yet, to ignore them altogether. To regard them as a comprehensive description of the army's interactions toward Native Americans, however, would be just as inaccurate. Actually, the worst outrages and atrocities on the frontier were committed not by the U.S. Army but by civilians or militia forces, including Colorado's Sand Creek massacre and the wholesale war of extermination launched by the state of California—and subsidized long after its conclusion by the U.S. government—against its Native inhabitants in the 1850s. In the moment itself, officers and enlisted men who encountered Native Americans regarded the indigenous inhabitants of North America and their experiences in a far more nuanced manner than most historians and American popular culture would have it.

Moreover, within limits, those who served in the U.S. Army could be astute observers of Indian cultures, Indian motivations, and federal policy. Generally dismissive of the moral arguments advanced by easterners concerning federal Indian policy, soldiers usually reacted to the tangled issues of Indian relations with the almost instinctive pragmatism of those attempting to implement a vexing and confused policy "on the ground." To most officers, blame for conflict with Western Indians rested with both sides but could ultimately be attributed to the expanding Anglo-American population—"the reckless, the idle, and the dissolute," in one lieutenant's description—whose flaws they had ample exposure to on the frontier. E. O. C. Ord, who would reach the upper echelons of the army's frontier command structure after the Civil War, wrote as a young officer that Indians in California were "infested with vermin, incorrigibly addicted to vice and the gratification of savage passions," but he concluded that "the volunteers who are trying to drive them from this, their country are not much better—not as brave—with a worse cause" (Smith 1995, p. 214 n. 8).

Officers generally concluded that unscrupulous settlers, and those who supported them, placed the army and Indians in an untenable relationship in which conflict was forced upon both, though desired by neither. General William T. Sherman maintained, for instance, that the army stood between "two classes of people, one demanding the utter extinction of the Indians, and the other full of love for their conversion to civilization and Christianity. Unfortunately the army . . . gets the cuffs from both sides" (Hutton 1985, p. 195). Frustration over this state of affairs led officers constantly to complain about the situation they found themselves in. In fact, rarely in U.S. history have so many top commanders *in the midst of a conflict* publicly questioned the case for war. General John Pope, commanding the Department of the Missouri, wrote this in his annual report for 1875:

> It is with painful reluctance that the military forces take the field against
> Indians, who only leave their reservations because they are starved there, and
> who must hunt food for themselves and their families, or see them perish with

hunger. . . . It is revolting to any humane man to see such things done, and far more so to be required to be the active party to commit violence upon forlorn Indians who, under the pressure of such necessity, only do what any man would do under like circumstances. (*Annual Report* 1875, p. 124)

Soldiers of varying ranks expressed similar sentiments throughout the nineteenth century. What is most striking about the criticism of the Indian wars proffered by soldiers, however, was their ultimate belief in the necessity and inevitability of Western expansion. The men who composed the U.S. Army during the period of Western expansion often voiced doubts about the particular rationale underlying any specific conflict, but even after intense soul-searching, few ultimately questioned the cause. "No human hand could stay that rolling tide of progress," General Nelson Miles asserted, while Sherman defended Major Baker's massacre of the Piegans by telling Congress in 1870 that "[t]he Army cannot resist the tide of immigration that is flowing toward these Indian lands, nor is it our province to determine the question of boundaries. When called on we must, to the extent of our power, protect the settlers, and, on proper demand we have to protect the Indian lands from the intrusion of the settlers. Thus we are placed between two fires, a most unpleasant dilemma from which we cannot escape, and we must sustain officers on the spot who fulfill their orders" (Smith 1995, p. 134; Andrews 1968, p. 79).

Custer Died for His Sins: The Little Big Horn, June 1876

Many Americans know the frontier army primarily through the tale of General George Custer's famous last stand with elements of the 7th Cavalry on the Little Big Horn in June of 1876. As it did with other imperial states (for example, the United Kingdom in the aftermath of the Zulu triumph over British regulars at the Battle of Isandhlwana), the "iconography of imperial death" resonated with the contemporary public (Johnson 1993). Lithographs depicting the denouement dominated nineteenth- and early-twentieth-century bars and journals, while heated debates and an official inquiry over responsibility for the disaster caught the national press, making the Last Stand a paradigmatic representation of the American West and Native Americans (invariably stylized as a savage and merciless horde ready to pounce upon the numerical weaknesses of Custer's noble soldiers).

The reality of the Last Stand, as shown through careful examination of the archaeological record and reconsideration of oral testimonies left by both Native and military sources in light of that record, was at the same time more and less complicated than the popular narrative would have it. Custer divided the 7th Cavalry into four cooperating wings: a battalion commanded by Captain Frederick Benteen, a decorated veteran who openly detested Custer, scouted to the southwest; a battalion led by Major Marcus Reno, a former staff officer relatively new to line command and frontier service, was charged with the task of launching the initial assault against the southern end of the Sioux/Cheyenne encampment; Company I, commanded by Captain Thomas McDougall, was in charge of the pack train, which was removed from the field thanks to its slower traveling pace; and Custer himself would lead a battalion along the ridgeline across the river from the Indian encampment. His apparent plan (if one can infer motive from the forensic record left by his firing troopers and the archaeological assemblage and his earlier battle record, most notably on the Southern Plains several years earlier) was to execute a rough "hammer and anvil" operation, modified by the additional attacks of the companies he had left dispersed along the ridgeline as he himself headed for the end of the massive camp (Fox 1993).

It is hard to imagine, even at this late remove, how Custer, leading his battalion through the overgrown and demanding terrain of the hills opposite, could have underestimated his opposition. Although his intelligence was sketchy, he had apparently planned for confronting 1,500 warriors, a number derived from reports from Indian agents and analysis of the Indian trail, and camps seen the month before when General George Crook confronted a sizable Indian force on the Rosebud. The command did not see the village before the battle (Custer having searched for it in vain with his field glasses), but his scouts reported an exceptionally large concentration of Indians ahead, testimony that Custer reportedly scoffed at.

We know today that the village strength most likely fell between 1,500 and 2,000 warriors in the village, with perhaps 6,000 noncombatants (ibid.). Having stolen a march on the "hostiles" by marching all night, the thrill of the chase must have inspired Custer. Some commanders might have been given pause by the circumstances; some might have pulled back, reconsolidated their forces, and modified the plan, even at the risk of being discovered (a camp this large and unwieldy would have had some difficulty escaping even the jaded horses of the 7th Cavalry). Such proposals, however, would have been anathema to Custer's military core; an energetic, aggressive, and sometimes hasty officer, Custer had won a reputation as a hard-charging and effective commander on the basis of such moves as these.

This time, though, he overreached, and in so doing led more than 200 men to their deaths. Reno's attack achieved local tactical surprise, but it was quickly repelled by the quick work of warriors in the camp. Regardless of the cause (Reno remains a controversial figure to students of the battle), Reno's failed attack highlighted the tactical disintegration of various elements of the 7th Cavalry, a process repeated several times on the fateful day. As the best reconstruction of the battle puts it: "[P]anic, which developed from a harrowing but hardly hopeless experience, rather quickly overwhelmed all in the command" (p. 270). Dispersed along the ridge line, the five companies under the immediate command of Custer were split into two wings; one, which Custer led, attempted to ford the river, while the other remained ensconced as skirmishers and a tactical reserve on the heights above the village. The chain of events that led to "Last Stand Hill," began with this latter group; archaeological evidence suggests that Company L under the command of Captain Thomas Calhoun, which had been organized into an orderly skirmish line, soon found itself under siege by opportunistic infiltrators, who used cover to pick troopers and to attempt to stampede their horses. A charge launched to beat back the infiltrators proved ineffective, as continuous pressure exerted by a superior number of Indian warriors broke up the charge and led to demoralization. (In more than one oral testimony given after the battle, Sioux combatants describe Custer's men as being "drunk," a statement that instead refers to the immense terror and panic the breakdown of tactical order created among the poorly trained cavalrymen.) From here on, one by one, the companies on the hill absorbed Indian attacks and quickly broke, at which point they fled farther along the ridgeline toward the next company, looking, as a combatant named Runs the Enemy later related, like "a stampede of buffalo" (p. 160).

For most, the end came with terrifying swiftness. Encircled by foes who could move with virtual impunity in the tall summer grasses and hidden draws of the hill system, the soldiers faced an enemy who outnumbered them and who, a significant minority of the time, out-armed them. Forensics evidence collected on the battlefield in the mid-1980s detailed that approximately a third of the Sioux and Cheyenne carried repeating rifles, while soldiers were armed with only their single-shot Springfield carbines and pistols. Custer's cavalrymen were picked off one by one, then in large clusters as terrified soldiers ran for cover. The places where they fell, along with the wounds inflicted upon their skeletons, do not suggest anything approaching a "last stand." In terror, clusters of soldiers huddled together and were killed without offering much resistance, their bodies "scattered in irregular clumps and at intervals about like those in a slaughter of buffaloes," a lieutenant who viewed the field in 1877 wrote (p. 170). Dumbstruck with fear, some soldiers shook so much that they could not discharge their own weapons; surprisingly few bullets or cartridges were found by archaeologists on the battlefield, whereas Indian weaponry is well represented. Oral accounts—which generations of Custer scholars either ignored or dismissed in their entirety because they contained some errors—vindicate the conclusion of a recent study of the battle which argues that "most, if not all, recruits had experienced inadequate training in basic combat skills, a deficiency that detracted from their potential for moral persistence in battle" (p. 270). They describe desperate men throwing their fully loaded pieces at the encroaching Indians, others abandoning their arms because they could not be reloaded quickly enough to be of use in close-order fighting, and still more troopers jerked off their horses as they tried to flee the action.

Instead of a last stand, Custer had, through his own tactical decisions and hubris, led a good portion of his regiment into a rout. Instead of displaying the leadership that had characterized him in earlier battles, Custer oversaw the tactical disintegration of his column—such dry words! If a key skill of the historian is establishing an empathetic connection with his subjects, students of both the Native American and U.S. Army perspective who attempt such a task are bound to encounter the historian pondering the Little Big Horn and confronting an experience disturbing, terrifying, and gruesome in myriad ways. (And it should be observed that making such a connection with the Sioux and Northern Cheyenne is also important; though they left the field victorious, nothing good came out of a day when they were violently driven out of their homes by Reno's advance.) Gravely wounded, many of the sol-

Pile of bones on the Little Bighorn battlefield from the most famous battle in the history of the American Indian Wars, fought from June 25–27, 1876. The Battle of the Little Bighorn (Custer's Last Stand) was costly on both sides, as the Sioux inflicted a great loss to the 7th Cavalry but suffered heavy casualties as well. (*National Archives and Records Administration*)

diers were dispatched by clubs and tomahawks by the Sioux and Cheyenne and then ritually mutilated—although a series of burial parties asserted the opposite, presumably in an attempt to spare the feelings of next-of-kin and to avoid offending Victorian propriety.

Custer Reconsidered:
Nation-Builders, not Indian Fighters

Little Bighorn served as a focused snapshot of the unfolding process of Euro-American expansion into the Native lands of the trans-Mississippi West. But the Battle of Little Bighorn was only a solitary day in decades of frontier service, and seen from the vantage point of everyday life in the army meant less than it might appear. Slightly more than 900 U.S. soldiers died fighting Indians after the Civil War, a figure that computes to about 40 per annum

Members of the Twenty-fifth U.S. Infantry on bicycles at Yellowstone National Park, 1896. (*National Archives and Records Administration*)

(Utley, 1973). Not quite a fourth of those deaths occurred on a single day in Montana in the summer of 1876. Although American culture (and American historians) have gotten quite a bit of mileage out of the "Indian War" as a veritable trope of nineteenth-century frontier existence, a closer look at the individual and institutional experience of the army illustrates the fact that frontier conflicts occupied a remarkably small portion of a frontier soldier's time. It was instead, to use an anachronistic term, a "nation-building" force. For most soldiers, daily life revolved around the mundane duties common to a nineteenth-century garrison: fatigue and policing duties, the care of animals, the procurement of water and supplies from local contractors. In the field, the army was just as likely to lay telegraph lines, blaze trails, conduct scientific expeditions, aid overland travelers, protect national parks, and extend relief to civilian victims of natural disasters such as earthquakes or droughts (Tate, 1999).

In undertaking these activities, the army was following a long tradition that had been begun in the first years of the American Republic. Despite a century of technological and geopolitical change, the U.S. Army of 1895 was not terribly distinct from the U.S. Army of 1795. That resemblance, however, would soon vanish, for Turner's canonical closing of the frontier indeed represented the end of a stage in the army's history. With the interior of the American West settled and Indian tribes "pacified," the army found itself casting about for a new mission. It would not have to wait long. Ironically, however, its new mission was both very similar to and very different from its historical antecedents. Once again the army served as a frontier constabulary, but this time the frontier had moved even farther afield thanks to the new geopolitical reality of imperialism. Not until World War I would U.S. soldiers truly leave their frontier past behind.

References and Further Reading

Adams, Kevin. *Caste and Class: Military Life on the Post–Civil War Frontier.* Norman: University of Oklahoma Press, forthcoming.

Andrews, Richard Allen. "Years of Frustration: William T. Sherman, the Army, and Reform, 1869–1883." Ph.D. diss., Northwestern University, 1968.

Ball, Durwood. *Army Regulars on the Western Frontier, 1848–1861.* Norman: University of Oklahoma Press, 2001.

Brininstool, E. A. *A Trooper with Custer.* Columbus, OH: Hunter-Trader-Trapper Company, 1926.

Coffman, Edward. *The Old Army: A Portrait of the American Army in Peacetime, 1784–1898.* New York: Oxford University Press, 1986.

Cooper, Jerry. *The Army and Civil Disorder: Federal Military Intervention in Labor Disputes, 1877–1900.* Westport, CT: Greenwood Press, 1980.

Delo, David. *Peddlers and Post Traders: The Army Sutler on the Frontier.* Helena: Kingfisher Press, 1998.

Dobak, William A. and Thomas D. Phillips, *The Black Regulars, 1866–1898.* Norman: University of Oklahoma Press, 2001.

Foos, Paul. *A Short Offhand Killing Affair: Soldiers and Social Conflict during the Mexican-American War.* Chapel Hill: University of North Carolina Press, 2002.

Fowler, Arlen. *The Black Infantry in the West, 1869–1891.* Norman: University of Oklahoma Press, 1971.

Fox, Richard Wightman. *Archaeology, History, and Custer's Last Battle.* Norman: University of Oklahoma Press, 1993.

Grant, U. S. *Personal Memoirs of U. S. Grant.* New York: Konecky & Konecky, 1992.

Hutton, Paul. *Phil Sheridan and His Army.* Lincoln: University of Nebraska Press, 1985.

Johnson, Susan Lee. "'A Memory Sweet to Soldiers': The Significance of Gender in the American West." *Western Historical Quarterly* 24, no. 4 (1993): 495–517.

Kenner, Charles. *Buffalo Soldiers and Officers of the 9th Cavalry, 1867–1898: Black and White Together.* Norman: University of Oklahoma Press, 1999.

King, Charles. *Campaigning with Crook, and Stories of Army Life.* New York: Harper Brothers, 1890.

Leckie, William. *The Buffalo Soldiers: A Narrative of Negro Cavalry in the West.* Norman: University of Oklahoma Press, 1967.

Meyerson, Harvey. *Nature's Army: When Soldiers Fought for Yosemite*. Lawrence: University Press of Kansas, 2001.

Mulford, Ami Frank. *Fighting Indians in the Seventh U.S. Cavalry: Custer's Favorite Regiment*. Fairfield, WA: Ye Galleon, 1972.

Prucha, Francis Paul. *Broadax and Bayonet: The Role of the United States Army in the Development of the Northwest, 1815–1860*. Madison: State Historical Society of Wisconsin, 1953.

Prucha, Francis Paul. *The Sword of the Republic: The United States Army on the Frontier, 1783–1846*. New York: Macmillan, 1968.

Rickey, Don. *Forty Miles a Day on Beans and Hay: The Enlisted Soldier Fighting the Indian Wars*. Norman: University of Oklahoma Press, 1963.

Schubert, Frank. *Buffalo Soldiers, the Braves, and the Brass: The Story of Fort Robinson, Nebraska*. Shippensberg, PA: White Mane, 1993.

Scott, Douglas D., P. Willey, and Melissa A. Conner. *They Died with Custer: Soldiers' Bones from the Battle of the Little Bighorn*. Norman: University of Oklahoma Press, 1998.

Smith, Sherry. *The View from Officers' Row: Army Perceptions of Western Indians*. Tucson: University of Arizona Press, 1995.

Smith, Sherry, ed. *Sagebrush Soldier: Private William Earl Smith's View of the Sioux War of 1876*. Norman: University of Oklahoma Press, 1989.

Smith, Thomas, ed. *A Dose of Frontier Soldiering: The Memoirs of Corporal E. A. Bode*. Lincoln: University of Nebraska Press, 1994.

Tate, Michael. *The Frontier Army in the Settlement of the West*. Norman: University of Oklahoma Press, 1999.

Tindall, George Brown, and David E. Shi. *America: A Narrative History*. New York: Norton, 2004.

Utley, Robert. *Frontiersmen in Blue: The United States Army and the Indian, 1848–1865*. Lincoln: University of Nebraska Press, 1967.

Utley, Robert. *Frontier Regulars: The United States Army and the Indian, 1866–1891*. Lincoln: University of Nebraska Press, 1973

Walker, Henry P., ed. "The Reluctant Corporal: The Autobiography of William Bladen Jett." *Journal of Arizona History* 12, no. 1 (1971): 4–44.

War Department. *Annual Report of the Secretary of War*. Washington, DC: Government Publishing Office, 1865–1890.

Wooster, Robert. *The Military and United States Indian Policy, 1865–1903*. New Haven: Yale University Press, 1988.

Mormon Settlement | 6

Jessie L. Embry

Many Americans associate the West with rugged individualism, wild open spaces, cowboys, and Indians. The Church of Jesus Christ of Latter-day Saints (Mormon or Latter-day Saint) differed. Brigham Young, "the American Moses," envisioned communities and cooperation (Arrington 1985). His influence extended throughout the intermountain West, California, and even into Canada and Mexico.

How did the Mormon experience differ from that of the rest of the settlement of the West? It does not take long to recognize some major differences. Mormons came west for religious reasons; many others came because of economics. Mormons carefully laid out towns; other settlers built homes on their property or near mines. Mormons struggled for statehood to escape federal control over the Utah territory. Most territories (except New Mexico and Arizona, which had their own unique features) became states sooner. This chapter will explore some of the most significant differences: organized migration, established communities, cooperation, polygamy, and political and economic control. These factors set Mormons apart not only from the rest of the West but also from the rest of the United States at least until Utah's statehood in 1896. But even afterward, what some called "the Americanization of Utah" did not happen all at once. The period between 1890 and 1930 can be understood as a transitional one for Mormonism, and many unique characteristics remain in the twenty-first century (Larsen 1971; Alexander 1986).

Mormon Background

Founder Joseph Smith, Jr., never saw the Mormon settlements in the West, but he had an impact on every aspect of their development. A visionary young man, Smith organized a church in New York State in 1830 and

Joseph Smith (1805–1844) founded The Church of Jesus Christ of Latter-day Saints (the Mormon Church), a home-grown church in the United States that today is one of the fastest-growing denominations, with a world membership of 7 million. (*Library of Congress*)

orchestrated his followers' moves to the Mississippi River. He initially moved to Kirtland (near Cleveland), Ohio, when a group of the Disciple of Christ (Campbellites) joined his church. Mormons moved to western Missouri in response to Smith's revelation that this was the location of the Garden of Eden and where Christ would return in glory. Smith developed a city plan, the Plat of Zion, where uniform blocks surrounded temples. He introduced an economic way of life, the law of consecration, whereby members shared everything in common. He sent missionaries to share his message of a restoration of Christ's church. He encouraged the converts to "gather" to church headquarters, where they could support each other and prepare for Christ's coming.

Smith's beliefs and practices were not popular on the 1830s Missouri frontier. The Mormon settlers were from the Northeast and opposed slavery. Other Missourians were from the South. The Mormons declared the area their promised land, and previous settlers felt that the Mormons were trying to run them off their lands. Smith's followers voted as a bloc and threatened to take over the government. As a result, Mormons and other Missourians clashed. Compromise attempts to provide one place for Mormon settlements failed because Mormons expanded behind the county boundaries, and Missourians questioned setting aside a place for the religious group. Eventually the Mormons left, feeling that they had been forced to flee their homes.

Smith established a new community, Nauvoo, Illinois, along the banks of the Mississippi River. The state granted Smith a liberal city charter including a militia. In a peaceful environment the church members gathered, creating a city of approximately 11,000. But the quiet did not last. For example, rumors of a unique marriage practice, polygamy, spread. Mormons and non-Mormons reacted to Smith's control. After Smith ordered the printing press which published a newspaper against him in 1844 to be destroyed, Illinois officials arrested him. The governor concluded that Nauvoo was too tightly connected to Smith, so he moved the trial to Carthage, the county seat. Although there were rumors that a mob might attack and kill Smith, the governor dismissed all but the Carthage group of the state militia, which was guarding the jail. A group of the dismissed Warsaw regiment came to the jail, and the Carthage soldiers let them pass. They started firing guns at Smith, his brother Hyrum, and two other Mormons—John Taylor and Willard Richards—who were in the upper room. Hyrum was shot in the face and the back and died. Other bullets hit him as well. John Taylor and Willard Richards were also hit but survived. Joseph Smith fired five shots at the mob and then attempted to escape through the window. He was hit and fell to the ground, where he died.

Many expected the church to disintegrate, but after some debate Brigham Young, head of the church's twelve apostles, assumed leadership. Young followed through on Smith's plans to move his people west, where they could be isolated. He studied explorer John C. Fremont's maps and considered settling in the Great Basin region. Smith's death speeded up the plans, and it was up to Young to fulfill the founder's vision. The first Mormons left Nauvoo in February 1846; others followed through September. By the time the Mormons crossed Iowa, it was too late in the year to continue west. Life at Winter Quarters on the Missouri River near Omaha was hard. Many, especially children, died. But the church members saw this as a holding place. When the weather warmed, Young led his vanguard group west, arriving in the Great Salt Lake Valley in July 1847.

Organized Migration

While Joseph Smith had been a visionary man, Brigham Young was very pragmatic. Smith recorded his revelations in a book of scripture, the *Doctrine and Covenants*, which outlined the church's organization and beliefs. Young added only one revelation to that book, a practical guide organizing the Mormons for the trip west. This set a pattern that continued as the rest of the Latter-day Saints followed Young into a new promised land in the Rocky Mountains.

Unlike many immigrant groups, Mormons traveled together and made sure that there was no one left behind. To help the poor, Young created the Perpetual Emigrating Fund, a revolving loan whereby church members received travel money that in theory they returned to the principal after they became established. Young used these funds to charter ships for use by English and northern European converts and to help the Mormons continue to Utah.

At first emigrants purchased wagons and animals to travel from the Missouri River to Utah, but that proved expensive. Young suggested handcarts—small wagons that the members pulled. The plan worked. More emigrants arrived in Utah. A popular nineteenth-century folk song described this experience:

> Ye saints who dwell on Europe's shore
> Prepare yourselves for many more,
> To leave behind your native land,
> For sure God's judgements are at hand.
> For you must cross the raging main
> Before the promised land you gain
> And with the faithful make a start
> To cross the plains in your handcart
> For some must push and some must pull
> As we go marching up the hill
> So merrily on our way we go
> Until we reach the Valley-o. (Cheney 1968, pp. 64–65)

Most handcart companies arrived in the Salt Lake Valley successfully. The plan met its goal: an inexpensive way to help poor Latter-day Saints arrive in Utah. Mormons often focus on two unfortunate groups, the 1856 Martin and Willie companies. They started too late in the season with carts made of green wood. Many died in Wyoming. But the Mormons tell the story not to condemn the idea but to show the faith and determination of their pioneer ancestors and their willingness to help. As soon as Young learned of the groups' struggles, he asked members to leave their comfortable homes in Salt Lake City to rescue the stranded Saints. And the members responded. The story represented Mormon cooperation and willingness to help each other.

Young eventually developed another cooperative plan to send young men with wagons east to pick up supplies and emigrants. But he did not see that as the final solution. When the Union Pacific and Central Pacific completed the transcontinental railroad, he applauded the new transportation method. The railroads united at Promontory Point north of Salt Lake City in 1869, refusing to come to the Mormon headquarters. So Young completed his own line. After that, railroad was the preferred means of transportation. The Daughters of Utah Pioneers, a hereditary society similar to the Daughters of the American Revolution, created to celebrate the early Mormons, considered 1869 the end of the pioneer period, because travel thereafter became too easy. About 90,000 Mormons immigrated to Utah during the nineteenth

century. Of those, estimates are that 60,000 to 70,000 came before the railroad (Allen and Leonard 1992, pp. 321–322).

Communities

Wherever Mormons settled, they first established communities using Smith's
Plat of Zion. Shortly after Brigham Young arrived in the Salt Lake Valley, he
marked the place to build a temple. Surveyors marked off 10-acre blocks,
divided by large streets, large enough to turn an ox team in. Carefully laid
lots provided space for gardens, fruit trees, and small domestic animals.
Houses sat on the blocks in such a way that neighbors did not look into each
other's windows. Residents traveled to outlying farms.

In some places the plan did not work. Just east of Salt Lake City's center
(now known as the Avenues), the slope was too steep for 10-acre blocks.
Merchants who did not have gardens and animals moved to that area to be
close to their stores and businesses (Haglund and Notarianni 1980). After
having settled Salt Lake City, Young expanded outward. He called upon
members to create new communities throughout the intermountain West.
His goal was to be self-sufficient. He asked some to go to southern Utah, the
area's Dixie, to grow cotton. (The experiment was not very successful, but
the warmer area has become a senior citizen retreat.) Like Thomas Jefferson,
Young's ideal was the yeoman farmer. Being close to the land promoted self-
sufficiency and closeness to God. He first called upon farmers to start a community, but he also recognized the need for blacksmiths, merchants, potters,
and choir leaders (Arrington and Bitton 1979, p. 311).

Young saw mining as a get-rich scheme that could not last. However,
he recognized a need for metals and some valuable ores. So he sent a group
to Cedar City in southern Utah to mine iron ore. (It was not very successful, although there was iron ore there.) He also called gold missionaries to
go to California. Some Mormons worked in the mines, but the goal was
always to be close to the land. To obtain workers, mine owners recruited
non-Mormons, many from southern Europe, to work in the coal mines.
Carbon County became a non-Mormon haven in a Mormon state (Notarianni 1981).

But not all Mormons responded to the call. Some refused to go, and some
sought permission to go to places Young was not ready to settle. Others moved
on their own. A few examples will demonstrate the settlement types.

As mentioned, Brigham Young called settlers to southern Utah in the
1860s, and most agreed to leave their new and comfortable homes. John
Pulsipher ignored the call for volunteers at a church meeting because "I had
a good home. . . . But when Apostle George A. Smith said I was selected to go
I saw the importance of the mission to sustain Israel in the mountains—we
had need of a possession in a warmer climate." Pulsipher went, "thank[ing]
the Lord that I was worthy to go (Allen and Leonard 1992, pp. 331–332).

Life in St. George was hard, but the residents did not give up. They
laughed at their misfortune and stayed on.

The reason why it is so hot,
Is just because it is, Sir.
The wind like fury here does blow
That when we plant or sow, Sir,
We place one foot upon the side
And hold it till it grows, Sir.

Chorus

Mesquite, soap root, prickly pears and briars.
St. George ere long will be a place that everyone admires.

(Charles L. Walker, "St. George and the Drag-on," quoted in Cheney 1968, pp. 114–115. The St. George Mormon pioneer named this song "St. George and the Drag-on" because it took so long to establish the settlement. The title was a play on words on the English folksong "Saint George and the Dragon.")

St. George life was difficult enough, but the 200 families asked to settle on the Muddy River, a few miles southwest of St. George, faced even greater problems. Arriving between 1865 and 1867, they attempted to raise cotton and figs. Weather spoiled the crops, Native Americans attacked, and then a survey placed them in Nevada. The government charged the settlers back taxes in cash. The settlers were willing to stay, but they left when Young released them to go in 1871 (Allen and Leonard 1992, pp. 331–332).

While the St. George and Muddy River settlers answered a call, other Mormons moved on their own. Those going to Utah County received permission. When the Mormons visited with Jim Bridger at his Wyoming fort, he suggested that the area around Utah Lake, 45 miles south of Salt Lake City, would be a better place than the Salt Lake Valley to raise crops. But he warned that the Utes fished and wintered in the area and might cause trouble. Based on this advice, Young avoided the area until some enterprising Mormons told him in 1849 that it was a good place to settle and offered to take his cattle. Young agreed but warned the men of Native American trouble.

The first Utah County residents went with reluctant approval, but having Mormons there helped. They fished Utah Lake and provided food during crop failures. When the U.S. Army came with a new governor to replace Young, the Mormons moved south to the Provo area in 1856.

Even though settling Utah County helped Young's programs, he worried about the Provo residents. They never seemed to follow instructions. Young did not like their fort placement. He did not like the selected city center and had them move the tabernacle, the central church building for Provo, about a half-mile east. The residents spent more time working on their homes than the church, so Young complained, "Build that house." Eventually Provo residents completed it, but by then it was too small. Young was so concerned that he sent former Salt Lake City mayor Abraham Smoot as stake president ("stake" is the Mormon term for a group of congregations). Young hoped that Smoot could convince the Provo citizens to follow church counsel. Although Smoot got a larger tabernacle built, he was not always successful in getting Provo Mormons to conform to Young's desires.

The first Provo residents asked for permission to depart; some from that area just left. As the easy valleys to settle filled up, Mormons needed more farmland. Explorers liked a high mountain valley up Provo Canyon, but travel was impossible. That changed when Young encouraged Provo residents to build a road so the U.S. Army supplies could reach Camp Floyd near Utah Lake without going through Salt Lake City. Utah County residents then moved to Heber Valley at the top of the canyon and established small communities. Most followed the Plat of Zion plan. So Heber City had square blocks. Midway was originally two towns—one a string town along the river. The two towns came together during conflicts with the Native Americans (Embry 1996, pp. 20–62).

Mormon communities remained basically the same even when outside influences threatened the pattern. The first settlers were squatters; technically, they did not own the land. Eventually the federal government deeded the land to the probate judges (usually also Mormon leaders) who deeded it to those who were already using the property. So the Wasatch County property records started when Abram Hatch, the Mormon stake president in Heber City, deeded the land to the residents.

The Homestead Act of 1862 required applicants to live on the land. Mormons responded in several ways in Cache Valley, near the Utah-Idaho border. In Lewiston, Utah, residents filed on a homestead for the downtown area in 1869. They deeded it to those who were living in the village. In North Logan, Utah (settled in the late 1870s), residents lived on their land but gathered for church and school. Still, assistant church historian Andrew Jenson recorded with dismay that the residents were scattered. It did not meet the Mormon village ideal (Embry 2000, pp. 2–7).

Cooperation

While North Logan did not physically match Joseph Smith's and Brigham Young's plan, it was very similar in other ways. An important part of all Mormon towns was cooperation. That included constructing public buildings, digging irrigation canals, and supporting Mormon merchants. Young encouraged residents to buy from the Mormon-owned cooperatives and not from the non-Mormon "Gentle" merchants. (Mormon country is probably the only place where a Jew is considered a Gentile.)

Irrigation demonstrated the Mormons' cooperation. Wilford Woodruff recalled the first group of settlers—"nearly the whole of us were born and raised in New England States, had no experience in irrigation." They flooded the land with water from City Creek and then had to wait for it to dry enough to plow. Gradually the Mormons learned how to divert water from the mountain streams. Brigham Young declared water a common property, replacing riparian rights that gave the water to the landowners on the streams or prior appropriation that gave it to the first settlers who used the land. Under this arrangement, old and new comers had access to water during a drought (Arrington and Bitton 1979, pp. 115–116).

Men dig the Strawberry Tunnel to transport water from the Strawberry reservoir through the Wasatch Divide, which eventually flows into the southern Utah Valley, ca. 1907. Still in operation, the tunnel itself is 3.8 miles long and has the capacity to contain 600 cubic feet of water per second. (*Library of Congress*)

The first irrigation efforts were done by trial and error. Scientist and Mormon leader John A. Widstoe learned from these experiments and expanded them in the early 1900s, becoming one of the founders of irrigation science. Mormon scientists and engineers shared their knowledge throughout the world during the mid-twentieth century. For example, Mormons Franklin S. Harris and Luther Winsor advised Iranian leaders on agriculture and irrigation methods in the 1930s. Mormon engineers from Utah State University returned there as part of U.S. president Harry S. Truman's 1950 Point Four program (ibid., pp. 311, 314–316).

Young especially promoted Mormon cooperation when outsiders threatened to change his economic and political control. In the 1850s he encouraged the Mormons to return to Smith's economic law. In the 1830s Smith announced revelations from God that the church members should live communally. Mormons donated their property to the church and received an assignment, a "stewardship," in return. This practice, called the Law of Consecration, was never successful. So Smith instead asked church members to give 10 percent, a tithing to the church. Brigham Young recognized that most Mormons were not willing to share everything in a commune. So the United Orders (another term used for Smith's economic policies) took several forms. One was the Brigham City model, in which business owners united and owned stock in cooperatives. In larger cities, owners formed individual industry coops. The best-known community example was Orderville. Residents donated everything they had and then received specific responsibilities, a "stewardship." The first twenty-four families in 1874 grew to 700 people in five years. Initially they ate in a common dining room, made their own clothing, and marketed furniture. Eventually, however, the young people rebelled and wanted to be like those in surrounding communities. Nevertheless, the order lasted until 1880 (Allen and Leonard 1992, pp. 369–371).

Eventually the Latter-day Saints had adapted to the American lifestyle, but they had interesting twists of working together. From 1890 to 1898, North Logan had one public building that the school used on weekdays and the church used on Sundays. After 1898 the school and church separated, but the two one-room buildings stood side by side. Neither had a gymnasium. During the 1930s educators throughout the United States believed that the best schools had indoor play areas. The school board's bond election that would have provided a gym for North Logan failed. So the town board, the school board, and the Mormon ward leaders pooled their resources and applied for a Public Works Administration grant to build a gym. Until 1951, the Mormon Church rented the gym for its church activities (Embry 2000, pp. 41–43).

This cooperative continued in Mormon towns. In the 1950s sociologists Evon Z. Vogt and Thomas F. O'Dea studied two New Mexico communities, Rimrock and Homestead (pseudonyms). They found that Mormon cultural views were more important than the environment. Mormons settled Rimrock in the 1870s, and Texas ranchers established Homestead in the 1930s. Mormon cooperation led to improved roads, a high school gymnasium, and more peaceful dances than those in Homestead. For example, a construction company improved the state highway in the 1950s and offered to gravel the roads in Rimrock and Homestead. Rimrock residents met at the Mormon Church and figured out how much each family would have to pay. Only one prominent resident complained, and he changed his mind when a poorer resident pledged $25, $5 more than the requested amount. Homestead residents, on the other hand, refused the offer. A few businesses bought gravel and spread it near their stores, but most Homestead roads remained muddy (Vogt and O'Dea 1953, pp. 645–654). More recent examples were Mormon assistance when the Teton Dam in southeastern Idaho broke in the 1980s, when the Mormons volunteered during the 2002 Winter Olympics in Salt Lake City, and when the Mormon Church sends relief in the United States and around the world following natural disasters.

This concept of community-building that started under Brigham Young and extended to the twentieth century gave the Mormon corridor, as a geographer dubbed the region, a different feel than other parts of the West (Meinig 1965). Mormons avoided much of the boom and bust of the West. One study contrasted the fortunes of towns in the Mormon corridor and other regions of the intermountain West between 1860 and 1870. During that time residents' personal wealth increased dramatically, but not nearly as much in Utah. Yet Utah towns were more stable. Between 1870 and 1910, 75 percent of Utah communities survived, while only 33 percent of Montana, 48 percent of Nevada, and 52 percent of Idaho settlements lasted. The religious motivation for settlement and the focus on building the City of God made the difference (May 1994, pp. 93–94).

The towns' layout increased social interaction, and Young encouraged recreation. Neighbors not only worshiped together but they also participated in social and recreational activities. Nineteenth-century Mormons supported the theater, dance, and the arts. Young explained: "I built the Salt Lake Theater, to attract the young of our community and to provide amusement for the boys and girls, rather than to have them running all over creation for recreation." He built a gymnasium for his children. He sent missionaries to Paris to take art classes. They returned to paint murals in the temples. For Mormons all activities were a part of worship ("Mutual Messages" 1941, p. 239; "Brigham Young" 1950, p. 529).

Young's organized migration, his establishment of communities, and his focus on cooperation thus made Mormon settlements different from others in the American West. It is with good reason that he has been called one of "the most successful commonwealth builders of the English-speaking world" (Morrison 1965, p. 549).

Polygamy

While some Americans know Mormons for their successful communities and irrigation, nearly everyone has heard of polygamy. But how many Mormon families were polygamous? Studies vary from 2 to 3 percent of the men to 20 to 30 percent of the families. These figures also varied by community. According to one study, 63 percent of the men in the Mormon colonies in Chihuahua, Mexico, were polygamous, because polygamists escaping U.S. laws settled there. But even towns next to each other in Kane County varied—10 percent in Rockville, and 67 percent in Orderville (quoted in Embry 1987, p. 38).

Why did Mormons accept this unusual marital practice? Mormons believe that God commanded them to do so. They also came up with other possibilities, such as a shortage of good men, a need to rise up righteous children, and a way to prevent prostitution. Non-Mormons saw the practice as religiously accepted prostitution. Scholars have suggested that polygamy moved Mormons' focus from family life to religious communities.

Whatever the numbers or the reasons, polygamy became the defining practice that separated Mormons from the rest of the United States during the nineteenth century. For many the marriage practice represented the community and theology in Utah. And no one outside of Mormondom liked the idea (although many enjoyed hearing the stories). Mormons defended their religious freedom, even arguing the point in the Supreme Court. Non-members disagreed, explaining that it destroyed the family. Congress passed laws against polygamy and sent marshals to arrest those who disobeyed. Mormons participated in civil disobedience and went on the "underground" to escape. Church leaders determined to continue this unique practice.

But the laws became stricter. The federal government placed Mormon property into receivership. Mormon men in Idaho had to take an oath that they did not support polygamy if they wanted to vote. Women in Utah received the vote because many non-Mormons assumed that they would

A Mormon family of the 1870s, with a husband, two wives, and nine children. (*Bettmann/Corbis*)

vote against polygamy. When they did not, Congress took away the women's right. In 1890, Church president Wilford Woodruff issued a press release, a "Manifesto," which said that there were no new marriages "contrary to the laws of the land."

The Manifesto did not completely end polygamy, however. Some church-sanctioned plural marriages were performed in Mexico, Canada, and even in the United States. But they were few, and the participants kept a low profile. The practice continued to be an issue when the U.S. Congress refused to sit Brigham H. Roberts, a church leader and polygamist, after Utah elected him to the House of Representatives in 1899. The Senate threatened not to include Reed Smoot, also a church leader but a monogamist, in 1904. Church president Joseph F. Smith testified at the hearing. He also issued what historians call the Second Manifesto, prohibiting plural marriages and threatening excommunication for those who did not obey.

Despite the fact that Mormons have not practiced polygamy for more than a century, the memory continues. There are break-off groups in Utah and Arizona who still continue to practice polygamy. Attempts to eliminate them failed with raids at Short Creek (now Colorado City), Arizona, in the 1950s. Recently there has been a renewed interest in men who marry under-age minors, abuse children, and misuse welfare funds.

Political and Economic Conflict

But was polygamy the real issue? Perhaps not. It certainly shocked many Americans, but Mormonism raised greater concerns. Just as they had in Missouri, Mormons in Utah voted as a bloc and controlled the elections. Brigham Young encouraged members to settle their disputes in church courts. Political parties divided on religious lines. By stirring up Americans about polygamy, political leaders also hoped to change the LDS theocracy (Lyman 1986).

When the Mormons first arrived in Salt Lake City, they had complete control. While the area became part of the United States, it was not a territory or a state. So Mormons created their own state of Deseret (a *Book of Mormon* term) that included all of present-day Utah, Nevada, parts of Idaho, Wyoming, and Colorado. It even extended to the coast in California. The residents elected a legislature and started passing laws.

Deseret did not last long. The U.S. Congress created territories in the newly acquired Mexico area. Slowly Deseret lost much of its size, and the remaining area became Utah, named after the Utes. But the new territory did not eliminate the Mormon control. The U.S. Congress appointed Brigham Young the first governor and Indian agent. Mormon leaders were judges, religious leaders, and territorial legislature members. There was no separation of church and state in Utah.

But change came quickly. First, the Gold Rush 49ers often passed through Salt Lake City, bringing needed supplies and a market for goods. But their presence threatened the Mormons' economic control. The railroad brought even more outside commerce. Besides the United Orders, Brigham Young encouraged men and women to be self-sufficient. He encouraged women to raise their own silk worms and to store grain.

Church control started disappearing, partially in reaction to polygamy. In 1852, Orson Pratt publicly announced that the church believed in plural marriage. Just four years later the Republican Party condemned the "twin relics of barbarism, slavery and polygamy." The U.S. Congress passed the first law against the practice in 1862. When that law did not control plural marriages, the Congress passed other laws. The U.S. president sent non-Mormons to hold some territorial positions. Many reported negatively about their experiences, claiming that they had to flee the area for their lives.

With such reactions, U.S. president James Buchanan appointed a new territorial governor, Alfred Cumming, and sent him to Utah in 1857 with nearly 2,000 soldiers to protect him. Young received word that the army was coming at the tenth anniversary of his arrival in the Great Salt Lake Valley. He immediately issued a scorched earth policy to slow the army's arrival and to destroy the Mormon communities if needed. A non-Mormon friend, Thomas Kane, worked out a compromise. The army entered Utah but promised to settle west of Utah Lake. The army remained until the Civil War started.

This time period, sometimes referred to as the Utah War or Buchanan's Folly, put the Mormons on the defensive. It resulted in one of the greatest tragedies in western American history, the Mountain Meadows Massacre. At the same time that the army was coming, the Fancher-Baker party, a group of immigrants from Arkansas and Missouri, places where Mormons had conflicts, came through Utah driving cattle they hoped to sell in California. Utah was undergoing a drought at the time and the cattle ate the limited grasses. Rumors spread that they had poisoned the streams. The

Mormons responded to the immigrants with violence and convinced the Paiutes to assist. Mormon John D. Lee promised to escort the immigrants to safety in an area called Mountain Meadows. A militiaman marched by each male immigrant, and when given the order, the militiaman killed him. The militia and the Paiutes also killed the women and all but the youngest children. Did Brigham Young order the attack, or at least create an atmosphere that made possible the attack? Did the emigrant party poison water, killing Native American and Mormon animals? No one knows for certain. The Mormon militia and religious leaders asked for Young's advice. His reply to leave them alone came too late. Years later, Lee, who was not the only Mormon involved, was blamed for the entire incident and executed.

The Mormons first denied any involvement, then blamed Lee. Several histories discuss this complex story. The first was Juanita Brooks, *The Mountain Meadows Massacre* (Norman: University of Oklahoma Press, 1991), a reprint of the 1962 edition. Brooks for the first time identified the Mormons involved. She denies that Brigham Young agreed to the murders. A more recent study by Will Bagley, *Blood of the Prophets: Brigham Young and the Massacre at Mountain Meadows* (Norman: University of Oklahoma Press, 2002), puts the blame on Young. If he did not order the massacre, he at least created a climate that led to it. Richard Turley, Ronald W. Walker, and Glen M. Leonard are completing a book on the subject to be published by Oxford University Press (Brooks 1962; Bagley 2002).

The Civil War moved much of the nation's attention away from the Mormons. Abraham Lincoln's policy was to avoid them, much as he would plow around a stump in a field. Patrick Connor, a U.S. military officer, had other ideas. While his official assignment was to protect travelers from Indians, he believed that he was to watch the Mormons. Connor built Fort Douglas above the city, sent his men out to mine, and murdered Shoshone men, women, and children at the Bear River Massacre. Mormons viewed the Civil War as the beginning of the end—wars and rumors of war predicted in the Bible before Christ's second coming.

The war's end changed the U.S. focus toward Utah. Additional legislation and federal marshals ended Mormon polygamy. Non-Mormon merchants came in, and Mormons such as the Godbeites (named for William S. Godbe) rebelled against Young's economic control and mining policy. They formed the Liberal Party in opposition to the Mormon People's Party. They started a publication that became the *Salt Lake Tribune* that competed against the Mormon's *Deseret News*. With pressure, Mormons broke up the People's Party and joined the Republican and Democratic parties. The church also changed its economic focus. As a result, Congress agreed to admit Utah as a state in 1896 (Alexander 2003, pp. 186–217).

The Transformation

Utah did not immediately fit into the American mainstream after statehood. True, the transformation had started, but it was not immediately complete. There were elements that demonstrated a change. Prohibition provided an

Lemuel H. Redd Jr.

Historian Leonard J. Arrington explained: "L. H. Jr. was part of the Mormon kingdom but also very much in the world" (Arrington 1995, p. 3). His father, Lemuel Hardison Redd, Sr., drove an ox team from Missouri to the Salt Lake Valley as a teenager. His mother, Keziah Jane Butler, also came to Utah as a child. His father married a plural wife and participated in the United Order in New Harmony, Utah, where they "wrung a harsh subsistence out of a small farm" (Redd 1984, p. 104).

In 1875 church leaders called Lem Jr. to attend the Normal School at the University of Deseret. There he met Eliza Ann Westover from Pinto, a town near New Harmony. After they graduated, they returned to their home towns to teach. In 1878 they married and moved to Leeds, where Lem and his father-in-law owned a butcher shop.

In August 1877, a year and a half after Brigham Young's death, church president John Taylor asked Mormons to move to the southeastern Utah San Juan area to work with the Native Americans and control the "outlaws" in the area. Lem Sr. and Jr. were asked to go in 1879. Jr. told his father that he did not want to leave his business. His father, who believed in following church leaders, told him, "You can't afford not to go."

The eighty families started out late in the season. The possible routes all had problems. Going north required crossing the Green River and Colorado River and traveling through Ute country. Going south through Arizona and New Mexico was also long, with little water and many dangers. So the group attempted a shortcut east from Escalante. They hoped to make the trip in six weeks.

The route looked short on a map but was almost impossible in fact. The group created a chute down the "Hole-in-the Rock" to the Colorado River. Visitors to Lake Powell can see part of their impossible trail. The difficulty continued. When they reached San Juan Hill, the last great obstacle, the group was exhausted. They had already been on the road for six months. Charles Redd, Lem Jr.'s son, recalled, "My father

---

important link between Mormons and Gentiles. Joseph Smith recorded a revelation, the Word of Wisdom, discouraging liquor and tobacco. While many recommended compliance, many Mormons—including leaders—believed that they could drink in moderation. But church presidents Joseph F. Smith and Heber J. Grant disagreed. They eliminated liquor at church-owned Saltair, a dance hall on the Great Salt Lake. They invited evangelical Protestant ministers to share the Prohibition message. Grant became an officer to Utah in the Anti-Saloon League of America. Those who had fought against polygamy became the Mormon allies in the fight against liquor. Grant made obedience to the Word of Wisdom a requirement for entering the temple.

Not all Mormons agreed with Grant's position on prohibition, a clear sign that Mormons no longer voted as a bloc. Senator Reed Smoot spoke against local option and national prohibition. Utah eventually passed prohibition and then approved the amendment to the Constitution. That could suggest that Mormons followed their church president. But Grant opposed the repeal and was upset when Utah became the final state needed to repeal the amendment. It was one reason that he became a Republican (Alexander 1986, pp. 258–271).

was a strong man, and reluctant to display emotion; but whenever in later years the full pathos of San Juan Hill was recalled . . . the memory of the bitter struggle was too much for him and he wept" (Arrington 1995, p. 16).

Life in the new area was rough. In 1882, 1884, and 1897 the settlers asked church leaders to let them leave. Each time the authorities told the settlers to "carry on." Lem and Eliza became community leaders. In 1883 church authorities advised Lem to marry a plural wife, and Eliza agreed. He married Lucy Zina Lyman that year.

Lem worked in the cattle and sheep business and became a wealthy man. In the 1900s and 1910s, when cash was scarce, a wool dealer received Lem's checks in change from a hotel. Lem was a delegate to the Utah Constitutional Convention in 1896 and served in the Utah legislature for four years. He became the Mormon stake president in the area. He won the respect of federal officials, non-Mormon ranchers, Utes, and Mormons.

Lem fathered eight children by his first wife and four by his second. During his last years, following World War I, he amassed a large debt, and his families struggled to get along. His dying wish to his son Charles was: "I wish my debt to be paid and my two families would get along." Charles said he would "try" (Redd 1984, p. 108). Lem passed away in 1923.

Lem saw the transformation of Utah from a Mormon settlement to a U.S. colony. He followed church leaders' requests to settle and marry a plural wife. He never lost faith in the church. In 1971 his son Charles established the Lemuel Hardison Redd, Jr., Chair of Western History at Brigham Young University in his memory.

References

Arrington, Leonard J. *Utah's Audacious Stockman: Charlie Redd.* Logan: Utah State University Press, 1995.

Redd, Charles. "As I Remember Him—My Father, L. H. Redd, Jr." In Jessie L. Embry, ed., *La Sal Reflections: A Redd Family Journal.* La Sal, Utah: Charles Redd Foundation, 1984.

Another example demonstrated that Mormons had differing political views. Smoot opposed the United States joining the League of Nations, but B. H. Roberts supported it. Both sides used the *Book of Mormon* to defend their beliefs, until Grant finally said that the book said nothing on the subject. Eventually church leaders stopped taking stands except on what they considered moral issues. They encouraged Mormons to vote for the best candidate regardless of party. J. Reuben Clark, for example, spoke against the League of Nations when he was a U.S. government official. He also expressed his opposition to the United Nations when he was a church leader, but he carefully added that it was his personal opinion (Allen and Leonard 1992, pp. 513–514).

There were other elements of change as well. Young and the leaders who followed him encouraged the gathering to Zion. That was where the other members were; that was where they built temples, and where members received ordinances needed for the next life. That gathering ideal changed in the twentieth century. In the 1920s, as the Church grew, Church president Joseph F. Smith—the nephew of Joseph Smith, Jr.—discouraged members from coming to Utah. He explained that Mormons could establish Zion where they were. The church's shelter did not have to be in one place. The stakes holding up the church's tent could be spread out to cover the entire world. During the 1920s and 1930s, Mormons moved to larger cities in California and the Midwest, looking for better jobs.

The Mormon Church eventually completely distanced itself from polygamy. Church leaders excommunicated men and women who continued the practice. Mormon families supported the Victorian ideals of the nineteenth century—the man as a breadwinner, the wife as a homemaker, with children learning and not simply little adults. Mormon families eventually would match the ideal more than other Americans.

Mormon support of the United States at war also demonstrated a change. Utahans volunteered to fight in the Spanish American War in 1898. Like the rest of the nation, Mormons were neutral when World War I started. But once the United States entered the war, they supported the effort through volunteers in the service and buying bonds and conserving supplies on the homefront. Mormons sold carefully guarded Relief Society grain as a public relations statement.

One historian argues that the Mormon transition was complete by 1930 (Alexander 1986). It took years for Mormons to let go of the political and economic control of Utah and surrounding areas. Others maintain that the church never ceded such control. In 2005, for example, Salt Lake City mayor Rocky Anderson complained that the city's council had too many Mormons on it and that the state legislature was nearly all Mormon. There is still a Mormon-Gentile division in the city, although Mormons and Gentiles are working together to improve downtown Salt Lake City.

Conclusion

In many ways Mormons are part of the American mainstream; in others they still cling to a religion that is a way of life. Some of the changes came quickly; others came much more slowly. A Wasatch County experience demonstrates how much of a change took place over the nineteenth century. Abram Hatch was the stake president in Heber City from 1877 to 1901. During the time when Mormons focused on community building, cooperation, polygamy, and political and economic control, Hatch was constantly out of step with general church leaders and more faithful local Mormons. Church leaders asked Mormons to trade with a Mormon cooperative, Zion's Cooperative Mercantile Institution (ZCMI). Hatch asked for Gentile businesses to move to Heber. Mormon educational leaders asked the Wasatch Stake to support a church academy, essentially a high school. Hatch promoted public or Protestant schools. While many stake presidents were polygamous, Hatch refused to be so. As a result, Hatch experienced conflicts with William Forman, the leader of a local congregation (a bishop of one of the Heber City wards) and general church leaders.

In 1901 general church leaders replaced Hatch with an outsider, William Smart. Smart felt that his mission was to create a better religious atmosphere in the county. He reintroduced policies that the church had changed. He created a cooperative, Brigham Young–style United Order, the Wasatch Development Company, with his counselors in the stake presidency and interested businessmen. They formed the Heber Mercantile Company. Even without the support of Abram Hatch and his sons, some leading businessmen, Smart's business became the largest in town. Some residents believed that they were disloyal to the church if they did not trade there. Hatch actively supported Mormons for the public school elections. He encouraged LDS teenagers to go to the BY Academy in Provo, rather than the developing public high school. He even married a plural wife before the Second Manifesto. He attempted to control the opening of the Uintah Indian Reservation. Smart was as much out of step with the church leaders as Hatch had been and experienced conflict as a result (Embry 1985, pp. 163–181).

The comparison of these two leaders shows how much Mormonism changed around 1900. From a church-run political and economic system, Mormons became more republican and capitalist. They eliminated polygamy and stressed Victorian family values. They built subdivisions that followed the typical American plan. Mormon leaders encouraged church members to vote but rarely spoke out on political issues, except for what they viewed as pressing moral issues. Over the years these have included opposition to a nuclear defensive project, MX, planned for Utah's west desert, the Equal Rights Amendment, and gay marriage.

The first Mormons in the West were unique because of their political, family, and economic views. Their migration and communities differed from those of other Western settlers. Although a majority of Mormons now live outside of the West—and indeed outside of the United States altogether—their cultural core in the intermountain West remains a distinct and critical part of the region.

References and Further Reading

Alexander, Thomas G. *Mormonism in Transition: A History of the Latter-day Saints.* Urbana: University of Illinois Press, 1986.

Alexander, Thomas G. *Utah: The Right Place.* Layton, UT: Gibbs Smith Publishers, 2003.

Allen, James B., and Glen M. Leonard. *The Story of the Latter-day Saints.* Salt Lake City: Deseret Book, 1992.

Arrington, Leonard J. *Brigham Young: American Moses.* New York: Knopf, 1985.

Arrington, Leonard J. *Utah's Audacious Stockman: Charles Redd.* Logan: Utah State University Press, 1995.

Arrington, Leonard, and Davis Bitton. *The Mormon Experience: A History of the Latter-day Saints.* New York: Knopf, 1979.

Bagley, Will. *Blood of the Prophets: Brigham Young and the Massacre at Mountain Meadows.* Norman: University of Oklahoma Press, 2002.

"Brigham Young Said: On Recreation." *Improvement Era* (June 1950): 529.

Brooks, Juanita. *The Mountain Meadows Massacre* [1962]. Norman: University of Oklahoma Press, 1991.

Cheney, Thomas E. *Mormon Songs from the Rocky Mountains: A Compilation of Mormon Folksong.* Austin: University of Texas Press, 1968.

Embry, Jessie L. "'All Things unto Me Are Spiritual': Contrasting Religious and Temporal Leadership Styles in Heber City, Utah." In Jessie L. Embry and Howard A. Christy, eds., *Community Development in the American West: Past and Present Nineteenth and Twentieth Century Frontiers.* Provo, UT: Charles Redd Center for Western Studies, 1985, 163–181.

Embry, Jessie L. *Mormon Polygamous Families: Life in the Principle.* Salt Lake City: University of Utah Press, 1987.

Embry, Jessie L. *A History of Wasatch County.* Salt Lake City and Heber City: Utah State Historical Society and Wasatch County Commission, 1996.

Embry, Jessie L. *North Logan Town, 1934–1970.* North Logan, UT: North Logan City, 2000.

Haglund, Karl T., and Phillip F. Notarianni. *The Avenues of Salt Lake City.* Salt Lake City: Utah State Historical Society, 1980.

Larsen, Gustive. *The "Americanization" of Utah for Statehood, 1897–1978.* San Marino, CA: Huntington Library, 1971.

Lyman, Edward Leo. *Political Deliverance: The Mormon Quest for Utah Statehood.* Urbana: University of Illinois Press, 1986.

May, Dean L. *Three Frontiers: Family, Land and Society in the American West, 1850–1900.* Cambridge: Cambridge University Press, 1994.

Meinig, Donald William. "Mormon Culture Region: Strategies and Patterns in the Geography of the American West." *Association of American Geographers* 5 (June 1965): 191–220.

Morrison, Samuel Eliot. *The Oxford History of the American People.* New York: Oxford University Press, 1965.

"Mutual Messages." *Improvement Era* (April 1941): 239.

Notarianni, Phillip F., ed. *Carbon County: Eastern Utah's Industrial Island.* Salt Lake City: Utah State Historical Society, 1981.

Redd, Charles. "As I Remember Him—My Father, L. H. Redd, Jr." *La Sal Reflections: A Redd Family Journal.* La Sal, UT: Charles Redd Foundation, 1984.

Vogt, Evon Z., and Thomas F. O'Dea. "A Comparative Study of the Role of Values in Social Action in Two Southwestern Communities." *American Sociological Review* 18 (December 1953), 645–654.

The Black West | 7

Dwayne Mack

Black Pioneers of the West

In 1893, Frederick Jackson Turner documented the importance of the settling of the West in U.S. history. According to the historian Quintard Taylor, Turner's scholarship promoted a story of "rugged Euro-American pioneers constantly challenging a westward moving frontier, bringing civilization, taming the wilderness, and, in the process, reinventing themselves as Americans and creating an egalitarian society that nurtured the fundamental democratic values that shaped contemporary American society" (Taylor 1999, p. 19). Turner's study appealed to most scholars, who, along with Turner, ignored the contribution of blacks to the settlement and development of the Western frontier. His thesis remained unchallenged for more than fifty years. However, by the early 1950s historians like W. Sherman Savage and Wendell G. Addington had begun producing scholarship on slavery in the West, black pioneers, Buffalo Soldiers, black cowboys, and other African Americans who participated in settling the Western frontier. After that, the number of books and articles produced on the black experience in the West continued to increase, refuting Turner's narrow frontier thesis. The scholarship proved that African Americans were present at all stages of Western history. They made key contributions and earned some triumphs amid great struggle.

The black presence in the West commenced in 1528, when a party of Spanish explorers wrecked their boats off the Texas Coast in the Gulf of Mexico. Of the handful of Spanish conquistadors in the group, an African slave named Estevanico emerged from one vessel. Estevanico and the soldiers roamed across the American southwest and Mexican north until the Spanish military rescued them in 1536. Before the Spanish found them, Estevanico and his cohorts heard stories about cities with gold mines from the indigenous peoples they encountered. In 1539 these fascinating stories convinced Spanish authorities in Mexico City to send a group, guided by Estevanico, to locate the legendary cities. The towns were there, but the gold failed to materialize. Furthermore, the inhabitants of one of these cities murdered Estevanico, thus ending an important phase of European exploration that was led by the first person of African descent to travel to Western areas later known as Arizona and New Mexico (Franklin 2000, pp. 37–38; Billington and Hardaway 1998, p. 1; Taylor 1999, pp. 27–28).

As a result of Estevanico's discoveries, over the next several centuries other people of African ancestry traveled to or resided in the region later known as the American West. When white Americans settled or explored the Western frontier, they frequently brought blacks as slaves or servants. Centuries after the Spanish explored North America, migrating Americans continued the practice of bringing slaves to the West. From 1804 to 1806, a slave named York was a member of the Meriwether Lewis and William Clark expedition that traveled under orders from President Thomas Jefferson overland from St. Louis to the Pacific, where they explored the Oregon Coast. York's expert hunting skills provided sustenance for his team. His invaluable aid to the expedition as a trader, hunter, and guide enabled the party to survive. Along the way, York traded items with Native Americans for food and supplies, and the explorers followed his recommendations of where to establish a winter camp along the Pacific coastline. Upon their return to Missouri at the conclusion of the expedition, Clark manumitted York (Billington and Hardaway 1998, p. 1; Katz 1987, pp. 13–15; Katz 1977, pp. 14–17; Betts 2002; Taylor 1999, pp. 48–49).

Besides opening the West to future exploration and settlement, the Lewis and Clark Expedition initiated a profitable fur trade on the frontier. Some blacks took advantage of this opportunity, migrating west with white fur trappers and traders. In 1806, Edward Rose, an African American from Kentucky, worked as an expert hunter, trapper, guide, and interpreter for the Missouri-based Manuel Lisa fur trading company. He led the company's expedition to the Bighorn River in Wyoming. Once in the West, Rose became an important member of two Native American communities—the Absaroka (Crows) and the Arikara. Natives as well as white traders and trappers embraced Rose because he served as a liaison between the groups (Blenkinsop 1972, pp. 338–341; Franklin 2000, pp. 120–121).

James Beckwourth was perhaps the most well-known black explorer, trapper, and trader in the West. He was born in 1798 in Virginia to a slave mother and a Caucasian father. In 1810 his father transported the entire family to St. Charles, Missouri. As an adult, Beckwourth became skilled with a bowie knife and tomahawk, making him an expert fur trapper in the Rocky Mountains, Idaho, and Wyoming. In 1835, Beckwourth participated in an expedition with Thomas Smith, who traveled along the Old Spanish Trail that stretched from Utah to southern California. Between his journeys Beckwourth temporarily settled in other Western territories, such as Colorado, Montana, and New Mexico (where he became a notorious horse thief), explored and claimed land, and worked as a scout for the Colorado Volunteer Calvary. In the late 1840s he set out for California as a miner in search of gold. En route, he found a trail through the Sierra Nevada Mountains. He claimed the land on the California side, near Reno, which became Beckwourth Pass, a wagon train trail (Bonner 1981; Taylor 1999, p. 51; de Graaf Mulroy, and Taylor 2001, p. 7; Katz 1987, pp. 31–34; Katz 1977, pp. 27–32).

James Beckwourth,
African-American
explorer, trapper,
trader (1798–1867).
(*Courtesy Mercaldo
Archives*)

Beckwourth's success in the West was also attributed to his relationship with Native communities. They embraced Beckwourth as they had Edward Rose. He became a member of the Crows of Wyoming and Montana, and he participated in numerous raids against their enemies, the Blackfoot tribe (Katz 1987, p. 32; Katz 1977, pp. 30–31).

Blacks who were neither trappers nor traders also continued to explore the West. In 1843 and again in 1845 and 1846, Jacob Dodson, a young free black from Washington, D.C., made two journeys west with John C. Fremont's party of seventeen that included Kit Carson. On the first expedition they traveled from Missouri to Fort Vancouver in the Oregon territory—the route that would become the Oregon Trail. During their return to Missouri, the pioneers traveled south into the western section of Nevada as well as into California's Central Valley, Utah, Colorado, and Kansas. During his other expedition with Fremont's group, they became involved in the U.S. occupation of California (Fremont 1845; Taylor 1999, p. 49). Beckwourth, Dodson, and other black explorers opened the frontier for thousands of African-American cowboys who in the nineteenth century earned decent wages while participating in numerous roundups and cattle drives and as "bronco busters" and cattle and horse rustlers. Cowboys like expert bulldoggers Bill Pickett and Lon Sealy earned respectable salaries at the 101 Ranch in Oklahoma. Cattle and horse rustler Isom Dart worked at various ranches in Wyoming, Utah, and Colorado. Notorious gunslingers like Dart, Cherokee Bill, and Nat Love (who became the legendary Nat Deadwood Dick) also shared the Western range with cowboys (Durham 1965; Porter 1998, pp. 110–127).

Slavery in the Antebellum West

Along with black explorers taming and settling the West, slave owners brought their black bondsmen to the area. The question of slavery in new territories hung over the nation as the institution expanded westward, however. Although the 1787 Northwest Ordinance prohibited slavery in the territory northwest of the Ohio River, a significant number of blacks traveled to and remained in the West as bondsmen. The slavery controversy in the West paralleled the debate back East. Northerners demanded the elimination of slavery in the Western frontier, particularly north of the Missouri Compromise line. White westerners denied their involvement in promoting slavery. Unfortunately, the Western frontier's "claims of innocence on slavery" are false, since slaves labored in almost every U.S. territory and state before 1861, and heated debate occurred over its appropriateness in Utah, Oregon, and California. In Kansas, political debates in the 1850s over slavery evolved into tragic incidents resulting in bloodshed (Savage p. 9; Taylor 1999, p. 53).

Slavery existed in the West because white people who migrated there transported their chattel property with them. The majority of the slave owners who moved west came from Southern states: Kentucky, Tennessee, Virginia, Georgia, and the Carolinas. Before the Civil War, most of the African Americans who moved west did so as slaves. In this enormous and diverse part of the country, each state and territory dealt with the slavery issue differently. Despite significant opposition, slave owners poured into the Western frontier. But when Euro-Americans began migrating westward, abolitionists and others opposed to slavery argued for a region free of the practice. Many Americans believed that the financial system of slavery would collapse in the West. Those opposed to slavery contended that profitable Southern crops such as rice, sugarcane, cotton, and tobacco could not grow there (Taylor 1999, p. 53; Savage 1998, pp. 8–9). But slaves in the West performed much of the labor necessary to guarantee the survival of its pioneers, such as harvesting crops, cooking, herding cattle, collecting firewood, nursing children, hunting, constructing shelter, and a myriad of other labor-intensive tasks.

Western slavery persisted despite most of the governments' adoption of Article VI, the antislavery provision of the Ordinance of 1787, which established a territorial governing system in the Northwest. The provision stated that "there shall be neither slavery nor involuntary servitude in said territory, otherwise than in punishment whereof the party shall have been duly convicted. Provided always that any person escaping into same, from whom labor or service is lawfully claimed, such fugitive may be lawfully reclaimed and conveyed to the person claiming his or her labor or service." By 1850 more than a quarter of the population in Oregon came from the South, and these whites were dedicated to promoting slavery in the Western frontier (Savage 1998, p. 9; Savage 1976, pp. 22–23).

In 1850, Congress organized and defined slavery in the land that the United States had acquired during the Mexican-American War. The Compromise of 1850 permitted California to enter the Union as a free state and created the territories of New Mexico and Utah. They included Nevada, Arizona, half of Colorado, and a section of Wyoming, with settlers in those areas determining through popular sovereignty whether to allow slavery. In the decade prior to the compromise, the United States had acquired Texas, the Oregon region, and the Mexican Cession. Congress granted statehood to Texas and founded the Oregon Territory. These areas almost doubled the nation's size. As for slavery, Oregonians decided that any states formed from their region would remain "free of the peculiar institution." Texans, however, immediately made slavery legal (Billington and Hardaway 1998, p. 7).

The Compromise of 1850 failed to immediately free African Americans in the West. In 1852 the territory of Utah followed the example of Texas, creating a constitution that legalized slavery. Even in California, a number of slaveholders disregarded the compromise and their own constitution, which outlawed slavery. They defied federal law, keeping their slaves in bondage until courts forced emancipation. For example, in 1856, Bridget "Biddy" Mason initiated a major lawsuit in California. She had lived half a decade as a slave there. In a groundbreaking decision, a judge ruled that slavery was prohibited in California. This precedent encouraged slaveholders to consider either selling or manumitting their slaves before moving to California (Savage 1998, p. 20; Hayden 1989, pp. 86–89; Franklin 1963, pp. 137–154; Taylor 1999, p. 79).

California was not the only Western state or territory in which whites illegally kept slaves; some resided in the Oregon Territory, which included present-day Washington, Idaho, Wyoming, and Montana. In addition, Congress in 1854 passed the Kansas-Nebraska Act. Besides opening the territory to settlers, the law permitted the residents of the area to decide through popular sovereignty whether to allow slavery. Finally, in 1857 the U.S. Supreme Court, in the monumental Dred Scott decision, ruled that slave owners could transport their slaves into any U.S. territory. This decision made the forced migration of slaves to the West easier (Billington and Hardaway 1998, p. 8).

Although slavery in California was less brutal than slavery in the South, a number of slaves in the Golden State absconded to coastal areas. The California judicial system was erratic; sometimes it enforced the Southern fugitive slave laws, while at other times it emancipated fugitive slaves or those suing for freedom. In April of 1852, the state legislature passed a fugitive slave law which declared that any black person who had migrated to California before it joined the Union either as a fugitive or with a slaveholder was considered property and faced jail or a fine. All runaway slaves were returned to their masters. However, a slave entering California after statehood became emancipated. Unfortunately, de facto slavery existed in California for several years after passage of the law. One custom that miners adhered to held that all gold found by a prospector belonged to that individual—unless that individual was a slave. If a slave found gold while mining for his master, the slaveholder became owner of the precious metal (Ravage 1997, pp. 86–87).

Unlike in California, slavery became legal in Texas. Immediately after Texas gained its independence from Mexico in 1836, slaveholders flooded the independent republic. Anglo Americans in the area justified slavery by explaining both the agricultural necessity for free black labor and their religious right to own blacks. In 1860, District Court Judge C. A. Frazier argued to an Upshur County grand jury in Texas that "I have no more doubt of the right of a civilized Christian nation to capture the African wherever he may be found and subject him to labor, enlightenment and religion, than I have of one of our people to capture a wild horse on the prairies of the West, and domesticate and reduce him to labor" (Campbell 1989, p. 213; Taylor 1999, p. 54).

Utah became the only other territory besides Texas to make slavery legal. Despite soil and weather that was not conducive to slave labor, several Mormon pioneers brought slaves to the territory. On January 10, 1847, a small number of slaves began a migration from Mississippi to Salt Lake City with a group of one hundred Mormons, led by Brigham Young. They came into the Salt Lake Valley to establish "Zion." Many of the white settlers in the group, such as John Bankhead, William Lay, and William Crosby, each brought a slave. Daniel Thomas transported his slave, Toby. Another white pioneer, William Matthews, brought his slave, "Uncle" Phil; William Lay had his servant Hark, whose name was on a list of original Utah pioneers. James Flake owned a couple of slaves, Martha and Green. Another early settler, William Smith, owned Lawrence and Herman. In sum, slave owners and their slaves were the Salt Lake City pioneers who organized and developed the area to prepare it for future Mormon migration (Savage 1998, p. 13; Beller 1929; Christensen 1957).

The Mormon colony in Utah failed to avoid the slavery controversy. The existence of slavery in the Salt Lake Valley forced a national debate over slavery's westward expansion, despite the relatively small numbers: by 1850, Utah had approximately twenty-six slaves and twenty-four free blacks. In 1852, Brigham Young and his followers decided the slavery question for themselves. The Compromise of 1850 had established for the Mormons a territorial government, and allowed the inhabitants of Utah to decide through popular sovereignty the "status of slavery." In 1851, the Utah residents appointed Young as their first territorial governor and they elected their first territorial legislature. When the legislature first assembled in 1851, it discussed the legality of slavery in the territory. In 1852, Young asked the legislature to legalize slavery. On February 4, 1852, Governor Young's request was granted, and Utah emerged as the lone territory west of the Missouri River and north of the Missouri Compromise line to permit slavery (Bringhurst 1998, p. 25).

The 1852 law reflected the racial attitudes of most Mormon residents. Young and other Mormons considered blacks "as inherently inferior and therefore fit subjects for involuntary servitude." The Mormons "traced the inferiority of black people to their alleged descent from Ham and Canaan," an ancestry that designated them "to occupy the position of 'servant of servants'" (ibid., p. 31; Coleman 1980, pp. 40–41, 45–47). Governor Young defended the 1852 act when he argued: "The seed of Canaan, will inevitably carry the curse which has placed upon them until the same authority, which placed it there, shall see proper to have it removed" (Bringhurst 1998, p. 32).

In addition to Texas and Utah, a significantly smaller number of slaves resided in Idaho, Montana, Nevada, North and South Dakota, New Mexico, and Arizona. The majority of slaves in Arizona labored as domestics, while others worked for fur companies.

Overall, Texas had the largest number of slaves of all the Western states and territories. White settlers, upon migrating, immediately created familiar racially based political and economic restrictions. Texas, instead of offering freedom to African Americans, entered the Union in 1845 as a slave state. In 1860 the state had 182,500, about a quarter of the state's total population. Texas was the lone Western state or territory to depend on slavery for survival before the territory gained independence from Mexico in the Texas Revolution of 1835–1836. The flood of fugitive bondspeople from nearby states during the Civil War caused Texas's total slave population to exceed 250,000 by the spring of 1865 (Taylor 1999, pp. 53–54; Campbell 1989, pp. 55–56, 251). Although many blacks experienced slavery in the West, some enjoyed freedom. Most free black migrants traveled west either in small bands with wagon trains or independently. They journeyed to places like California to look for gold in the integrated mines with Chinese, Europeans, and Latin Americans. Peter Brown, a free black from Missouri, mined in Sacramento City, where he became prosperous in a short time. He wrote back home to his wife: "California is the best country in the world to make money. It is also the best place for black folks on the globe. All a man has to do is to work, and he'll make money" (Brown 1851). The success of Brown and other free black California migrants spurred a tremendous population increase. By 1852 the number of blacks in the state had reached 2,000; a decade later the census recorded 4,000 blacks (U.S. Census 1853; U.S. Census 1864; Taylor 1999, p. 84). California had the largest number of free blacks in the West. State legislators, however, enacted an "extensive body of discriminatory laws." Some of these laws prohibited black court testimony, black homesteading, black jurors, black voting rights, and interracial marriage (Johnson 1992, pp. 121–122, 125–127; Berwanger 1967, pp. 70–77, 118–121; Edwards 1977, p. 36). The territorial governments of Colorado, Utah, Oregon, Nebraska, New Mexico, and Kansas all passed comparable restrictive laws.

In addition to the gold mines, black Californians found work in trades similar to those of their Eastern counterparts. The men labored as stewards on river steamboats, cooks, and barbers; both men and women found positions as waiters, whitewashers, maids, and servants. Although most blacks worked at labor-intensive jobs, a black middle class emerged in places like San Francisco. Mary Ellen Pleasant, for example, became a wealthy black property owner with three laundries and significant investments in mining stocks.

In 1850, Mifflin Gibbs moved from Philadelphia to San Francisco. The following year he cofounded with Peter Lester the Pioneer Boot and Shoe Emporium, selling to customers as far away as Oregon and southern California. As

George Washington

Although most blacks lived in bondage as slaves in the early 1800s, some blacks prospered outside the "peculiar institution." In 1817 the black Pacific Northwest pioneer George Washington was born in Virginia to a Caucasian mother and slave father. He was given up for adoption to James and Anna Cochran, a white couple. The family lived first in Ohio and then moved to northern Missouri. Washington prospered in Missouri and, in 1843, by an act of the state legislature, he achieved legal citizenship. But that status did not protect him from racial prejudice. As a Missouri resident, he owned a store, where he permitted his patrons to purchase items with credit. One day a white customer refused to pay his debt, and Washington took the man to court. Washington was unable to win his case because the courts refused to

recognize his citizenship, thus nullifying his suit (Hayes, pp. 4–5; Katz 1987, p. 73).

By the 1850s, Manifest Destiny was in full swing. Waves of Americans migrated westward to participate in U.S. continental expansion. In 1850, Washington and his aging adopted parents left Missouri in a train of fifteen wagons, participating in the great migration west. Their four-month-long journey ended in the Oregon Territory. As a landowner on a sizable 640-acre plot purchased for him by James Cochran, the young George Washington prospered by growing cereal and various vegetable crops (Katz 1987, p. 73; Hayes 1994, p. 5).

Later, in 1872, during the Reconstruction era, the Northern Pacific Railroad built across his land, and Washington benefited financially. With his earnings, he established the town Cen-

blacks found economic success, the African-American population increased. As a result, free black communities sprang up in San Francisco, Sacramento, and Los Angeles. In those cities African Americans established churches, which galvanized them. In 1851, the Reverend Bernard Fletcher founded St. Andrews A.M.E. in Sacramento, and a year later the former slave John Jamison Moore established A.M.E. Zion Church of San Francisco.

As the black population in California grew, white lawmakers imposed rigid social restrictions on African Americans. During the Civil War, however, blacks fought back, making use of legal methods to combat discriminatory laws. For example, in 1863 black San Franciscan William Bowen was removed from a North Beach and Mission Railroad trolley. Bowen responded by suing the trolley company for $10,000 in damages. The following year a district court judge awarded him $3,199 (Taylor 1999, pp. 92–93). Other blacks, such as Charlotte Brown, Mary E. Pleasant, and Emma J. Turner, filed similar antidiscriminatory lawsuits. These legal victories failed to end streetcar restrictions against blacks in California, but they did encourage the state to pass a progressive antidiscrimination law in 1893.

Reconstruction in the West

With the Union victory and the abolition of slavery, African Americans in the South and West gained their freedom. Following the Civil War, African Americans sought better social, economic, and political opportunities.

terville, which eventually became Centralia. To facilitate his town's growth he sold inexpensively priced lots to buyers who agreed to build houses worth at least $100 each. Washington donated most of the land sale proceeds to the construction of churches and a cemetery, the design of a public square, and the assistance of struggling settlers. In 1905, when Washington died at the age of eighty-eight, his property holdings were valued in the thousands (Katz 1987, p. 73; Hayes 1994, p. 5; Bleeg 1970, p. 58).

Some social and financial prosperity for these pioneers came after the state of Washington passed progressive civil rights laws near the turn of the twentieth century. The legislation prohibited discrimination in public accommodations based on race, creed, or color. One explanation for the late-nineteenth-century general migration into Washington was the South's post Civil War deteriorating economy. For most blacks, the South's discriminatory Jim Crow laws prevented them from achieving economic prosperity. Because of fewer racial restrictions in the Northwest, black migration into that area increased. The region's small population also allowed blacks to purchase acres of reasonably priced land, where some prospered as farmers.

References

Bleeg, Joanne Wagner. "Black People in the Territory of Washington." MA thesis, University of Washington, 1970.

Hayes, Ralph, and Joseph Franklin. *Northwest Black Pioneers: A Centennial Tribute*. Bon Marche Corporate Sponsor, 1994.

Katz, William Loren. *The Black West*. Seattle, WA: Open Hand Publishing, 1986.

They sought escape from racially repressive areas like the Jim Crow South, initiating a great exodus. As a result, the West experienced another tremendous wave of black immigration, permanently changing that region's demographic landscape. But before free black people could carve out better lives for themselves in the West, several states and territories had to ensure them citizenship rights. The battle over those rights raged on from 1865 to 1870, culminating in the passage of the Fifteenth Amendment. Moreover, the battle over Reconstruction in the West paralleled the crises in the East, making Reconstruction a national issue centered on states' rights (p. 105).

Like easterners, white westerners denied former slaves the opportunity to exercise the right to vote, attend public schools with whites, use public facilities, marry a white person, hold public office, or serve on a jury. Former slaves in places like Texas found it difficult to adjust to freedom. Irate landowners evicted blacks from their plantations. The state legislature passed a Homestead Act that gave white settlers 160 acres of land but prohibited African-American land claims. Despite the law some blacks purchased land, but former Confederates forced the majority of former slaves to continue living in poverty, without land ownership (pp. 106–107).

For a brief interval, an interracial group of Unionists controlled Texas government. In the late 1800s, African Americans George Ruby and Matt Gaines served in the state senate, and a dozen blacks won seats in the House of Representatives. African Americans served in other political offices in Texas: Walter Burton served two terms as sheriff of Fort Bend County, and Waller County residents elected Matt Kilpatrick treasurer (p. 110).

Reconstruction was a critical period in our nation's history. Despite its successes, the federal government failed to stem the tide of violence against blacks or to repeal the repressive codes. The Ku Klux Klan killed hundreds of newly freed blacks in Texas, including African-American politician Goldstein Dupree in 1873. White supremacists killed former slaves simply for enjoying their freedom or for failure to comply with racist social customs. DeWitt County's sheriff shot an African American for whistling "Yankee Doodle Dandy" (p. 111).

Despite the civil unrest and social restraints in Texas, African Americans created some semblance of community structure by establishing their own churches. African-American communities developed around African Episcopal Methodist, Baptist, and Methodist Episcopal churches. These served not only as meeting places for spiritual and social comfort but also as locations for Freedmen's Bureau schools. Some churches were even directly involved in founding colleges. In 1872, the African Methodist Episcopal Church Conference founded Paul Quinn College in Austin (in 1881 the school moved to Waco).

The prosperity that some blacks experienced in Texas faded quickly. By 1872, conservative Democrats had seized the state legislature. Over the next three years the Democrats restored former Confederate rule. In 1875, Democrats enacted a new constitution that recognized black suffrage but implemented Jim Crow legislation. Suffrage was the most important battle that African Americans faced during Reconstruction, and among the Western states and territories, Texas was the major battleground for that fight.

African Americans in the Colorado Territory would wage a similar suffrage campaign. On December 11, 1865, a group of three African-American barbers led by William Jefferson Hardin submitted a petition with the signatures of 137 other black Coloradans to Territorial Governor Alexander Cummings to delay Colorado statehood because the territorial legislature had given only white males the right to vote. The actions of blacks in Colorado spurred Congress to pass the Territorial Suffrage Act on January 31, 1867. That law gave blacks the right to vote in Colorado and the other territories some three years before Congress ratified the Fifteenth Amendment, which gave black men throughout the nation the same rights (Berwanger 1981, pp. 144–150).

Buffalo Soldiers

More than 180,000 African Americans served with distinction and honor in the Union Army during the Civil War, and more than 38,000 died in the war that won freedom for more than 4 million blacks. After the Civil War, the United States focused on securing its Western territories. African-American soldiers, whom the Cheyenne and Comanche of the plains referred to as "Buffalo Soldiers," helped in fulfilling what many Americans were calling "manifest destiny." Most had served in the Civil War. Through the Army Reorganization Act of 1866, the government authorized the formation of the Ninth and Tenth Cavalry and Twenty-fourth and Twenty-fifth Infantry.

These black units were under the leadership of white commissioned officers and African-American noncommissioned officers. The recruitment of white officers was difficult. Despite the opportunity of quick promotion, many officers, including George Armstrong Custer, refused to command black soldiers (Leckie 2003, pp. 5–8; Fowler 1996, p. 115).

During the late nineteenth century, Buffalo Soldiers represented 20 percent of all cavalry forces on the Western frontier. In an effort to accelerate the induction of black soldiers, the army established recruiting offices in New Orleans, Louisiana, and Louisville, Kentucky. The majority of the original recruits came from those two states and had bravely served during the Civil War. The new recruits enlisted for five years, receiving a monthly salary of thirteen dollars in addition to room, board, and clothing (Leckie 2003, p. 9). The Buffalo Soldiers experienced inadequate living conditions. They slept in dilapidated, poorly ventilated, dirt or mud floor, pest-infested barracks. The soldiers bathed in creeks, which often caused tuberculosis, dysentery, or diarrhea. Their diet consisted of meat, potatoes, beans, vegetables, and fruit. They worked every day of the week and had days off only on Independence Day and Christmas (ibid., pp. 99–100; Fowler 1996, pp. 9–10, 20–22). The infantry regiments served at different locations throughout the western frontier, including more than ten forts in Texas during the decade of the 1870s (Billington 1998, p. 57).

In 1867 the Ninth Cavalry moved to Texas to protect stage and mail routes, build and maintain forts, and establish law and order in an immense area dominated by Mexican revolutionaries and raiding Comanches, Cheyennes, Kiowas, and Apaches. While attempting to keep the peace, the Buffalo Soldiers experienced racial discrimination from white communities. In 1870 in a town near Fort McKavett in Texas, John Jackson, a Caucasian settler, unmercifully murdered three Buffalo Soldiers. After a speedy trial an all white jury acquitted him. Still, despite experiencing racial prejudice and being faced with the arduous assignment of maintaining order in such an immense region, the Ninth succeeded.

The Buffalo Soldiers conducted routine garrison duties, including escorting trains and stages; building roads and telegraph lines; constructing and repairing buildings; digging water wells and cellars for storing perishable items; chopping and collecting firewood; guarding water holes; and protecting lines of military supply. Infantries frequently provided invaluable service to quartermaster departments as teamsters, blacksmith assistants, and corral builders. The work of the Buffalo Soldiers prepared the Southwestern frontier for white settlement by protecting survey and mapping teams. They constructed and repaired posts and protected railroad construction crews from marauding Indians and outlaws (ibid., pp. 57–58; Fowler 1996, p. 23).

Perhaps in no area did the Buffalo Soldiers distinguish themselves more conspicuously than in policing the Western frontier. The Ninth and Tenth cavalries chased—over some of the most treacherous terrain in the Western frontier—and brought to justice Mexican criminals, absconding Native Americans, and white outlaws. Some of these included Billy the Kid, Sitting Bull, Geronimo, and Pancho Villa. The soldiers' duties carried them to New Mexico, Texas, Arizona, and Colorado, where they beat and relocated

Ninth Cavalry on horseback, ca. 1898. (*Library of Congress*)

to reservations Arapahoe, Comanches, Kiowas, Kiowa-Apaches, and other Native American groups (Leckie 2003).

In 1879 and 1880, the Ninth and Tenth cavalries battled Chief Victorio and his Warm Springs Apache absconders. In 1879, Victorio and his warriors escaped from their Fort Stanton reservation in New Mexico, reeking havoc throughout the Southwest while en route to Mexico. Their rebellion initiated the so-called Victorio War. The Buffalo Soldiers tried to prevent Victorio's return to the United States, especially to New Mexico, where he could encourage other Apaches on reservations to rebel. The soldiers of the black units understood the importance of water in the hot climate of the region, and the soldiers seized the water holes along Victorio's route. The strategy stopped Victorio's progress toward Texas and forced him to retreat south to Mexico. Similarly, the Buffalo Soldiers contained the Apaches' advance. On October 14, 1880, as Victorio and his warriors reached the border in retreat, Mexican troops killed the majority of the band. According to historian Arlen Fowler, "[T]he efforts of the black soldiers in their dogged pursuit of the elusive Victorio added an important and decisive chapter to the pacification of the Texas frontier" (Fowler 1996, pp. 36–38; Billington 1998, pp. 59–60; Leckie 2003, pp. 211–233).

The policing responsibilities of the Buffalo Soldiers were not limited to battling Native Americans. The soldiers also apprehended revolutionaries and "border scum": bootleggers, cattle rustlers, horse thieves, "crooked government contractors, heartless Indian agents, and land-hungry homesteaders" (Leckie 2003, p. 18).

Like a number of former slaves in the South during Reconstruction, some black soldiers received a more comprehensive education. A limited number of posts established evening schools to reduce the high illiteracy rate caused by slavery. Chaplains assigned to African-American units served as teachers. Many of these new students had never learned to read or write. This educational program made it possible for some Buffalo Soldiers to overcome their academic deficiencies: some soldiers, after finishing their duty on the frontier, gained formal academic training. The program, albeit marginal, did induce some veterans to continue their educational pursuits and secure employment after their tours of duty (ibid., pp. 244–245; Billington 2003, p. 62; Fowler 1996, pp. 92–113).

Because of the harsh conditions, only a small number of enlisted soldiers brought their families with them to the military outposts. Those wives and children who came to live with the soldiers at the posts alleviated some of their loneliness. Along with the families, unmarried blacks of both sexes—cooks, laundry workers, gamblers, prostitutes, and unskilled laborers traveled with the soldiers—developed into small traveling communities. The married officers resided with their families in on-post housing. Enlisted men and their families lived outside the posts in shacks and shanties. These communities contained gambling saloons (Taylor 1999, p. 184).

After the Civil War, the military gave some African-American men the opportunity to "prove their manhood in a nation that, by and large, but particularly in the South, denigrated their worth as human beings," as one historian put it. Despite having inadequate artillery, mounts, clothing, shelter, and food, the "Ninth and Tenth Cavalry had an outstanding record for faithful service, with a desertion rate well below any units of the army" (Leckie 2003, p. 10, 164). Desertions among white soldiers were several times more frequent than among Buffalo Soldiers. In addition to a low desertion rate, black units had a lower rate of alcoholism than white units (Fowler 1996, pp. 60, 78–79, 138; Taylor 1999, p. 185).

The Great Black Exodus

Because of the social, economic, and political failures of Reconstruction (1865–1877), thousands of blacks sought to improve their lives by relocating to other cities. As a result, the sparsely populated Western states and territories appealed to blacks who had lived in the segregated South. African Americans used railroads, steamboats, and their feet to migrate to rural states and the Kansas Indian Territory and Texas from the South. For the most part, they migrated west in search of greater economic, social, political, and economic opportunities. In Texas, some African Americans earned a monthly salary of $20, more than what blacks in most Southeastern states could earn in a month (Taylor 1999, pp. 134–135). As race relations in the South worsened during the post-Reconstruction period, African-American migration from

Texas and the South increased. Black North Carolinians who had migrated to Texas in 1879 sought land to farm. However, the Texas Homestead Act prohibited them from claiming public lands, and white Texans refused to sell land to them. As a result, African Americans who remained in the state became cotton sharecroppers or low-wage cotton pickers (Taylor 1999, pp. 135–136). African Americans in Texas, like white settlers in Turner's thesis, hoped for freedom and opportunity in the West as well.

The inability of blacks to homestead in Texas prompted them to migrate. In the words of one historian, Kansas offered African Americans "the prospect of political equality, freedom from violence, access to education, economic opportunity, and liberation from the presence of the old slave holding class—in sum, the *practical independence*' that Reconstruction had failed to secure" (Foner 1990, p. 252). Kansas also appealed to blacks because it was the former home of the martyred abolitionist John Brown. Furthermore, Kansas had never allowed slavery, and its electorate had voted for the party of Lincoln, the Republican Party. As a result, between 1860 and 1870, African-American communities in Kansas swelled as thousands of newly freed slaves settled in the state.

Many of the newcomers had left the South at the request of former slaves—and emigration specialists Benjamin "Pap" Singleton from Tennessee and Henry Adams from Georgia (Marable 1991, pp. 9–10). They led hundreds of impoverished migrants to Kansas. In 1878, Singleton founded the predominantly black Dunlap Colony. A year earlier other settlers had established Morton City, Hodgeman, and Nicodemus. Black migration to Kansas peaked around 1879 as thousands of destitute African Americans from Louisiana, Mississippi, and Texas arrived in St. Louis. From there they settled in more urban areas such as Lawrence, Topeka, Atchison, Kansas City, and Leavenworth. In those cities they found labor-intensive unskilled employment.

Most of these new arrivals took advantage of the 1882 Homestead Law. Unlike the restrictive Texas Homestead Act, which prevented blacks from claiming land, the 1882 Act gave 160 acres of land to any settler in Kansas and other western regions who paid a nominal filing fee and lived on and enhanced the land for half a decade. A homesteader had the option of buying the property for $1.25 an acre after residing on it for half a year, however (Taylor 1999, p. 136; White 1991, pp. 143–145).

Other blacks began life in other Western cities. From 1875 to 1900, blacks migrated to Montana, Idaho, Utah, Wyoming, Oregon, Colorado, Washington, Texas, and New Mexico. By then, Oklahoma was even more alluring than Kansas. By the start of the twentieth century, African-American farmers in Oklahoma owned more than 1 million acres of land, either by meeting the requirements of homesteading or by purchasing allotments of land Indians abandoned because of the Dawes Act (Taylor 1999, p. 147; Debo 1984).

Although blacks settled thousands of acres in Oklahoma, Kansas remained the most tolerant of the post-Reconstruction states. In 1870, Kansas ratified the Fifteenth Amendment, enfranchising African Americans. In the late 1870s blacks consisted of only 6 percent of the population, but during the last fifteen years of the nineteenth century, approximately 20 percent of them voted in statewide elections (Woods 1998, pp. 132–133).

Black voters cast their ballots in large numbers. In the 1880s, the Democratic, Republican, and Populist parties vied for their votes. As a result, blacks wielded considerable power. Although blacks remained loyal to the Republican Party, Democrats and Populists courted black votes by nominating blacks to city, county, and state positions. African Americans used this leverage to gain government posts and to force Republicans to include them in policymaking (ibid., p. 133).

The right to vote did not prevent de facto segregation. In Kansas, however, segregation was not legally institutionalized as it was in the South. In Leavenworth, black and white children were educated in separate elementary schools. The black schoolhouses and supplies were inferior to those for whites. Some high schools and colleges, however, were integrated. Several times during the late 1800s, the Kansas legislature amended school segregation. Although the Kansas constitution of 1859 mandated separated schools for whites and blacks, in 1874 the legislature passed a civil rights law that prohibited state educational institutions from admitting students based on "race, color, or previous condition of servitude" (Wilson 1954, pp. 3–4; Woods 1998, pp. 133–134). Four years later the legislature deleted "whites only" from the educational policy, eliminating separate schools. In 1879 the Republican-dominated legislature chose to allow cities of 10,000 or more to re-establish separate primary schools, but not secondary schools or colleges, a policy that remained in place until the 1954 U.S. Supreme Court ruling in *Brown v. Board of Education of Topeka* (Woods 1998, p. 134).

Nicodemus became the first predominantly black town in the West to gain national recognition. Founded by blacks from Lexington, Kentucky, who wanted to create a black farming community, the town would represent the pinnacle of black political, economic, and social success in Kansas and the rural West (Painter 1992, pp. 149–150; Taylor 1999, pp. 140–141). Nicodemus, located on the Solomon River, attracted blacks from the South. W. H. Smith and Benjamin Carr served as president and vice president of the Nicodemus Town Company of Graham County, and the Reverend Simon P. Roundtree became the town's first secretary. The early Nicodemus settlers encouraged blacks from Lexington, Kentucky, to settle with them in Kansas. Most arrived in two migration waves in 1877 and 1878. By 1880, Nicodemus's black population peaked at 700 (Painter 1992, pp. 149–151; Taylor 1999, pp. 138–141).

Several black entrepreneurs contributed to the success of the new city. In 1879, S. G. Wilson, who had arrived from New York, constructed the town's first two-story stone building where he operated a general store. A diverse small number of black churches ministered to the spiritual and social needs of the town. By the late 1880s, Nicodemus had Baptist, Free Methodist, and African Methodist Episcopal congregations. Nicodemus was a model of racial relations, but African Americans in other Kansas towns endured blatant racism. In Leavenworth, Topeka, and Kansas City whites forced blacks to live in segregated neighborhoods. These dirty and neglected areas lacked sidewalks, and the roads were poorly maintained. To make matters worse, city fire departments responded slowly to fires in these areas (Woods 1998, p. 137).

View of Washington Street in Nicodemus, Kansas, ca. 1885. (*Library of Congress*)

African Americans, however, fared slightly better in terms of employment. Blacks worked as firemen, police officers, and janitors. A few city
police and fire departments were integrated. In the 1880s Kansas City had
an entirely black fire department, and Topeka employed a dozen black police
officers and nine black firefighters (ibid.).

From November 1879 to March of 1880, approximately 4,000 blacks settled in Kansas. By 1880 the stream had slowed to a trickle because potential
settlers recognized that land was becoming scarce and that life on the prairie was difficult (Painter 1992, pp. 200–201; Taylor 1999, p. 143). Instead,
blacks were looking at migrating to predominantly white states like Montana, Wyoming, Idaho, Oregon, Utah, New Mexico, Nevada, Colorado, California, and Washington.

Early-Twentieth-Century Migration and Settlement

In addition to settling in the rural cities and towns like Nicodemus, African
Americans migrated to urban areas during the late nineteenth and early twen-
tieth centuries. Although by the end of the first decade of the twentieth century
San Francisco, Los Angeles, Seattle, Portland, and Denver had a combined
African-American population of approximately 18,000, they still migrated West
(Taylor 1999, p. 193; U.S. Census 1900). In San Francisco, Oakland, Portland,
Spokane, Seattle, and other urban areas, black men found positions as jani-

tors, porters, waiters, bartenders, restaurant kitchen helpers, counterworkers, chauffeurs, bellhops, busboys, and coat and hat checkers. Black women found work as cooks, janitors, hairdressers, manicurists, housekeepers, and waitresses. Most black women worked in private households as domestics.

Some blacks became entrepreneurs. They owned and operated their own auto body shops, laundromats, hotels, restaurants, taverns, construction companies, apartment buildings, and barbershops. Most of these businesses served both white and black clienteles. In these cities, as in most urban areas, some black-owned financial-service-oriented companies emerged. For example, by the early twentieth century, Golden State Mutual in Los Angeles became one of the nation's largest black-owned businesses.

As the black population continued to grow, its members formed the same kind of social, cultural, and religious institutions that existed in other parts of the country. These institutions forged alliances between the longtime residents and new arrivals that allowed them to endure or combat racism. Several black churches addressed the spiritual and social needs of San Francisco, Los Angeles, Seattle, Portland, Spokane, and other urban black communities. The churches sponsored picnics, dances, plays, carnivals, athletic teams, and literary clubs—social outlets that shaped and sustained the African-American community. Churches also formed and supported the social and political agenda of the black working class (Kelley 1993, p. 80).

Black pastors and churches united the community by extending their services throughout the community. In the early 1890s, Emma Ray, a member of Jones Street A.M.E. Church in Seattle, organized the women of her congregation into the Frances Harper division of the Women's Christian Temperance Union. The women worked in the city's red light district and at the King County Jail, assisting the indigent, criminals, prostitutes, and drug addicts of all races (Taylor 1994 p. 39).

Black churches also helped newcomers adjust to their new environment by helping them find employment and housing. More important, they directed them about how to avoid businesses that discriminated against blacks and how to conduct themselves in public. Following the advice of the established residents, most African-American migrants avoided jail or physical and verbal abuse.

In addition, the black church also served as an unofficial welfare agency for African Americans who needed financial assistance, especially during times of unemployment or bereavement. Spokane churches such as Calvary, Bethel A.M.E., and Morning Star maintained a "Sinking Fund" that helped its members pay off delinquent bills. Some churches donated money for heating fuel to members who needed it. At Christmas time, West Coast churches, including those of prominent ministers Father Divine and Daddy Grace, prepared and distributed food and clothing baskets to less fortunate families in Los Angeles.

Around the turn of the century several secular black groups, including, political clubs, fraternal organizations, cultural associations, social clubs, and literary societies, evolved from churches (ibid., pp. 136, 138). In San Francisco these included the Prince Hall Masons, the Amateur Literary and Drama Association, the Young Men's Union Beneficial Society, the Elliot

Literary Institute, and the West Indian Benevolent Association (Taylor 1999, p. 200). Often, those who did not belong to the same religious congregation nevertheless became members of the same club, fraternal order, or socialized at barbecues or dances or sporting events (Taylor 1994, p.136).

Next to churches, black fraternal orders had the most diverse membership in the West. The members of these strictly bourgeois organizations included people from all social, economic, and religious categories (ibid., p. 139). For example, on April 13, 1903, the all-black Inland Empire Number Three Masonic Lodge of Spokane, Washington, was founded (DeBow and Pitter 1927, p. 10). Its counterpart in Seattle had established ten lodges by the mid-1920s. Some of these orders that had women's auxiliaries included the Masons, the Odd Fellows, and the Knights of Pythias. The Spokane and Seattle Masons and other West Coast orders also aided their respective communities by providing financial assistance to individuals suffering from economic hardship. During the Great Depression, welfare agencies in Phoenix denied help to destitute black families. In response, the black residents of the city established the Phoenix Protective League, which collaborated with African-American fraternal organizations to help the poor (Taylor 1999, p. 228).

The women's auxiliary of the Masons, the Eastern Star, was an organization of black women. The organization adhered to a strict code of ethics that included a strong belief in God, honesty, charity, loving people in a Christian manner, protecting members during misfortune, promoting community growth, and understanding world events and the changing society. In cities like Spokane, the Eastern Star was primarily a charitable agency that provided hospice care and college scholarships, and also gave financial assistance and donated money to the March of Dimes. On the West Coast and nationally, the organization was one of the earliest supporters of the national civil rights struggle and of the National Association for the Advancement of Colored People.

Black women continued to be instrumental in improving social conditions in the West. Women's clubs contributed to the growth of the Los Angeles, Topeka, Pasadena, Berkeley, Denver, Kansas, and other Western urban communities. Many of these groups contained people who wanted to pursue their recreational, cultural, political, and social interests with others of the same race. In 1894 the Heart's Ease Circle of King's Daughters was formed in Austin, Texas, to create homes for elderly citizens. In Spokane, the Wednesday Art Club exhibited its artists' watercolor and oil paintings. The artist Mamie Lee was the curator of many of these exhibits. The club also featured its work at several national art exhibits, and its members won several first prizes. In 1936, the organization's greatest achievement occurred when it locally showed the Harmon Foundation's collection of several outstanding works by black artists.

The NAACP in the West

Black westerners participated in the burgeoning nationwide civil rights movement. A few years after the founding of the National Association for

African-American families lost everything in the Tulsa Race Riot of 1921, if not their lives. Many fled the city, not to return. Reparations to the families were never made and the perpetrators were never prosecuted. (*Library of Congress*)

the Advancement of Colored People (NAACP) in New York in 1910, African Americans in the West created local chapters of this leading black civil rights organization. Concerned blacks in San Francisco, Los Angeles, Houston, San Antonio, Topeka, Denver, Portland, Albuquerque, Salt Lake City, Boise, Omaha, Spokane, and other cities founded chapters. The Los Angeles NAACP branch led other Western cities such as Seattle, Portland, Denver, Dallas, Wichita, and Topeka in organized protests against the racist film *The Birth of a Nation* in 1915. As an alternative, organizations like the Universal Negro Improvement Association (UNIA) and National Urban League attracted thousands of loyal followers. Some black communities in Mill City, Texas, Colorado Springs, Colorado, and Ogden, Utah, had embraced the black nationalist message of Marcus A. Garvey and founded UNIA chapters. Los Angeles boasted the largest West Coast UNIA chapter. These organizations were committed to the protection and legal defense of black westerners (ibid., p. 242).

Moreover, these community institutions provided a stable base for West Coast blacks as they faced impending civil rights struggles. The NAACP and organizations like the National Urban League fought racial discrimination. Although African Americans in this part of the country experienced less outright violence than their Southeastern counterparts, sporadic outbursts of white rage were not unknown. During the "Red Summer" of 1919, twenty-five race riots claimed the lives of thousands of African Americans and inflicted millions in property damage. The summer of rioting began in Longview, Texas, when a mob of whites raided the black section of town, flogging a school principal, destroying homes and businesses, and forcing prominent blacks to flee. In 1921 lynch mobs in Tulsa, Oklahoma, killed scores of black residents and completely destroyed their communities.

Depression and World War II

Black migration to the West resumed during the Great Depression. Following the lead of black pioneers of the West, African Americans arrived during this period of economic crisis in search of racial equality and financial relief. President Franklin Delano Roosevelt signed into law an economic stimulus program known as the New Deal. The program created government agencies and projects to create jobs and strengthen the economy. The hope of benefiting from New Deal programs eluded most black westerners. However, some African Americans gained from Roosevelt's economic initiatives. In 1933, a small percentage of African-American enrollees in the Civilian Conservation Corps (CCC) began attending to the country's neglected woodlands. They fought fires, dug firebreaks, planted trees, restored parks and recreational areas, strung telephone and electrical wires, laid roads, truck trails, and airport runways, and erected lookout towers. In addition, some enrollees cultivated a cordial relationship with the neighboring white communities by participating in athletic competitions. Black enrollees often formed basketball and baseball teams, competing against local residents or other nearby white CCC camps (Mack 2003, pp. 236–245).

In no area did African-American corpsmen distinguish themselves more conspicuously than in construction. Since most enrollees had limited labor experience working outdoors before finding themselves in Montana, Utah, California, Oregon, or South Dakota, their accomplishments were all the more impressive. In predominantly white towns such as Libby and Troy, Montana, the minimally trained black corpsmen completed dozens of conservation projects. As their first major project, the enrollees in the Pipe Creek camp built an airport for the Libby community (ibid.; Cole 1999).

Undoubtedly, the African-American enrollees' hard work and dedication enriched the quality of life for the residents. Within a few years, they had transformed the West Coast's infrastructure. Furthermore, the use of African Americans in a predominantly white region indirectly improved race relations. Racism, however, brought their service in the white West Coast towns to a premature end. In 1934, racist local and federal government officials authorized a permanent transfer of all African-American enrollees from white towns. The legacy of the African-American enrollees is still visible in the structures they built and the forests they saved.

The new influx of blacks into the West generated a resurgence of violent racism. These tensions increased as more Southern blacks appeared. The newcomers were unaccustomed to the relative absence of social restrictions.

Under the tutelage of long-time residents many of the newcomers became integrated into the black community, but some continued to struggle.

White efforts to exclude blacks were relatively isolated, but frequent. Just as in the American South, in the West blacks were routinely denied service at most white-owned hotels, motels, restaurants, department stores, barbershops, beauty parlors, real estate and employment agencies, and nightclubs. Throughout Spokane and Pasco, Washington, for example, window signs reading "We Reserve the Right to Serve" and "We Won't Serve Colored" were not uncommon. Likewise, movie houses and public swimming pools in Los Angeles, Denver, Dallas, and Oklahoma City permitted blacks only in designated sections.

Western retail stores were known for making African Americans feel unwelcome. Some clerks served all of their white customers first. Many clothing stores would not allow black women access to dressing rooms to try on clothing, unless they purchased the clothing first. Some stores did not permit blacks to try on shoes before buying them. Finding a place to live could be very discouraging. In an attempt to exclude blacks, most real estate agencies and private home-sellers engaged in unfair housing practices. Restrictive housing covenants, the most popular method of excluding blacks from white neighborhoods, existed throughout the nation. These covenants consisted of language in property deeds of sale in which "owners agreed not to sell or lease to an undesirable." These covenants prevented countless numbers of blacks, Jews, Mexicans, Japanese, Chinese, and Indians from using or buying available tracts of land (To Secure These Rights 1947, p. 68). By the early 1940s, most of Los Angeles's blacks resided in Watts; Denver's settled in the Five Points District; Spokane restricted blacks to the eastern section of the city; and Phoenix's black population were relegated to the southwestern part of the city.

The U.S. entry into World War II encouraged more black migration to the West. As Americans successfully fought to promote freedom and democracy abroad, black Americans campaigned for a double victory: to secure and ensure their civil rights on the home front. For African Americans, the war brought a ray of hope that their appeal for racial equality would end racism. According to historian Neil A. Wynn: "[A]long with this desire of most blacks to fight for equal rights was the feeling that participation in the war effort would be rewarded; in fact the two were inextricably interwoven" (Wynn 1993, p. 101). However, the pleas of blacks who served in the armed forces and who sought upward mobility and racial justice were largely ignored. The "double victory" campaign failed to secure the civil rights of most blacks who lived in the South and the rest of the nation.

Nevada, Washington, Oregon, and California experienced the greatest black population growth. By 1945, most of these migrants lived in the urban cities of Seattle and Portland in the Pacific Northwest, and, in California, around San Francisco, Los Angeles, and San Diego. Black population growth ranged from 168 percent in Los Angeles to 798 percent in San Francisco (Taylor 1999, p. 251; Schmid 1968, pp. 911).

Comparably, between 1940 and 1950 the black population in Washington grew tremendously, from 7,424 to 30,691, a 312 percent increase.

Blacks migrated in large numbers to the cities of Seattle and Tacoma and even formed new communities in smaller western Washington cities like Pasco, Bremerton, and Vancouver. The influx brought significant changes, such as a "visible increase in black political influence in the larger cities, the strengthening of black civil rights organizations and black-related social groups, and the passage of civil rights and anti-discrimination legislation at the state level." Migration, however, caused "increased racial tension in many Washington cities and severe overcrowding in black residential areas, which accelerated the pace of the physical deterioration in those communities." Tensions arose between longtime residents and newcomers as they grappled for leadership positions in these newly expanded black neighborhoods (Taylor 1977, p. 65; Schmid 1968, p. 9).

In large part, black movement to the Pacific Northwest was part of a nationwide migration that reflected wartime and postwar employment opportunities. World War II created better economic conditions and thousands of African Americans, after decades of menial jobs, entered West Coast factories and shipyards. Moreover, a combination of increased wartime production, white worker shortages, and pressure from the federal government's Fair Employment Practices Committee (FEPC) allowed thousands of blacks to gain employment in defense-related industries, which were once closed to them. The Pacific Northwest region became a significant builder of aircrafts and ships. Some eighty-eight shipyards, twenty-nine in Seattle, constructed a variety of watercrafts for the navy, coast guard, and merchant marine. The largest Washington State companies included the Todd Shipbuilding Corporation of Tacoma and the Kaiser Company in Vancouver. Besides working in the defense industry, African Americans also came to the region to serve at military bases. The majority of Tacoma's African American population, for example, were soldiers and their families who lived on base at nearby Fort Lewis (Taylor 1977, pp. 65–66). Following the war, African Americans continued to migrate and settle in the Pacific Northwest and other urban West Coast areas.

The African-American presence in the West frontier disproves Turner's narrow thesis. Blacks migrated to the region as explorers, slaves, laborers, cowboys, and soldiers. Along with Caucasians, they contributed to taming and settling the West. As slaves, for example, blacks mined gold in California, and as explorers they opened the frontier for whites to settlement. Black migration to the West continued after 1865 and Reconstruction, through the Great Depression and World War II. During the years following the war, as African Americans in the West attempted to improve their own situation, they closely monitored press coverage of Southern resistance to African-American protests and the federal government's desegregation efforts. Black westerners mounted a similar frontal attack on racial discrimination during the 1950s and 1960s that paralleled the civil rights movement in the South. By the 1970s and 1980s, some African-American westerners benefited from the civil rights movement. Like their East Coast counterparts, blacks in the West were elected to important state and local political offices. In Spokane, in 1981, James Chase became the first African American to become mayor in Washington State. Chase's triumph and that of other blacks during the twentieth century drew upon the groundwork laid by African-American Western pioneers years earlier.

References and Further Reading

Beller, Jack. "Negro Slaves in Utah." *Utah Historical Quarterly* 2, no. 4 (October 1929): 122–126.

Berwanger, Eugene H. *The West and Reconstruction.* Chicago: University of Illinois Press, 1981.

Berwanger, Eugene H. "Reconstruction on the Frontier: The Equal Rights Struggle in Colorado, 1865–1867." In Monroe Lee Billington and Roger D. Hardaway, eds., *African Americans on the Western Frontier.* Niwot: University Press of Colorado, 1998.

———. *The Frontier Against Slavery: Western Anti-Negro Prejudice and the Slavery Extension Controversy.* Chicago: University of Illinois Press, 1967.

Betts, Robert B. *In Search of York: The Slave Who Went to the Pacific with Lewis and Clark.* Boulder: University Press of Colorado, 2002.

Billington, Monroe Lee, and Roger D. Hardaway, eds. *African Americans on the Western Frontier.* Niwot: University Press of Colorado, 1998.

Bleeg, Joanne Wagner. "Black People in the Territory of Washington." MA thesis, University of Washington, 1970.

Blenkinshop, Willis. "Edward Rose." In LeRoy Hafen, ed., *The Mountain Men and the Fur Trade.* Glendale, CA: Arthur H. Clark Company, 1972, vol. 9.

Bonner, Thomas D., ed. *Life and Adventures of James P. Beckwourth.* Lincoln: University of Nebraska Press, 1981.

Bringhurst, Newell G. "The Mormons and Slavery: A Closer Look." In Monroe Lee Billington and Roger D. Hardaway, eds., *African Americans on the Western Frontier.* Niwot: University Press of Colorado, 1998, 24–36.

Brown, Peter, to Alley Brown, December 1851, California-Oregon Collection, Missouri Historical Society, St. Louis, Missouri, quoted in Taylor, Quintard, *In Search of the Racial Frontier*, 84.

Campbell, Randolph B. *An Empire for Slavery: The Peculiar Institution in Texas, 1821–1865.* Baton Rouge: Louisiana State University Press, 1989.

Census Bureau. *Seventh Census of the United States, 1850.* Washington, DC: Robert Armstrong, Public Printer, 1853.

Census Bureau. *Twelfth Census of the United States, 1900, Population Part 1.* Washington, DC: U.S. Government Printing Office, 1901.

Christensen, James B. "Negro Slavery in the Utah Territory." *Phylon* 18, no. 3. (1957): 298–305.

Cole, Olen. *The African American Experience in the Civilian Conservation Corps.* Gainesville: University of Florida Press, 1999.

Coleman, Ronald. "A History of Blacks in Utah, 1825–1910." Ph.D. diss., University of Utah, 1980.

Debo, Angie. *And Still the Waters Run: The Betrayal of the Five Civilized Tribes.* Princeton: Princeton University Press, 1984.

DeBow, Samuel P., and Edward A. Pitter, eds. *Who's Who in Religious, Fraternal, Social, Civic and Commercial Life on the Pacific Coast.* Seattle: Searchlight Publishing Company, 1927.

deGraaf, Lawrence B., Kevin Mulroy, and Quintard Taylor, eds. *Seeking El Dorado: African Americans in California.* Seattle: University of Washington Press, 2001.

Durham, Philip, and Everett L. Jones. *The Negro Cowboys.* Lincoln: University of Nebraska Press, 1965.

Edwards, Malcolm Edwards. "The War of Complexional Distinction: Blacks in Gold Rush California and British Columbia." *California Historical Quarterly* 56, no. 1 (spring 1977): 34–45.

Foner, Eric. *A Short History of Reconstruction.* New York: Harper and Row Publishers, 1990.

Fowler, Arlen L. *The Black Infantry in the West, 1869–1891.* Norman: University of Oklahoma Press, 1996.

Franklin, John Hope, and Alfred A. Moss. *From Slavery to Freedom: A History of African Americans.* 8th ed. New York: McGraw Hill, 2000.

Franklin, William E. "The Archy Case: The California Supreme Court Refuses to Free a Slave." *Pacific Northwest Historical Review* 32 (May 1963): 137–154.

Fremont, John Charles. "A Report of the Exploring Expedition to Oregon and North California in the Years 1843–44." U.S. 28th Congress, 2d Session, House Document 166, December 2, 1844–March 3, 1845.

Gibbs, Mifflin W. *Shadow and Light: An Autobiography.* New York: Arno Press and the New York Times, 1868.

Hayden, Delores. "Biddy Mason's Los Angeles, 1851–1891." *California History* 68, no. 3 (fall 1989): 86–99.

Hayes, Ralph. *Northwest Black Pioneers: A Centennial Tribute.* Seattle: The Bon Marche Department Store, 1994.

Johnson, David Alan. *Founding the Far West: California, Oregon, and Nevada, 1840–1890.* Berkeley: University of California Press, 1992.

Katz, William Loren. *Black People Who Made the Old West.* New York: Thomas Y. Cowell Company, 1977.

Katz, William Loren. *The Black West.* Seattle, WA: Open Hand Publishing, 1987.

Kelley, Robin D. G. "We Are Not What We Seem: Rethinking Black Working-Class Opposition in the Jim Crow South." *Journal of American History* 80, no. 1(June 1993): 75–112.

Leckie, William H. *Buffalo Soldiers: A Narrative of the Negro Cavalry in the West.* Norman: University of Oklahoma Press, 2003.

Mack, Dwayne A. "'May the Work I've Done Speak for Me': African American Civilian Conservation Corps Enrollees in Libby and Troy, Montana, 1933–34." *Western Journal of Black Studies* 27, no. 4 (winter 2003): 236–245.

Marable, Manning. *Race, Reform, and Rebellion: The Second Reconstruction in Black America, 1945–1990.* Jackson: University Press of Mississippi, 1991.

National Association for the Advancement of Colored People, Branch Files, NAACP Spokane, Washington, Manuscript Division, Library of Congress, Washington, DC.

Painter, Nell Irvin. *Exodusters: Black Migration to Kansas after Reconstruction.* New York: W. W. Norton and Company, 1992.

Porter, Kenneth W. "Black Cowboys in the American West." In Monroe Lee Billington and Roger D. Hardaway, eds., *African Americans on the Western Frontier.* Niwot: University Press of Colorado, 1998, 110–127.

Ravage, John W. *Black Pioneers: Images of the Black Experience on the North American Frontier.* Salt Lake City: University of Utah Press, 1997.

The Report of the President's Committee on Civil Rights. *To Secure These Rights.* Washington, DC: United States Government Printing Office, 1947.

Savage, W. Sherman. *Blacks in the West.* Westport, CT: Greenwood Press, 1976.

Savage, W. Sherman. "Slavery in the West." In Monroe Lee Billington and Roger D. Hardaway, eds., *African Americans on the Western Frontier.* Niwot: University Press of Colorado, 1998, 7–23.

Schmid, Calvin F., Charles E. Nobbe, and Arlene E. Mitchell. *Non-White Races: State of Washington.* Olympia: Washington State Planning and Community Affairs Council, 1968.

Schwantes, Carlos A. The *Pacific Northwest: An Interpretive History.* Lincoln: University of Nebraska Press, 1996, 72–73.

Taylor, Quintard. "Migration of Blacks and Resulting Discriminatory Practices in Washington State between 1940 and 1950." *Western Journal of Black Studies* 2, no. 1 (1977), 65–71.

Taylor, Quintard. *The Forging of a Black Community: Seattle's Central District from 1870 through the Civil Rights Era.* Seattle: University of Washington Press, 1999.

Taylor, Quintard. *In Search of the Racial Frontier: African Americans in the American West, 1528–1990.* New York: Norton, 1998.

U.S. Census, *Seventh Census of the United States, 1850.* Washington, DC: Robert Armstrong Public Printer, 1853.

U.S. Bureau of the Census. *Eighth Census of the United States, 1860, Population.* Washington, DC: Government Printing Office, 1864.

U.S. Bureau of the Census. *Twelfth Census of the United States, 1900, Population Part 1.* Washington, DC: Government Printing Office, 1901.

White, Richard. *"It's Your Misfortune and None of My Own": A New History of the American West.* Norman: University of Oklahoma Press, 1991.

Wilson, Paul. Memorandum, Files *re Brown vs. Topeka Board of Education* (1954), 3–4, Kansas Historical Society.

Woods, Randall B. "Integration, Exclusion, or Segregation? The 'Color Line' in Kansas, 1878–1900." In Monroe Lee Billington and Roger D. Hardaway, eds., *African Americans on the Western Frontier.* Niwot: University Press of Colorado, 1998, 128–146.

Wynn, Neil A. *The Afro-American and the Second World War.* New York: Homes and Meier, 1993.

Asians and Asian Americans in the West | 8

Lisa Hsia

Introduction

From the early 1850s until the 1920s, almost 1 million Asians immigrated to the United States and Hawaii, mainly from China, Japan, Korea, India, and the Philippines. Asian immigrants first appeared in the United States at a crucial time in Western history. When the first Chinese came during the California Gold Rush, they entered territory that was still in the midst of rough-and-tumble frontier conditions. By the 1880s, when more Japanese began to arrive on the mainland, California (as well as Hawaii) was a rapidly transforming region. Many of the immigrants were workers, who played a major role in the development of the West as a region. In some places, in some industries, they made up the majority of the labor force. Some had been urged to come by recruiters who told them of opportunities in the United States. Their exertions were a significant contribution to the building of the West; yet, when it came time for recognition, they were often passed over.

All Asians who came to this country, not just the workers, found them-selves and their livelihoods limited by restrictions placed upon them by the larger U.S. society. Even the basics of survival were often denied them because of their race: by discriminatory legislation, immigration exclusion, or, where those failed or did not yet exist, threats and violence. White Americans had welcomed Asian labor, but beyond their labor, they were not yet willing to offer them a place in society. Motivated by a desire to keep the United States the way it was, and bolstered by a belief that Asians could never be successfully integrated into that society, they sought ways to prevent Asian immigrants from gaining a foothold in the United States.

The number of Asian Americans in this country's history has been numerically small, and chronologically recent, but the events and responses generated by their presence show that discriminatory sentiments have always lurked below the surface of democracy, equality, and all else that this country has promised to its people. But besides that, their story also shows the resilience of individuals and communities in the face of opposition, and how people found places for themselves in the West in spite of oppression and prejudice.

Who Were the Immigrants?

Until the Immigration Act of 1965 loosened restrictions on immigration, there were five main groups of Asians who came to the United States: Chinese, Japanese, Koreans, Asian Indians, and Filipinos. Because of various events in both their home countries and in the United States, these groups also fall fairly neatly into separate time periods. The Asians who came to the mainland United States during the nineteenth century were almost exclusively Chinese. Chinese immigrants began to come in the 1840s, but their numbers decreased sharply after the Chinese Exclusion Act of 1882. Other groups started to arrive in the early twentieth century, but until the 1920s, the Chinese remained by far the most numerous group of Asians in the United States. The Japanese, while they immigrated in large numbers to Hawaii from the 1880s onward, did not start coming to the mainland in significant numbers until after the turn of the century. Their immigration would be severely limited by the 1907 so-called Gentlemen's Agreement between the United States and Japan, then curtailed by the Immigration Act of 1924. Likewise, Koreans, Asian Indians, and Filipinos all started to immigrate to the mainland United States during the first decades of the twentieth century, but also suffered from immigration restrictions until their numbers, too, diminished. After the effective exclusion of Filipino immigrants with the Tydings-McDuffie Act in 1934, Asian immigration was extremely limited until 1965.

Chinese

The Chinese were the first group of Asians to immigrate to the mainland United States, as well as to Hawaii. Between the late 1840s, when the first Chinese joined the Gold Rush to California, and the early 1880s, when Chinese exclusion went into effect, roughly 370,000 Chinese immigrated to California and Hawaii. The first Chinese to set foot in the United States went to California; by 1860, nearly all the Chinese in the continental United States lived in that state. Within a decade, although they were still coming to California each year by the thousands, they had branched out to other states as well. By 1900, only about half of them lived in California (Chan 1991, p. 28).

Many factors combined to push Chinese to emigrate. From the 1840s onward, China was racked by political and religious upheaval as well as natural disaster, much of which directly affected the residents of southern regions of China—the areas from which most immigrants came. Between 1846 and 1850, a series of floods and droughts devastated food supplies and gave rise to widespread banditry. Added to this, in the 1850s, rebellions, uprisings, and ethnic warfare caused further instability and suffering. Many young men sought a better future for themselves and their families by migrat-

Chinese miner with sluice box in California. (*California Historical Society*)

ing abroad. They had heard of the Gold Rush in California; representatives of Western industries, who suffered from a shortage of white labor in the 1850s and 1860s, also recruited Chinese workers. In the late 1860s, heavy recruiting by the Central Pacific Railroad Company was partly responsible for a sharp upswing in emigration from China. Hawaii, independent until its 1898 annexation, boasted a profitable U.S.-dominated sugar industry that also attracted tens of thousands of Chinese laborers (ibid., p. 27).

At first, responses to the Chinese presence were favorable or neutral. In the highly diverse atmosphere of the Gold Rush, the foreign customs and appearance of the Chinese sparked curiosity and wonder in many European Americans. One man wrote in his diary in 1855:

> [The] Americans salute [the Chinese] all indiscriminately by the easy and euphonious appellation of "John," to which they reply as readily as if they

were addressed by their true names; and they . . . [apply] the same term to us, equally indiscriminately. A great number of them think "John" is the only name white people have . . . But their own vernacular cognomens . . . sound certainly very odd to occidental ears. The following may be taken as fair specimens: Kal Chow, Chum Fi, Yah Wah, Si Ta, Hom Fong, Dack Mung, Gee Foo. (Helper 1855, p. 91)

Nearly all Chinese who emigrated abroad at this time came from the same six regions of southeastern China. Most of those who ended up in California came from Guangdong Province, an area with a unique role as the center of Western trade in China. Within Guangdong emigrants, three subgroups were most prominent. The Sanyi (Sam Yup) people came from three districts north and west of Guangzhou (Canton). These districts were more urbanized than their counterparts, and people from these areas tended to become entrepreneurs: merchants, grocers, and so forth. The Siyi (Sze Yup) came from poorer districts to the south and west of Canton, and most of them worked as laborers. The vast majority of California's Chinese population were Sze Yup until the 1950s. The third subgroup were the Xiangshan (Heungsan) people, who came from a district between Canton and Macao and tended to work in agriculture (Chan 1991, p. 64). Although the immigrants all came from China, it is likely that they identified themselves as people of their particular region, rather than citizens of the larger country. The dialects they spoke were different, and there were differences in culture as well. When they began building communities in California, they would continue to separate themselves regionally, associating primarily with others who had come from the same place they had.

Most of the migrants were young men in the prime of their working life. They left wives and families behind when they left China, hoping to make enough money in America to provide for them from afar. These men have been characterized as "sojourners," not settlers, since many of them intended to stay in America only as long as was necessary to get back their economic footing. However, it was not always as easy to make a living in the United States as they expected it to be. One man later recalled: "Coming to America [was] one of the better ways perhaps to have a better future. So everybody told you it's good here. They don't tell you [about] the laundrymen, [or that] people work eighteen hours a day, they don't tell you this. They only tell you, it's a lot of gold, go and dig." Popular conceptions of the ease of making a fortune in the United States may have resulted from immigrants' unwillingness to reveal to their families the true nature of their work. For example, some laundrymen would say that they worked in clothing stores, instead of admitting to their relatives that the money they sent them came from washing other people's dirty clothes. One laundryman remembered how he felt before he emigrated: "When I heard about a chance to go to America, the hardship just didn't occur to me. All I got excited about was to take the chance—going to America! . . . Now I am here, I begin to feel America is work, work, work" (Hsu 2000, p. 53). Many immigrants, while they continued to send their earnings to their families, never saved up enough to return to China as they had hoped.

Many early Chinese immigrants came seeking their fortunes in the California Gold Rush. But within a decade of the initial discovery, the rush had subsided. Surface deposits of gold had been severely depleted, so that most independent prospectors could not glean much profit from them. Large mining companies turned to a new method, hydraulic mining, which extracted gold from the rock on a larger scale by means of directed, pressurized flows of water—at great cost to the environment. Chinese miners, however, did not have enough capital to invest in hydraulic mining, and they continued to mine the surface deposits by panning or digging. They remained in the mining districts for decades after the others had moved on.

Their lack of capital was not the only factor holding Chinese miners back. In 1852, the state legislature passed the Foreign Miners' Tax. Although the tax was, in theory, applicable to all foreign miners, it was most often enforced against the Chinese. (An 1850 version of the tax, which was repealed in 1851, was enforced primarily against Mexican miners.) Many tax collectors took advantage of their power to intimidate, rob, extort, or physically attack Chinese miners. By 1862, at least eleven Chinese miners were known to have been killed by collectors of the tax (Chan 1991, p. 48). Between 1850 and 1870, the Foreign Miners' Tax generated at least half of all California state revenues (Tchen 1984, p. 5).

Chinese found their way into two other important occupations during the Gold Rush, when the near-total lack of women meant that men would have to take on "women's work." Like white men, Chinese men had traditionally left the duties of cooking and washing clothing to women, but in California they saw these tasks as a means of survival. Chinese restaurants and laundries were both highly visible service jobs that catered to a large white clientele, so they served as sites for Chinese-white interaction on a regular basis.

From the beginning, Chinese restaurants developed a reputation for good food and low prices. On the Gold Rush frontier, goods could command far higher prices than they did in a more settled country: a drink that had cost five cents in St. Louis might go for fifty cents in San Francisco (Lee 1992, pp. 257–258). Hungry miners were grateful for the Chinese restaurants that provided them with generous helpings of food at decent prices. Although the restaurants quickly learned how to prepare and serve American food, many served Chinese food as well, and employed Chinese wait staff. Then as now, for many of their customers, restaurants served as an introduction to Chinese people and culture.

Alongside the success of their restaurants, Chinese soon became the most visible group in the laundry business. Many Chinese entered the business because, unlike stores or restaurants, the initial outlay of capital could be relatively small; also, laundrymen could run a successful trade without knowing much English. By 1860 there were almost 900 Chinese laundrymen in California, a number that shot up to 3,000 by 1870 and 5,000 a decade after that (Chan 1991, p. 33). Laundries provided a livelihood for many Chinese men, but the work was lonely and isolating. For anti-Chinese groups, laundries seemed to serve as a symbol of all Chinese businesses and people. Chinese laundries were often targets for violence or arson, and between

1870 and 1884 the San Francisco Board of Supervisors passed a series of discriminatory laws that hurt Chinese laundries but left white-owned laundries unaffected. Those laws were eventually declared unconstitutional, but the negative sentiments that had inspired them remained unchecked.

After the Gold Rush was over, large numbers of Chinese found work on the railroads. The transcontinental railroad, completed in 1869, was a major engineering feat and a milestone in the history of American transportation. It played an extremely important role in shaping U.S. history, by linking California and other Western states to the rest of the country. Before the railroad, goods and people often had to be transported by sea to get from the East Coast to the West; that meant a lengthy trip around South America (until the completion of the Panama Canal in 1914). Overland routes existed, but they were difficult and expensive to traverse. With completion of the first transcontinental railroad in 1869 and the second in the 1880s, people and goods could be moved overland quickly and cheaply, thus not only boosting the economy but also drastically shifting patterns of settlement across the nation.

The transcontinental railroad was built simultaneously from two ends: the Union Pacific Railroad built west from the Missouri River, and the Central Pacific built east from Sacramento. The Central Pacific's section was the more difficult to build, since it had to go through several mountain ranges.

The Central Pacific company first hired Chinese workers in 1865. Initially, many people were skeptical about their ability to do hard physical labor. (To this criticism, one Central Pacific official countered: "They built the Great Wall, didn't they?") Soon the company was hiring Chinese to do most of the work. Chinese workers received less pay than white Americans, and they all received the same wage regardless of skill level. The work was difficult and often very dangerous. In 1866 and 1867 the company had the men continue work even through heavy winter snowfalls. Many died or fell by the wayside, and their bodies remained frozen in the snow until they could be dug out for burial in the spring. In 1867, thousands of Chinese workers went on strike. "Eight hours a day good for white men, all the same good for Chinamen," they said, demanding more pay, a limited work day (from eight to ten hours), and a stop to whippings from overseers. After a week, the strike failed. "I stopped the provisions on them," said a company superintendent, "stopped the butchers from butchering, and used such coercive measures" (Takaki 1998, p. 86). For want of food, the men were forced to resume work. After that, the company prepared to have black workers ready as strikebreakers in case of another strike.

When work ended in 1869, Chinese were not invited to the completion ceremonies. Almost 10,000 Chinese workers were now unemployed. Most of them sought whatever jobs were available, since they could not afford to ride the train back to California (and they were not allowed to ride for free) (Chan 1991, p. 32).

California's success in agriculture also owed much to Chinese labor. In the Sacramento and San Joaquin deltas, Chinese laborers performed the strenuous task of making the swampy marshland fit for cultivation. The *Overland Monthly* recognized their accomplishments in 1869: "The descendants of the people who drained those almost limitless marshes on either

side of their own swiftly flowing Yellow River, and turned them into luxuriant fields, are able to do the same thing on the banks of the Sacramento
and the San Joaquin" (Takaki 1998, p. 89). Often standing up to their waists
in water, using equipment as basic as shovels, Chinese workers drained the
marshes and built irrigation networks, dikes, ditches, and levees.

Most Chinese did not own their farms, working instead for other people.
Large growers liked to hire Chinese contract laborers because it was easy
to arrange for them. Instead of talking to individual independent workers,
they made negotiations with Chinese crew leaders or labor contractors, who
provided a given number of workers for a lump sum. Chinese workers were
also easier to support, since they boarded themselves (by cooking for themselves, or pooling money to hire a cook) and used their own tents (or none
at all) (Chan 1991, p. 32). They grew, picked, and packed fruit on farms and
orchards. By the 1880s, Chinese made up more than half of California's agricultural labor force (Matsumoto 1993, p. 20). Many Chinese tenant farmers
specialized in labor-intensive vegetables, fruits, and nuts. Some were farm
cooks, and others made a living selling other growers' crops (including those
of white farmers).

From the 1860s onward, Chinese in towns and cities all along the Pacific
Coast found jobs in light manufacturing. During the 1860s, Chinese workers
made up almost half of the workforce in the four most important industries
in San Francisco: boots and shoes, woolens, cigars and tobacco, and sewing.
By 1872, nearly half of the workers employed in all of San Francisco's factories were Chinese (Takaki 1998, p. 87).

Japanese

Until the time of exclusion, the Chinese were virtually the only Asians living
in the mainland United States. However, in the last decades of the nineteenth
century, Japanese also began to immigrate. During the late 1860s, Japan's
Meiji government began programs of "Westernization" and modernization. As a part of those efforts, the government encouraged people to move
abroad. The first of these went to Hawaii, Guam, and California in 1869, but
they met with such hardship and bad treatment that emigration ceased until
1885. After that, it started up again. The numbers on the mainland were far
smaller than those in Hawaii, where the Japanese population surpassed the
Chinese early in the twentieth century, but they grew steadily. By the early
twentieth century, the Japanese began to attract much of the same kind of
discriminatory sentiment that had led to the exclusion of the Chinese.

As late as 1900, only about 2,000 Japanese lived on the mainland, for
movement to Hawaii constituted the bulk of early Japanese emigration
(ibid., pp. 44–45). In the two decades following the turn of the century, however, the numbers increased. From 1902 to 1906, about 34,000 Japanese left
Hawaii for the mainland, while others came from Japan (Chan 1991, p. 37).
Like the Chinese, most Japanese emigrants originated from the same place,
a small area of southwest Japan that included prefectures on Honshu and
Kyushu islands (however, this area was not as poverty-stricken as China's
Guangdong Province). Japanese laborers were recruited for work in railroad

companies and lumber mills and on farms along the Pacific Coast. By 1920, Japanese outnumbered Chinese on the mainland.

Although the Japanese arrived too late to take advantage of the Gold Rush, they were able to find work in many other areas. Agriculture would soon become their primary occupation. Chinese workers had long constituted the bulk of California's agricultural labor force, but after their exclusion in 1882, Japanese workers took their place. The first Japanese to enter the California migrant farm workforce were students, harvesting crops over their summer vacation. Over time, the number of Japanese working in other industries declined as most of them turned to agricultural jobs. By 1910, agricultural work would become the dominant occupation of Japanese immigrants, employing two-thirds of them in California (about 16,000 people), and still more in other states (ibid., p. 38). Over the next decade, this number stayed more or less the same: while the Gentlemen's Agreement cut off the immigration of more male workers, immigrants maintained the continuity of their community by sending for wives and younger relatives from Japan.

Japanese farmworkers met discrimination early on, but they fought back. In Oxnard, California, Japanese and Mexican farmworkers joined together in a Japanese-Mexican Labor Association (JMLA). In 1903 more than a thousand JMLA members went on strike against the growers, protesting wage cuts and a new labor contracting system. Two secretaries of the organization, one Japanese and one Mexican, prepared a statement on the strike:

> Many of us have family, were born in the country, and are lawfully seeking to protect the only property that we have—our labor. It is just as necessary for the welfare of the valley that we get a decent living wage, as it is that the machines in the great sugar factory be properly oiled—if the machines stop, the wealth of the valley stops, and likewise if the laborers are not given a decent wage, they too, must stop work and the whole people of this country suffer with them. (Takaki 1998, pp. 198–199)

Although four workers were injured during the strike and one worker was killed, the strike was eventually successful. Afterward, the Mexican secretary of the JMLA applied for the organization to become part of the American Federation of Labor (AFL). However, AFL president Samuel Gompers would not grant a charter to an organization that had Asian members. (This was not the first time that Gompers had spoken out against Asian labor. In 1902 he had written a pamphlet dramatically entitled: "Meat vs. Rice: American Manhood against Asiatic Coolieism. Which Shall Survive?" In it, he asserted that white and Asian workers could never exist alongside one another, and therefore Asian workers must be expelled.) Although the AFL refused to grant the new union admission, the episode was important for the way in which two Western ethnic groups came together to work in solidarity for the same cause.

For many Japanese farm laborers, the end goal of their work was to own land. Many of the immigrants had come from agricultural backgrounds in Japan, where farming was a well-respected occupation. Most of them started out as tenant farmers and slowly worked their way up until they had land of their own, saving their wages and often pooling their resources. One famously successful Japanese farmer was Kinji Ushijima, later known

George Shima, known as the "Potato King," plows land, ca. 1900. (*Agricultural Laborers in California, 1905.02724, The Bancroft Library, University of California, Berkeley*)

as George Shima, or the "Potato King." Shima came to the United States in 1887. He worked as a potato picker in the San Joaquin valley, then became a labor contractor. Soon he leased and then purchased his own land in that region, draining and diking the swampy land the way Chinese laborers had done earlier. By 1912, he owned 10,000 acres of potatoes (ibid., p. 192). Shima's success epitomizes the dream of many Japanese farm laborers. For them, farming promised greater opportunities for advancement than many other industries—that is, until the first alien land law in 1913 prevented Asians from owning land. Still, many found loopholes in the laws and maintained control of their land. Japanese farm production reached a peak in 1917 because of the demands of World War I (Chan 1991, p. 38).

Having come to the mainland United States after Chinese exclusion, the Japanese realized the precarious position of Asians in America, and they struggled to present a positive image. In the early years, Japanese immigrants did receive better treatment than the Chinese, in part because of the difference between the two nations' status. Japan was a more powerful country than China, and the U.S. government did not wish to antagonize it. Nevertheless, even that fact could not stop the ever-increasing tide of anti-Asian sentiment. People grew more and more vociferous on the subject of Japanese immigration. Finally, in 1907, the United States negotiated a Gentlemen's Agreement with Japan to limit immigration. Under the terms of this agreement, Japanese laborers could no longer immigrate to the United States, but the laborers who were already living on U.S. soil could send for their wives to join them.

Koreans, Indians, and Filipinos

Three other groups of Asians immigrated to the United States in the early years of the twentieth century. They came in smaller numbers than the Chinese or

Japanese, but their general trajectory was the same. Most of them came to the United States seeking opportunities for economic advancement, and they worked in a variety of occupations upon arrival. But before long, they too would be caught by the flood of anti-Asian feeling and would find themselves barred from entering the country.

For a long time, Korea, like Japan, was closed to the outside world. It closed its borders after suffering Japanese and Manchurian invasions during the late sixteenth and early seventeenth centuries and began interacting with other nations again only during the 1860s. In 1876, a treaty between Korea and Japan granted Japan some trade rights within Korea. After that first treaty, others followed: Korea made a treaty with the United States in 1882, and then Great Britain, Germany, Russia, Italy, and France. Shortly after the turn of the century, Koreans began to emigrate abroad, mostly to other areas of Asia and the Russian maritime provinces, but also to Hawaii, where sugar planters and Christian missionaries encouraged them to come. U.S. Protestant missionaries had begun to proselytize in Korea not long after the United States and Korea signed their treaty, and they had gained many followers. Of the 7,000 emigrants who left Korea between 1902 and 1905, 40 percent were Christian converts. About 1,000 of those would eventually find their way to the U.S. mainland (ibid., p. 15).

Unlike the Chinese and Japanese immigrants, who had come from concentrated areas in their homeland, Koreans came from all over their country, especially seaports and their vicinities. They were mostly laborers, former soldiers, or artisans, though many of them became agricultural contract laborers or tenant farmers once they reached the United States. Many of those who emigrated for religious reasons brought their families with them to resettle in a Christian country. But the Korean government put a stop to emigration in 1905, and subsequent laws in the United States soon barred all Asians from entering this country, so the Korean American population during this time remained very small.

As with Koreans, the number of Asian Indians in the United States during this early period was very low. Most of them came from the same region of northwestern India, Punjab, which had been annexed by the British in 1849. They came to the United States in search of work, paying their own passage and traveling mostly in small bands of several individuals. Most were men (fewer than twelve Indian women had immigrated to the United States before World War II!) of the Sikh religion; some of them had left their wives behind in India, as many Chinese men had also done (p. 104). They settled in scattered locations throughout the West and worked in agricultural jobs, lumbering, and on railroads.

Indian immigrants were received curiously by the white population. They were not clearly Asian in the way that the Chinese or Japanese were, and yet they were not white or black. Their traditional dress also set them apart, since turbans were a highly visible requirement of the Sikh religion. While many people recognized that their stature and features marked them as Caucasian, popular conceptions of their "inferior" character led them to be categorized with other Asians, and they suffered the same racism, violence, and discrimination. The Immigration Act of 1917 invalidated all question of their racial or ethnographic status by drawing an imaginary line through the continent of Eurasia and prohibiting entry to the people of all countries to the east of that line, including India (p. 55).

Like Indians, Filipino immigrants presented a special challenge to anti-Asian groups, though not for the same reasons. Ever since the 1570s, the Philippines had been a Spanish colony. However, when the Spanish American War ended in 1898, the United States acquired the islands in the peace settlement. Filipino nationalists resisted the U.S. presence, and the Philippine-American War ensued, with the two nations fighting several years of guerrilla warfare in the Philippines. In the end, however, the Philippines remained a U.S. possession. That gave Filipino immigrants a different status than all other Asian immigrants.

In the first three decades of the twentieth century, many thousands of Filipinos poured into Hawaii and the mainland United States; in Hawaii, especially, they were heavily recruited by sugar planters after other Asians had been excluded. By the 1920s, Filipinos would be the largest ethnic group in both the Hawaiian plantation and the Pacific Coast farm labor force, and they would endure racism and discrimination just as terrible as that of all the Asians who had come earlier (p. 39). In 1934 the Tydings-McDuffie Act gave the Philippines their independence, thus ending Filipinos' privileged immigration status as U.S. nationals and drastically curtailed the entry of Filipino immigrants.

Ethnic Enclaves and Community Formation

Patterns of settlement and community-building among Asian immigrants were different from those that had developed in their homelands. They had to be, for conditions in the United States were different. Instead of building the kinds of villages that many of them had known back home, the constant danger of racism led them to settle in clusters for protection. Ethnic enclaves, such as Chinatowns, could be confining, since they prevented their residents from interacting fully with the larger society, and confined them to limited areas. But enclaves also provided security and community. Within these boundaries, immigrants knew that they would be among other people who looked like them and spoke their language, where familiar customs and things existed. Street and shop signs were written in their native language. Buildings were constructed to resemble traditional architecture and were decorated accordingly. Residents could spend time talking with friends, eat their favorite comfort foods, or buy newspapers with the latest news of the home country. They enjoyed a freedom that they could not find in the outside world, for here they were not constantly reminded that they were different-looking and unwelcome foreigners. Outsiders who visited Chinatowns and other enclaves often felt that they had been transported away from the United States—which was a large part of the appeal for enclave residents.

The oldest and largest Chinatown in North America was in San Francisco. Its construction began in the 1850s, and within a couple of decades

Fish merchant weighs fish in Chinatown, ca. 1900. (*Library of Congress*)

it was a thriving community. Like other ethnic enclaves all over the West, San Francisco's Chinatown was both haven and confinement for its residents. However, unlike many of the smaller Chinatowns, it also developed a highly successful tourist trade. Other westerners considered San Francisco's China-town a mysterious, perhaps dangerous, maze of opium dens, gambling houses, and places of prostitution, navigable only by the Chinese residents—or by licensed (non-Chinese) guides who profited from taking tourists around the neighborhood. With its Chinese signs and architecture, men in traditional clothing and queues, and shops selling curios and other Chinese goods, China-town appealed to these visitors as something exotic. When Chinatown was destroyed in the earthquake and fire of 1906, many white residents cam-paigned to stop it from being rebuilt, but eventually it was.

Besides creating Chinatowns, "Little Tokyos," and other enclaves, Asians also relied on ethnic associations for support, strength, and social networking. These associations were usually centered around common ties, such as place of origin, dialect, kinship, or religion; or common interests, as with political groups and trade guilds. Such organizations provided their members with critical assistance and support in times of need, and they also served as venues for social interaction within the community. Associational leadership posi-tions gave individuals the chance to rise in status within the ethnic commu-nity, but also outside of it, as associations helped to arrange communication between immigrant communities and the larger society. Chinese, Japanese, and Korean immigrants all formed associations, and though these varied in their roles within their communities, they all had a lasting impact.

For Chinese immigrants, the most important associations were those based on common place of origin. Chinese tended to settle with other people from their same district, so they formed district associations, called *huiguan*. As early as 1851, two district associations existed in San Francisco: the Sanyi Huiguan (Sam Yup Association), also known as the Canton Company, and the Siyi Huiguan (Sze Yup Association). Similar to these were kinship-based associations based on family or clan lineage. Each type served a similar function for its members. They were there when new immigrants arrived, to help them with adjusting to their new life: they met them at the docks and provided temporary housing for them in association-owned buildings. Then, when the immigrants had found work, they helped prepare them with equipment and advice. They took care of people who were ill or indisposed, and helped immigrants to send letters or money back to China. They also saw to the continuation of traditional rites by building altars and temples, and maintaining cemeteries. Associations provided economic assistance as well, largely through rotating credit associations (members pooled funds regularly, then took turns using the money). Before long, the huiguan decided to unite for greater strength. In 1862 officers from the six California huiguan drew together representatives from each to form a loose organization, which whites called the Six Chinese Companies. Twenty years later, in response to the Exclusion Act and encouragement from the San Francisco Chinese consul general, community leaders formed an even stronger coalition called the Zhonghua Huiguan (Chinese Consolidated Benevolent Association), or the Chinese Six Companies. Throughout the 1880s, other Consolidated Chinese Benevolent Associations were founded in other areas, including Portland and Seattle. These all looked to the San Francisco organization for leadership (p. 66).

It was partly the organizational structure of these associations that made community structure in the United States different from that in China. In China, the elite class was composed of scholar-gentry, but in the United States merchants rose to the top. The leadership positions in almost all Chinese organizations were occupied by merchants. They were the wealthiest occupational class among Chinese immigrants, and they also enjoyed a privileged status under the terms of the 1882 Exclusion Act. Hence, in the United States they became the leaders and frequent spokespeople for their communities.

Besides the huiguan and kinship associations, Chinese also formed organizations based on common interests. Fraternal orders, known as *tangs,* or *tongs,* were among the most important of this type of organization. Tong members swore brotherhood to one another and held secret initiation rites. Many of them had participated in similar organizations in China, called triads. Soon tongs would become infamous outside of the Chinese community because of some of their violent activities in the Chinese immigrant underworld.

Other common-interest groups were not so notorious, but just as important. Craft and labor guilds, which had a long history in China, were already in existence in San Francisco by the 1860s (p. 67). There were guilds for shoemakers and cigarmakers, but the laundrymen's guild, the Tongxingtang (Tung Hing Tong), was the most effective. It decreased competition by standardizing prices, and helped increase each laundry's chances of success by dividing up neighborhoods among members. It also played an important role in fighting anti-Chinese laundry laws by raising money and hiring lawyers to defend its members. The laundrymen's guild scored a major triumph in 1886 in the *Yick Wo v. Hopkins* case. When some 200 Chinese laundrymen resisted a new ordinance that discriminated against them, the guild hired a well-known trial lawyer to defend them in a class action suit. The Supreme Court ruled in their favor, citing the Fourteenth Amendment's guarantee of equal protection under the law.

Like the Chinese, the Japanese also formed many associations. Their counterpart to the Chinese huiguan were the *kenjinkai*, prefectural associations, and they also served both aid and social functions. After 1893 they also set up trade associations, including agricultural associations. These would be very important in Japanese immigrant life as more and more immigrants entered agricultural work. Like the other associations, these served two main functions. They sponsored social functions, such as picnics, fairs, festival celebrations, and youth groups, and they also provided vital support to their members. They helped the agricultural community to unite by bringing together Japanese growers, merchants, wholesalers, and retailers, and they created channels of communication for sharing information and research. Many of the men who served as officers in these associations took on elite status within their communities.

The most important Japanese-American institution to exist before World War II was the Japanese Association of America, founded in 1908. Like the Chinese Six Companies, it was founded right after exclusion (in the Japanese case, the 1907 Gentlemen's Agreement), and many of its activities centered around fighting discriminatory laws. The association's headquarters in San Francisco covered members' activities in northern and central California and Nevada; during the decade beginning in 1910, other chapters were founded in behalf of Japanese in southern California, Oregon, Idaho, Washington, Montana, New Mexico, and Arizona. Eventually, the organization would expand still further to include Colorado, Utah, Texas, Illinois, and New York.

Families, Women, and Children

In early Asian communities, particularly among the Chinese, family formation was slow. Before exclusion there were only about 9,000 Chinese women in the continental United States, and many were prostitutes. Because of the skewed sex ratio, there were not many families among early Chinese population. In addition, antimiscegenation laws meant that Asians could not seek marriage partners outside their ethnic group. At California's 1878 constitutional convention, one delegate expressed a common belief when he declared that a child of Chinese and white parents would be "a hybrid of the most despicable, a mongrel of the most detestable that has ever afflicted the earth" (Okihiro 1994, p. 51). Antimiscegenation laws affected all Asians, but among Japanese and Korean immigrants the sex ratio was more even and there were more families.

Many of the women who emigrated were prostitutes, especially in the early stages of Chinese immigration. Some were independent prostitutes or madams, but from the 1850s to the 1870s most Chinese prostitutes were bonded women who had been sold, kidnapped, or tricked into prostitution. Upon arrival in the United States, they took up work in squalid conditions. Among the worst were those in the "cribs," four-by-six-foot cells at street level from which the women called out their prices to passersby: "Two bittee lookee, flo bittee feelee, six bittee doee!" The men who owned and controlled them took their earnings, but kept them fed, clothed, and housed in the most basic way, thus extracting as much profit as they could (Takaki 1998, p. 122).

White Americans objected strongly to the existence of Chinese prostitutes, even though the women catered to white men as well as Chinese. The Gold Rush had brought prostitutes of all nationalities to San Francisco, but the Chinese prostitutes received undue attention, for they were seen as evidence of Oriental depravity. Many saw them as erotically exotic, passive by nature and sexually submissive. In 1866, the San Francisco board of health recommended that Chinese prostitutes live only in certain areas outside of the city limits, doing their best to confine what they could not eradicate (Chan 1991, p. 56).

The prevalence of Chinese prostitutes had a negative effect on all Chinese women. The U.S. government's first significant attempt to stop the immigration of Chinese prostitutes was the Page Law of 1875. This law prohibited the entry of Asian (at this time mostly Chinese) prostitutes, felons, and contract workers. Thereafter, since prostitutes were not allowed into the country, immigration officials became more vigilant about checking every entering Chinese woman to determine if she was a prostitute—that is to say, all Chinese women were now suspected of being prostitutes. Between 1875 and 1885, fewer than 1,400 Chinese women were allowed into the country, and those who were allowed in were subjected to humiliating scrutiny of their character (ibid., p. 105). The lack of women in the Chinese immigrant community severely limited the community's growth.

For the immigrant women who were not prostitutes, life in the United States was still difficult. The necessities of making a living meant that nearly all of them worked, except the well-to-do merchants' wives. However, there were few opportunities for waged work outside of the home, so they found ways to make money while staying at home. Some of them took in laundry or sewing, while others cooked or took in boarders. Others raised flowers, vegetables, or chickens, in the yard or even in the house—some women grew bean sprouts in the bathtub. At the same time, married women had to care for the household and raise children. The sex ratio among Asians in the United States deprived most women of the female companionship they had enjoyed in their home countries, and their confinement within the home isolated them still further.

Lalu Nathoy

When the first Asian immigrants came to the West, they often faced the harsh physical conditions of the frontier as well as the mental and spiritual ordeal of discrimination and oppression. That was true for the men who made up the vast majority of this population, but it was perhaps even more true for the few women who found their way here in the early years. Even more than their male counterparts, women found very limited opportunities to pursue their own livelihoods, and much more so than men, were in positions of dependence and physical vulnerability. But even within these circumstances, women found ways to shape their own lives into lasting testaments to their strength and character.

Lalu Nathoy was one of these pioneer women. She was born in 1853, the daughter of poor farmers in northern China. When she was eighteen years old, a long drought drove her desperate parents to sell her to bandits in exchange for two bags of seed, which they hoped would save the rest of the family. When she arrived in San Francisco in 1872, she was auctioned off as a slave. An old man named Hong King bought her for $2,500 and brought her to the Idaho mining town of Warrens, where he kept a saloon. There, Lalu was renamed Polly and put to work in the saloon.

The vast majority of Chinese women in the western United States at this time were smuggled in as prostitutes, and that may have been the purpose for which Polly was intended. It is likely, though not certain, that Polly served Hong King in that respect, though she also cooked, cleaned, and served food and drinks in his saloon. In this way, King's customers came to know Polly. They admired both her beauty and her sense of humor, and she earned a good reputation among them.

Polly developed a special friendship with one of the men in Warrens, another saloon keeper named Charlie Bemis. Bemis helped to protect and support Polly whenever she felt threatened or overwhelmed at King's saloon, and she in turn helped him with some household duties. Bemis slept in a room behind his saloon, and after Polly noticed how messy it was, she went over from time to time to tidy it up. According to local legend, Bemis won Polly's freedom for her in a poker game with Hong King. By the 1880s, Polly and Bemis were living together.

Through her relationship with Charlie Bemis, Polly gained much more control over her own life. After she was freed, she became financially independent through Bemis's assistance and her own initiative. She took in miners' laundry, taking care to mend their clothes before she washed them—a gesture that they appreciated. She also earned a fine reputation for hospitality. Bemis built her a two-story boarding house close to his own saloon, with a bedroom, a sitting and dining room, and a kitchen. She learned to cook the local fare by watching the white women cook in Warrens, and her food was especially popular among young people.

Over time, Polly and Bemis built a comfortable life together. In 1894 they were married, even though Idaho law prohibited the marriage of whites to nonwhites. (The justice of the peace who officiated over their ceremony was himself married to an Indian woman.) Two

Inasmuch as there were few women among Asian immigrants, there were not many children. Where children existed, though, they encountered the same prejudice and discrimination that affected their parents. A colored school for black children had been established in San Francisco in the 1850s, and by 1859 the city had also started a school for Chinese children. After the school closed because of low enrollment, there were not many educational options

years later, Polly obtained a certificate for legal residence in the United States. Polly and Bemis then moved about seventeen miles away from Warrens, to a site on the Salmon River. There they set up a garden and orchard, and raised chickens, ducks, cows, and horses. Polly also grew herbs for the two Chinese doctors who lived in Warrens. Bemis returned to Warrens every so often to sell their produce.

Before long, the Bemis's ranch became known as Polly's Place. The couple was as well loved in their new home as they had been in Warrens, especially Polly. Bemis helped to ferry people across the river, and often invited them to spend the night at Polly's Place. When they departed, Polly gave them pies, cakes, and produce, for their own enjoyment, and to be delivered to their old friends in Warrens. When people were injured or ill Polly cared for them, and she came to be as well respected for her nursing skill as for her personality.

By all accounts, Polly was a strong-willed and physically tough woman who proved well able to withstand the rugged conditions of her life in Idaho. While she was keeping her boarding house in Warrens, she once responded to boarders' complaints about her coffee by brandishing a butcher knife and asking, "Who no like my coffee?" (McCunn 1981, p. 318). After moving to the Salmon River, she hunted with Bemis and went fishing with worms she slipped into her apron pocket while working in the garden. When she and Bemis found an orphaned cougar cub on one of their hunting trips, they brought it home. Polly nailed a metal plate to the table, and the cougar ate there alongside

visitors to the ranch. If the cougar frightened visitors, Polly would take it outdoors.

Even in the later years of her life, Polly remained active. She survived her husband by more than a decade, continuing to live on the river up until her death. Charlie Bemis died in 1922, after several years of being bedridden from illness. Her neighbors brought her back to Warrens, thinking that she might be happier there. Indeed, Polly was well acquainted with many of the town's residents, and children were especially fond of her. She boarded many children from outlying areas at her cabin when they came in to Warrens to go to school. But she grew homesick for her riverside home, and one day she decided to return there, walking the entire seventeen miles back to the ranch. Back at the river she made a deal with her neighbors, in which she offered them her property in exchange for their assistance in helping her to live out the rest of her life there. They built her a single-room cabin, and furniture for it, and Polly lived there until she died in 1933. Although it has been many years since Polly's death, her presence remains. In 1987, the Department of the Interior and the governor of Idaho honored Polly's role as one of the pioneers of the region. Her cabin, which still stands, is now a museum and a dedicated historic site.

References

McCunn, Ruthanne Lum. *Thousand Pieces of Gold*. Boston: Beacon Press, 1981.
McCunn, Ruthanne Lum. *Chinese American Portraits: Personal Histories 1828–1988*. Seattle: University of Washington Press, 1988.

for Chinese children. They had to turn to private tutors, or the English and Bible classes that Protestant missionaries taught in Chinatown (ibid., p. 57).

In 1884, Joseph and Mary Tape challenged school segregation in behalf of their daughter Mamie. The Tapes were an unusual couple for the time. Joseph Tape had immigrated to the United States at the age of thirteen, cut his queue, and adopted U.S. clothes and manners. Mary had come to San

Francisco from China with missionaries when she was eleven. She had been brought up by the Ladies' Relief Society and spoke very little Chinese. Both Tapes spoke excellent English. Since they did not live in Chinatown, it was not convenient for them to send Mamie to the Bible schools that were held there. When they tried to enroll her in a white public school and she was refused, they took their case to court (McCunn 1988, p. 41).

As the months passed, the city's educational authorities kept finding new reasons to keep Mamie out of the schools, including insisting that classes were full. Mary Tape wrote a furious letter to the Board of Education in 1885, berating them for their treatment of her daughter:

> I see that you are going to make all sorts of excuses to keep my child out of the Public Schools. Dear Sirs, will you please tell me! Is it a disgrace to be born a Chinese? Didn't God make us all!!! What right! have you to bar my children out of the school because she is a chinese Descend . . . Do you call that a Christian act . . . You have expended a lot of the Public money foolishly, all because of one poor little Child. Her playmates is all Caucasians ever since she could toddle around. If she is good enough to play with them! Then is she not good enough to be in the same room and studie with them? . . . It seems no matter how a Chinese may live and dress so long as you know they Chinese then they are hated as one. There is not any right or justice for them . . . I will let the world see sir What justice there is When it is govern by the Race prejudice men! (Yung 1995, p. 49)

Finally, later that year, a new Oriental school was built for Chinese children, and Mamie was enrolled there. At first, this school was the subject of great public curiosity: so many people came to see it that classes were disrupted until the teacher set aside one day per week to satisfy their curiosity. But the visitors had not come to see neat, clean, well-behaved Chinese children wearing Western clothing and doing schoolwork in fluent English, and they soon lost interest in visiting. Chinese children in many areas of California (including San Francisco) were still being educated in segregated schools until the 1930s (Chan 1991, p. 58).

Many Methods of Discrimination

Like many other immigrants, Asians were subjected to intense prejudice, discrimination, and outright violence. The privileged category of "white" racial status has evolved over the years to encompass an increasing number of ethnicities; nearly all groups of European immigrants experienced violent opposition from the native-born American population when they first came to the United States. In that sense, Asian immigrants shared their struggles against intolerance with almost all Americans.

But Asian immigrants' experience also differed from that of European immigrants in a very significant way. While the latter were able to fight nativism and prejudice through political mobilization, for Asians those avenues were closed. Because they could not become naturalized citizens until the 1940s or later, Asian immigrants were particularly vulnerable; their inability to become citizens meant that they could not vote and therefore had very little political power.

It is perhaps a result of this fact that in these early years, Asian immigrants were the subject of many different types of discrimination. From legal restrictions to economic inequality, from Eurocentric attitudes to racialized violence, they were constantly impeded and threatened in their daily survival. That is not to say they never fought back. Often, not even the most dedicated or courageous fighters could escape the overwhelming odds stacked against them, but in spite of the limited resources available to them, Asian immigrants resisted the constraints that society attempted to place upon them.

The workplace was a locus for controversy over Asian migration, especially Chinese migration. Particularly in urban areas, white workers resented Chinese workers' willingness to work for significantly lower wages. In one factory in 1876, Chinese were paid ninety cents per day, when even child workers—the lowest class of white laborer—were paid one dollar per day (Nee 1972, p. 45). Chinese were also frequently called in to serve as strikebreakers. As the economy worsened, white workers' resentment deepened. In the cigar industry, manufacturers who employed white workers began to distinguish their products with a label: "The cigars herein contained are made by WHITE MEN. This label is issued by authority of the Cigar Makers' Association of the Pacific Coast" (Saxton 1971, p. 74). Soon, other manufacturers were using similar labels on their products, and businessmen committed to "anti-coolieism" began to display placards with similar messages on their premises. By 1890, white boycotts of Chinese-made goods had succeeded in effectively eliminating them from the market (Chan 1991, p. 40). The discrimination Chinese faced on the job was a symptom of a larger issue. As the nineteenth century progressed, white Americans became more and more vehement about expelling the Chinese in their midst. Prejudice against the Chinese had already made its appearance as early as the 1850s, but it had not yet become as widespread, as fervent, or as tightly organized as it would become. In fact, in 1850 the mayor of San Francisco and other community leaders gathered publicly to recognize and welcome Chinese immigrants to the city, while newspapers praised the Chinese as models of "sobriety, order, and obedience to law." When California became a state, Chinese San Franciscans were among those invited to participate in the ceremonies (Purdy 1924, pp. 40–41).

These displays of friendship and inclusion would become far rarer in coming decades, however, as increasing numbers of working-class citizens in the West blamed the Chinese for their hard lots in life. The frenzied state of anti-Chinese sentiment in California during the 1870s was partly a consequence of people's troubles. There was a nationwide economic depression, and in 1876 and 1877 the state experienced the lowest rainfall in decades. In the countryside, crops failed and livestock died. In San Francisco, the unemployment rate was estimated to be between one-fifth and one-quarter of the available white male labor force. Desperate workers began to cast about for a scapegoat on which to blame their problems. Before long, many of them felt that the Chinese were at fault. This view was fueled by mass meetings and fiery oratory that listed the reasons that Chinese immigrants were to blame, and exhorted listeners to push them out of the country. In San Francisco,

Workingmen's Party leader Denis Kearney ended all his speeches with the catch phrase: "The Chinese Must Go!" In Nevada, miners' unions presented a scenario of impending Chinese takeover to play on workers' fears and drum up anti-Chinese feeling:

> Capital has decreed that Chinese shall supplant and drive hence the present race of toilers. . . . Every branch of industry in the State of California swarms with Chinese. . . . Can we compete with a barbarous race, devoid of energy and careless of the State's weal? Sunk in their own debasement, having no voice in government, how long would it be ere ruin would swamp the capitalist and the poor man together? . . . Here, then upon the threshold of a conflict which, if persevered in, will plunge the State into anarchy and ruin, we appeal to the working men to step to the front and hurl back the tide of barbarous invaders. (Saxton 1971, p. 59)

In all of these speeches, orators conveyed two ideas: that Chinese workers presented damaging competition to white workers, and that Chinese workers were precipitating white workers (or white society) into a worse state. It seems that the Chinese could never win, for if whites did not denounce their depravity, they criticized their success. One man expressed this fear: "If given an equal chance with our people, [the Chinese] would outdo [us] in the struggle for life and gain possession of the Pacific Coast of America. . . . We cannot compete with them, not because of their baser qualities, but because of their better" (McCunn 1988, p. 49). No matter what the Chinese did, many white laborers strongly believed that their presence was the root of many of their problems, and that getting rid of them was the key to a more secure future. Asian scapegoating would resurface again in other periods of economic difficulty: in the 1920s, after Chinese exclusion, whites began to blame economic problems on the Japanese.

The highly Eurocentric attitudes of the time reinforced working-class resentment of Asian labor. In general, nineteenth-century Americans believed that the course of human progress moved in a westerly direction. According to them, the ancient civilizations of the East, where human civilization had begun, were now in decay. Europe, too, had had its time of glory, but the enlightened future belonged to the nation farthest West: the United States. Correspondingly, "Orientals" were frequently thought of as backward, often even as incapable of taking part in Western society and culture. Even as early as 1852, the *Daily Alta California* asserted that the Chinese "are not of that kind that Americans can ever associate or sympathize with. They are not," the editorial continued, "of our people and never will be, though they remain here forever" (ibid., p. 41). The assumption that Asians were unassimilable was one of the most fundamental beliefs that underlay prejudice, violence, and discrimination against them.

As time went on and anti-Chinese sentiment increased, stereotypes of the Chinese became uglier and more degrading. Instead of being seen as merely backward and foreign, they were depicted as beasts of burden (coolies), deranged opium addicts, or, at worst, some sort of almost subhuman category, entirely different from other people. An 1885 San Francisco Board of Supervisors report on conditions in Chinatown found its subjects

BOYCOTT

A General Boycott has been declared upon all CHINESE and JAPANESE Restaurants, Tailor Shops and Wash Houses. Also all persons employing them in any capacity.

All Friends and Sympathizers of Organized Labor will assist us in this fight against the lowering Asiatic standards of living and of morals.

AMERICA vs. ASIA
Progress vs. Retrogression
Are the considerations involved.

BY ORDER OF
 Silver Bow Trades and Labor Assembly and Butte Miners' Union

Flyer calling for the boycott of Chinese and Japanese laborers in Butte, Montana, ca. 1898. The flyer threatens businesses owned by Chinese and Japanese residents as well as businesses employing Chinese or Japanese laborers. (*National Archives and Records Administration*)

depraved and disgusting: "foul odors [from toilets or sewers] . . . mingle with the Mongolian messes [simmering] upon the adjoining cooking device, nauseating the visitor but . . . adding zest to the appetite of the Celestials" (*Report of the Special Committee* 1885, p. 22). Such revulsion and hatred could not be appeased merely through discriminatory action, but found its outlet in more direct expressions of violence.

Violence

Partly fueled by frustrated economic scapegoating, partly the result of racism and a desire to harm or intimidate Asians, Asian immigrants were frequent targets for violence. This violence could be aimed at individuals or at ethnic enclaves such as Chinatowns, and occurred throughout the history of Asians in the United States.

Because the Chinese were the first group of Asians to settle widely, the earliest anti-Asian violence was directed against them. It started in the early 1850s and continued thereafter. In 1862, records showed that eighty-eight Chinese had been killed by white Americans, including eleven collectors of the foreign Miners' tax. The first documented instance of violent action against a Chinatown took place in 1871 in Los Angeles. Police and an armed crowd were involved, shooting, lynching, and burning innocent Chinese residents. When the incident was over, nineteen Chinese were dead and two were wounded. The perpetrators were jailed but released after one year. Six years later, in Chico, California, members of a white supremacist group used arson on the town's Chinatown—and some of its residents. They burned Chinese homes and a Chinese laundry, and also a factory that employed Chinese and property belonging to a person who leased farmland to Chinese. They caught and set four Chinese on fire; two died, but two escaped. Those responsible for the attacks were released on parole (Chan 1991, p. 49). Many other similar incidents occurred throughout the West, continuing well into the 1880s (after the Exclusion Act had been passed). Most attacks were committed with the intent of driving the Chinese from the area. In 1885, residents of Washington made a plan to drive out the Chinese from the territory. They set a deadline and gathered committees to do the job. Chinatown residents found unsigned notices posted through the quarter ordering them to leave, while employers with Chinese workers received threats of violence against their families if they did not immediately fire those workers. Some whites rejected the expulsion plan and the ensuing violence. Among those were eight pastors, who denounced the plan to their congregations, and a Tacoma woman named Mrs. Bowen: when a mob gathered at her house and ordered her to "put out" her Chinese servant, she replied, "Put him out nothing!" and attacked the would-be assailants with her broom. But the mob and the committees succeeded in driving out almost all of the Chinese residents of Tacoma. President Cleveland sent the military to Seattle to protect the Chinese and maintain order, but some of the soldiers participated in beating up Chinese or extorting money from them. By 1886, almost all the Chinese in Washington had been expelled (though some would begin coming back a few years later) (McCunn 1988, p. 49).

Attacks also occurred against other Asian groups. The first recorded one against Japanese was in San Francisco in 1906, following the earthquake. In 1908 a mob in Live Oak, California, drove 100 Indian farmworkers out of their camp, robbed them, and set their camp on fire; local officials said that the actions were the result of the Indians' own misbehavior. Incidents against Korean farmworkers began in 1909, and in 1928 the first attempt to drive Filipinos from an area occurred in Washington (Chan 1991, p. 53). These often extremely brutal acts of violence show the anger and frustration that many white Americans felt about having Asians in their midst; even people who did not participate directly in the violent incidents may still have shared the participants' sentiments toward Asians.

The feelings that lay behind these attacks also prompted lawmakers to try to make efforts to restrict Asians legally. Prohibitions on court testimony began early on. Inspired by laws denying Native Americans the right to give court testimony, lawyers and judges interpreted these laws to include Chinese; thus it became very difficult for Chinese to take advantage of the legal system to redress their wrongs. Other laws restricted Asians in other ways. In 1898, some whites even attempted to deny American-born Asians the rights of citizenship; the Supreme Court, however, upheld this right in *Wong Kim Ark v. United States*, maintaining that Wong, having been born in the United States, was a U.S. citizen.

Toward Exclusion

The violence and hatred directed at Asians culminated in efforts to exclude them entirely from U.S. society. Attempts at limiting Chinese immigration occurred as early as 1855, when a tax was proposed on immigrants who could not become citizens—meaning Asians. This attempt, and several that followed it, were declared unconstitutional, since the Supreme Court deemed immigration regulatable only by the federal government. Anti-Chinese groups therefore began to turn their energies toward the creation of a federal exclusion law. An 1875 law, then a treaty in 1880, started to set limits on the Chinese entering the country.

In 1882, the Chinese Exclusion Act became the first U.S. law to explicitly prohibit immigration based on race. The law banned the entry of all Chinese immigrants, except for a select few categories: merchants, students, teachers, diplomats, and travelers were all permitted. But laborers (and their wives) could no longer enter the country. The act was followed by other laws that further narrowed these allowances, laws that left many laborers who were out of the country at the time stranded and unable to return. The Exclusion Act dramatically affected the Chinese population in the United States. Five years after the act was passed, in 1887, Chinese immigration into this country reached an all-time low of ten people. Between 1890 and 1920, the act decreased the nation's Chinese population by about half (Takaki 1998, pp. 111–112).

After the Chinese were excluded, other groups would suffer similarly. The 1907 Gentlemen's Agreement halted the influx of Japanese laborers, the group that whites were most concerned about after the Chinese had gone. A decade or more later, the immigration acts of 1917 and 1924 refused access to Asian Indians and Koreans, respectively; the 1924 act ended all Asian immigration by prohibiting the entry of immigrants who could not become citizens. Filipino immigration effectively ended in 1934, with the Tydings-McDuffie Act. Although Asians had played a key role in building much of the West, white Americans had succeeded in dramatically limiting the numbers of Asians and their ability to perpetuate their communities. Immigration from Asia, today a major force in the American West, would not resume in significant numbers until 1965.

Conclusion

During the second half of the nineteenth century and the first decades of the twentieth, Asian immigrants and white Americans encountered one another for the first time in the West. In the earliest years, they were able to meet without incident, still forming perceptions about each other. Within a short period, however, the majority population had decided that the Asian newcomers were an unwelcome threat that needed to be expelled. But the exclusionary legislation passed in 1882 and afterward was not enough to completely eliminate the Asian "problem" from the country. Asians continued to live in the United States, working, organizing, and raising future generations.

For new generations of immigrants, some things changed, but others remained the same. The second generation did not have their parents' defining experience of leaving an old life behind to start anew in a foreign country. The United States was their only home, and its language, people, and culture were familiar to them. As citizens, they also had rights and powers that the first generation had not, giving them the freedom to accomplish more than their parents had. And yet, many of the restrictions that their parents had suffered under still carried over to them. They remained subject to discriminatory legislation, and were still susceptible to racism and violence.

Asians and Asian Americans have never made up more than a small minority of the U.S. population. But their story is larger than their numbers. The history of their treatment in the American West shows the often-hidden, unequal side to U.S. democracy and "justice for all." It reveals Americans' unspoken prejudices and desires and the lengths to which they will go to maintain their vision of the future. On the other side of the story, the experience of Asians in this country is a testament to the human ability to survive and live in spite of opposition. Despite racism, despite oppression, despite the uncertainty of trying to live in a strange place and keep ahead of ever-changing rules, the early immigrants managed to find a place for themselves in this land—so they hoped—of opportunity.

References and Further Reading

Chan, Sucheng. *This Bittersweet Soil: The Chinese in California Agriculture, 1860–1910.* Berkeley: University of California Press, 1987.

Chan, Sucheng. *Asian Americans: An Interpretive History.* Boston: Twayne Publishers, 1991.

Chinn, Thomas W., ed. *A History of the Chinese in California; A Syllabus.* San Francisco: CHSA, 1969.

Helper, Hinton Rowan. *The Land of Gold: Reality Versus Fiction.* Baltimore: H. Taylor, 1855. Online at Library of Congress, *"California as I Saw It": First-Person Narratives of California's Early Years, 184–1900.* http://memory.loc.gov/ammem/cbhtml/

Hsu, Madeline. *Dreaming of Gold, Dreaming of Home: Transnationalism and Migration between the United States and South China, 1882–1943.* Stanford: Stanford University Press, 2000.

Hune, Shirley, and Gail Nomura. *Asian/Pacific Islander American Women: A Historical Anthology.* New York: New York University Press, 2003.

Ichioka, Yuji. *The Issei: The World of the First Generation Japanese Immigrants 1885–1924.* New York: Free Press, 1988.

Lee, Erika. *At America's Gates: Chinese Immigration during the Exclusion Era, 1882–1943.* Chapel Hill: University of North Carolina Press, 2003.

Lee, Mary Paik. *Quiet Odyssey: A Pioneer Korean Woman in America.* Seattle: University of Washington Press, 1990.

Pai, Margaret K. *Dreams of Two Yi-Min.* Honolulu: University of Hawaii Press, 1989.

Matsumoto, Valerie J. *Farming the Home Place: A Japanese American Community in California, 1919–1982.* Ithaca: Cornell University Press, 1993.

McCunn, Ruthanne Lum. *Thousand Pieces of Gold.* Boston: Beacon Press, 1981.

McCunn, Ruthanne Lum. *Chinese American Portraits: Personal Histories 1828–1988.* Seattle: University of Washington Press, 1988.

Nee, Victor G., and Brett de Bary Nee. *Longtime Californ'.* Stanford: Stanford University Press, 1972.

Okihiro, Gary. *Margins and Mainstreams: Asians in American History and Culture.* Seattle: University of Washington Press, 1994.

Purdy, Helen Throop. "Portsmouth Square." *Quarterly of the California Historical Society* 3.1 (1924): 30–44.

Report of the Special Committee of the Board of Supervisors of San Francisco on the condition of the Chinese quarter and the Chinese in San Francisco, July, 1885. San Francisco: P.J. Thomas, 1885.

Saxton, Alexander. *The Indispensable Enemy: Labor and the Anti-Chinese Movement in California.* Berkeley: University of California Press, 1971.

Shah, Nayan. *Contagious Divides: Epidemics and Race in San Francisco's Chinatown.* Berkeley: University of California Press, 2001.

Takaki, Ronald. *Strangers from a Different Shore*: *A History of Asian Americans.* Rev. ed. Boston: Little, Brown and Company, 1998.

Tchen, John Kuo Wei. Arnold Genthe, photographs. *Genthe's Photographs of San Francisco's Old Chinatown.* New York: Dover, 1984.

Entrepreneurs | 9

Ryan Carey

No place in the United States is more synonymous with "making it on your own" than the American West. Throughout the nineteenth and twentieth centuries, Americans have understood the West as the land of unlimited opportunity. Whether it is making a name for oneself, making a fortune, or just "making it," somehow the West has seemed more "American" than the rest of the country. It is a mythic place where individuals can become whatever they want to be; where grit, determination, and hard work will pay off with fame, fortune, and success. Indeed, Western history seems to provide no shortage of examples of this kind of success story, from clothing magnate Levi Strauss, who built an empire of denim in San Francisco, to software magnate Bill Gates, who built an empire of information in Seattle. Yet, for every Levi Strauss and Bill Gates, there are tens of thousands of individuals who had just as much grit, who had just as much determination, and who worked just as hard, but who didn't make it.

As with much of Western history, the myth doesn't quite match up to the reality, though in business and other realms, the successful and powerful did their best to propagate that myth to their political advantage. For the most part, the history of entrepreneurs and business in the West looks like a photo negative of the popular perception. Less a story of individual determination and hard work, the history of business in the West involves corruption, politics, connections, and class. And most important, rather than the individual playing the central role, institutions such as corporations, the federal government, and big banks made success in the West a reality.

There were at least three factors that explain success in Western enterprise. The first was the ability to take advantage of connections to the East. Businesses that did the best created corporate structures that accessed Eastern markets, goods, money, and labor. In the sparsely populated but resource-rich American West, high costs of doing business demanded that companies do business with established markets across the continent and across the Atlantic Ocean. The third key to success was the ability to rely on, take advantage of, and manipulate the significant federal presence in the West. Although popular perception holds that the "West was won" by the people who settled it, the federal government played a crucial role in the process of integrating the American West into the nation as a whole. Consider the near constant military presence, which relied on civilian contractors to keep them fed and clothed, and the creation of innumerable federal subsidies for economic activity, such as the mail and railroad construction. In the mid-nineteenth century, when a significant amount of the economic activity in the region was directed to keeping the government presence up and running, federal subsidies gave the upper hand to many businesses that went on to dominate Western economic life. Finally, for all the talk of individual opportunity that the West seemed to inspire, the Western entrepreneurs that we remember and celebrate—whether it be in mining, timber, ranching, or transportation, as well as banking and mercantile schemes—were successful because of their ability to monopolize the industries of their choosing and eliminate all competition. A reliance on corporate, not individual, enterprise ruled Western business. There are, of course, stories that will confound these generalizations, but it is important to note which elements came to dominate Western economic life.

When one looks hard at the history of Western business, it begins to look a lot less "Western" and much more like what we would call "Eastern," or just American, capitalism, a relationship that isn't coincidental. The history of U.S. business and the history of the American West joined in a kind of confluence in the nineteenth century in two important ways. First, as corporations began to take advantage of the opportunities the West provided, they had to learn how to operate on an ever larger scale and over an ever increasing expanse of space. Whether it be the novel corporate structure of John Jacob Astor's American Fur Company, or the significant role played by managers in the operation of railroads, doing business in the West (which often meant doing business in or with the East) demanded innovative business structures. Many of these innovations led to the modern corporate structure that has come to dominate U.S. business today. Second, American expansion into, and domination of, the West was largely a product of entrepreneurial and corporate development of Western markets and resources. Nineteenth-century corporations encouraged and even undertook much of the exploration, mapping, and even settlement that came to define Western history. In other words, the westward push of the American empire and the capitalist development of that frontier went hand in hand.

The Fur Trade

The case of the fur trade in the American West offers a good introduction to the history of entrepreneurs and big business, because it demonstrates, in a microcosm, the important elements of business in the West. The French and the British had both been engaged in the Fur Trade for more than two centuries by the time American businessmen entered the fray. By 1650, the

French enjoyed a thriving trade in pelts centered on the St. Lawrence River and the lands beyond the Great Lakes. So, too, were the British interested in furs, and in 1670 the British monarchy created the Hudson's Bay Company (HBC). The company was granted a monopoly of all the British fur trade for the entire watershed of Hudson's Bay. The fur monopoly grew so influential that it engendered criticism from independent trappers and traders as well as colonists, who complained that its initials, HBC, stood for "Here Before Christ" (Hine and Faragher 2000, p. 144). In the final decade of the eighteenth century Americans tentatively entered the race for North American furs, increasing their activities after the Lewis and Clark Expedition.

Although American firms did not have the same state-sponsored monopolistic sanctions as their British and French rivals, they nonetheless took advantage of the federal presence in the West. In fact, the national government first tried to regulate the fur trade with a well-intentioned but ill-conceived "factory system." In 1796, President George Washington urged Congress to establish government-run "factories" in the hopes of regulating the trade and quieting tension between whites and Indians along the frontier. However, the government was not able to supply the actual demands of either Indians or whites, which often confounded the idealized visions of government factors (Haeger 1991).

The first successful entrepreneurs in the fur trade were those who capitalized on their connections with federal efforts in the West, especially the first notable government exploration of the region, the Lewis and Clark Expedition. In 1803 the United States obtained title to the Louisiana Territory, running west of the Mississippi River and encompassing the watershed of the Missouri River, a purchase that nearly doubled the size of the nation. President Thomas Jefferson sent Meriwether Lewis and William Clark to explore the new territory in order (1) to find a water route across the continent that would open up trade in the Pacific, (2) to assess the territory's value and possible uses, and (3) to make peaceful trading alliances with the region's Native American population. Although the explorers failed to find a navigable river route, they were successful in their other goals. Upon the expedition's return in 1806, Meriwether Lewis wrote to Jefferson explaining that both the upper reaches of the Missouri as well as the Rocky Mountains were "richer in beaver and otter than any country on earth" (DeVoto 1952, p. 527).

The first to take advantage of Lewis and Clark's reconnaissance were individuals connected with the expedition. Manuel Lisa, a merchant who had supplied the explorers, quickly moved into the fur trade, establishing relations with the Indians along the Missouri River as well as at the confluence of the Bighorn and Yellowstone rivers. Within two years, Lisa had partnered with William Clark as well as August Pierre and Jean Pierre Chouteau to form the Missouri Fur Company. The Chouteaus brought a historical monopoly with the Osage granted by the former Spanish governor of Louisiana, while Clark brought personal knowledge from his exploration. The company also employed John Colter and George Drouillard, both of whom had served in the Lewis and Clark Expedition and who used the geographical insight gained in the expedition in their search for furs.

The Missouri Company was only the first American enterprise to take advantage of Western fur resources. It was quickly surpassed by John Jacob Astor's American Fur Company in 1808. Astor was a master of political connections (Haeger 1991). He convinced Congress to put an end to the factory system while using federal Indian agents to secure Indian labor for trapping animals. Based in New York, Astor also made alliances with capitalists interested in investing in the lucrative fur trade, allowing the American Fur Company to swallow up rival firms. By 1834 the American Fur Company was a near monopoly, controlling more than three-fourths of the fur exports from the United States. At the same time, William Henry Ashley, Missouri's first lieutenant governor, sent "enterprising young men" overland to the Rockies where they revolutionized the industry by setting up yearly rendezvous on the Green River (Goetzmann 1963, p. 407). The company was profitable but changed hands repeatedly in the decade following its inception. Finally, however, Astor and the American Fur Company managed to drive the Rocky Mountain firm out of business.

The era of the fur trade lasted until the beginning of the 1840s (the last rendezvous was in 1840). Decline in resources as well as changes in the global market (by midcentury European fashion no longer held such a high demand for beaver fur) eventually brought an end to the trade. However, the significance of the trade was long lasting. It shed light on the West as a place of entrepreneurial possibility. Trappers themselves became critical guides to the many government exploring expeditions of the 1840s and 1850s that catalogued the immense agricultural, mineral, and timber wealth of the region, creating a reciprocal relationship between commerce and empire. The fur trade also set the standard for both Western as well as American business practice by defining the elements of monopolistic enterprise: large corporate structures aimed at extracting natural resources; the cooperative help of the federal government; and ready access to Eastern capital. Ordinary Americans saw the fur trade primarily as a colorful enterprise in the "primal wilderness," but U.S. businessmen benefited from the commercial knowledge created in the fur trade.

The Business of Mining

Remembered as a moment of wide-open opportunity, when a rough-and-tumble crowd came West to strike it rich, the Gold Rush, like the fur trade, exemplifies the chasm between popular myth and historical reality. Although thousands went west hoping to secure a fortune, the vast majority found only disappointment at the end of their journey. The rumors of gold were overplayed and the opportunities for wealth were much more limited. After the lucky success of a handful of early miners, the era of the lone gold digger came to a shockingly abrupt end. In a few short years, successful and profitable mining in California demanded corporate structures, capital-intensive investments, and gangs of wage laborers. Within three years of the initial rush, California seemed about as far from the Gold Rush Garden of Eden as it could possibly be.

There were fortunes to be made in California, but the mines were only one place to do so. Out of the tens of thousands who came to California to find their fortune, only a small proportion of the miners did indeed strike it rich. As miner-turned-merchant Henry Kent explained: "I find that all shrewd calculating men, if they can git one or two thousand dollars either go home, or git into other business besides mining either trade or farming" (Rohrbough 1997, p. 128). California's elite heeded Kent's advice and became merchants. In the heady days of the Gold Rush merchants were able to charge exorbitant prices on anything from shovels to flour. Those with foresight immediately put their stock into importing and selling the necessities of mining life.

Leland Stanford, Charles Crocker, Mark Hopkins, and Collis P. Huntington, the four men who would come to control the Central Pacific Railroad, all had their start as merchants. After a brief stint in the mines, the New York–born Leland Stanford joined his brothers, who were already operating a successful store in Sacramento. The crush of miners and their constant demands for groceries and supplies meant that the Stanford brothers were soon making money hand-over-fist. The brothers branched out, opening stores outside of Sacramento, including one in Michigan Bluff in the Sierra Nevada Mountains, which Leland operated by himself. He was successful enough to buy out his brothers just three years after he got to California. Stanford's story was echoed in that of his later Central Pacific partners. Like many of his generation, the lure of the gold fields proved too much for Charles Crocker, who led a party of gold seekers west in 1850. But like Stanford, he found work in the mines dull and unending with little opportunity for a payoff. After two years he opened a dry goods store in Sacramento and soon became one of the wealthiest men in the city. Both Huntington and Hopkins had mercantile experience before they came to California. Huntington had been a general merchant with his brother in upstate New York before he left by steamer to try his luck in the mines. In Panama, while he was waiting for a ship to take him north along the Pacific Coast, he fell back on his mercantile skills and bought and sold merchandise for others in his predicament. Huntington made nearly $4,000 during his time in Panama. When he came to Sacramento, he immediately opened a hardware store. Not long afterward, he entered into a partnership with former New York merchant Mark Hopkins. Hopkins, like Huntington, had come west in 1849 but had also immediately opened a store rather than toil in the mines. Together, their partnership made them two of the wealthiest residents on the Pacific Coast by the mid-1850s. Within a decade, Stanford, Crocker, Huntington, and Hopkins had invested their fortunes made off of the miners, and the influence that those fortunes bought, in the new industry of railroading, which quickly transformed them from merchant elites to industrial tycoons.

California's merchant elite during the Gold Rush capitalized on its connections to Eastern goods. With so many workers in the diggings, few Californians spent much time producing consumer goods, so merchants had to import goods from Eastern and European manufacturing centers. But successful merchants like Stanford were not agents of Eastern capital; rather, they were "petty resident capitalists" (Pomeroy 1965, p. 88). Their advantages came from their local residency—truly the right place at the right time—and the fact that they were able to perceive scarcity in the consumer markets created by the thousands of gold seekers. The merchant capitalists of the first few years of the Gold Rush created an economic system "that may not have been democratic but was not colonial in the sense of the absentee capitalism that prevailed in most new and far-off lands." Indeed, California's merchant elite took the vast sums they made selling to miners and put it in local banks, or became bankers themselves and began to fund a broader economic base beyond mining for gold (Schweikart and Doti 1999). For a very brief time, the region could be described as a relatively autonomous economy. But as we will see later, those merchants like Stanford, Crocker, Hopkins, and Huntington soon invested in other industries that ushered in an economic phase in which federal power and Eastern capital eroded that autonomy.

The chances of finding a paying claim in the Gold Rush were indeed slim, yet some men did. But within two or three years of the initial rush of '49, mining began to change. As one '49er put it: "[M]ining will pay here for some time to come but it will have to be conducted differently than what it now is." For him, that meant corporate gold mining that "will yet pay millions of dollars . . . but Capitalists will take hold of it" (Rohrbough 1997, p. 197). Indeed, by 1852 capitalists had taken hold. Only corporate firms could unlock the wealth buried deep in the mountains. Costly technology was needed to sink deeper shafts into the ground or fund the huge hydraulic pressure systems—hoses—to blast away the mountainsides to get to the gold-bearing ore. The rock they removed was a tangled knot of quartz and gold that needed expensive mills to crush the ore and elaborate chemical processes to extract the gold. Independent prospectors did not have the capital for such a venture. Instead, money from San Francisco capitalists as well as Eastern and European financiers poured into corporate mining firms in this second wave of the Gold Rush. In the blink of an eye, the mountains of the Sierra Nevada became dominated by large corporations, worked by gangs of wage laborers. The days of the independent prospector were all but gone (Jung 1999).

Soon these miners were looking beyond California for the next big claim. In the Washoe Mountains beyond the Sierras, a group of prospectors found the Ophir silver vein in 1869, which came to be known as the Comstock lode, named after Henry T. P. Comstock, who alleged that he had a claim on the spring the prospectors were using. As prospectors heard of the Comstock, people poured into the Washoe to stake claims. But the metals were locked deep inside quartz veins; no single prospector could make it pay. Individuals quickly sold their claims to men like San Francisco capitalist George Hearst, who could make the Comstock a paying mine.

Hearst had learned the trade in the lead mines of Missouri, but he had come to California in 1850 like so many to strike it rich. A short time in the diggings, however, had convinced him that money could be made elsewhere, so he began speculating in claims, buying and selling ownership of mining claims as though they were stocks and bonds. When he found out about the riches of the Comstock load he sold all of his California claims, borrowed heavily, and bought as much of the Ophir mine as he was able. Hearst's

Cars coming out of a shaft at the Comstock Mine in Virginia City, Nevada, in 1868, taken by Timothy O'Sullivan. (*National Archives and Records Administration*)

years of trading claims in California had prepared him well for the rush to the Washoe, where he created a mining syndicate to capitalize on the heavy fixed costs inherent in the Comstock load. The mine was so rich that Hearst and his business partners quickly set up a full operation on site in Virginia City, Nevada, where the ore could be crushed and smelted (James 1998).

The quartz mining like that of the Ophir mine brought big capital to the gold fields of the West. Although much of the initial money to fund these corporate mines came from San Francisco capitalists, their real role was to act as funnels, conduits through which nonlocal funds could flow. They acted as the "men-on-the-spot" who could channel vast sums of corporate capital into paying mines such as the Ophir. In addition, they acted as corporate managers, not just directing capital but also organizing labor and technology to make nature pay. They needed experienced Cornish and Welsh miners to work the complex vein, German smelters to extract the ore, as well as cheap labor for the unskilled work above ground; much of it came from Latin America or China. The "Kings of the Comstock," as they were known, helped to bring wage labor to the West, where they soon learned both how to discipline and make money from a large industrial workforce. The result was that the West quickly became one of the most heavily industrialized regions in the nation. Much of the region's economy was run by new corporations that set the standard for how large operations, dependent upon international capital and relying on an army of wage workers, could make vast sums of money in this new industrial era (Cornford 1999). One of their innovations was to remove themselves to San Francisco and leave the daily operation of the mines to a new class of workers, the corporate manager, whose job it was to make the miners' toil profit the company. In metaphoric fashion, the Comstock owners set up mansions atop San Francisco's Nob Hill, above the bustle of the city. Their vantage point allowed them to survey their domain. From their drawing rooms and billiard tables, they increasingly directed and monopolized the economic development of the mining West.

Transporting Wealth by Stagecoach and Steamboat

The pattern of California was repeated throughout the West as gold rushes spawned a number of urban centers into which Eastern and European capital flowed. Mining rushes to mountains beyond Denver and Portland helped to establish those towns and the elites residing in them; the process turned small villages into urban centers with the power to direct these new economic hinterlands. Merchants and bankers arose to capitalize on both the natural resources as well as the crush of people who flooded the region to strike it rich. Using their financial contacts in the East, men like Jerome Chaffe in Denver and William S. Ladd in Portland worked to monopolize the economic life of these many "Wests," creating small banks and amassing large fortunes funding early Western enterprise. In addition to banking and storekeeping, these men added transportation to their list of economic ventures. The most successful were nearly able to freeze out competition, becoming the sole means of transportation and shipping, even before the era of the railroads. And like their more prominent San Francisco counterparts, they too built fabulous mansions, great halls, and other monuments to their supposed economic and cultural superiority. It was architectural proof of their hard work in the land of possibility. But their mansions and halls also covered over the fact that without connections to Eastern capital and control of political influence, none of this prosperity would have been possible.

Federal support was essential to success in the transportation business. The government anticipated and encouraged Western emigration by building stable overland routes to connect the new far-Western territories to Eastern and Midwestern cities and towns. The sizable Western military presence also needed Eastern connections, so Congress and the Department of the Interior hired private companies to survey and build wagon roads across the West while at the same time offering sizable federal subsidies to firms willing to transport federal mail and military supplies. The first transportation entrepreneurs to strike it rich, New Yorkers John Butterfield, William Fargo, and Henry Wells, capitalized on this federal largess. The three controlled the powerful Eastern shipping company known as the American Express Company. Wells and Fargo also had experience in the West, where their firm, Wells, Fargo, and Company, had all but monopolized California stagecoach service by the mid-1850s. Together with Butterfield, the three created the Overland Mail Company, which received a federal subsidy of $600,000 per year to transport people and mail from Missouri to San Francisco. Their route had regular stops along the way where the stage would change horses or mules and the passengers would be able to eat and rest from the hot, dusty, and generally uncomfortable ride. Overland Mail made its first connection in 1858; the trip from Missouri to San Francisco took twenty-four days, and twenty-one days on the return journey. In addition to their federal subsidy and profitable mail contract, private shipping and passenger fares soon began to pay. Together, American Express, Overland Mail, and Wells, Fargo, and Company were able to drive out competition in the West, or else subcontract smaller firms and incorporate them into their empire. Their stable income from federal subsidies allowed them to engage in rate wars when new competitors arrived. If they failed to undercut rival companies, they simply bought them out. The result was almost always capitulation by competing firms. When Overland Mail suffered a credit crisis, Wells, Fargo purchased the firm and achieved dominance in Western transportation (Schwantes 1999).

Before Wells, Fargo and Overland Mail were able to monopolize the region, other companies had been successful in garnering government contracts—if only for a short time. During the 1850s, the firm of Russell, Majors, and Waddell successfully capitalized on the needs of the U.S. Army, becoming the sole shippers to all of the Western army posts after the Mexican War. The firm shipped supplies from the more densely settled Midwest to army posts in the newly acquired Mexican session, at the same time that they used the stable income from the military to monopolize Southwestern trade. From 1855 to 1860, the firm steadily grew, employing 4,000 men operating 3,500 wagons. They branched out into passenger service but failed to get a governmental subsidy like that of the Overland Mail. Without federal funding, their passenger service failed. In order to save the firm, the men began the ill-fated Pony Express. Although we remember the Pony Express today as an essential Western enterprise, it was in fact a dismal failure that limped along for the two years it was in existence. Like their stage scheme, the express also lacked a federal contract or subsidy. Unlike the gentlemen at Wells, Fargo, the partners at Russell, Majors, and Waddell never truly learned the key to success in Western shipping—a robust system of corporate welfare. In order to make it rich, you needed the financial support of the federal government.

As Russell, Majors, and Waddell were in decline, they enlisted the help of fellow transportation entrepreneur Ben Holladay (see inset for details). When the firm went bankrupt in 1862, Holladay reorganized their business and subcontracted with Overland Mail to operate the Eastern portion of the trans-Mississippi mail and stage line. In the middle of the 1860s, the government awarded him a contract for branch lines into the new Pacific Northwest. At the height of his success, Holladay was one of the largest employers in the nation: more than 15,000 employees labored on 20,000 stagecoaches and wagons. But Holladay suffered financial reversals in 1865 and sold his interests to Wells, Fargo, and Company. Using money from that sale, however, he invested heavily in steamship and regional rail lines on the Pacific Coast, where he prospered for another ten years.

Upon the failure of Russell, Majors, and Waddell, and with the success over Holladay, Wells, Fargo and Company became one of the biggest corporations in the United States, with enough capital to withstand the competition that ensued once the transcontinental railroads were built in the 1860s,

Ben Holladay

Ben Holladay was born on the Kentucky frontier in 1819. He first achieved financial success with the help of the federal government. He got his start as a wagon-shipper during the Mexican War. Taking advantage of war demands, Holladay made handsome sums supplying and shipping supplies for the Army of the West commanded by Stephen Watts Kearney. Holladay freighted goods across the barren expanses of the Southwest while the U.S. Army fought for California. With his war profits, Holladay stood poised to take advantage of the new markets the United States gained in the Southwest. The Mexican session opened up California, Santa Fe, and the southern Rockies to U.S. interests, and Holladay was interested in them all. To realize his goal, Holladay followed the lead of many shippers: he purchased surplus army wagons and stock at cut rate prices as the military scaled back from wartime preparedness. With inexpensive wagons and stock, as well as a small fortune gained from wartime shipping, Holladay set about to become the "Stagecoach King" and the "Napoleon of the West" as admirers and critics alike referred to him later in life.

Holladay built his empire on tried and true methods. Directly after the war, he continued to profit from government contracts by supplying dry goods to the military in Utah. Along with overland shipping magnate William Russell, Holladay had a contract to deliver flour to Utah military posts. He also capitalized on his military connections to get into public trade. In 1849, he sent fifty wagonloads to Salt Lake City along with a letter of introduction to Mormon leader Brigham Young from Colonel A. W. Doniphan. Unlike many of his colleagues, Doniphan was friendly with the Salt Lake Mormons; he recommended Holladay, which helped the hard-drinking, brusque Holladay establish a foothold in the Mormon trade when it might have been more difficult.

Like many Western entrepreneurs, Holladay branched out from his initial ventures, in his case stagecoach and freighting, to the realm of finance. Holladay's success continued when he used his considerable wealth to aid the shipping firm of Russell, Majors, and Waddell. In 1858, he began supplying the firm with livestock. Two years later he became the financier for one of the firm's ill-fated schemes, the Pony Express. When the Central Overland California, and Pike's Peak Express, owned by Russell, Majors, and Waddell, went bankrupt, Holladay stepped in and assumed a mortgage on the firm's properties. In 1862, he assumed control of the perennially slumping firm for the bargain price of $100,000. Purchase of Russell, Majors, and Waddell vaulted Holladay into the ranks of stagecoach king. He immediately created the Overland Stage Line, a vast freighting and coach company that operated all over the West. His most lucrative line was the eastern section of the trans-Missouri Stage mail route, running to Salt Lake City, which he operated as a subcontractor for the federally subsidized Overland Mail Company. Holladay added other lucrative government subsidies, running lines to Nebraska and Colorado. In 1864, the federal government granted Holladay his own four-year contract to run the mail east of Salt Lake City. More important, the government granted him contracts for new branchlines to the New Northwest—Oregon, Washington, Idaho, and Montana. Truly a "Stagecoach King," Holladay employed 15,000 men and ran ten times that many livestock for his coaches, which, it was reported, numbered some 20,000 vehicles.

Holladay was at his financial peak at the end of the Civil War, when he suffered financial setbacks: he blamed Indian attacks for losses of coaches and stock. The next year he sold his entire stage empire to Wells, Fargo, and Company. Although it might appear as if Holladay was beaten by Wells, Fargo, in truth he simply shifted industries. With his profits won by selling to the ubiquitous stagecoach company, Holladay traveled to the Pacific slope, only to interest himself in burgeoning steamship and railroad ventures. Three years before he sold out to Wells, Fargo, he had invested considerable sums in Pacific shipping. He incorporated the California, Oregon, and Mexican Steamship Company, which ran freight up and down the Pacific Coast south of the Canadian border. With the money from Wells, Fargo, he expanded his operations and bought into ships traveling as far north as Alaska.

Secure in his coastal properties, or so he thought, Holladay then turned inland, trying his hand at railroading. In 1866, Congress created a 3.7-million-acre land grant in Oregon's Willamette River Valley, containing both rich farmland and a wealth of timber resources. The state legislature had the power to assign the grant to any company they chose, and two Portland syndicates began constructing rail lines, one on each side of the river, in hopes of obtaining the grant. The legislators chose the Oregon Central Railroad (OCRR), the line traveling down the west side of the river, but the east-side line, known as the Oregon and California Railroad (O&C), did not give up. When Holladay arrived in Oregon, the two were frantically trying to outbuild each other. Holladay threw his weight (and money) in with the east-side line, and in 1868, Holladay bought out the O&C and folded it into his North Pacific Transportation Company, a financial conglomerate that owned the individual companies in Holladay's empire. He bombarded the public with newspaper broadsides and sent aggressive lawyers to intimidate the opposition, all in hopes of recapturing the grant. Known for his vulgar boasting and keen political corruption, Holladay reportedly spent $35,000 in the 1868

Oregon legislature to achieve his aims. Using outlandish political corruption—Oregonians remembered the incident as the "Great Barbecue"—Holladay effectively purchased the land grant: the legislature passed a bill that reallocated the land to the Oregon and California road. Then Holladay purchased the west-side line, the OCRR, just to freeze out any further possible competition.

Holladay needed the O&C to complete more than 200 miles of track within a specified time, or he would forfeit the grant. To accomplish his goals, he engaged in questionable financial practices, specifically selling cut-rate mortgage bonds to English and German financiers hoping to cash in on the railroad riches the United States supposedly had to offer. After the O&C completed a line to Roseburg, Oregon, and secured the grant, Holladay bought out competing Willamette River steamship companies, thus securing a monopoly on the rich and densely settled valley. By 1871 he had reorganized his holdings, created the Oregon Steamship Company, and rightly claimed dominion over the Pacific Slope north of California.

Even as Holladay celebrated his success, however, his empire was crumbling beneath him. In a rush to complete the railroad down the Willamette, he had overextended himself. Although he realized great profits, they were not great enough to make good on the mortgage bonds he owed to holders in London and Frankfort. When the nation experienced a financial panic in 1873, Holladay had to forfeit on his bonds. Henry Villard, representing the German capitalists, came to Oregon in 1874 and within two years had forced Holladay to sell his entire empire on the cheap. Holladay died in 1887, embroiled in lawsuits by numerous investors who had put their faith in the "Napoleon of the West." Their faith, it seemed, had been misguided.

1870s, and 1880s. When the railroad companies began encroaching on the shipping and passenger service of Wells, Fargo, the company simply cut back its overland service and focused on serving places outside of the railroad's territory. At the same time it poured capital into its banking wing, and eventually it all but left the transportation business.

Other prerailroad transportation entrepreneurs cooperated with the transcontinental railroad economy that developed in the 1860s and 1870s. The Oregon Steam Navigation Company controlled not stagecoaches but steamships along the Columbia River in Oregon. During the initial rush of the Oregon Trail, most emigrants took advantage of government land grants to settle fertile federal land in the Willamette Valley. However, a few enterprising entrepreneurs decided to settle lands along the Columbia River at the Cascade Rapids, which blocked navigation along the river. Using the Oregon Donation Land Claim act, these men were able to obtain strategic riverfront lands for next to nothing while monopolizing all river traffic along the rapids. They built portage roads and eventually tramways to transship the belongings of the many emigrants coming down the river. Eventually, Portland steamship entrepreneurs John C. Ainsworth, Simeon Reed, and R. R. Thompson incorporated with the Columbia River landowners to form the Oregon Steam Navigation Company, or the OSN (Schwantes 1999).

The OSN took advantage of the federal land policy in the West, as well as the region's unique geography. With steamships running the length of the Columbia River and exclusive control of the lands surrounding the river's rapids, the OSN was able to make the Columbia River its own private highway. The firm bought out competing firms and waged freight wars, lowering prices so dramatically that the smaller firms could not compete. At one point the company simply stopped shipping all freight along the portages that did not come on OSN boats. As mining rushes and large-scale farming came to the Pacific Northwest, the OSN was there to capitalize on the need for transportation. For some twenty years the company paid handsome dividends, sometimes as much as 25 percent on its $5 million capitalization. While the company's owners became wealthy beyond their wildest dreams, the region's residents became resentful of its exclusive power and monopoly. Soon, locals hoped, the transcontinental railroad would come and break the back of the OSN. Unfortunately, their dreams went unfulfilled. As we will see, the company was so powerful that it was able to dictate terms to the incoming railroad. The OSN directorate sold out to the transcontinental lines, making a handsome profit, receiving large amounts of railroad stock, as well as positions in the new firm. Rather than compete with the railroad, Ainsworth, Reed, and Thompson simply joined it, thereby prolonging their status as rulers of the Northwestern economy.

Transcontinental Connections

By the end of the Civil War, the trans-Mississippi West held well more than 2 million people. Westerners clamored for a transcontinental rail connection to service this ever-growing section of the nation—if only because the shipping monopolies made overland travel so expensive. In addition, wartime demands suggested that a rail link would help preclude another sectional conflict. The federal government thus set out to integrate the West into the national economy and political structure. In the 1860s, two transcontinental schemes were born. The first, articulated in the Pacific Railroad Act, which linked the Union Pacific and Central Pacific railroads, would be finished by the end of the decade. The other, the Northern Pacific Railroad, would languish for nearly two decades, mired in financial mismanagement, before an Eastern financier could connect with Western entrepreneurs and finish the road. Railroads transformed the Western and national economies at the same time that they modernized U.S. business practices. Yet, for all of their innovation, the railroads built on time-honored traditions of Western entrepreneurship, including monopolistic practices, connections to Eastern capital, and federal support.

In 1861, Leland Stanford, Mark Hopkins, Collis Huntington, and Charles Crocker, all four of whom had become wealthy buying and selling supplies during the Gold Rush, proposed a transcontinental railroad connection between San Francisco and the Missouri River. As California's status grew, the four wanted a more immediate connection to Eastern markets (Bain 1999). They incorporated the Central Pacific Railroad, which they intended to build east from San Francisco across the Sierra Nevada mountains. In the spring of 1861, with the help of Rep. Oakes Ames, a congressman keenly interested in the project, they convinced Congress to pass the Pacific Railroad Act. The legislature created the Union Pacific Railroad, with Ames as one of the directors, to run westward from the Missouri River to a connection with the CP.

Although other railroads had been built without the aid of the federal government, most had had some state support. In this case, however, the cost would be immense. The federal government was short on capital (it was, after all, fighting the Civil War) but long on assets. To fund the construction, the government gave the two companies real estate: free right-of-way as well as 10 square miles of land along the railway line for every mile of track completed. The company could sell the land as it built the railroad, bringing in the cash necessary for construction. To sweeten the deal, Congress guaranteed the companies' mortgage, and agreed to subsidize construction at $16,000 per mile of flat terrain, up to $48,000 per mile in the mountains. In 1864 the government doubled the land grant, liberalized the mortgage terms, and increased the amount of available stock to 1 million shares. Without this federal largess, the transcontinental railroad would have remained a far-off dream (ibid.).

Even with such liberal federal funding, the transcontinental railroad almost didn't happen. Although a link to Western markets would surely pay, no one knew *when* it would pay. The high construction costs and operating costs for the railroad far outweighed the available market, and investors were wary of such a risky scheme. The railroad men got "creative." The Central Pacific directorate, or "big four" as they were known—Stanford, Hopkins, Huntington, and Crocker—managed to secure more than $1.5 million from the state of California, where Stanford was governor. More important, they

Leland Stanford
(1824–1893), railroad
tycoon, politician,
and philanthropist.
(*Bettmann/Corbis*)

convinced the federal government that the Sierra Nevada mountains started
at Sacramento (which they did not), thus enjoying an inflated $48,000 per
mile subsidy. Finally, the company used a complex system of subcontractors,
many of whom were simply dummy corporations owned by the big four,
to make it rich off the construction of the line. The CP would pay construction companies more than the cost of construction. With the profits from
such deals, the big four would then buy CP stock, thus giving the company
enough capital to fund the line (White 2003).

Such deceit and government manipulation was not unique to the CP. The
Union Pacific engaged in similarly corrupt business practices. Lacking the capital necessary to build (not enough shares of UP were sold to pay for construction), the UP's directorate—Oakes Ames, Thomas Durant, and others—created
a sister company, called the Credit Mobilier of America, to fund the road. The
UP contracted with nonexistent third-party builders who then contracted
with Credit Mobilier to build the road. Credit Mobilier, however, inflated
the costs of construction, sometimes charging more than double the actual

costs. As a result, Credit Mobilier realized fantastic profits and attracted outside investors. Then Credit Mobilier's directorate (also the UP's directorate) purchased UP stock with the profits from the inflated construction costs.

The shady deals of Credit Mobilier did answer one of the problems of the UP: the railroad directorate could sell their ill-gotten stock on the open market, well below the congressionally mandated price, but high enough to pay for construction. In addition, the directorate also managed to realize a handsome profit for themselves—somewhere between $13 million and $16 million for the Credit Mobilier stockholders. These men justified their dealings by noting the considerable risk they were taking in undertaking the project as a whole. Even after their actions were revealed, many men continued to enjoy a good business reputation, at least among investors, because of the fact that they had made such fantastic profits. At the same time, many federal and state politicians invested in the UP and Credit Mobilier. Although not officially state sanctioned, the corporation's influence in the government was undeniable. Not exactly hidden, but not quite open to public knowledge, this kind of corruption was essential to the building and running of large corporations in the United States. It played an important role in funneling and concentrating the capital that made possible U.S. industrialization (ibid.).

Only 40 miles of the UP had been built when the Confederacy surrendered in 1865. The war had locked up material, capital, and labor. The completion of the war made materials available, and Credit Mobilier provided funding, but neither guaranteed workers. Laying track was hard, dirty, and poorly paid work. To solve this problem, the company hired subcontractors to recruit gangs of laborers. The most successful of these men, Jack Casement, had been a general during the Civil War, and he organized his labor force like an army (Bain 1999). When surveyors finished mapping out where the road would go, his army, many of whom were Irish-American war veterans, would grade the site. Soon after, horse-drawn carts laden with rails would come by while workers removed the steel and laid them upon the ties. Finally, a crew with spikes and hammers would fix the rails to the ties. In the first six months, they laid 250 miles of track. And for the next two years, "Casement's army" averaged two to seven miles of track *per day*. The CP also turned to subcontractors to recruit labor. Thousands of Chinese immigrants blasted rock, graded roadbeds, and laid track for the CP. They did not come on their own, however: the CP hired Chinese labor contractors to recruit and control their own countrymen, and the contractors, entrepreneurs in their own right, profited nicely.

The first transcontinental, completed in 1869 at Promontory Point, Utah, provides one example of how massive railroad projects were completed. The Union Pacific was financed largely by Eastern capital and run by Eastern capitalists, a fact that westerners noted with bitterness. However, the CP was run by Western capitalists, even if they utilized some Eastern capital. Although many contemporary observers tried to argue that railroads made the West a colony of Eastern capital, a plundered province, the example of Stanford, Crocker, Hopkins, and Huntington demonstrate that the reality was more complex.

The second major transcontinental project further complicates that economic picture. In 1864, Congress created the Northern Pacific Railroad

In 1862, the U.S. Congress chartered the Central Pacific Company to build east from Sacramento, and the Union Pacific Railroad to build west from Omaha. Here, workers join the tracks at Promontory Point in Utah in 1869, creating the first transcontinental railroad. (*National Archives and Records Administration*)

(NP). Seen as a Northern counterpart to the Union Pacific-Central Pacific Transcontinental, the Northern Pacific was instructed to connect the city of St. Paul, Minnesota, with "some point on Puget Sound" in Washington Territory. Although Congress was less generous in terms of cash subsidies (none were granted) and government loans (Congress refused to guarantee the company's mortgage bonds), it did endow the railroad with the largest government land grant in history, some 55 million acres, roughly the size of New England! Even with such federal aid, however, the Northern Pacific struggled for nearly two decades before construction began in earnest. It was finally completed in 1883. The solution lay in creative Eastern financiers who grafted themselves onto the powerful Western elites. It was only after this successful union that the Northern Pacific railroad was completed.

The NP was funded by a joint combination of Eastern and Western entrepreneurs eager to cash in on the enormous federal land grant. In 1873, steamship and stagecoach entrepreneur Ben Holladay had defaulted on bond payments to a group of German and English capitalists. Henry Villard, a German immigrant representing the Frankfurt bondholders, forced Holladay to sell his crumbling empire at a reduced cost. To save the failing companies, Villard combined with the Portland-based Oregon Steam Navigation Company (Schwantes 1993). Armed with both Eastern as well as Western capital and management, Villard's new company, the Oregon Railway & Navigation Company (OR&N), held a firm grasp on the Columbia River, as well as regional rail lines throughout the Northwest, and it hoped to dominate the region in the same way that the Central Pacific dominated the San Francisco trade. By the end of the 1870s the company was jealously eyeing the Northern Pacific land grant, and Villard managed to convince New York investors to join him in a hostile takeover of the Northern Pacific. In 1880 he sent a letter to his closest Wall Street allies asking them to subscribe some $8 million for an undisclosed scheme. Within twenty-four hours, he had double that amount! With help from the Portland syndicate, Villard formed one of the first financial holding companies in U.S. history, the Oregon and Transcontinental, bringing together multiple companies under one organization, including a controlling interest in the NP. Within three years, the Northern Pacific transcontinental connection was complete (ibid.).

The Northern Pacific had a grand ceremony in 1883 to celebrate completion of the line. But even as champagne corks were popping from St. Paul to Portland, Villard was receiving news that the Northern Pacific was in financial ruin. In haste to complete the line, the company had overextended itself, and Villard was forced to sell his interest in the scheme. The Western directors faired much better, however. They had put only their own money into the combination, while letting Villard, the New York financier, assume the risk of attracting outside investors. While Villard lost much of his personal fortune (though not nearly all), Ainsworth, Reed, and Thompson were able to weather the storm as a new generation of Eastern capitalists took advantage of their considerable knowledge and economic authority. Ainsworth, Reed, and Thompson slowly sold their interests in the Northern Pacific, but they did so on their own terms, thus ending nearly three decades of economic dominance over a region whose development they had literally funded out of their own pocket.

The example of the Northern Pacific, though, demonstrates a third entrepreneurial strategy available in the era of large industrial corporations. In addition to the nonlocal control represented by the Union Pacific, local control represented by the Central Pacific, nonlocal financiers had the option to graft themselves onto the considerable power enjoyed by indigenous elites in the era of industrialization. Other examples of big railroad power exist to further complicate this picture, but it is safe to say that land, money, and power were essential ingredients for success in Western railroading.

Extracting Wealth in an Industrial Age

Railroads ushered in a new phase of Western development by providing access as well as capital to a host of new industrial activities. The roads spurred mining activities, logging concerns, and aided in the rise of industrial agriculture and ranching corporations in the American West. The region had always been a nexus for outside capital and local resources, but the advent of the transcontinentals brought change to the Western economy in both scale and scope.

Industrial mining had come to the West before the railroad, but the transcontinentals helped push Western mining beyond precious metals. San Francisco investors who had become rich on precious metals began looking for more opportunities when Marcus Daly, an Irish immigrant who had been in Butte for almost a decade, convinced the San Franciscans that the mountains of Montana held riches galore. When his Anaconda mines began to run out of silver, Daly and fellow Montanan William A. Clark began to exploit the vast copper reserves in the region. Electricity was becoming more important to the U.S. economy, and Montana provided an abundant supply of the necessary copper wire. Daly, Clark, and the San Francisco capitalists put $4 million into the Anaconda mines, an investment that paid off. Dubbed "the Richest Hill on Earth," the Anaconda mines created the Montana "Copper Kings" (Malone 1981, p. 11). Producing 5,000 tons of copper in 1882, Montana had contributed more than 175,000 tons to the nation's economy by 1916. The story was repeated in Utah, at the Kennecott copper mine, in Arizona, at Bisbee where Phelps-Dodge set up operations, and all across the West as corporations began to investigate and exploit the mineral wealth of the region.

Using the riches gained from mining, these men turned to territorial and state politics as a means to secure their position at the top of Montana society. The Copper Kings were not a monolithic group, however. Clark and Daly developed an intense political rivalry. At the end of the nineteenth century, conflict erupted between the mining magnates. Known as the war of the copper kings, these political battles centered over who would control the Democratic Party and represent Montana in Washington, D.C. The result was a period of intense corruption in Montana politics and the creation of fabulous fortunes for those at the top of society. As Montana became one of the nation's leading copper producers, Eastern investors began to funnel capital into the state. Eventually, the Montana elite lost control of Anaconda to investors from Standard Oil, including John D. Rockefeller.

At the same time that elites were struggling with one another for control over Montana's riches, they were also struggling to control the workers they employed. Western industries depended upon huge labor forces to bring the wealth from the earth. Mining, like many Western extractive industries, was a dirty, difficult, and dangerous job, and corporate profits depended on keeping wages at a bare minimum. The situation bred conflict. One of the reasons that the executives turned to politics was as an attempt to control an increasingly fractured Western society that was split between rich corporate owners and poorly paid industrial workers. Mine owners developed means to control workers on the job as well, such as playing on and reproducing the workers' racial and ethnic prejudices. A multiethnic workforce, companies hoped, would keep workers from uniting under the auspices of a union. Owners subcontracted with labor *padrones*, ethnic entrepreneurs who used their contacts in Europe or Asia to funnel workers to the United States. Gangs of laborers from Greece, Italy, Mexico, and China, among other nations, came to the United States through these padrones. For their services, the companies paid padrones for each worker they imported, as well as the exclusive right to hire and fire. As entrepreneurs, the padrones learned how to make money from worker's movements, and though little known in the annals of Western history, they played important roles in the development of the West (Peck 2000).

Try as they might, however, the mine owners were only marginally successful in controlling their workers. Strikes occurred in Western mining routinely, and workers banded together to resist the owners' intentions. Work slowdowns and stoppages remained the most potent tool available for miners. Often, corporations turned to the federal government to aid them in putting down worker actions. In Idaho, Colorado, and Washington, striking workers met violent resistance by federal troops and private hired guns; strikes could end up in pitched battles. But relying on federal troops to protect corporate interests only demonstrated how weak the mine owners' were. Presented with militant anticapitalists, corporations often accommodated less radical workers in "company unions." Both cases, however, demonstrate the considerable role played by workers in Western industry; though corporate directors wanted to believe that they were in control of the region's economy, unionism and worker actions often demonstrated how tenuous that hold really was.

Similar corporate stories characterize other Western extractive industries. Timber companies poured into the region after the completion of the transcontinentals. Early firms such as Pope and Talbot arose to meet the demands of the initial Western gold and land rushes, but they made up a relatively small proportion of the Western economy. Bigger firms arose after the transcontinentals, as financiers from New England, the Great Lakes, and San Francisco began to exploit the region's resources. Timber firms also benefited from unofficial federal subsidies, such as the incredibly cheap land prices charged for the public domain. Frederick Weyerhaeuser was a relatively prosperous lumberman from St. Paul who by 1900 had purchased more than 900,000 acres of Western forests. He bought most of his land from the Northern Pacific, which was desperate to sell large portions of its land grant. Weyerhaeuser eagerly bought up NP land on the cheap, hired workers, and began logging the West in earnest. Following the lead of the Western mining magnates, he sought young, unmarried men to work his lumber camps. And, like the work in mines, logging was difficult, dangerous, and poorly paid. When the radical union the International Workers of the World, or the IWW, came to the timber camps in 1905, the workers became quick converts. Yet loggers never achieved even the modest gains that their fellow Western industrial workers would. Although the timber camps of the Pacific Northwest were awash in labor radicalism the timber companies managed to crush the IWW by playing up the union's links to the supposedly "un-American" concept of socialism (Cornford 1987).

Corporate Ranchers and Industrial Wage Hands

It is surprising to us that the most mythologized of Western heroes, the independent, self-sufficient cowboy, was part of one of the most heavily corporate industries in the West. After an initial period of smaller entrepreneurship in the 1870s, the cattle industry began to corporatize, taking advantage of the market connections provided by the railroad (Igler 2001). Eastern and European investors saw the cattle industry as a good get-rich-quick scheme, thanks to the industry's well-publicized high profits. James Brisbin's *Beef Bonanza: How to Get Rich on the Plains,* and other books like it, compared the cattle industry to the Gold Rush, with profits as high as 40 percent a year. Capital heeded the call and poured in from New York, London, and Edinburgh. Teddy Roosevelt, before he became president, was one of the many easterners who turned to ranching for fun and profit, investing $82,500 in a badlands ranch in the Dakota Territory. Scottish investors alone poured some $2.5 million into the immense Swan Land Cattle Company, which controlled more than 600,000 acres of Nebraska and Wyoming. British investors bankrolled Charlie Goodnight's JA ranch in Texas's Palo Duro Canyon. These investors created the "super ranch," consolidated industrial ranches where hundreds of wage laborers (cowboys) worked with thousands of cattle for million-dollar profits (Hine and Faragher 2000, p. 321). The XIT ranch, for example, covered more than 3 million acres across ten Texas counties. XIT, standing for Ten in Texas, was controlled by the Capital Syndicate, a group of Chicago investors. John Chisum's Bosque Grande on the Texas and New Mexico border, covered an area nearly the size of Connecticut, Massachusetts, and Rhode Island. Wranglers on the ranch branded more than 18,000 calves in a single season.

If the railroads helped the ranchers by providing a market, so too did the federal government. During the Civil War, Chisum got a deferment from fighting and began selling his cattle at a premium to the Confederate Army. After the war, Chisum sold beef to the U.S. Army and then to the Indian bureau. In 1866 he and Charles Goodnight began driving cattle to feed Navajo Indians on the Bosque Redondo reservation near Fort Sumner, New Mexico. In the summer of 1874, Chisum won a contract to provide beef to several Apache reservations in New Mexico. The federal government, in the form of the Indian reservations, helped to concentrate capital in the cattle industry by providing a steady and stable market for the industry when it was just getting off the ground.

Armed with huge tracts of land and steady government contracts, ranchers had only to control competitors and workers to cement their power. Cowhands increasingly found themselves working in what was truly an industry. When Karl Marx's daughter and son-in-law toured U.S. labor conditions in 1886, it was the cowboys, they noted, that best represented a true proletariat: "[No] class is harder worked," they said, reiterating what one cowboy had told them, and "none so poor paid for their services." Cowboys, far from the individualistic men of the range, worked hard to come together to fight the power of the big ranchers. In New Mexico, cowboys organized the Northern New Mexico Small Cattlemen and Cowboy's Union. Their demands sound familiar to us: "[T]he working season of the average cowboy is only about five months, and we think it nothing but justice that the cowmen should give us living wages the year round." Cowhands, like many workers in the industrializing United States, struck for higher pay and better working conditions. In the spring of 1883, a Denver newspaper reported that a demand for a wage increase to $50 per month resulted in "an extensive strike" among

Branding cattle on the XIT Ranch in Texas, ca. 1904. (*Library of Congress*)

the cowboys of Texas, including Goodnight's JA Ranch and the XIT. Three hundred men held out for more than a year against paid gunmen and Texas Rangers, but they lost in the end when the cattlemen replaced them with scabs (ibid., pp. 321–322).

Cowboys didn't want to remain wage hands the rest of their lives. Those that tried to become cattlemen themselves came into conflict with their former bosses, and the struggles that they fought on the job carried over into violent conflicts as competitors. Large ranching operations organized themselves in cattle cartels, corporate organizations aimed at freezing out competition from small ranchers. The cattle cartels were notorious for their violence. The peak came in Wyoming when members of the Wyoming Stockgrowers Association moved to eliminate small ranchers. The roots of this violence lay in conflicts over maverick cattle, unbranded calves found without their mother on the open range. The big ranchers who made up the association had been in the habit of simply appropriating the mavericks and dividing them up among themselves, but during the cattle boom their own cowboys began branding mavericks to form small herds. To eliminate competition, the Stockgrowers Association began pressuring local communities to prosecute "cattle rustling," which the big ranchers began to define as branding of maverick cattle. Local communities, unsympathetic to the big ranchers, tended to let rustlers off. War broke out in 1891, when the Stockgrowers Association began to organize lynching bees to "clean out the rustlers." In April 1892, a special train left Cheyenne, Wyoming, for Casper carrying twenty-five Texas gunmen and twenty-four regulators: ranch owners, managers, foremen, and privately hired "detectives." The stockgrowers' men carried a "death list" of small ranchers they planned to execute, but they were thwarted by local resistance after assassinating only two. Locals forced the illegal army to hole up at a local ranch where the two sides shot at each other for three days. In the end no one else was killed except for one Texas gunman, who had shot himself in the groin and died days later from the wound (White 1991).

Conclusion

Many historians have noted that Western myths and Western reality bear little resemblance to each other. The story of the cattle industry is one of the most glaring examples of the gap between the two, but the rest of our understanding of business in the West is similarly clouded by the region's mythic nature. The qualities of individualism and autonomy that mark the "grit-and-determination" stories of the American West may be useful in the neat and tidy world of myth but fail to capture the complexity that was business in the West. From afar, the West seems like a land of open opportunity. However, like much of the United States, when viewed up close, the story changes dramatically. Success in the region was not dependent upon abundant opportunity, competition, and good luck; rather, it was dependent on connections to financiers, political influence, government subsidies, monopolistic business practices, and hard-bitten control of wage workers. In that way, business in the West came to resemble business in the United States.

References and Further Reading

Bain, David Howard. *Empire Express: Building the First Transcontinental Railroad.* New York: Viking, 1999.

Cornford, Daniel. *Workers and Dissent in the Redwood Empire.* Philadelphia: Temple University Press, 1987.

Cornford, Daniel. "'We All Live More Like Brutes than Like Humans': Labor and Capital in the Gold Rush." In James J. Rawls and Richard J. Orsi, eds., *A Golden State: Mining and Economic Development of Gold Rush California.* Berkeley: University of California Press, 1999, 78–104.

Deverell, William. *Railroad Crossing: Californians and the Railroad, 1850–1910.* Berkeley: University of California Press, 1994.

DeVoto, Bernard. *The Course of Empire.* Boston: Houghton Mifflin, 1952.

Goetzmann, William H. "The Mountain Man as Jacksonian Man." *American Quarterly* 15 (1963): 402–415.

Haeger, John Denis. *John Jacob Astor: Business and Finance in the Early Republic.* Detroit: Wayne State University Press, 1991.

Hine, Robert V., and John Mack Faragher. *The American West: A New Interpretive History.* New Haven: Yale University Press, 2000.

Igler, David. *Industrial Cowboys: Miller & Lux and the Transformation of the Far West, 1850–1920*. Berkeley: University of California Press, 2001.

James, Ronald M. *The Roar and the Silence: A History of Virginia City and the Comstock Lode*. Reno: University of Nevada Press, 1998.

Jung, Maureen A. "Capitalism Comes to the Diggings: From Gold Rush Adventure to Corporate Enterprise." In James J. Rawls and Richard J. Orsi, eds., *A Golden State: Mining and Economic Development of Gold Rush California*. Berkeley: University of California Press, 1999, 52–77.

Malone, Michael P. *The Battle for Butte: Mining and Politics on the Northern Frontier, 1864–1906*. Seattle: University of Washington Press, 1981.

Peck, Gunther. *Reinventing Free Labor: Padrones and Immigrant Workers in the North American West*. New York: Cambridge University Press, 2000.

Pomeroy, Earl. *The Pacific Slope: A History of California, Oregon, Washington, Idaho, Utah, and Nevada*. New York: Knopf, 1965.

Rohrbough, Malcolm J. *Days of Gold: The California Gold Rush and the American Nation*. Berkeley: University of California Press, 1997.

Schweikart, Larry, and Lynn Pierson Doti. "From Hard Money to Branch Banking: California Banking in the Gold Rush Economy." In James J. Rawls and Richard J. Orsi, eds., *A Golden State: Mining and Economic Development of Gold Rush California*. Berkeley: University of California Press, 1999, 209–232.

Schwantes, Carlos. *Railroad Signatures across the Pacific Northwest*. Seattle: University of Washington Press, 1993.

Schwantes, Carlos. *Long Day's Journey: The Steamboat & Stagecoach Era in the Northern West*. Seattle: University of Washington Press, 1999.

White, Richard. *"It's Your Misfortune and None of My Own": A New History of the American West*. Norman: University of Oklahoma Press, 1991.

White, Richard. "Information, Markets, and Corruption: Transcontinental Railroads in the Gilded Age." *Journal of American History* 90 (2003): 19–43.

Working the American West | 10

Greg Hall

At the beginning of the nineteenth century, working for wages was not a common experience for most American men. Journeymen considered wage work a temporary phase before reaching the status of master craftsman, opening their own shops, and then becoming self-employed. The same was true of the hired farmhand, who expected to become self-sufficient by climbing the "agricultural ladder" from wageworker to tenant farmer to farm owner, and thus economic independence. By the end of the century, however, working for wages or for a salary became common for men in the United States. The transition of working for someone else rather than being self-employed as a farmer, merchant, or skilled craftsman coincided with the settlement of the American West. Working for wages is not necessarily the first image that may come to mind when one thinks about Western history. Nevertheless, wageworkers were important historical participants given the dominant role that heavily capitalized extractive industries, commercial farming, and ranching played in the region's economy. For these workers, the West was a "wageworkers' frontier" that began soon after the California Gold Rush and extended into the early decades of the twentieth century.

The wageworkers' frontier possessed several features that grew out of the distinctive nature of the West's economy, especially in regard to periodic cycles of boom and bust. With a relatively small population, the West could not consume all that it produced, requiring industrial production to be shipped out. Fluctuations in the market price of silver or consumer demand for wheat could send wage-working men into periods of unemployment. Creating the region's infrastructure had a similar effect on employment as the start and completion of construction projects such as railroad lines stimulated a demand for thousands of manual laborers who were no longer needed once the project was completed. Furthermore, production stops caused by limits in quartz mining technology could bring gainful employment suddenly to a halt. All of these factors led to a temporary and seasonal quality to workplaces throughout the region. Therefore, workers had to be mobile and travel to where job opportunities arose. Areas of employment could resemble industrial islands in a sea of an undeveloped Western landscape. The labor of wageworkers could be a precious commodity during labor shortages, forcing wages up throughout the region. High wages and geographic mobility enabled laborers to leave dissatisfying work environments and seek better wages and working conditions. Overall, laborers in the wageworkers' frontier were largely young, male, white, and native-born, making for a higher male proportion of the population than in any other region of the country. Immigrants, though, did make up a considerable portion of the heavily male workforce, depending on the sector under consideration. In fact, by 1900 the American West was the most ethnically and racially diverse region in the United States. Concomitant with the frontier labor experience was an urban environment in cities such as San Francisco, Denver, and Seattle that would grow with time and resemble their Midwestern and Eastern equivalents, though with some distinctive Western qualities of their own. This chapter, then, is an examination of the world of work on the wageworkers' frontier in mining, cattle, agriculture, railroad construction, and logging, as well as a study of Western urban work environments from the mid-nineteenth century to the 1920s. Also coming under analysis are the unions and labor federations that grew out of the work life of the men and women in the West. Of course, not all industries, workers, or the labor movement as a whole can be treated in full here. Nevertheless, a representative sample of major occupations, social groups, and examples of historical agency can help the reader arrive at a more thorough understanding of wage work in the rural and urban West (Schwantes 1987, pp. 39–55; Robbins 1994).

From Prospector to Miner

The first industry on the wageworkers' frontier to attract a large labor force was mining. Early mining, as in the case of the California Gold Rush, was surface placer mining. In January 1848, the discovery of gold in the American River excited a stampede of prospectors to the Sierra foothills of California. Very quickly, gold seekers learned that the "mother lode" spread along a 500-mile stretch of the Sierra Nevada Mountains. Within the first year, 10 million dollars worth of gold was taken out of Sierra streams. By 1860, a half-billion dollars in gold had been taken out of California. From California, prospectors spread out across the West's mountains and deserts, making strikes and initiating numerous rushes for the next forty years. For a brief period, a unique culture developed in the West where mining camps took hold. The early camps were made up of independent prospectors who filed claims on public domain land and then began to placer mine. The only equipment they needed was a pick, shovel, and a pan. Miners "panning" for gold simply washed gravel that they hoped contained gold. Any gold sank to the bottom of the pan as the lighter gravel was washed away by the water. Prospectors eventually developed other tools of their trade, such as the rocker, "long tom," and sluice. They also used quicksilver or mercury, which would amalgamate with gold and not other material, in conjunction with these early techniques (Paul 1963, pp. 12–36; Hine and Faragher 2000, pp. 234–247).

In the spring of 1849, some 80,000 gold seekers journeyed to California, with 50,000 of them taking the overland route. The Gold Rush participants were a diverse lot, though overwhelmingly male. Most of the men were in their twenties and thirties. About 80 percent of the prospectors were white, American-born men, equally Southerners and Northerners. Within this group of American immigrants to California were a number of slaves and free blacks. Californios—the native Latino population—participated in the Gold Rush as well, though they were overwhelmed by the influx of new-comers such as immigrants from Australia, Hawaii, France, England, Ireland, Mexico, Chile, and China. Referring to California as the "Gold Mountain," the Chinese began to pour in to San Francisco in 1849 by the thousands. Ten years later, 35,000 of them were laboring as miners throughout the state. Like many placer miners, they arrived to labor temporarily for gold, make their fortune, and then return home. Most Chinese were married, but few brought their wives to North America. The 1852 California census listed only seven Chinese women in the state, and over the next three decades most of the women who emigrated from China were prostitutes; many of them were held as bound labor (Johnson 2000, pp. 57–95; White 1991, pp. 191–194).

By the middle of the 1850s, California gold miners had to use increasingly elaborate means to reach gold deposits, leading to the heavy capitalization and corporatization of hard-rock mining. Miners employed hydraulic systems that used great amounts of water under high pressure to demolish entire mountainsides. Eventually, gold encased in veins, or lodes, had to be extracted with rock-crushing devices. Miners used the stamp mill, which had a heavy, iron stamp that rose and fell, crushing the rock on an iron slab. In most parts of the West, the exhaustion of surface deposits led to the construction of shafts and tunnels deep underground, allowing miners to follow the veins of ore. Ore that contained gold, silver, or some other profitable metal had to be blasted and then worked with hand tools or crushing tools. In Butte, Montana, a gold discovery in 1864 led to additional discoveries of copper, silver, and zinc in what has been called the richest hill on earth. Mine shafts there reached depths of a mile and required 3,000 miles of underground rail lines. Such operations required machinery to move hard rock miners and equipment thousands of feet into the earth. Dealing with the intense heat of the mines and the problems of underground water were constant problems faced by miners. These conditions required the technical innovations of elevators, scaffolding, drills, fans, and pumps. This type of mining required millions in investment capital, as huge amounts of ore needed to be extracted in order to make a profit. These mining operations fed the growing industrial sectors in the Midwest and East and the developing Western urban environments. Despite gainful employment, boom and bust cycles predominated because of price fluctuations of metals on the market and the exhaustion of deposits. Either occurrence could cost workers their jobs (Hine and Faragher 2000, p. 239; Wyman 1979, pp. 3–31).

Mining towns that survived the boom and bust periods developed stable social structures and a complex cultural life. Unlike mining towns in the Midwest and East, Western mining towns maintained their frontier quality of having a majority male population throughout much of the nineteenth century. At the apex of the social hierarchy were the elite of mine owners, managers, engineers, and supervisors. Next were the leading merchants, doctors, lawyers, editors, and ministers. Forming the core of the town was its ethnically diverse labor population of skilled and unskilled workers. These workers could be Greek, Serbian, Irish, Welsh, Cornish, German, Italian, and many other nationalities. Most of the managerial positions were held by native-born white men. Not only were these towns heavily male, they also possessed vestiges of the mining camp with saloons, brothels, and gambling establishments. With town populations of primarily single men, women's domestic labor was in high demand. The few women who made their way to these towns and had capital could establish boarding houses, hotels, laundry businesses, restaurants, and taverns. Many women, though, in these early mining communities were forced into prostitution to survive. If one includes all of the frontier towns and cities of the West, about 50,000 women worked as prostitutes during the second half of the nineteenth century. As these towns became permanent, the ratio between men and women evened out, and families resulted. The towns established newspapers, local main street businesses, entertainment such as opera houses and vaudeville performance halls, and schools and churches. Furthermore, some of these towns either evolved into or started off as company towns: a town completely owned and controlled by the mining company, including the housing, stores, doctors, saloons, newspapers, schools, churches, and fraternal associations. By controlling wages and the cost of living in the towns, mine owners could reap fabulous profits (White 1991, p. 304; Emmons 1989; Christensen 2002).

Working the Range

On the wageworkers' frontier, probably the most distinctive laboring environment was raising and driving cattle on the range. Spaniards brought the practice of open-range herding by men on horseback to the Americas during their first century of colonization. The tradition of raising cattle for meat, hides, and tallow in what is today the American Southwest began when Juan de Onate's men drove more than a thousand head into the Rio Grande Valley in 1598. Spanish settlers and mission friars raised large herds in New Mexico, and later rancheros in California and Texas had herds numbering into the thousands. California and Texas proved to have a climate and grasses that helped the stock to thrive. Open-range ranching allowed for the cattle to become semiwild and for evolution to take hold: the result was the Texas longhorn. By the 1760s, Tejanos were driving their cattle to market in New Orleans. The vaqueros along with the rancheros are historically significant figures because together they developed the work life culture and pastoral economy that American cowboys and cattlemen would later emulate throughout the West. Vaqueros established roping techniques, branding, corrals, and roundups to create a viable means to manage cattle enterprises in the region. Vaqueros developed lightweight leather saddles with a horn for roping cattle on horseback, and their clothing such as the broad-brimmed hat, chaps, and spurs were well adapted to the work of the hacienda, to weather and climate conditions, and to the topography. Open-range herding on horseback made sense on the plains, and the practice of driving herds to market for customers was an innovative means of turning arid grasslands of California and Texas into a pastoral economy that could serve consumers locally, in Mexico, and in the young United States of the late eighteenth and early nineteenth centuries (Slatta 1990, pp. 18–23, 39–44).

With heavy U.S. colonization of Mexican Texas in the 1830s, Anglos and African-American slaves began to learn and adapt ranchero and vaquero traditions of ranching and horsemanship. After the Texas Revolution, ranches replaced ranchos. Initially, these early Texas ranchers followed the lead of Tejanos and shipped their cattle out of port cities such as Brownsville or Galveston to ship to market centers, but by the early 1840s, Anglo ranchers had discovered new markets and drove their cattle up to Missouri. With the outbreak of the Civil War, however, the Texas cattle drives to the North were closed off, as were outlets to the sea by the Union naval blockade. With Texans off fighting the war, their herds were neglected and scattered across the countryside, resulting in an estimated 5 to 6 million feral longhorns grazing on the Texas range at the war's end (White 1991, pp. 220–221).

In 1865, the major market centers of the South were commercial wrecks. Texans, though, soon discovered a new and more secure Northern market west of Missouri in Abilene, Kansas, where the Kansas Pacific Railroad (KPR) established a stockyard and depot in 1867. That year 35,000 head of cattle arrived at the railhead, but over the next five years 1.5 million arrived. Other rail lines and towns rivaled Abilene and the KPR, including Wichita and Dodge City, with the Santa Fe line taking a larger number of cattle east. Kansas City, St. Louis, and Chicago were the primary destinations for cattle from the West. In Chicago, the Union Stockyard was capable of handling up to 21,000 cattle each day. Even though the primary meat diet of 1860s America was pork, meat packers Philip Armour and Gustavus Swift used "disassembly" lines in their slaughterhouses, the introduction of refrigerated railroad cars, and advertising and marketing techniques to change Americans' meat diets.

For ranchers and meat processors, profits were in their favor well into the 1880s, triggering the great cattle drives of Western legend. Each spring from the 1860s to the 1880s, cowboys would round up herds, brand the calves, and select steers to send to market. Before railroads made the cattle drive obsolete, cattle had to be driven great distances to get to a market place or a rail center that could take them the rest of the way. Trails such as the Chisholm (from San Antonio to Abilene and Ellsworth) and Goodnight-Loving (to Pueblo and Denver) were hundreds of miles long. Half a dozen cowboys, a cook, and a trail boss could drive 1,000 to 2,000 head of cattle. Not all the animals survived the drive, but enough did to yield a good profit. In all, roughly 4 million cattle had walked north from Texas by 1890. Although most Texas cattle were eventually loaded onto trains to go east for slaughtering, some

Roundup on the Sherman Ranch in Genesee, Kansas ca. 1902. The cattle industry was at its height during the 1880s, as cattle grazed on about 44 percent of the land in the entire nation. (*National Archives and Records Administration*)

continued north to ranges where cattlemen had virtually free access to vast lands still in the public domain. A result of these "long drives" was an extension of open-range cattle ranching from Texas to the northern Great Plains, making Wyoming, the Dakotas, and Montana important cattle territories and then states (Hine and Faragher 2000, pp. 220–223; White 1991, pp. 220–223).

For the wage working cowboys, their work life on the saddle was rough. Drives of hundreds of miles took several months to complete. Hours were long, and it was difficult to manage animals that could panic and stampede. Cowboys had to be on the lookout for strays and guard against predatory animals. Heavy amounts of dust collected in the lungs of experienced hands. At the trail's end they had to force the steers into cramped railroad cars, prodding them forward with steel rods (hence the name "cow-puncher"). Cowboys did not make a lot of money. Around $30 to $40 a month was their pay, and, typical of the wageworkers' frontier, many did not have year-round employment; most made only one or two drives before they left the trade for more long-term employment. Overall, cowboys tended to be young white men from a variety of backgrounds. Many were former Confederate soldiers who made their way west looking for a new start. Texas supplied a large number of these men who returned from the war to their home state and initially could find work only in cattle. George Saunders, president of the Old Time Trail Drivers Association, in 1925 estimated that perhaps as many as one-third of the cowboys were African American, Mexican, and Native American. Contemporary scholars think that this figure may be a little high, though all contemporary Western historians agree that there was far more racial and ethnic diversity among cowboys than was portrayed in popular literature and film or even in much of the historical literature of previous generations (Slatta 1990, pp. 45–50; Hine and Faragher 2000, p. 310; Hunter 2003).

Bindle Stiffs

Sod busting Western pioneer farm families did not remain subsistence farmers for long. Very quickly farming in the West became commercial, having tremendous impact on farm labor practices. As Americans and immigrants settled the Great Plains and Far West after the Civil War, the U.S. economy became increasingly more industrial and urban. In the last third of the nineteenth century and continuing into the next century, Western farming moved to an overwhelmingly market-oriented enterprise to supply the growing urban demand for agricultural products. Large, medium, and even small farmers focused on monocrop agriculture for economic survival. With new technological innovations, farming became increasingly mechanized. New technology, particularly in wheat production, made it possible for farmers to plant thousands of acres. Even a small farmer, however, who took advantage of new farming technology and planted several hundred acres of wheat could not harvest the crop without seasonal help. In California, Washington, and other parts of the West, railroad expansion, irrigation, and new refrigeration technology helped to make commercial monocrop agriculture in fruits, vegetables, sugar beets and other crops possible. Still, limits in harvest technology required farmers to employ seasonal workers. Year-round farmhands were essential to the harvest in the plains and Far West, and some of these wageworkers were able to climb the agricultural ladder. The ladder, however, broke down in many areas as arable land filled up with farmers and as prices for farmland and the necessary mechanized equipment for a profitable farm rose beyond what a farmhand could save to purchase. In fact, in some areas of the West, particularly in parts of California, the ladder never existed (Schob 1975, pp. 267–271; Applen 1974, pp. 1–3; Martin 1988, pp. 4–5; Schwantes 1994, pp. 28–29; Higbie 1997, p. 394).

Even by employing several farmhands, Western farmers in the late nineteenth century needed to supplement that labor with migrant and local seasonal wageworkers: men, and sometimes women and children, who would never become farm owners. These workers became as indispensable to farmers for the crop harvest as the railroad was for transporting crops to market. Stretching from west Texas to central Canada was the North American "wheat belt," where well more than 100,000 migrant and seasonal workers traversed the plains, harvesting and threshing wheat before 1920. In other subregions of the West, farmers developed extensive and intensive agriculture requiring such workers, too. Eastern Washington's wheat-producing Palouse and the fruit-growing areas of the Yakima and Wenatchee valleys were some of the earliest Western agricultural zones that grew to require tens of thousands of seasonal workers every harvest and packing season. As early as the 1870s, California with its bonanza farms located in fertile central river valleys required migrant and seasonal wage laborers. California's commercial agriculture would grow only with time, and it would evolve into the state with the largest number of migrant and seasonal farmworkers in the West (Robbins 1994, p. x; Limerick 1991, pp. 70–71; Worster 1992, pp. 23–24; Street 2004).

These wageworkers developed distinctive cultures of work and life on the road in search of employment in this segment of the wageworkers' frontier. Before the advent of the automobile, migrant workers carrying their belongings on their backs in a bedroll had to travel by freight train. When stopping in area farm towns to find employment, it was customary for these "bindle stiffs" to go to the center of town and wait for farmers from the countryside to arrive and offer employment. Workers would have to determine whether to accept the wages, board, and hours offered. Once they completed the harvesting job, workers had to move on to find other employment. In the wheat belt, workers could find jobs beginning in June and extending to fall from the South Plains to central Canada. Between jobs workers stayed in "jungles." Jungles were temporary communities situated well outside of towns but near a railroad line and a stream or some other water source. In these camps, a worker could make a meal, sleep, socialize, and become informed about other employment. The vast majority of these wheat belt harvesters were young, single, white, native-born men. In the Pacific Northwest, the wheat-harvesting workforce was similar in population and culture. Yet the region was more diverse with women, children, Asians, and Native Americans laboring in hop, berry, and tree fruit harvesting. These particular workers, before the automobile, tended to be local residents. California possessed the most diverse of workforces, with Latinos, Asians, women, children, European immigrants, and native-born white men working for wages on the industrial farms in the state. California had a resident population for some agricultural harvesting, but it was not sufficient. Therefore the state relied upon a migrant labor force that would move through as an army of harvesters, with the majority being white, native-born, and male before World War I (Hall 2001, pp. 10–47).

Building the Iron Roads

Other significant forms of employment on the wageworkers' frontier were the great railroad construction projects that created the transportation infrastructure of the region. Most Western railroads were built first to connect the Pacific Coast to the eastern half of the country. Railroad promoters knew that building the first transcontinental railroad was going to be very expensive. The railroad would help spur economic development in the West, but it would take time for there to be enough freight to haul in order to turn a profit. Therefore railroad companies turned to the federal government for assistance for the cost of construction. The Pacific Railroad Act of 1862 provided loans and also 10 square miles (later increased to 20) of public domain for every mile of track laid. Congress promoted railroad construction to tie California and Nevada, with their rich deposits of gold and silver, to the Union and to stimulate the rapid economic development of other parts of the West. Western entrepreneurs—not just eastern or European corporations—were responsible for some of the railroad building. Collis P. Huntington was one such businessman. He went west to make his fortune not in mining but in selling supplies to miners in California. He and several other business leaders of the Sacramento area, known as the "big four," created the Central Pacific Railroad (CP) in 1862. The CP won from Congress the right to build the Western link of the transcontinental railroad eastward from San Francisco. The Union Pacific Corporation (UP) was given the right to construct the section from Omaha westward. The tracks of the two companies finally met at Promontory Summit, north of the Great Salt Lake, on May 10, 1869 (White 1991, pp. 246–252).

Massive building enterprises such as these required thousands of laborers out on the wageworkers' frontier. The companies needed primarily unskilled day laborers. In the East, the UP employed European immigrants, especially Irish, but also former Confederate soldiers, African Americans, and Mexicans. In the West, the CP had a difficult time recruiting workers because the gold fields and mines siphoned off precious labor sources. Also, white workers, whether native-born or immigrant, had a variety of laboring opportunities. The difficult working conditions of railroad construction motivated many to quit the construction job site and move on to greener pastures. Therefore, in order to supplement an anemic labor pool, Charles Crocker, one of the "big four" of the CP, decided to employ Chinese workers. Very quickly Chinese laborers became the wageworkers of choice by the CP. The Chinese possessed a tremendous work ethic and the capacity to learn a variety of skills necessary to build the railroad over deep gorges and through the granite-mountains of the Sierras. As of 1867, nearly 90 percent of the CP workforce was Chinese, which numbered around 12,000 workers.

The two workforces of the CP and UP had several distinguishing characteristics. The Chinese preferred to supply their own food rather than partake of the company fare of beef, potatoes, and bread. Chinese merchants and vendors supplied the workers with foods similar to what the workers would prepare in their homeland: fish, cabbage, rice, and so forth. Chinese workers also drank green tea instead of the less than safe water supplied by the company. Some Chinese workers also smoked opium when off the worksite rather than drink whiskey. Chinese food preferences saved the CP money, and their behavior off the worksite rarely interfered with productivity. The UP, in contrast, had a workforce that ate the company fare but also patronized purveyors of vice, those who supplied the workers with gambling, prostitutes, and whiskey. In fact, a tent city followed the UP as it laid track west. According to one source, "by a ratio of four to one, more Union Pacific workers died from exposure, violence, and disease in these 'Hell-on-Wheels' tent towns than the many industrial accidents." However, despite the different cultural worlds of the railroad construction workers, they were an impressive workforce that could lay miles of track in a day (Hine and Faragher 2000, pp. 280–288).

Timber Beasts

Growing up alongside mining, agriculture, and railroad construction was the West's lumber industry. It had its earliest beginnings in California in the 1850s, particularly with companies that could supply San Francisco with necessary lumber. The city rapidly emerged as the most significant urban center of the Far West, and it required lumber to expand. As area lumber sources depleted, new sources needed to be found. One of these new sources was the redwood forests to the north. Humboldt County emerged in the 1870s and 1880s as the primary locus of lumber company activity. The lumber industry in California centralized rather quickly in comparison to other regions. Large corporations sought to integrate their operations vertically, so that they owned mills and vast tracts of timber lands where they could establish their own logging operations. Logging and milling the timber into lumber, of course, required a workforce. At first many of the workers who journeyed to the logging camps and mills in this sector of the wageworkers' frontier were frustrated gold field miners, the independent prospector type who had hoped to get rich in the Gold Rush. Finding their gold fortune too elusive, some of these workers fell back on logging and milling skills that they had learned in New England or eastern Canada, their home regions.

Working and living conditions for lumber workers varied in California. Wages for logging and mill workers were higher than back East. For example, the Dolbeer and Carson Company in Humboldt County paid its workers between $40 and $70 a month. These wage rates were considerably higher than what the same worker could earn on the job in Maine or Nova Scotia. Still, the work was seasonal. Logging operations began in spring and continued through the fall until heavy rains brought production to a halt. The supply of raw timber then reduced output in the mills, which led to layoffs. During the off season lumber workers had to find other employment or hole up for the winter in San Francisco or another city until work commenced again in the spring. Turnover at logging sites in particular could be high. The work was difficult and dangerous. Days were typically twelve hours, with mill workers gaining the ten-hour day in 1890 (Cornford 1987, pp. 7–27).

Although logging and milling would continue to be important in California and other areas of the West, the Northwest became the most important lumber producing region. At first the lumber industry served local needs, but with the exhaustion of forest lands in the Great Lakes area toward the end of the nineteenth century, lumber companies looked to the forests of Washington, Oregon, northern Idaho, and western Montana to exploit. Transportation connections between the Northwest and the transcontinental railroads were also important for the development of the lumber industry because they provided access to large lumber markets in Midwestern and

Eastern states. The owners of the saw mills and logging camps tended to be few in number. The giants of the industry included Weyerhauser and the Southern Pacific and the Northern Pacific railroads. The concentration of ownership was extreme, especially in Washington and Oregon. The larger companies employed hundreds of loggers in numerous logging camps and hundreds of mills. Independent logging operators did exist in the Northwest more so than in California. These operators, who supplied timber to saw mill companies that could not afford to establish their own logging camps, were known as gyppos, and they could be found more in the inland regions of the Northwest than along the coast (Schwantes 1996, pp. 215–222; Jensen 1945, pp. 99–102; Robbins 1988, p. 7; Mittelman 1923, pp. 315–316).

The labor force that logged the Northwest woods and drove logs down river to the mills shared many of the experiences of mill workers. The ten-hour day and the seven-day work week were the standard for the industry at the end of the nineteenth century. Unlike California, wages were not unusually high. However, as in California, working conditions were unsafe and unsanitary, particularly in the logging camps. Some of the most dangerous aspects of the loggers' employment were the huge saws they operated and a concomitant lack of company safety regulations. Furthermore, in many instances workers were forced to find employment through employment agents. It was common for lumber companies to hire only workers who had paid the employment service for the job. Living conditions in the logging camps were especially difficult for workers. Although some employers had healthful and sanitary bunkhouses and cooking facilities, most did not. In fact, most logging camps lacked showers or bathing accommodations for the workers, drying rooms for rain-soaked clothing, a place to wash soiled work clothes, or nutritional food. The common bunkhouse was usually overcrowded. Bunk beds were often made of wood and sometimes slept two men to a bunk. A blanket covering a loose bed of straw was what usually passed for mattresses. Body lice were rampant in such camps because of the inability of the workers to bathe adequately and because of the lack of sanitary beds. Also, as employers did not provide adequate bedding, workers had to carry a bedroll from job site to job site. The "bindle stiff" culture of agricultural labor could be found in the logging camps as well. Moreover, the harvest workers and logger could be one and the same person, depending on seasonal employment opportunities (*Industrial Worker*, May 13, 1916; *West Coast Lumberman*, September 15, 1917; O'Connor 1964, p. 60; Hyman 1963; Kornbluh 1964, pp. 257–259).

Laboring in the City

Augmenting the wageworkers' frontier in the countryside was an ethnically and racially diverse Western urban workforce that included women and children. Unlike cities in the Midwest and Northeast, the West had few truly complex industrial manufacturing cities until well into the twentieth century. Urban centers in the West tended to focus on regional industries such as mining, lumber, fishing, canneries, commerce, and transportation.

For several decades, San Francisco stood alone as a city comparable to major cities east of the Mississippi River. Toward the end of the century, Denver, Seattle, Portland, and other Western cities began to add to their regional industrial specializations, becoming manufacturing centers in their own right. Even though Western cities never reached the level of manufacturing complexity of Chicago or New York before World War II, the formation of an urban Western working class did possess attributes similar to those of its counterpart in the Midwest and Northeast. Western cities required skilled printers, tailors, carpenters, masons, and machinists, as well as unskilled day laborers. Towns devoted to one major industry such as mining and smelting required a competent specialized workforce. Advertisements, boosterism, recruitment, and word of mouth brought wage laborers to the West from other parts of the United States and from overseas. In most cases, Western emigrants found that the Rocky Mountain and Pacific states paid higher wages for both skilled and unskilled work. Moreover, despite a higher cost of living in the West, workers' real wages still were the highest in the country (Brundage 1994, pp. 8–9; White 1991, pp. 277–280).

San Francisco epitomized the ethnic and racial diversity of the West. From the late nineteenth to the early twentieth century, 50 and sometimes 70 percent of the city's population was either foreign born or children of foreign-born parents. The Irish were the dominant ethnic group from the Gold Rush to late in the century, with Germans "including Protestants, Catholics, and Jews" being a close second. At the end of the century and continuing into the early decades of the twentieth, Scandinavians and Italians became large immigrant groups. Like many Western cities, San Francisco's most significant nonwhite population was Asian. The city had the largest Chinese immigrant population in the West. Although some of these immigrant groups found avenues to self-employment as merchants, grocers, manufacturers, owner-operators of fishing boats, and in other entrepreneurial ventures, many had to find employment as wageworkers. Using occupational categories and birthplace of workers' parents for 1900, a breakdown of ethnicity and employment becomes clear. For example, native-born whites controlled the salaried professions and white-collar jobs. Germans dominated the skilled trades with Irish working in both skilled and unskilled capacities. High percentages of Italians could be found employed as fishermen, while many Scandinavians found employment as sailors and boatman. Because of discriminatory hiring practices, Chinese workers congregated in laundry, cigar making, textiles, and service jobs (Issel and Cherny 1986, pp. 53–58).

Even though women and children also worked for wages, most often their work life tended to be unpaid in the family home, farm, or business. Nonetheless, in small to large Western cities, native-born and immigrant women and children could be found working for wages in a variety of occupations. One sector in which they found gainful employment was in fruit and vegetable canneries. Employers tended to prefer women's and children's labor to that of men. Therefore, women and children very quickly came to dominate the workforce in the canning industries of the West Coast. A typical breakdown of labor employment tasks is revealed in a U.S. Department of Agriculture study of a plant in Eugene, Oregon, circa 1915. Here girls

Women size lemons by hand before packing them, Lamanda Park, California, ca. 1923. (*Library of Congress*)

worked at the preparing tables while women cleaned and canned the fruit with a female supervisor as a "forewoman." The smaller number of men and boys in the plant worked as helpers, receivers, clerks, and warehousemen. The employment practices were very similar in Washington and California, where as much as three-quarters of the fruit and vegetable cannery workforce was female (*Sacramento Bee*, August 18, 1908; "Forrest Grove" and "Eugene," USDA Cannery Survey OSU Archives; U.S. Census 1904, pp. 140–141, 150–151; U.S. Census 1913, 289, pp. 381–382).

In California, cannery syndicates proved highly effective in sharing the risks associated with this seasonal, consumer-driven industry. The largest of these combinations was the California Packing Corporation, or Calpak, better known by its label Del Monte. By 1916 it was the largest canning operation in the world. One of the major syndicates associated with Del Monte was the California Fruit Canners Association (CFCA). Owned by an Italian immigrant, Marc Fontana, the CFCA had the world's largest cannery as early as 1913, with the Santa Clara Valley as the source of the fruits and vegetables and the immigrant neighborhoods in San Francisco, San Jose, and Oakland supplying the labor. Overall, Calpak or Del Monte had associated canning operations and fruit packing plants—numbering over seventy—in other parts of the state as well as in Oregon and Washington, where it employed thousands of women and girls (Greenberg 1985, pp. 51–53; Braznell 1982, pp. 29–30, 43; Reis 1985, p. 177).

As early as the 1880s, California's cannery workforce was fairly diverse, especially in Bay Area canneries. Workers came from the ranks of native-born whites, African Americans, and Latinos and from immigrant groups from Europe and Mexico. In some canneries, half the women wageworkers were Italian. Women's ages ranged from the early teens to the early seventies: most were single, but more were married with each passing decade and always a few were widowed. For these and other cannery workers, the canning season tended to be longer in urban areas than in rural areas. The turnover rate was high, and many did not work the entire season from spring to fall. The reasons for their desire to work in the canneries varied dramatically from women wanting "pin money," to supplementing their families' income, to making this trade part of their year-round employment cycle. One of the overriding reasons that they chose canning was that it was one of the few well-paying occupations for women with limited skills and modest education. The temporary nature of the employment gave women additional flexibility in regard to their family responsibilities. This was true for single as well as married women, as many single women and girls were still living with their parents, siblings, or extended family members. Contributing to the larger "family income" was significant for the family's standard of living (*Third Biennial Report* 1888, pp. 20–21, 57–58, 72–74; Reis 1985, p. 179; Industrial Welfare Commission 1917, p. 9).

A Labor Movement for the Few

Growing out of the wageworkers' frontier and the urban Western labor experience was a labor movement forced to deal with the power of employers, ethnic and racial diversity in workplaces, and the various skill levels of wageworkers. The ethnic and racial diversity of the West in both rural and urban communities made heterogeneous labor organizations difficult to establish. Therefore, early labor unions were exclusionary, with organization focused on the skilled trades practiced chiefly by white American-born men and male immigrants from Europe. It was thought by organizers that these workers were better able to negotiate with employers because their labor was not easily replaceable. The political expression of the labor movement could be both progressive in dealing with workplace issues and racist when it came to Asian immigrants. One of the most divisive immigration issues of the day involved Chinese workers in the West. Hostility to Chinese immigration occurred during the earliest period of the California Gold Rush, but it reached its high point later in the century. In California, the 1870s brought dramatic economic changes, especially with the onset of the Panic of 1873 and subsequent depression. As unemployed workers from the East made their way to California to find employment, Chinese immigration reached its peak in 1876. Wages were falling, and the numbers of unemployed white men increased in San Francisco. Also, in 1877, the effects of the country's first national railroad strike began to ripple through the West. Rising out of these difficult economic circumstances, the "Chinese Question" made its way into the labor movement's political expression. The Working Man's Party of California (WPC) galvanized working and some middle-class support for political and economic reforms and simultaneously reactionary social legislation. Led by the Irish immigrant and former drayman Dennis Kearney, the WPC's 1878 platform called for the "eight-hour day; direct election of United States Senators; compulsory education; abolition of contract labor on public works; state regulation of banks, industry, and railroads; and a more equitable tax system." Coupled with these calls for substantial reforms was an effort to expel the Chinese from the state and forbid new Chinese immigrants from entering California. The third party soon fell apart in the early 1880s, along with its reform agenda. Nevertheless, the anti-Chinese sentiment found great resonance throughout the state and in other parts of the West. Even though violence was associated with the anti-Chinese movement as early as 1849, it was a series of riots that broke out in the 1870s and 1880s that amounted to something similar to anti-Jewish pogroms in Europe that left hundreds of Chinese workers dead and injured. The culmination of this hostility and political agitation led to Congress's passage of the Chinese Exclusion Act in 1882, which prohibited Chinese immigration and naturalization and placed limits on the civil rights of those currently residing in the country (Johnson 2000, pp. 247–249; Schwantes 1996, pp. 156–157; McWilliams 1949, pp. 171–176; White 1991, pp. 354–355).

The labor movement of the West engaged in political action across the spectrum of party politics, including support for the union labor parties in California and Colorado and the Socialist Party in a variety of Western states in the first two decades of the twentieth century. For the most part, however, labor tended to work with the two major political parties on a nonpartisan basis before the 1930s. Union leaders and the rank and file were much more focused on economic power through creating and maintaining strong trade unions rather than committing to one or another party to gain political power. Trade unionism—in the West like its counterpart in the East—consisted of workers in specific trades such as printers, carpenters, stonemasons, and teamsters. These union members were largely skilled workers, native-born white or European immigrant men. Their trade union affiliations translated into trade councils at the city level and federations of labor at the state level. These organizations could be rather progressive, especially in regard to supporting the eight-hour day, compulsory education, and state regulation of industry, to mention just a few reforms (McWilliams 1949, pp. 128–130; Issel and Cherny 1986, pp. 81–83; Schwantes 1991, pp. 129–130; Johnston 2003, pp. 78–79, 100–102).

Large cities such as San Francisco and Denver and smaller cities such as Spokane and Portland established a strong trade union movement with a central labor assembly. Other industrial towns that centered on one industry, such as the mining community in Butte, Montana, established a strong union consciousness among workers. Despite these labor institutions, most wageworkers in the West remained unorganized for a variety of reasons. For example, the heterogeneous nature of the wage workforce created a number of racial and ethnic divisions. Unionized, skilled workers prevented Chinese, Japanese, Latinos, African Americans, and other minorities from taking part in their trades and from joining their unions. In many ways, trade unions could be very conservative in terms of whom they allowed to be employed in their sector of the economy and whom they would permit into their organizations. Furthermore, women were not welcomed into the skilled trades, and those women who did work for wages tended to work temporarily in canneries, packinghouses, and in field and orchard harvesting. Male trade unionists believed that women would eventually marry and cease wage employment to work in the home. They also thought that women who did work full time as waitresses, laundresses, domestics, and at other unskilled jobs lacked sufficient commitment to their trades to be organized. Even when these wageworkers went on strike or tried to organize into their own unions, urban trade councils gave them little long-term support.

Racism and sexism help to explain why white, male trade unionists failed to organize these particular workers, but prejudice such as this was not unique to the West. What was unique to the region was a split in the wage workforce between the "home guard" and "migratory" workers and the nature of their employment. Home guard workers tended to be wage or salary workers who were either skilled tradesmen or professional and managerial employees. These men had roots in the community with family ties and economic and social connections. Moreover, as the American Federation of Labor (AFL) gained strength in the 1880s and 1890s, the federation's rather conservative philosophy of organizing primarily skilled male workers and advancing the political interests of these workers within the existing political structure of party politics came to heavily influence city labor councils and state federations of labor. The AFL leadership tended to seek an accommodation with capitalism and saw skilled workers as permanent members of the capitalist system who simply required fair compensation for their labor. The temporary and seasonal migratory workers in agriculture, mining, logging, and construction, however, did not easily fit into that type of a labor movement. They worked and lived within the wageworkers' frontier or at the margins of urban employment as unskilled laborers. These workers required a different kind of labor organization. For many of them and for those who would become their leaders, an accommodation with capitalism was unrealistic, especially when employers sought autocratic control of a workplace manned by unskilled and therefore replaceable labor (Schwantes 1987, pp. 44–45).

A Union for All

Wageworkers in the West were ripe for a labor organization that could speak to their distinctive work life. The Knights of Labor, the most important labor federation in the United States in the 1870s and 1880s, became that organization. The Knights possessed a labor movement philosophy that had strong resonance among itinerant men in the wageworkers' frontier. The federation focused on union organizing in the workplace rather than on party politics, which made sense to mobile Western men who did not reside in a community long enough to vote. The Knights argued that wageworkers as a class of wealth producers deserved the full fruits of their labor and that the developing industrial capitalist system channeled that wealth into the hands of the few who did not do the work. The Knights argued for unity among the producing classes, so that all workers regardless of trade, gender, race, ethnicity, religion, or national origin should join together into one great house of labor. Even small businessmen and farmers were permitted as members. The Knights, however, did not welcome the Chinese. They believed that the Chinese refused to assimilate into U.S. society and that they worked at rates that undercut white workingmen. The Knights wholeheartedly supported Chinese exclusion. Still, the thrust of the Knights' agitation was against big business and industrialization. Before their very eyes, they could see independent, self-employed skilled workers become a dependent class of wage laborers (Lingenfelter 1974, p. 127; Hine and Faragher 2000, pp. 298–299; Schwantes 1991, pp. 129–130; Fink 1994, p. 27).

The Knights' challenge to industrial capitalism in the West manifested itself in unexpected places, such as with cowboys out on the range. During the 1880s, ranching moved dramatically from small- and medium-size family-owned operations to corporate ranching. Heavy Eastern and foreign investment had moved into the region. With the peak of the cattle boom in the first half of the decade, big profits were possible for investors. The absentee owners of these corporate ranching operations employed hundreds of cowboys and an onsite management team. In the 1880s, cowboys became Knights, forming locals in order to address their economic concerns. In the spring of 1883, 300 cowboys struck for $50 a month on the XIT ("Ten in Texas") and on other ranches simultaneously. They held out for more than a year against paid gunmen and Texas Rangers, but in the end they were replaced by scabs. In 1886, a Wyoming cowboy strike was more effective over a wage cut. The owners raised the wage to its original level, but the leaders of the strike were fired and blacklisted. In the mid-1880s, ranch hands organized the Northern New Mexico Small Cattlemen and Cowboys' Union. They argued that as "the working season of the average cowboy is only about five months, and we think it nothing but justice that the cowmen should give us living wages the year round." But the cattlemen organized into powerful stockmen's associations and broke any efforts by workers to organize and demand improvements in wages and working conditions. Although cowboys were ineffective in creating long-lived unions or more victorious strike actions, the fact that some did try to organize underscores the industrial and corporate nature of some sectors of Western ranching. Few cowboys or ranch hands for that matter could save enough of their wages to become ranch owners and thus attain economic independence (Lopez 1999, pp. 164–178; Robbins 1994, pp. 70–71; Igler 2001).

Miners, like cowboys, had little hope of becoming owners of mines. Permanent wage labor was the future for most miners in the late nineteenth century. The Knights, though, spread the message that miners as a class were the true wealth producers in that industry and that they deserved the full fruits of their labor. Unfortunately, the lack of legal protections for unionized miners and the determination of employers to maintain their control over the workplace engendered a great deal of class conflict. Labor's challenge to management's autocratic control led to some of the most spectacular examples of class warfare in the West. For example, scholars have termed a series of conflicts between management and labor in northern Idaho in the

1880s and 1890s the Coeur d'Alene mining wars. These wars involved two major episodes of industrial violence that wracked the new state of Idaho. Starting in the late 1880s, in the mining towns of Wardner, Gem, Burke, and Mullan, Idaho, hard-rock miners met secretly to form unions. At about the same time, mine owners formed the Mine Owners Protective Association (MOPA). Mine owners did have a variety of economic problems to face, such as the falling price of silver and rising railroad rates. But the chief concern of those in the association was union power. Mine owners, like most employers in the late nineteenth century and beyond, thought of labor as a variable cost that they could manipulate to their own economic advantage. Unions stood in the way of owners having control of the wages that they paid their workers (Wyman 1979, pp. 161–166; Lingenfelter 1974, pp. 219–228; Brundage 1994, pp. 2–3; Schwantes 1996, pp. 317–318).

Coeur d'Alene miners struck when the MOPA reduced wages in 1892. The miners walked out, and the owners vowed never to hire a union man and set about to destroy the union. The MOPA, knowing that local government officials were supportive of the union workers, hired a private force of armed guards to protect the mine and scab labor. Although initially peaceful, angry miners, frustrated over the length of the strike and the federal injunctions that mine owners obtained against them, took up arms in July 1892. They attacked the Frisco and Gem mines, destroyed the Frisco mill, and captured all the guards and scabs. They then marched on the Bunker Hill and Sullivan mines and captured the company's ore concentrator. They achieved the dismissal of all the scabs there, though the fighting left six men dead. Still, the miners achieved only a brief victory. The MOPA now easily obtained a declaration of martial law from Governor Norman Willey. Six companies of the Idaho National Guard marched in and made wholesale arrests of union members and of local businessmen and lawyers who sympathized with the union. The soldiers herded more than 300 men into crude stockades, or "bullpens." Many were held for almost two months. The local unions that conducted the strike were broken over the passing months. While in jail, however, leaders—including the Irish miner Edward Boyce—laid plans for the creation of a larger and more effective union. In Butte, delegates for local unions from Idaho, Colorado, Montana, and South Dakota met with the Butte Miners' Union and created the Western Federation of Miners (WFM) in 1893. Boyce, like much of the early leadership and rank and file of the WFM, had been influenced by, or were themselves, former members of the Knights (Lingenfelter 1974, pp. 196–218; Wyman 1979, pp. 165–166).

Between 1893 and 1899, the WFM persuaded the mine owners in the Coeur d'Alene area to pay union wages. They were unable to achieve this at the Bunker Hill and Sullivan Company mines. The owners of the mines were very skillful in using their spies to identify union organizers and their supporters to the owners, so that they could fire them and thereby prevent a successful union organizing effort. On Saturday, April 29, 1899, miners commandeered a train to the Bunker and Sullivan mines. Along the way they stopped at the Frisco powder house and more miners got on the train. By the time they reached their destination, nearly a thousand armed and masked miners were on the train dubbed the "Dynamite Express." When the

Dynamite Express approached the Bunker Hill and Sullivan complex, company guards fled along with the superintendent and manager. The workers burned the company's office and boardinghouse and placed 3,000 pounds of dynamite around the concentrator's support pilings. At 2:26 P.M. the dynamite was ignited, blowing the expensive structure into pieces. The miners celebrated their victory as they commandeered the train back to their mining towns. However, repercussions set in very quickly. Idaho's governor Frank Steunenberg declared a state of insurrection. He wired for federal troops, as most of Idaho's National Guard was in the Philippines. Brigadier General Henry Clay Merriam and about 800 troops, some of them all black units, arrived within a few days. Nearly a thousand men were arrested and placed in bullpens. Nevertheless, over the weeks many would be released after it proved difficult to link anyone specifically with the dynamite action. In the end, only twenty or so miners were convicted on reduced charges and sentenced to two years or less in San Quentin Prison (Schwantes 1996, pp. 320–322).

The Industrial Workers of the World

Despite the efforts of the WFM, AFL, and other unions and labor federations in the West, the labor movement effected little change in working conditions and wages. Miners did receive the eight-hour day in 1910 throughout much of the region either through law or contract, but safety regulations in mines and other industrial workplaces lacked any kind of comprehensive political support or could survive court challenges. Moreover, urban labor councils had a mixed record of success when one examines the full spectrum of the West's working class, whether in regard to the eight-hour day or other workplace issues. Out of this frustration with lack of reforms, both in the West and East, was born the Industrial Workers of the World (IWW). In 1905, William D. "Big Bill" Haywood—the secretary of the WFM—chaired a convention of disaffected labor organizations in Chicago that created the IWW. The West was well represented, with the WFM as a major constituency of this new labor federation. Although the IWW and their members, known as Wobblies, would have a presence in other parts of the country and engage in a series of spectacular strikes, it was in the West that their union would find its deepest resonance among wageworkers.

The IWW embraced much of the organizing strategy of the Knights, except that they would welcome Asians into their ranks. The Wobblies also adopted the industrial union model of the WFM in that they would organize by industry rather than by trade. The IWW was especially interested in organizing unskilled laborers of the West who worked in the extractive industries and had to roam the countryside hopping freight trains and living in jungle camps and flophouses between jobs. Eventually, Wobblies, through their industrial unions, hoped to overthrow capitalism and the state through a general strike, bringing working-class exploitation to an end and ushering in a new society controlled by and for the benefit of the world's working classes. Even though the IWW had very lofty goals, it had problems from its birth in both holding itself together and defending itself from the onslaught

William D. "Big Bill" Haywood: Union Man of the American West

It was a warm, smoke-filled meeting hall in Chicago at midmorning on June 27, 1905. The room was filled with two hundred labor leaders, radicals, and revolutionaries from across the United States. Bill Haywood climbed up to the platform and walked to the podium in front of the crowd and with a board in his hand gaveled the group to order. "Fellow Workers," he announced to the men and women before him, "this is the Continental Congress of the Working Class. We are here to confederate the workers of this country into a working-class movement in possession of the economic powers, the means of life, in control of the machinery of production and distribution without regard to capitalist masters" (Kornbluh 1988, p. 1). The Industrial Workers of the World (IWW) was born that day, and it was no coincidence that the midwife was Bill Haywood, secretary-treasurer of the most militant labor union in the West, the Western Federation of Miners (WFM).

Bill Haywood was born in Salt Lake City on a cold February day in 1869. He was a first generation westerner. His Midwestern father came out in search of gold, and his Scot-Irish mother emigrated from South Africa in search of a better life. Haywood's father, like many placer miners, became a hard rock miner and had to leave his family behind as he traveled to find work. He died while working at a British-owned mine when Haywood was just a boy. His mother married another miner, and Haywood's family moved to the mining town of Ophir. There, Haywood grew up on the wageworkers' frontier in a mining town on the edge of wilderness. After moving back to Salt Lake City, he decided to leave home and find a trade for himself. In 1884, he chose mining and at fifteen years old went to work at a mine in northern Nevada.

Haywood's career as a miner began with mentoring by fellow miner and Irish immigrant Pat Reynolds. Reynolds, a member of the Knights of Labor, imparted to the young apprentice the necessity of unions for workers' self-protection.

William "Big Bill" Haywood (1869–1928) was the secretary-treasurer of the Western Federation of Miners at the time it joined the Industrial Workers of the World. (*Library of Congress*)

He and Reynolds discussed much of the labor news of the day, including the Haymarket Riot in Chicago and the subsequent trial and execution of the Haymarket anarchists. Although he never had an opportunity to join the Knights, he wrote years later that he "was a member in the making." The mine soon closed, and Haywood had to move on to find other employment. A mining job brought Haywood back to Utah where he met, fell in love, and married Nevada Jane. Their life together was difficult at best. Jane lost her first child and suffered from a lifelong debilitating illness. Haywood brought his wife out to Nevada and left mining to work briefly as a ranch hand. But the better pay of mining beckoned him. After several jobs, he landed a position at a mine in Silver City, Idaho. Ed Boyce, president of the WFM, easily organized the camp in

1896. Haywood was ripe for the WFM's industrial union message, and he quickly rose up the ranks of his local to a seat on the federation's national executive board (Haywood 1974, p. 31).

Working as a union operative came naturally to Haywood. His work in the WFM, whether negotiating for higher wages, overseeing a union medical plan, or building a hospital for miners, created a loyal following. In 1901, Haywood's fellow miners elected him secretary-treasurer for the WFM. He relocated to Denver and helped the union move through several very difficult years. In 1904, violence broke out in Cripple Creek, Colorado. Miners dynamited a train of strike breakers and fled to the hills, where they engaged in firefights with state troops. Haywood was forced to make frequent trips out to the camps of striking miners. Law enforcement arrested him repeatedly, and he had to defend himself from so many physical attacks that he took to carrying a pistol. Despite his energetic commitment to striking miners in Colorado, the WFM kept losing strikes. In an effort to create greater support for industrial unionism, Haywood and the WFM leadership helped to create the IWW.

For all practical purposes, Haywood would finish out his labor movement career as a Wobbly. Slowly his close ties to the West would become strained and eventually break. He spent little time with Nevada Jane and his children as his union activities took him into direct confrontation with the powers of the capitalist system. In 1905, Frank Steunenberg, former governor of Idaho, was killed by an assassin's bomb blast. Harry Orchard confessed to the killing and implicated Haywood and other members of the WFM leadership in the assassination. Haywood, WFM president Charles Moyer, and former union organizer George Pettibone were kidnapped in Colorado and brought to stand trial in Idaho. Haywood, ably defended by Clarence Darrow, was found not guilty, and the prosecution dropped their case against the other two defendants. Haywood, though, would be forced to leave the WFM as his ties to the IWW grew stronger.

Plunging into socialist politics and IWW organizing, Haywood became a major figure in the radical wing of the American labor movement. However, it was his election to secretary-treasurer of the IWW in 1914 that bought him to the leadership of the famed Wobblies. Haywood did not forget his roots. He worked tirelessly to organize the unskilled laborers of the United States regardless of race, ethnicity, or sex. He promoted the producer ethic and inclusiveness of the Knights and the industrial unionism of WFM in his organizing efforts. By the summer of 1917, he presided over a union of perhaps 100,000 strong that had members in agriculture, mining, logging, construction, railroads, and many other industries, with the most successful industrial unions being in the West. Haywood's challenge to the forces of capitalism and the state would engender serious repression in wartime America. He was arrested, tried, and convicted of violating wartime statutes. He continued to advocate for the workers of the world while free on appeal, but in the end he decided to flee in 1921 to the Soviet Union, never to return to the West or anywhere else in the United States.

References and Further Reading

Carlson, Peter. *Roughneck: The Life and Times of Big Bill Haywood*. New York: W. W. Norton and Company, 1983.

Conlin, Joseph R. "William D. 'Big Bill' Haywood: The Westerner as Labor Radical." In Melvyn Dubofsky and Warren Van Tine, eds., *Labor Leaders in America*. Urbana: University of Illinois Press, 1987.

Dubofsky, Melvyn. *"Big Bill" Haywood*. New York: St. Martin's Press, 1987.

Haywood, William D. *Bill Haywood's Book: The Autobiography of William D. Haywood* [1929]. New York: International Publishers, 1974.

Kornbluh, Joyce. *Rebel Voices: An IWW Anthology*. Chicago: Charles H. Kerr Publishing, 1988.

of employer and government oppression. The WFM left the new federation soon after it was founded, and Wobblies lost most of the strikes that they instigated. Even bringing their message to the working class of the West was a struggle in itself. The Wobblies were forced to engage in a series of "free speech fights" from 1908 to 1916 in cities throughout the West where migrant workers passed through looking for jobs or living on their stake until new employment came their way. The free speech fights advanced the cause of free speech and later helped to inspire the creation of the American Civil Liberties Union. These fights, though, had little success in organizing wage-workers (Hall 2001, pp. 4–8; White 1991, pp. 290–293).

Western Wobblies were most successful when they adapted to the cultural world of the workers they sought to reach. With many men on the wageworkers' frontier engaged in a variety of different trades annually, the union set up mixed locals rather than locals for one specific industry. These mixed locals served as recruitment center, social club, lecture hall, flophouse, soup kitchen, and post office for workers in any industry or trade. Moreover, Wobbly job delegates rode the rails, lived in the jungles, and worked the job sites side by side with their fellow wageworkers. These delegates signed up new members with union supplies that they carried in their own bindles and distributed IWW literature throughout the countryside. The IWW union card became a free pass on freight train travel, and the IWW songbook was filled with songs that reflected the work life experiences of laborers out on the wageworkers' frontier. Many IWW songs were "zipper songs," a working-class songwriting tradition of using a popular melody and substituting different lyrics to reflect particular issues in working-class life. Other songs were written specifically to address frustrations on the job site that resulted in a tried and true form of working-class protest: sabotage. A case in point is "Ta-Ra-Ra Boom De-Ay," written by the popular song writer and Wobbly martyr Joe Hill.

> I had a job once threshing wheat, worked sixteen hours
> with hands and feet.
> And when the moon was shining bright, they kept me
> working all the night.
> One moonlight night, I hate to tell, I "accidentally"
> slipped and fell.
> My pitchfork went right in between some cog wheels of
> that threshing-machine.
> Ta-ra-ra-boom-de-ay!
> It made a noise that way,
> And wheels and bolts and hay,
> Went flying every way.
> That stingy rube said, "Well!
> A thousand gone to hell."
> But I did sleep that night,
> I needed it all right.

The IWW tried to find a niche for itself in industries that the AFL tended to avoid, such as agriculture, construction, and logging. For most wageworkers, logging was a dirty, lice-infested, wet, cold, dangerous, low-paying, long-hour job. Still, those in need of work took these jobs in the mountains of the Pacific and Inland Northwest. Wobblies began organizing drives in 1907 but for ten years struggled. Then, in the summer of 1917, a strike by river drivers began in northern Idaho. They struck for the eight-hour day and for $5.00 a day. That strike spread to the logging camps throughout the Inland Northwest. In August the IWW took leadership of the strike, and it continued to spread west. By September 1917, 75 percent or more of all logging operations in the Northwest came to a stop and resulted in slowing and even halting milling operations. The federal government urged the lumber corporations to give in to the demands of the workers, which included the eight-hour day, laundry and bathing facilities in the camps, increase in wages, and better food and living conditions. The corporations balked. The Department of War, however, grew impatient because the timber used was necessary for the war effort, especially the spruce timber in the Cascade Range in Washington. By fall, the army had entered the forests to harvest the timber and work with local law enforcement to arrest striking workers. Eventually, the IWW came up with an ingenious strategy of striking on the job. Members would go back to work, but only for eight-hour shifts. If fired, then the next crew worked for eight hours only. Their goal was to force the eight-hour day. In spring of 1918, the corporations finally capitulated. The eight-hour day became the standard, and living conditions in the work camps greatly improved over the next decade, making logging a highly sought after occupation. Although the IWW could take some responsibility for these changes in the logging workplace, pressure from the federal government and the Loyal Legion of Loggers and Lumbermen (a company union of sorts) also played a significant role in establishing the eight-hour day and improvement in working conditions (Brazier 1968, pp. 91–105; Kornbluh 1988, pp. 65–66; *Songs of the Workers* 1917, pp. 7, 27, 12; *I.W.W. Songs,* 1918, p. 13; Tyler 1967).

The IWW did not have a long-term organizing presence in the West's labor movement. The federation's radicalism and the antiwar position of many members gave the federal government the excuse it needed to suppress the union beginning in the fall of 1917. The United States had entered World War I in the spring of that year, and eventually Congress passed war-time legislation that federal authorities claimed Wobblies violated. The entire first-, second-, and even most of the third-tier leadership of the union was arrested, tried, and sentenced to long prison terms. The IWW held together in the postwar years, but Wobblies had to deal with state criminal syndicalism laws that were an effort to make the union illegal. Hundreds of IWW members spent years in state penitentiaries in the late 1910s and 1920s. The union did rebound in the early 1920s, but only to suffer from internal divisions in 1924. The demise of the IWW out West, though, had more to do with changes in the wageworkers' frontier than with government oppression or internal conflicts. The IWW's Agricultural Workers Industrial Union (AWIU) is a good example. The AWIU, like the IWW as a whole, was a union made for the largely white, male, migrant labor force. The AWIU supplied half of the federation's treasury and perhaps one-third of its overall membership in 1923. However, it went into steep decline after 1925, not because migrant and seasonal wageworkers were no longer necessary for Western agricultural harvests but because the culture and social makeup of the workforce dramatically changed. In the wheat belt, young men began to own and drive their secondhand "tin lizzes" and trucks throughout the countryside and solicit work directly from the farmer, circumventing the freight train and the jungle. In the fruit and vegetable harvests in West Coast states, white, Latino, and Asian families traveled to different worksites, avoiding the all-male and largely Anglo culture of the IWW union hall. Wobblies simply never successfully adapted their organizing strategy to these changes (Hall 2001, pp. 150–158; Dubofsky 1988).

The Closing of the Wageworkers' Frontier

The wageworkers' frontier was changing dramatically by 1920. It did not end at the same time and in the same industries and trades simultaneously, nor did the West became heavily urban overnight and emulate Midwestern and Eastern cities. These changes were gradual, with some industries losing their frontier quality early and other trades retaining a frontier quality deeper into the twentieth century. The boom and bust nature of the Western economy was fading at the end of the turn of the century, and technology was having a greater impact on labor needs. Migratory and seasonal labor in a variety of industries became less and less significant to the West's economy over the decades, too. For example, electrification and other technological advances in hard-rock and coal mining helped stabilize the industry. As early as the 1890s, more mines could stay open "year-round instead of shutting down when winter weather froze the water power." Mechanization of grain harvests in the 1920s and the spread of the tractor and truck on the farm reduced the need for migrant laborers. Local wageworkers could more sufficiently supply the seasonal labor needs of Great Plains farmers. Also, farmers of fruit, vegetables, sugar beets, potatoes, and other crops increasingly began to provide camps for families of workers to reside in during the harvest seasons. These harvest families drove to the farms and made it part of their annual family work cycles. Road travel was simply replacing freight train travel by workers, which made women and children an ever greater part of wage working in the countryside (Schwantes 1987, pp. 53–55; Deutsch 1987).

Over the course of the late nineteenth and early twentieth centuries, the home guard worker in the urban and rural areas grew to become a standard feature of the Western economy as employment grew more stable in major industries. Railroad companies, for example, still needed construction and maintenance crews, but those crews became permanent employees. As road replaced railroad construction in the early twentieth century, temporary laborers were required, but those workers had homes in the West to return to after the construction job ended. Cattle owners still needed cowhands, but raising cattle on the open range rapidly came to an end by the turn of the century. Ranch hands simply replaced cowboys. The jobs became more stable, and these wageworkers stayed with the same ranch family or corporation year after year. The rural West was fading as a large draw of

Western employment as urban areas grew in complexity and population. Workers heading west had to go to cities to find employment, and there they put down roots. Moreover, the urban labor movement had a conservative edge during the 1920s as the AFL continued to grow in dominance. Its bread and butter unionism eschewed radicalism in favor of pragmatic gains for its membership. The West's wageworkers, even though they processed an ethnic and radical diversity different from other parts of the country and labored in some distinctively Western trades, overall began to resemble the workforce in other regions. The working classes of the West simply became much more similar to those of the rest of the country as the twentieth century unfolded.

References and Further Reading

Applen, Allen. "Migratory Harvest Labor in the Midwestern Wheat Belt, 1870–1940." Ph.D. diss., Kansas State University, 1974.

Braznell, William. *California's Finest: The History of Del Monte Corporation and the Del Monte Brand.* San Francisco: Del Monte Corporation, 1982.

Brundage, David. *The Making of Western Labor Radicalism: Denver's Organized Workers, 1878–1905.* Urbana: University of Illinois Press, 1994.

Carlson, Peter. *Roughneck: The Life and Times of Big Bill Haywood.* New York: W. W. Norton and Company, 1983.

Christensen, Bonnie. *Red Lodge and the Mythic West: Coal Miners to Cowboys.* Lawrence: University of Kansas, 2002.

Conlin, Joseph R. "William D. 'Big Bill' Haywood: The Westerner as Labor Radical." In Melvyn Dubofsky and Warren Van Tine, eds., *Labor Leaders in America.* Urbana: University of Illinois Press, 1987.

Cornford, Daniel A. *Workers and Dissent in the Redwood Empire.* Philadelphia: Temple University Press, 1987.

Deutsch, Sarah. *No Separate Refuge: Culture, Class, and Gender on an Anglo-Hispanic Frontier in the American Southwest, 1880–1940.* New York: Oxford University Press, 1987.

Dubofsky, Melvyn. *We Shall Be All: A History of the Industrial Workers of the World.* 2d ed. Urbana: University of Illinois Press, 1988.

Emmons, David M. *The Butte Irish: Class and Ethnicity in an American Mining Town, 1875–1925.* Urbana: University of Illinois, 1989.

Fink, Leon. *In Search of the Working Class: Essays in American Labor History.* Urbana: University of Illinois Press, 1994.

Greenberg, Jaclyn. "Industry in the Garden: A Social History of the Canning Industry and Cannery Workers in the Santa Clara Valley, California, 1870–1920." Ph.D. diss., University of California, Los Angeles, 1985.

Hall, Greg. *Harvest Wobblies: The Industrial Workers of the World and Agricultural Laborers in the American West, 1905–1930.* Corvallis: Oregon State University, 2001.

Haywood, William D. *Bill Haywood's Book: The Autobiography of William D. Haywood* [1929]. New York: International Publishers, 1974.

Higbie, Toby. "Indispensable Outcasts: Harvest Laborers in the Wheat Belt of the Middle West, 1890–1925." *Labor History* 38 (fall 1997): 393–412.

Hine, Robert V., and John Mack Faragher. *The American West: A New Interpretive History.* New Haven: Yale University Press, 2000.

Hunter, J. Marvin. *The Trail Drivers of Texas.* Austin: University of Texas Press, 2003.

Hyman, Harold M. *Soldiers and Spruce: Origins of the Loyal Legion of Loggers & Lumbermen.* Los Angeles: Institute of Industrial Relations, 1963.

Igler, David. *Industrial Cowboys: Miller & Lux and the Transformation of the Far West, 1850–1920.* Berkeley: University of California Press, 2001.

Industrial Welfare Commission. *The Regulation of the Fruit and Vegetable Canning Industry of California.* Sacramento: California State Printing Office, 1917.

Industrial Worker (Seattle, Washington).

Issel, William, and Robert W. Cherny. *San Francisco, 1865–1932: Politics, Power, and Urban Development.* Berkeley: University of California Press, 1986.

I.W.W. Songs: To Fan the Flames of Discontent. Chicago: I.W.W. Publishing Bureau, 1917.

I.W.W. Songs: To Fan the Flames of Discontent. General Defense Edition. Chicago: I.W.W. Publishing Bureau, 1918.

Jensen, Vernon H. *Lumber and Labor.* New York: Farrar and Rinehart, 1945.

Johnston, Robert D. *The Radical Middle Class: Populist Democracy and the Question of Capitalism in Progressive Era Portland, Oregon.* Princeton: Princeton University Press, 2003.

Johnson, Susan Lee. *Roaring Camp: The Social World of the California Gold Rush.* W. W. Norton and Company, 2000.

Kornbluh, Joyce L., ed. *Rebel Voices: An I.W.W. Anthology.* Ann Arbor: University of Michigan Press, 1964.

Limerick, Patricia Nelson. "The Trail to Santa Fe: The Unleashing of the Western Public Intellectual." In Patricia Nelson Limerick, Clyde A. Milner II, and Charles E. Rankin, eds., *Trails: Toward a New Western History.* Lawrence: University Press of Kansas, 1991, 59–80.

Lingenfelter, Richard E. *The Hardrock Miners: A History of the Mining Labor Movement in the American West, 1863–1893.* Berkeley: University of California Press, 1974.

Lopez, David E. "Cowboy Strikes and Unions." In Walter Nugent and Martin Ridge, eds., *The American West: The Reader.* Bloomington: Indiana University Press, 1999.

Martin, Philip L. *Harvest of Confusion: Migrant Workers in U.S. Agriculture.* Boulder, CO: Westview Press, 1988.

McWilliams, Carey. *California: The Great Exception.* Westport, CT: Greenwood Press, 1949.

Mittelman, Edward B. "The Loyal Legion of Loggers and Lumberman: An Experiment in Industrial Relations." *Journal of Political Economy* 31 (June 1923): 313–341.

O'Connor, Harvey. *Revolution in Seattle: A Memoir.* New York: Monthly Review Press, 1964.

Paul, Rodman Wilson. *Mining Frontiers of the Far West.* New York: Holt, Rinehart and Winston, 1963.

Reis, Elizabeth. "AFL, the IWW, and Bay Area Italian Cannery Workers." *California History* 64 (summer 1985): 174–191.

Robbins, William G. *Hard Times in Paradise: Coos Bay, Oregon, 1850–1986.* Seattle: University of Washington Press, 1988.

Robbins, William G. *Colony & Empire: The Capitalist Transformation of the American West.* Lawrence: University of Kansas Press, 1994.

Sacramento Bee (Sacramento, CA).

Schob, David E. *Hired Hands and Plowboys: Farm Labor in the Midwest, 1815–60.* Urbana: University of Illinois Press, 1975.

Schwantes, Carlos A. "The Concept of the Wageworkers' Frontier: A Framework for Future Research." *Western Historical Quarterly* 18 (January 1987): 39–55.

Schwantes, Carlos A. "Spokane and the Wageworkers' Frontier: A Labor History to World War I." In David H. Stratton, ed., *Spokane and the Inland Empire: An Interior Pacific Northwest Anthology.* Pullman: Washington State University Press, 1991.

Schwantes, Carlos A. *Hard Traveling: A Portrait of Work Life in the New Northwest.* Lincoln: University of Nebraska Press, 1994.

Schwantes, Carlos A. *The Pacific Northwest: An Interpretive History.* Lincoln: University of Nebraska Press, 1996.

Slatta, Richard W. *Cowboys of the Americas.* New Haven: Yale University Press, 1990.

Songs of the Workers: On the Road, in the Jungles and in the Shops. Spokane, WA: Spokane Local of the I.W.W., 1912.

Street, Richard S. *Beasts of the Field: A Narrative History of California Farmworkers, 1769–1913.* Stanford: Stanford University Press, 2004.

Third Biennial Report of the Bureau of Labor Statistics of the State of California for the Years 1887–1888. Sacramento: State Office, J. D. Young, Supt. State Printing, 1888.

Tyler, Robert L. *Rebels of the Woods: The I.W.W. in the Pacific Northwest.* Eugene: University of Oregon, 1967.

U.S. Agriculture Department. Northwest Cannery Survey Collection, Box 1, Folder "Forrest Grove," and Box 2, Folder "Eugene." Oregon State University Archives, Corvallis.

U.S. Agriculture Department. Department of Commerce and Labor, Bureau of the Census. *Special Reports: Occupations at the Twelfth Census.* Washington, DC: Government Printing Office, 1904.

U.S. Agriculture Department. Department of Commerce, Bureau of the Census. *Thirteenth Census of the United States: Volume III, Manufactures 1909 General Report and Analysis.* Washington, DC: Government Printing Office, 1913.

West Coast Lumberman (Tacoma, WA).

White, Richard. *"It's Your Misfortune and None of My Own": A New History of the American West.* Norman: University of Oklahoma Press, 1991.

Worster, Donald. *Under Western Skies: Nature and History in the American West.* New York: Oxford University Press, 1992.

Wyman, Mark. *Hard Rock Epic: Western Miners and the Industrial Revolution, 1860–1910.* Berkeley: University of California Press, 1979.

Women in the West | 11

Martin Padget

On March 30, 1850, an Anglo woman named Margaret Frink set out from Martinsville, Indiana, with a small party of gold-seekers bound for the West Coast. The Frinks, like so many thousands of their fellow Americans, had decided to go west after hearing confirmation of the rumored abundance of gold in California. The group was led by Margaret's husband, Ledyard, a successful merchant. In her journal of the five-month trip across the plains, deserts, and mountains of the West, Frink did not find it necessary to explain in any great detail the motivation behind her trip. It was enough to note that despite the wealth and comfort the Frinks had achieved in Indiana, they "were not yet satisfied" (Frink 1850, p. 59).

Margaret Frink's diary was published in 1897, several years after her death, and it has long been regarded as one of the classic accounts of travel along the California and Oregon trails in the mid-nineteenth century. Written in a literate and accessible style, Frink's account not only provides copious information about the practicalities of day-to-day travel on the overland journey but also creates a window through which the expectations, fears, and disappointments of emigrants can be viewed. Frink shared with so many others the hope that riches would result from the search for gold, although once in California neither she nor her husband headed for the gold fields. Instead, upon arriving in California in September 1850, the couple exploited the booming demand among thousands of emigrants-turned-miners for accommodations and the goods necessary to set out for the gold diggings. Unlike other women on the trail, Frink was not a half-willing accomplice to her husband's vision of what might be achieved in California. Nor did she go west in the austere style that poorer women had to endure, traveling instead in a custom-made wagon fitted with "an India-rubber mattress that could be filled with either air or water, making a very comfortable bed," and with a large supply of clothes that had recently been sewn by her seamstress, not to mention generous stores of food (ibid., p. 60). But much of this luxury was of little account when all emigrants were faced with the aridity and heat of the high desert through modern-day Utah and Nevada and were forced to abandon precious possessions.

When historians first started in earnest to publish articles and books examining Western women thirty or so years ago, Margaret Frink was just the sort of individual who featured in their revisionist studies of the region. Although women like Frink had figured in previous historical accounts of the epic movement of emigrants west during the nineteenth century, their stories had never taken center stage. In Frederick Jackson Turner's frontier thesis it was the actions of men rather than women that were associated with "winning" the West. For Turner and succeeding historians of the frontier, women were featured as supporting characters to the masculine heroes of the main drama in which westward expansion and the extension of the state transformed the notionally free space of the West into the empire for liberty— the fully realized American nation—that Thomas Jefferson had envisaged stretching from the Atlantic to the Pacific.

As the frontier was deemed closed after the 1890 census, so in succeeding decades did American popular culture—in Wild West shows, dime novels, and movie Westerns—become suffused with images of male heroism. Not even in the more sober environment of scholarly education after World War II did major historians find much of substance to say about Western women. Having published the first edition of his large textbook *Westward Expansion: A History of the American Frontier* in 1949, Ray Allen Billington still did not deem it necessary to provide an entry for "women" when the 800-page fourth edition was published in 1974. Several exceptional women were mentioned, such as Anne Hutchinson for her role in the Puritan-era Antinomian Controversy, Narcissa Whitman for crossing the Rockies in 1836 to set up a mission among Cayuse Indians, and Helen Hunt Jackson for her outspoken calls to reform federal Indian policy in the 1870s and 1880s. In contrast to Billington's *Westward Expansion*, Richard White's major overview of Western history, *"It's Your Misfortune and None of My Own": A New History of the American West*, published in 1991, contains numerous entries on women. In composing his account, White was able to draw upon the work of many studies of women in the West that had been published since the mid-1970s. Today, with the benefit of another fifteen years' worth of articles and books on Western women, scholars and students of the West are well placed to appreciate the significance of women of all ethnicities to the history of the region.

This discussion pays attention to the experiences of a wide range of women who came to live in the West from the 1840s to the present day. To convey the diversity of the multicultural West, this chapter focuses on six individuals who can be regarded as representative of women within the communities into which they were born. Sarah Winnemucca, a Northern Paiute Indian, grew up in a culture that became heavily affected by travel along the California Trail during her girlhood in the 1840s and 1850s. In time she became a spokesperson for her people, lecturing to audiences in the East to raise public awareness about the need to provide funds for educational programs for Native people. Winnemucca's travels away from her tribe's homelands also left her partly estranged from her own people, so that she was fully a part neither of her tribal culture nor of the larger American world beyond the confines of tribal reserves in Nevada and Oregon. Sarah Davis, a young Quaker bride who hailed from Michigan, was one of the many thousands of emigrants who passed through Northern Paiute homelands in modern-day western Nevada while en route to the West Coast in 1850. The poet Walt Whitman celebrated such women in his poem "Pioneers! O Pioneers," when he wrote: "O you daughters of the West!/ O you young and elder daughters! O you mothers and you wives!/ Never must you be divided, in our ranks you move united,/ Pioneers! O pioneers!" (Whitman 1977, p. 260).

According to the 1850 census, only 90 African-American women dwelled in California; indeed the total number of black women west of the Mississippi River in that year was a mere 392, or 0.3 percent of all women in the West (Graaf 1980, p. 287). But by the late nineteenth century, African-American middle-class women such as Biddy Mason, a successful entrepreneur in Los Angeles, had forged a significant presence in the West's burgeoning urban centers. Some seventy years after Sarah Davis traveled west to California, a poor young Chinese woman, named Wong Ah So, set out from Guangdong Province in China to travel east to San Francisco. On arriving in California she was shocked to find that, instead of marrying a Chinese man, as she had expected, she was forced to become a prostitute. Between the mid-nineteenth and early twentieth centuries, this proved to be a common fate for the poorer Chinese women emigrants who set out for the United States. At a time of general hostility toward the Chinese on the West Coast, concerned Anglo women campaigned for the rights of Chinese women whom they regarded as victims of the white slave trade.

The story of Rosa Guerrero, a Mexican-American woman, born in El Paso in 1934, adds a further direction of immigrant travel to the West. Her parents met in the city after migrating north within Mexico to settle on the U.S.-Mexico border. During their lifetime El Paso grew into one of the West's largest urban centers and became home to a predominantly Latino population. Anna Moore Shaw, an Akimel O'odham (formerly known as the Pima Indians), left her reservation community to the south of Phoenix, Arizona, in order to attend a boarding school in Phoenix itself. Although she did not travel far geographically, her life experiences, from the late nineteenth century into the 1970s, demonstrate the great distance traveled by so many Native American women throughout the West as they came to terms with the great changes wrought to tribal cultures during the twentieth century.

The women mentioned are but a few of the great diversity of individuals that might have been considered in greater depth in this discussion. Today's students of history have a great array of information available to them regarding Western women. In the process of revising appropriate images of Western womanhood, historians have made a more complete portrayal of women's experiences in the West. For example, historians have created better informed and carefully nuanced images of prostitutes, charting the varying fortunes of women of different ethnicities who became sex workers in mining towns such as Butte, Montana. So too have historians come to appreciate the overlapping stories that explain the interaction of people of diverse backgrounds throughout the West over the past 150 or so years. It has become clear that through the waves of mass movement of people into the region, the cultures of migrants—and of Native people—have been changed, adapted, and re-created in all manner of ways in the process.

Women on the Overland Trail

When Margaret and Ledyard Frink took the Overland Trail in 1850 they joined a mass movement of people moving westward. Between 1840 and 1848, almost 19,000 Americans traveled west, the bulk of them heading for Oregon's Willamette Valley, while 4,600 concluded their journey in Utah and 2,735 reached California. During the succeeding decade more than 200,000 people made their way to California, a high proportion of them intending, as did the Frinks, to try their luck in the gold fields. Far fewer—just over 53,000—traveled to Oregon, but their number was still significant, as was that of the almost 43,000 emigrants who set out for Salt Lake City and other new settlements in the vicinity of the Great Salt Lake. Women and children constituted a significant proportion of the emigrants, although their numbers in the early years of travel were low and their presence was again marginalized during the male-dominated years of 1849 and 1850, when gold fever was at a height. Such anomalies aside, travel along the overland trails tended to be a family affair. In addition, the parties in which people traveled were often organized around extended family groups.

Sarah Davis, a twenty-three-year-old Quaker from Michigan, set out from St. Joseph, Missouri, with her husband, brother-in-law, and her eight-month old child in April 1850. Her diary, noteworthy for its highly idiosyncratic spelling, indicates some of the perils of travel on the Overland Trail. She notes the high incidence of mortality among travelers and describes numerous freshly dug graves seen along the way. It appears that at some point in the journey Davis took responsibility for caring for two young children whose mother had died of cholera. She also describes the death of emigrants at the hands of Indians, although we should note that reports of Indian violence were often based on hearsay rather than first-hand factual observation. Unlike Margaret Frink, who reported with a flourish the great number of abandoned possessions along the California Trail in the Humboldt Sink of modern-day Nevada, Davis simply wrote that "it is a sight to see the distruction [sic] here" (Davis 1850, p. 201). There is, perhaps, not a great deal that is different between these comments and those of many other women diarists on the Western trail. However, Davis does provide one extraordinary observation that indicates how relations between women and men became strained in the course of travel. On July 28, 1850, Davis reports that when a large emigrant party camped within a mile of her own group, a great argument took place: "[T]hey were whiping a man for whiping his wife he had whiped her every day since he joined the company and now they thought it was time for them to whip him and they caught him and striped him and took the ox gad to him and whiped him tremendous she screamed and hollerd for him till one might have hare him for three miles" (ibid., p. 186).

A family poses by their covered wagon in which they live and travel in pursuit of a homestead in Loup Valley, Nebraska, in 1886. (*National Archives and Records Administration*)

How might we make sense of this event, the severity of which is conveyed by the repetitious nature of the terms "whiping," "whip," and "whiped"? The historical evidence suggests that the decision for families to set out on the Overland Trail was overwhelmingly dictated by the husband. Women had little choice but to accompany their partners if they wished to keep their families intact; certainly, few women chose to remain behind as their husbands and main means of support headed west. The conflict that Davis observed came about because of the husband's violent actions toward a wife he regarded as intransigent and resistant to his authority. These beatings came to the attention of the company as a whole, and the decision was made—by whom exactly we do not know—to intervene in what had hitherto been the private concern of husband and wife. And so the men of the company publicly punished the husband. What makes this passage particularly interesting from a rhetorical point of view is the ambiguity of the final sentence, where the screams of the wife and husband appear to become conflated. It is unclear whether the wife remained angry at her husband after his beating, thus seeming to give her sanction to his punishment, or if she felt violated by the men's intervention, hence her possible rage at their actions.

What does appear certain from this episode is that travel on the Overland Trail could place considerable pressure on the traditional roles of husband and wife. Reading journals and letters written by pioneer women in the course of their travels across the continent leads us to consider several interconnected questions with regard to Western emigrants. To what extent did women share the urge of their husbands and male kin to take up stakes in the eastern half of the country and travel west in search of a better future?

In the mid-nineteenth century, a high proportion of middle-class women's lives were dominated by the tenets of the Cult of True Womanhood, which stressed the need for women to be pious, pure, and submissive, and to remain within the domestic sphere. How then did the balance of power within the family structure change when traditional work roles for women and men were transformed in the course of overland travel? Did women, through their actions if not through their stated thoughts, challenge the domestic roles prescribed for them? When emigrants encountered Native Americans on the trail, did women tend to view and interact with Indians differently than men traveling alone or in male-only groups?

African-American Women

One of the most compelling images from Margaret Frink's diary of her trip to California in 1850 is of an African woman glimpsed in the midst of a throng of emigrant travelers: "Among the crowds on foot, a negro woman came tramping along through the heat and dusty, carrying a cast-iron bake oven on her head, with her provisions and blanket piled on top—all she possessed in the world—bravely pushing on for California" (Frink 1850, p. 135). Frink's description conveys the impression of a strong, determined and lone individual, traveling to California to partake of the equal opportunity that mining for gold seemed to hold for migrants of all ethnicities and nationalities, at least initially. It may be that the woman, who remains unnamed in the historical record, had no intention at all of setting out for the gold fields, instead aiming to establish herself in one of the burgeoning cities of the West Coast. She could have been a fugitive slave, heading west with the knowledge that in the year of the Compromise of 1850, she would be free in California. Whether she labored for a pittance or became a successful entrepreneur is not known. Perhaps she was a figure akin to Mary Ellen Pleasant, a former slave who owned her own boarding house and was at the forefront of efforts to protect the threatened rights of African Americans in California during and after the Civil War (Riley 1992; Katz 1996).

We do know that while relatively few black women embarked on the Overland Trail during the 1840s and 1850s, parts of the West did become places of refuge for African Americans. Many African Americans sought a new life in the region in the aftermath of the Civil War, particularly so at the conclusion of Reconstruction, when white supremacists again took control of many facets of black people's lives in the South. Through the "Exodus of 1879," African Americans left the South to create new communities in Kansas, Nebraska, and many other parts of the West. The historian William Loren Katz notes that often it was women who motivated their immediate and extended families into leaving the South: "Mothers sought to rescue themselves and their children from southern officials who denied them an education, bounded their lives with restrictions and encouraged random acts of white terror" (Katz 1996, p. 183). Perhaps the most famous of the new Western settlements was Nicodemus, Kansas, where migrants endured their first winter while living in crude sod houses. For Williana Hickman, a child when she accompanied her family in their migration to Nicodemus, the tough conditions of the journey west and the inhospitable conditions on arrival in Kansas left an indelible impression: "The family lived in dugouts. We landed and once again struck tents. The scenery to me was not at all inviting, and I began to cry" (quoted in Graaf 1980, p. 290).

Towns and cities in general proved to be a more attractive environment for African-American women than homesteads. By the early twentieth century, black women had established a genuine presence in many Western urban locales. Many of these women became members of the National Association of Colored Women, a nationwide body that had 50,000 members within two decades of being established in 1896. Although this umbrella organization was created at a point when African-American and white women remained in separate spheres, black women having been denied equal membership rights in the white-dominated General Federation of Women's Clubs, nevertheless the NACW brought women together in common purpose. Social organizations—a high proportion of them drawing from local church congregations—provided the means for African-American women to improve the quality of life within their local communities. Before the Civil War, African-American women in Lawrence, Kansas, organized the first black women's club in the West to help individuals fleeing slavery. In the ensuing decades, as women came to outnumber men in the African-American populations of growing cities such as Kansas City, Denver, and Los Angeles, so black women's clubs became an increasingly common and prominent part of local communities. Typically it was middle-class women who assumed leadership of the organizations, creating a program of activities that might include opportunities for raised cultural awareness, vocational training, and childcare provision. Although the values espoused by many African-American club women echoed the Victorian-era and then Progressive-era values of white clubwomen, the latter did not seek to integrate the former into their own organizations. But for black middle-class women, who echoed the sentiments of the African-American spokesperson Booker T. Washington, the founder and principal of the Tuskegee Institute between 1881 and his death in 1915, working for the practical and moral improvement of local and regional black communities was a necessary step to their fuller integration into U.S. society on an equal par with their more privileged white counterparts.

Chinese Women

In 1922 a young woman named Wong Ah So traveled to San Francisco from Guangdong Province in China to San Francisco. She thought that she was following her mother's instruction to marry a Chinese man living in California; however, on arrival in the United States, she discovered that she was instead indentured to the man she had thought would be her husband. Wong Ah So's later testimony indicates the naive condition in which had she left China: "I thought that I was his wife, and was very grateful that he was taking me to such a grand, free country, where everyone was rich and happy" (quoted in Yung 1999, p. 203). Far from achieving freedom and wealth, the young woman was forced to become a prostitute. Such a fate had become significantly less common by the 1920s than a half-century before, when prostitutes constituted an exceptionally high proportion of female Chinese immigrants to the United States. Indeed, in 1870 the Chinese population of San Francisco numbered 1,410 women, of whom 1,132 were prostitutes and 18 brothel keepers (Chen 2000, pp. 55–56). Tongs—secret societies, created by Chinese immigrants that were often associated with criminal activities— exploited the demand for sexual partners among the overwhelming male population. Although in theory such women had the capacity to purchase their freedom through working the duration of their four-to-six-year con- tracts, it appears that relatively few women survived that long. Fortunately for Wong Ah So, her plight came to the attention of a reformer named Don- aldino Cameron, who organized her refuge in the Chinese Mission Home, located in San Francisco, which had been established by white Protestant missionaries in 1874.

The high number of Chinese prostitutes in California can be attributed to several factors. Most obviously, the high ratio of twenty-four men to a single woman within California's Chinese population in 1890 explains the high demand for female prostitutes. In the early decades of Chinese immigration, the primary allegiance of emigrants was to China. Those men who were already married when they left China tended not to bring their wives with them. Secondly, women within Chinese society had for hundreds of years been subordinate to men, making it easier for the male-dominated Chinese immigrant community to justify the sexual exploitation of women. Chinese proverbs echoed Confucius's statement that "[w]omen indeed are human beings, but they are of a lower state than men and can never attain full equality with them," with propositions such as these: "Daughters are goods upon which one loses money," and "A wife is like a pony bought; I'll ride her and whip her as I like" (Yung 1999, pp. 106, 108, 112). Finally many young women traveled west because they had little choice in the matter. They were propelled east to California by economic necessity. Impoverished parents wished to be relieved of the burden of providing for daughters, relying on arranged marriages with Chinese men in California (marriages that, as we have seen, often turned out to be fraudulent) or the sale of their daughters as indentured labor in order to generate sorely needed income. Typically daughters were imbued with a deep sense of filial duty and complied with their parents' instructions, although one suspects that they would have been rather less compliant if they had had a clear sense of the fate that awaited them once they arrived in California.

Wong Ah So's story is of interest today not only for highlighting the high degree of sexual exploitation within the Chinese immigrant community but also for illuminating the ways in which poor Chinese women and far more socially and economically privileged white women came to share common ground. The Protestant women reformers who established the Chinese Mis- sion Home regarded prostitution as a form of slavery for the women con- cerned and a vice that blighted California society. Imbued with Victorian-era beliefs regarding the moral authority of women and the sexual impropriety

Woman peers out of a doorway of a Chinatown bagnio, or a brothel, in San Francisco in the 1890s. (*Chinese in California, 1982.104, The Bancroft Library, University of California, Berkeley*)

of men, reformers such as Donaldino Cameron sought the rescue of Chinese women from their exploited status. The individuals that they rescued would not only be freed from prostitution but would also be taught new standards of female behavior, particularly piety and domesticity, which echoed the tenets of the Cult of True Womanhood that were noted earlier in the essay (Pascoe 1991).

In the course of being released from prostitution, women took part in a cultural transformation as they moved from being Chinese emigrants to Chinese Americans. From the brief glimpses that the historical record gives of Wong Ah So, we can trace the way in which her sense of identity changed over time as she called into question several different forms of authority in her life. After Wong Ah So became a resident of the Chinese Mission Home, she wrote a letter to her mother that remained unsent. She first noted her sense of filial duty: "At home, a daughter should be obedient to her parents; after marriage to her husband; after the death of her husband, to her son." But then she made clear the plight into which her contract had led her: "Your daughter's condition is very tragic, even when she is sick, she must practice prostitution [literally, do business with her own flesh and skin]. Daughter is not angry with you. It seems to be just my fate." Finally she criticized her mother more overtly for failing her: "Since daughter came to California, by right she should forsake you" (quoted in Yung 1999, pp. 205–206). Thus Wong Ah So challenged both the patriarchal logic governing a woman's place in Chinese society and a conventional sense of filial duty on the part of a daughter to her mother. In addition to these challenges, Wong Ah So, after experiencing marital problems in the aftermath of her time at the Chinese Mission Home, also called into question some of Donaldino Cameron's convictions regarding a woman's place within marriage. And so she also learned to challenge the authority of men in marriage.

Mexican-American Women

During the four decades between 1890 and 1929, it is estimated that from 1 million to 1.5 million Mexicans migrated north to the United States. Rosa Guerrero, a resident of El Paso, Texas, was born in 1934 during the Depression to Mexican parents who had both sought an improved livelihood north of the border at the tail end of this period. They were part of the great migration by thousands of Mexicans who were propelled north by the turmoil of the Mexican Revolution and pulled into the U.S. economy through its need for cheap labor. On arrival in the United States, Guerrero's mother had little formal education and spoke no English, although she shared her rich knowledge of Mexican folklore with her daughter. Because of the extraordinary circumstances of the Depression, Guerrero's mother went to work for at least part of the 1930s, while her husband stayed at home to look after the couple's children. Guerrero recalls her mother laboring as a domestic worker within wealthier El Paso households: "For a dollar a week, she used to work and scrub by hand, wash all the linen and boil them" (quoted in Ruiz 1987, p. 223). The necessity of working to provide sustenance for the family and, in time, the odd luxury for herself, was instilled in Guerrero at an early age. But work did not come at the expense of her formal education, and her achievements in high school and her college education were prized by her parents. So too did her family value her considerable achievement of forming and directing the Rosa Guerrero International Ballet Folklorico and becoming, what the historian Vicki Ruiz calls a "mujer de la gente" (woman of the people) (ibid., p. 220).

Rosa Guerrero's story resembles the experiences of many second-generation immigrants whose parents' values and actions created the foundation for their children's success in the United States. Looking back on her life in an interview in the early 1980s, when she was almost fifty years old, Guerrero took care to express her gratitude toward her parents. In so doing, she credited the family with being the social institution that explains the particular strength of interpersonal ties within the Mexican-American community: "I think that the family in Mexican culture, la cultura Hispana, the family (the immediate family, the extended family) is the greatest contribution that mankind can have" (quoted in ibid., pp. 222–223). Significantly, the family that Guerrero describes stretched south of the border to include members in Ciudad Juárez and other locations within Mexico. The incidence of families similarly living on both sides of the border is high among residents of El Paso, where the population is 76.6 percent Latino. The concentration of Latino residents is even higher, at over 91.3 percent and 94.1 percent, respectively, in the border communities of Brownsville and Laredo, Texas (see *Census 2000 Brief*). This situation, with the proximity of the border, along with the back-and-forth migration of Mexican nationals, helps to explain the maintenance of what is often referred to as a distinctively "Mexican-American" identity within the United States. And yet, since there has also been great internal stratification within the larger community along lines of region, social class, ethnicity, gender, and sexuality, it might well be more accurate to refer to the plural "identities" than to the singular "identity" when referring to Mexican Americans in general.

For all that Rosa Guerrero celebrates the family and the extended ties between people that she regards as characteristic of Mexican-American culture, she also provides a note of discord. She points out that tensions between women and men lie at the heart of the family, blaming "the machismo element" and the related "cycle of borracheras" (cycle of drunkenness) for social ills within Mexican culture (quoted in Ruiz 1987, p. 223). This observation that the exercise of unbridled masculinity threatens the equilibrium of family shares common ground with the radical gender politics of Chicana (or Mexican-American women) activist-writers, such as Gloria Anzaldúa and Cherríe Moraga, who came into prominence during the 1980s. In her highly influential book *Borderlands/La Frontera* (1987), Anzaldúa writes of being marginalized by her mestizo ethnicity, female gender, and queer sexuality. She states: "I am cultureless because, as a feminist, I challenge the collective cultural/religious male-derived beliefs of Indo-Hispanics and Anglos" (Anzaldúa 1987, pp. 102–103).

Native American Women

Elsewhere in this essay information has been relayed about Sarah Winnemucca's experiences as a spokesperson for Northern Paiutes in the second half of the nineteenth century. Had she been born fifty years later than 1844 and into a different environment, albeit another desert location, some 850 miles to the south, she might well have had a fate similar to that of Anna Moore Shaw, an Akimel O'odham, or Pima Indian. Unlike Winnemucca, Shaw grew up in a community that had already been placed on a reservation, along the Gila River, adjacent to what is now the vast metropolitan sprawl of Phoenix. Born in 1898, she experienced a new way of life that Winnemucca anticipated its being necessary for Northern Paiutes to embrace if they were to achieve a viable way of life in the late nineteenth century. Shaw, like a high percentage of her fellow Akimel O'odham, became a member of the Presbyterian Church and was educated at the Phoenix Indian Boarding School for ten years. After marrying her husband, Ross, another Akimel O'odham, she remained in Phoenix for more than forty years before the couple retired to the Salt River reservation, where Ross Shaw had been brought up.

Deliberating on certain aspects of Anna Moore Shaw's life helps us to appreciate how Akimel O'odham women negotiated profound changes in their livelihoods during the twentieth century. While it is difficult to make accurate generalizations about Western Native American women's lives collectively, certainly much of what Shaw has to say in her autobiography,

Sarah Winnemucca (ca. 1844–1891)

Around 1844 a child named Thocmetony, or Shell Flower, was born into the Northern Paiute tribe in what is now western Nevada. Sarah Winnemucca, as she became known to Americans, grew into an influential figure as she campaigned for the rights of Northern Paiutes in the midst of their forced transition to a new way of life on reservations. Historically her people had lived in bands situated through much of the northern part of the Great Basin. In the decades leading up to her death in 1891, Sarah witnessed profound changes to her tribe's livelihood. Her grandfather, a headman named Truckee, gave a warm welcome to the first white emigrants he met near Pyramid Lake, western Nevada, while they were traveling to California in the early 1840s. In succeeding years, Truckee sought accommodation with emigrants, including Captain John C. Fremont, at least partly because the arrival of whites had been prophesied within Northern Paiute culture. According to the tribe's oral tradition, in the beginning of the world there had existed only four humans—a white girl and boy, and a dark girl and boy. In time the two pairs of children fought and were eventually separated, the white pair being sent away across the ocean. It was thought that the return of whites would bring about reconciliation and prosperity for the Northern Paiutes.

Within several years the accommodationist stance toward Western emigrants that both Truckee and Sarah's father, Winnemucca, another headman, had advocated was breaking down, and increasingly hospitable relations gave way to violence between Indians and whites. Winnemucca recounted to his people a fearful vision he had dreamed of their future: "I saw the greatest emigration that has yet been

Sarah Winnemucca, a Paiute and the first Native American woman to publish in the English language (ca. 1844–1891). (*Nevada Historical Society*)

through our country. I looked North and South and East and West, and saw nothing but dust, and I heard a great weeping. I saw women crying, and I also saw my men shot down by the white people. They were killing my people with something that made a great noise like thunder and lightning, and I saw the blood streaming from the mouths of my men that lay all around me. I saw it as if it was real." So too did a shaman prophesy that the Northern Paiute population would be decimated by "a fearful disease that will cause us to die by hundreds." In the decades after Sarah's birth, the Northern Paiutes would become confined to reservations and increasingly divided among themselves over the degree to which they should resist the imposition of American power over their lives (Winnemucca 1994, pp. 14, 16).

Sarah played a crucial role in mediating between Northern Paiutes and official representatives of the U.S. government. As a child she had traveled with Truckee, her mother, and kinfolk from her tribe's homeland in western Nevada to California, where Truckee worked as a ranch hand. She spent much of the 1850s living with white families in California and western Nevada, becoming fluent in English and wearing American clothes. Because of her knowledge of both spoken and written English, she was employed by the U.S. Army and Indian agents as an interpreter, caught in the awkward position of explaining the rules associated with warfare and reservation life to her own people. After the Bannock War of 1878, Sarah traveled to Washington, D.C., to argue for the release of imprisoned Northern Paiutes. Having failed to convince Carl Schurz, the secretary of the interior, of the need to take action, she lectured extensively in the East to publicize the plight of her tribesmen in 1883–1884. Among many others attending her lectures were the poet-philosopher Ralph Waldo Emerson and the Indian reformers Senator Henry Dawes and Mary Mann, who edited Sarah's book, *Life among the Piutes* (1883).

Sarah Winnemucca is of particular interest today because her experiences positioned her on the historical boundary between two cultures and also because her life story places her at the intersection of the present-day disciplines of women's history, ethnohistory, anthropology, and literary and cultural studies. She is a liminal figure who lived fully in neither the realm of her own people nor that of American society, instead inhabiting the borderlands between two cultures during the decades of warfare and national expansion west of the Mississippi River. She was a victim of westward expansion, and yet in an important sense her career as an activist, teacher, and writer was enabled by the process of expansion. She commands our attention because she was an eloquent spokesperson for her people, but we cannot claim that in her lectures, writings, and action she represented a unified viewpoint for the Northern Paiutes. She supported the Dawes Act, which provided for the allotment of tribal lands to families and individuals as part of a government-sponsored effort to bring the core American values of individualism and property ownership into Native American lives. But the continuing value of her life story is that of an individual striving, at significant cost to her personal welfare, to forge for her people a means of continuing as a viable culture at a point when the forces of assimilation threatened the very survival of Northern Paiute society.

References and Further Reading

Bataille, Gretchen M., and Kathleen Mullen Sands. *American Indian Women: Telling Their Lives*. Lincoln: University of Nebraska Press, 1985.

Canfield, Gae Whitney. *Sarah Winnemucca of the Northern Paiutes*. Norman: University of Oklahoma Press, 1983.

Walker, Cheryl. *Indian Nation: Native American Literature and Nineteenth-Century Nationalisms*. Durham: Duke University Press, 1997.

Winnemucca, Sarah. *Life among the Piutes: Their Wrongs and Claims*. Reno: University of Nevada Press, 1994.

A Pima Past (1974), could apply to Lakota, Spokane, or Pomo women in, respectively, South Dakota, Washington, and California. She was born into a culture that until the decade of the Civil War had in many respects successfully withstood the struggle for dominance in the Southwestern borderlands of first the Spanish, then Mexicans, and finally Americans, who gained control of the extended homelands of the Akimel O'odham and related Tohono O'odham (formerly known as Papago) tribes through the Gadsden Purchase of 1853. From 1871 much of the flow of the Gila River, vital to the continuation of Akimel O'odham horticulture in a highly arid environment, was diverted by Anglo settlers in order to irrigate new farms and bring water to new settlements. This action spelled near catastrophe for the tribe as its former way of life—sustained through subsistence farming and trade—was undermined. Increasingly the Akimel O'odham were forced by necessity to become day laborers rather than independent farmers.

The Akimel O'odham experienced great duress as almost every facet of the traditional beliefs and practices and belief systems that underlay everyday life were transformed through a host of factors associated with their incorporation into U.S. society. Profound changes were made not only to subsistence and labor but also to the organization of land, education, and religious belief. Both Shaw's parents were converted to Christianity during her early childhood, joining the growing number of Akimel O'odham who followed the ministry of Dr. Charles H. Cook, a Presbyterian missionary who settled within the reservation community in 1870. Shaw's autobiography, written in her seventies, provides a positive image of Cook, who established the C. H. Cook Christian School in Phoenix, at which many Native American children were educated. So too does she speak highly of the Presbyterian influence in Akimel O'odham society in the early twentieth century. Indeed, at the age of eight, Shaw voluntarily joined an elder brother in attendance at the Tucson Indian School, an institution for Akimel O'odham and Tohono O'odham children, which had been established by the Presbyterian Board of Home Missions. Two years later she was a resident at the government-sponsored Phoenix Indian School, where she joined Indian children from not only Arizona but also places farther afield, such as California, the Dakotas, and Oklahoma.

As a result of first being educated away from the reservation community and then remaining in Phoenix after her marriage to her fellow Akimel O'odham, in 1920, Shaw became somewhat distanced from her own culture, although not wholly so. Simultaneously, because of the missionary influence within the community, traditional ceremonies were diminishing in influence. Looking back with qualified regret, Shaw comments: "I would have no puberty ceremonial, and Circle and Name-Calling dances were almost things of the past. When grandmother would tell me of an old festival like the Ho'ok, or Witch-Burning ceremony, I would wish I had been born in the days gone by" (Shaw 1974, p. 120). Yet Shaw did retain many distinctive aspects of the Akimel O'odham way of life. During summer vacations spent on the reservation, she continued to learn about the multiple responsibilities of a young woman in her community. Thus she learned how to grind corn, make tortillas, and prepare pinole at home as well as how to scrub floors, darn stockings, and sew dresses at the boarding school. She also learned how to harvest the sweet red fruit of the saguaro cactus, boiled into syrup that would be used throughout the year, and how to carry a heavy load of *wihog* (mesquite bean pods) in a *gioho*, a burden basket made of mescal fibers.

After her education at the Phoenix Indian School and her marriage in 1920, Shaw settled in Phoenix for the next forty years. Outwardly it would seem that she and her husband pursued an upwardly mobile way of life that took them a long way, economically and socially, from the reservation communities in which they had both been raised. After settling in one of the city's ethnically diverse neighborhoods, the family purchased a home in a more exclusively white residential area. There, despite experiencing some racial discrimination from local residents, the Shaws felt at home as they raised their three children in the years before World War II. Shaw joined the Parent Teacher Association at her youngest son's elementary school and participated in the activities of Church Women United, an evangelical Christian organization. Looking back on this period of her life, Shaw acknowledged that her children had grown away from the old ways that she had learned as a child on the Gila River reservation: "They were far more at home in the world of the white man, and they preferred hot dogs and fried chicken to succotash and pinole" (ibid., p. 172).

A superficial reading of Shaw's autobiography might well lead the reader to think that both mother and children left behind their cultural roots to embrace a more "progressive" lifestyle and assimilate into U.S. society. Yet the truth of the matter is rather more complicated. Shaw did not simply forsake the traditional beliefs and practices of her formative years in the course of her school education, church attendance, and suburban existence. After all, the proximity of the reservation to Phoenix meant that visits were possible on some weekends and during vacations. Instead, she, like so many Native people who dwelled in cities, pursued a livelihood informed as much by her own culture's beliefs as those of dominant U.S. society. For instance, Shaw's regular attendance at the Central Presbyterian Indian Church brought her into contact with the Hopi, Mohave, Tohono O'odham, and other Southwestern tribes. (Today the church continues to host services for Native Americans of all tribal affiliations.) On the one hand, the broad claim could be made that Shaw's immersion in evangelical Christianity is a sign of the success of the Presbyterian missionary who, in seeking to convert the Akimel O'odham from 1870 on, set about undermining the tribe's traditional religious belief system. But on the other hand, one could argue that Shaw's Christian activities provided the opportunity to forge a personal and collective identity in the modern world. Participation in a predominantly Native American congregation created alliances with a diverse group of Indian women, while her role in Church Women United brought her into contact with an even more ethnically diverse organization to which Christians of all denominations were invited. In addition to these considerations, it should also be noted that during her retirement years Shaw helped revive basket-making skills that were in danger of being lost, recorded traditional oral storytelling in her first book, *Pima Indian Legends* (1968), and played a proactive role in establishing a range of programs and initiatives to improve the quality of education, childcare, and housing for the Salt River reservation community.

Conclusion

One wonders what Margaret Frink would have thought of the modern West had she been able to leap forward to the twenty-first century after arriving in California in 1850. Perhaps for a woman who enthusiastically left her home in Indiana for the promise of a new life on the West Coast she might not have been too alarmed to witness the dramatic transformation of San Francisco and the surrounding Bay Area into a metropolitan cityscape. But just as the construction of modern cities, interstate freeways, and airports has dramatically changed the character of Western settlement and travel, so too has the social character of Western society been transformed since the nineteenth century. And it is intriguing to speculate how Frink might have responded to the ways in which social mores and gender roles have changed in U.S. society over the past 150 years. In San Francisco itself she would be able to view women of many ethnicities moving freely through the city to their places of work, unencumbered by the constraints of nineteenth-century ideas of domesticity. She would also see a thriving lesbian and gay community, and more generally witness a great liberalization of gender roles and sexual propriety in U.S. society.

The writing of history is rarely if ever a neutral endeavor. Historical studies of the West have reflected the broader social and political preoccupations of the decades in which Western historians wrote, starting from the publication of Frederick Jackson Turner's frontier thesis in 1894. Turner wrote at a point midway between the enfranchisement of women in the Territory of Wyoming, in 1869, and the passage of the Nineteenth Amendment to the Constitution in 1920, which secured the right of women to vote in all elections. But it was not until the publication of Dee Brown's popular study *The Gentle Tamers* (1958) that women took center stage in historical studies of the West. Although certain aspects of *The Gentle Tamers* now appear outmoded and even condescending toward women, nevertheless this was the first study to provide a sustained consideration of women in a variety of roles in the West, from Indian captives to woman's suffrage campaigners, and from women settlers on the sod-house frontier to female stage players.

When historians started to pay greater attention to women's experiences in the West during the 1970s, much of the momentum for their work came from the rise of the women's movement during the 1960s and the concomitant rise of radical feminism by the early 1970s. The influence of feminist authors of the 1960s and 1970s, such as Betty Friedan, Kate Millett, and Germaine Greer, together with the influence of the anti–Vietnam War movement during the same period, created an atmosphere in which feminist challenges to male social privilege extended to the classroom and the masculine bias of much Western American history was called into question (Friedan 1963; Greer 1970; and Millett 1970). Historians of women in the West concluded that by 1920 the West had become the region of the United States in which women were most fully enfranchised. But it also became clear that women's freedom and ability to exert power could not simply be calculated by whether or not they had the right to vote. So too did it become clear to historians that precious few women of color had experienced the freedom, rights, and power that Anglo women accrued during the late nineteenth and early twentieth centuries.

In recent years scholars in a number of related disciplines have paid increasing attention to the minority cultures within the United States. In the coming decades, as the demographic profile of the West, and the United States as a whole, continues to change, so too will scholarly attention, in all likelihood, continue to be focused on multicultural issues. But this is not simply a matter of recovering the stories of previously neglected individuals and communities, but also of reconfiguring the ways in which historians comprehend the interplay of gender, ethnicity and sexuality. For, in addition to the rise to prominence of multiculturalism in scholarly concerns in recent decades, so too have studies of sexuality assumed an increasing importance in the work of historians, literary scholars, and cultural critics (see Johnson 1996, 2000).

If there is one constant in the history of women in the West since the mid-nineteenth century, it is that of mobility and change. The West is, after all, the region where women were first enfranchised and where artists and writers, such as Georgia O'Keeffe and Mary Austin, most felt able to give expression to their creativity. It was in Taos, New Mexico, where the wealthy Anglo heiress Mabel Dodge married a Taos Indian named Tony Lujan in 1922, a union hard to imagine taking place in Mabel's native Buffalo. But the exact character of the mobility and change experienced by women has varied considerably according to their ethnicity and social class status. When Walt Whitman referred in his poem "Pioneers! O Pioneers!" to the "resistless, restless race" of Americans marching West in the nineteenth century, he captured the energy—both cooperative and competitive—of the movement westward. However the promise of improvement and upward social mobility contained within this image of the West came largely at the expense of Native Americans, while African Americans, Mexican Americans, and Asian Americans would struggle for decades to combat racism and overcome their subordinate status within U.S. society. Today we live in a period of historical obligation when the social, economic, and environmental costs of the epic movement westward are being assessed. But it remains to be seen how far the social freedom and economic opportunity long associated with the West will extend to all women in the coming decades as the region's population continues to diversify.

References and Further Reading

Anzaldúa, Gloria. *Borderlands/La Frontera: The New Mestiza.* San Francisco: Spinster/Aunt Lute, 1987.

Bataille, Gretchen M., and Kathleen Mullen Sands. *American Indian Women: Telling Their Lives.* Lincoln: University of Nebraska Press, 1985.

Billington, Ray Allen. *Westward Expansion: A History of the American Frontier.* 4th ed. New York: Macmillan, 1974.

Brown, Dee. *The Gentle Tamers.* London: Barrie and Jenkins, 1973.

Canfield, Gae Whitney. *Sarah Winnemucca of the Northern Paiutes*. Norman: University of Oklahoma Press, 1983.

Census 2000 Brief: The Hispanic Population, According to Census 2000 (http://www .census.gov/prod/2001pubs/c2kbr01–3).

Chen, Yong. *Chinese San Francisco, 1850–1943: A Transatlantic Community*. Stanford: Stanford University Press, 2000.

Davis, Sarah. "Diary from Missouri to California, 1850." In Kenneth L. Holmes, ed., *Covered Wagon Women: Diaries and Letters from the Western Trails, 1850*. Vol. 2. Lincoln: University of Nebraska Press, 1996, 174–204.

De Graaf, Lawrence B. "Race, Sex, and Region: Black Women in the American West, 1850–1920." *Pacific Historical Review* 49 (1980): 285–313.

Faragher, John Mack. *Women and Men on the Overland Trail*. New Haven: Yale University Press, 1979.

Faragher, Johnny, and Christine Stansell. "Women and Their Families on the Overland Trail to California and Oregon, 1842–1867." *Feminist Studies* 2, nos. 2, 3 (1975): 150–166.

Friedan, Betty. *The Feminine Mystique*. New York: W. W. Norton, 1963.

Frink, Margaret. "Diary of a Party of Goldseekers." In Kenneth L. Holmes, ed., *Covered Wagon Women: Diaries and Letters from the Western Trails, 1850*. Vol. 2. Lincoln: University of Nebraska Press, 1996, 58–167.

Greer, Germaine. *The Female Eunuch*. London: MacGibbon and Kee, 1970.

Gutiérrez, David G. *Walls and Mirrors: Mexican Americans, Mexican Immigrants, and the Politics of Ethnicity*. Berkeley: University of California Press, 1995.

Gutiérrez, Ramón A. "Unraveling America's Hispanic Past: Internal Stratification and Class Boundaries." *Aztlán* 17 (spring 1986): 79–102.

Jacobs, Margaret D. *Engendered Encounters: Feminism and Pueblo Cultures, 1879–1934*. Lincoln: University of Nebraska Press, 1999.

Jameson, Elizabeth. "Toward a Multicultural History of Women in the Western United States." *Signs* 13, no. 4 (summer 1988): 761–791.

Jameson, Elizabeth, and Susan Armitage, eds. *Writing the Range: Race, Class, and Culture in the Women's West*. Norman: University of Oklahoma Press, 1997.

Jeffrey, Julie Roy. *Frontier Women: The Trans-Mississippi West, 1840–1880*. New York: Hill and Wang, 1979.

Jensen, Joan M. *One Foot on the Rockies: Women and Creativity in the Modern American West*. Albuquerque: University of New Mexico Press, 1995.

Johnson, Susan Lee. "'A Memory Sweet to Soldiers': The Significance of Gender." In Clyde A. Milner II, ed., *A New Significance: Re-envisioning the History of the American West*. New York: Oxford University Press, 1996, 255–278.

Johnson, Susan Lee. *Roaring Camp: The Social World of the California Gold Rush*. New York: W. W. Norton, 2000.

Katz, William Loren. *The Black West*. New York: Touchstone, 1996, 138–139.

Limerick, Patricia Nelson. *The Legacy of Conquest: The Unbroken History of the American West*. New York: W. W. Norton, 1987.

Limerick, Patricia Nelson, Clyde A. Milner, II, and Charles E. Rankin, eds. *Trails: Toward a New Western History.* Lawrence: University Press of Kansas, 1991.

Matsumoto, Valerie. *Farming the Home Place: A Japanese American Community in California, 1919–1982*. Ithaca: Cornell University Press, 1993.

Millett, Kate. *Sexual Politics.* Garden City, NY: Doubleday, 1970.

Myres, Sandra L. *Westering Women and the Frontier Experience, 1800–1915.* Albuquerque: University of New Mexico Press, 1982.

Pascoe, Peggy. *Relations of Rescue: The Search for Female Moral Authority in the American West, 1874–1939*. New York: Oxford University Press, 1991.

Riley, Glenda. *A Place to Grow: Women in the American West.* Arlington Heights, IL: Harlan Davidson, 1992.

Ruiz, Vicki L. *Cannery Women, Cannery Lives: Mexican Women, Unionization, and the California Food Processing Industry, 1939–1950*. Albuquerque: University of New Mexico Press, 1987.

Ruiz, Vicki L. "Oral History and La Mujer: The Rosa Guerrero Story." In Vicki L. Ruiz and Susan Tiana, eds., *Women on the U.S.-Mexico Border: Responses to Change*. Boston: Allen and Unwin, 1987, 219–231.

Ruiz, Vicki L. *From out of the Shadows: Mexican Women in Twentieth-Century America*. New York: Oxford University Press, 1999.

Saldívar-Hull, Sonia. *Feminism on the Border: Chicana Gender Politics and Literature*. Berkeley: University of California Press, 2000.

Sánchez, George J. *Becoming Mexican American: Ethnicity, Culture, and Identity in Chicano Los Angeles, 1900–1945*. New York: Oxford University Press, 1993.

Sarris, Greg. *Mabel McKay, Weaving the Dream.* Berkeley: University of California Press, 1994.

Scharff, Virginia. *Twenty Thousand Roads: Women, Movement, and the West.* Berkeley: University of California Press, 2003.

Schlissel, Lilian. *Women's Diaries of the Westward Journey.* New York: Schocken Books, 1982.

Shaw, Anna Moore. *A Pima Past.* Tucson: University of Arizona Press, 1974.

Taylor, Quintard Taylor. *In Search of the Racial Frontier: African Americans in the American West, 1528–1990.* New York: Norton, 1998.

Unruh, John D., Jr. *The Plains Across: The Overland Emigrants and the Trans-Mississippi West, 1840–60.* Urbana: University of Illinois Press, 1979.

Walker, Cheryl. *Indian Nation: Native American Literature and Nineteenth-Century Nationalisms.* Durham: Duke University Press, 1997.

Welter, Barbara. "The Cult of True Womanhood: 1820–1860." *American Quarterly* 18, no. 2, part 1 (summer 1966): 151–174.

White, Richard. *"It's Your Misfortune and None of My Own": A New History of the American West.* Norman: University of Oklahoma Press, 1991.

Whitman, Walt. *Collected Poems.* New York: Penguin, 1977.

Winnemucca, Sarah. *Life among the Piutes: Their Wrongs and Claims.* Reno: University of Nevada Press, 1994.

Yung, Judy. *Unbound Feet: A Social History of Chinese Women in San Francisco.* Berkeley: University of California Press, 1995.

Yung, Judy. *Unbound Voices: A Documentary History of Chinese Women in San Francisco.* Berkeley: University of California Press, 1999.

Bad Men, Unsexed Women, and Good Citizens: Outlaws and Vigilantes in the American West

Helen McLure

12

Rough, bad, violent men and the fearless citizen posses who pursued and brought them to swift and certain justice at the end of a convenient rope gallop thunderously through the history, fiction, films, and television programs about the U.S. West. While Americans always believed that multitudes of ruffians, desperadoes, and ne'er-do-wells infested the ever-shifting margins of the nation's westward expansion, it is the mid-to-late nineteenth-century Western "outlaws" who have captivated the popular imagination. Billy the Kid, Jesse James, Butch Cassidy and the Sundance Kid, Joaquín Murrieta, Belle Starr—their names the stuff of legend, their real lives often the subject of fierce controversy before and long after their deaths. Were these men and women vicious criminals who preyed on law-abiding and respectable members of society, or "social bandits" like Robin Hood who stole from the rich to give to the poor? Some outlaws attracted public support and sympathy because they assailed unpopular targets like Yankees, railroads, and banks. Many of the most notorious outlaws, such as Murrieta, the James brothers, and Billy the Kid, participated directly in national, regional, and local political, economic, and social conflicts. Their restless, violent, and frequently short lives illuminate several of the most powerful themes and currents of U.S. Western history: Anglo conquest and dominance and native, Mexican-American, and African-American resistance; the impact and legacies of the Civil War and Reconstruction; and bitter contests for Western resources such as water, grass, animals, precious minerals, timber, and oil.

With the possible exception of Murrieta, none of those legendary Western outlaws died at the hands of posses or vigilantes, but thousands of other alleged lawbreakers were lynched—hanged, shot, or burned to death—by their fellow citizens during the nineteenth and early twentieth centuries. The rhetoric of crime and justice deployed to explain and justify Western lynching largely obscured its roots in complex issues of property, politics, class, gender, race, and ethnicity. American vigilantes frequently won approval and praise from contemporaries and later commentators for imposing order on lawless, violent frontiers. Owen Wister's 1902 novel *The Virginian*, a classic that set the mold for the Westerns of the twentieth century, presented the most enduring image and defense of Western vigilantism as a stern and orderly process performed by just and righteous men as an integral part of their civic duties. Speaking for the vigilantes, all the more powerfully because he is portrayed as a high-status member of the local judicial system, Judge Henry Dow declares:

> For in all sincerity I see no likeness in principle whatever between burning Southern negroes in public and hanging Wyoming horse-thieves in private. I consider the burning a proof that the South is semi-barbarous, and the hanging a proof that Wyoming is determined to become civilized. We do not torture our criminals when we lynch them. We do not invite spectators to enjoy their death agony. We put no such hideous disgrace upon the United States. We execute our criminals by the swiftest means, and in the quietest way. Do you think the principle is the same? (1902, 437)

Generations of Americans have responded, "No," and agreed that vigilantism and lynching in the West and Southwest served higher and nobler purposes than the racial antagonisms that fueled Southern extralegal violence. Western lynching was viewed as springing from the "natural environment" of the frontier—an instinctive response of good people to its primitive and dangerous social conditions. Vigilantes, posses, and necktie parties expressed the will and drive of the "best citizens" to control and repress the hopelessly bad "criminal element" in the new Western towns and cities, as the Anglo settlers tamed and subdued the primeval "wilderness" and its denizens, including the Native peoples.

Newspaper reports and travelers' accounts of episodes of extralegal violence indicate that many U.S. farmers, laborers, merchants, and professionals carried various concepts and memories of mob and Regulator actions against criminals and other immoral or dangerous individuals with them as they migrated to the ever-shifting Western and Southwestern frontiers from the early to mid-1800s. The backcountry settlers of Virginia, the Carolinas, and Pennsylvania moved to the Upper South, Midwest, and border West with their traditions of mobilizing citizen posses against the Indians. In addition to their human property, Southern slaveholders also brought fears of slave insurrection and both extralegal and legal institutions designed to suppress it, such as "Committees of Safety" and slave patrols. The words "regulator" and "regulating" continued to describe extralegal collective violence, but the new terms "lynch law" and "lynching" also became widely used. (According to the definition of the term finally agreed upon by antilynching activists in 1940, a "lynching" is an illegal homicide by a group purporting to act in defense of tradition, race, or justice [Brundage 1993, p. 17]).

However, these words usually referred to nonlethal corporal punishments such as whipping, tar-and-feathering, and branding, generally followed by expulsion from the community. By the mid-1830s, the word "lynching" increasingly came to signify an extralegal execution at the hands of a mob, particularly by hanging, and was strongly linked with the slave-holding South and the frontiers of Anglo settlement in what is now the Old Southwest, Midwest, and border West.

Early-nineteenth-century extralegal tribunals targeted primarily property offenses. Many frontier citizens believed that large, well-organized, secret networks of rustlers, counterfeiters, and slave stealers operated across the vast expanses of the West and Southwest, arousing additional anxieties about their potential subversive roles in foreign schemes, slave revolts, or local politics. Vigilante movements flourished in Mississippi, Alabama, Arkansas, Texas, Missouri, and Iowa during the 1830s and 1840s. In Massac County, Illinois, not far from the notorious Cave-in-Rock outlaw retreat, the Linn family allegedly formed the core of a wide network of horse thieves, robbers, and counterfeiters called the Flatheads during the 1840s. Their political opponents called themselves the "Regulators" and claimed that the county clerk, county sheriff, and a representative to the state legislature were also Flatheads. Thus, the Regulators insisted, the problem was not the absence of law, but rather the hopeless corruption of the local judicial system by the criminals. The Massac County Regulators did not focus on the resolution of a single crime, but waged a campaign against those individuals they identified as part of an extensive local criminal conspiracy, whipping, banishing, or killing dozens of men (Etcheson 1999).

The term "Regulator" remained in use for several more decades, and vigilantes frequently claimed that breakdowns in the formal legal machinery forced them to use extralegal methods to achieve justice. In the 1870s, Henry McCarty, also known as Billy the Kid, joined a group of Regulators who believed that the local justice system was under the control of the men who had assassinated their employer. During the 1850s, San Francisco's vigilantes argued that the city's police and courts had been hijacked by criminals and corrupt politicians. The massive, militarized San Francisco vigilance committee of 1856 attracted widespread national attention and set the pattern for Western vigilantism for the next fifty years.

In 1849, however, as people from across the nation and around the world sailed into the great harbor filled with the rotting hulks of dozens of deserted vessels, San Francisco was a city of "tents and canvas houses" (Ring 1849a); its new inhabitants, young Eugene Ring observed, had set forth "in a great crusade for self" (ibid., 1849b). During the long voyage from New York, the 300 passengers aboard Ring's ship amused themselves with a variety of activities, including "Mass meetings and stump speeches; militia training, headed by a band with instruments improvised from the cook's tinware . . . and [m]ock trials" (Ring 1849). These amusements reflected the intense political involvement common to American men of the period, as well as their familiarity with both legal and extralegal types of judicial proceedings. Many of those who arrived in San Francisco brought memories or knowledge of Regulator and mob actions in their own towns or states against alleged criminals or other "undesirables." They readily attended the types of large public gatherings called by local leaders such as Sam Brannan, who in February 1849 denounced a group of local politicians and their supporters, known as "the Hounds" (Abrahams 1998, pp. 56–57). A number of merchants, businessmen, and other elites formed companies of "special constables" that arrested, tried, and convicted about twenty Hounds, including their leader, Sam Roberts, and deported or banished more than a dozen men, resulting in the destruction of Roberts and his power base. Journalist and vigilante supporter Frank Soulé noted approvingly in 1855: "[T]he ease with which a number of respectable and determined men could thus put down a disorderly gang, afterward encouraged the formation of the famous 'Vigilance Committee' of the year 1851" (Soulé 1855).

In February 1851, a merchant named Jansen was clubbed unconscious in his store and robbed. Suspicions immediately focused on the city's Australian immigrant population, known generally as the "Sydney Ducks" and stigmatized by most Americans as former convicts because the British settlement of Australia began with penal colonies. San Franciscans also accused the Ducks of setting most of the fires that periodically devastated the city in order to use the ensuing confusion for robbery and looting. A secret vigilance committee was organized on August 8, and several days later the vigilantes "tried" Australian John Jenkins, sentenced him to death, and hanged him. The vigilance committee remained active throughout the summer, calling ninety-one people before it, most of them Australian laborers. The vigilantes hanged three more men, banished fourteen, and whipped a Mexican man. The committee's activities tapered off by the fall, usually a very busy season for the merchants who composed its leadership, but it never formally disbanded (Ricards and Blackburn 1991; Senkewicz 1985, p. 5).

There is no evidence of a genuine crime wave in the spring of 1851, and arson did not cause most of the fires (Senkewicz 1985, pp. 246–247). And for all of the vigilante complaints about a corrupt municipal government tyrannized by Democrat David Broderick's political machine, the Whigs had swept both the city administration and councils in April, just two months prior to the formation of the committee. The vigilantes "greatly exaggerated" the fraud and violence associated with the city's political system—they were primarily "hustlers" who became self-righteously outraged whenever they were bested by other, mostly Democratic, hustlers (ibid., p. 105). However, the Irish Catholic Ducks presented a clearly identifiable source of crime and corruption, particularly as Americans believed that an entire "class" of shiftless vagabonds and professional criminals had migrated to San Francisco, where they preyed on honest, hardworking, unwary native citizens. Soulé declared that the Ducks were embedded in a vast and intricate network of villainy (Soulé 1855). Moreover, during this period, Anglo Americans generally viewed all Irish immigrants with immense scorn and their religion, Catholicism, with deep hostility and suspicion. The 1851 committee's tight focus on the Ducks indicates that the vigilantes deliberately attempted to disrupt that immigration stream. Another age-old theme of American vigilantism, struggles over land and property, also played a crucial role, as "some of the [vigilantes'] wholesale condemnation of the courts was intended to undermine respect for certain judicial decisions regarding real estate" (Lotchin 1974, p. 236).

In 1856, business, politics, and religion again converged to create the largest and most powerful vigilance movement in U.S. history. A failed banker turned fiery newspaper editor who called himself James King of William began fulminating against crime and municipal corruption and predicting his own martyrdom at the hands of his enemies. One of them soon obliged him. Rival editor and Democratic city supervisor James P. Casey, incensed because King's paper, the *Bulletin*, raked up Casey's unsavory past, including a stint in Sing Sing Prison, shot and mortally wounded King. William Coleman and other former members reconstituted the 1851 committee and signed up thousands of new recruits (workingmen and Irish Catholics were largely excluded), organizing them into armed military units. The vigilantes seized Casey and an Italian gambler named Charles Cora from the authorities and took their captives to the vigilantes' headquarters, called Fort Gunnybags because it was fortified with sandbags and heavily armed, including with artillery pieces. As Casey and Cora were being "tried" by the executive committee, word arrived of King's death. Early on the morning of May 22, a priest was admitted to the vigilante headquarters and performed a marriage ceremony for Charles Cora and his lover, Arabella Ryan, who had been fighting desperately behind the scenes to save his life. Shortly afterward, the vigilantes hanged Cora and Casey from the second-floor windows of Fort Gunnybags (Senkewicz 1985, pp. 167–172).

Cora's death at the hands of the vigilantes resulted from a series of events that began with his relationship with Ryan, and highlighted the new significance of women in the city's affairs. Formerly notorious for its overwhelmingly male population, by the mid-1850s many more women, particularly middle- and upper-class Anglo women, had arrived, and they often found San Francisco's social conditions appalling. In their daily activities, as they left their middle-class neighborhoods and headed downtown, they were compelled to traverse the vice district. As one historian noted, "A trip to the dentist, the doctor, the milliner, the husband's office, and sometimes even to church kept the situation explosive by renewing the contact between housewives and harlots" (Lotchin 1974, p. 257). One evening at the theater, U.S.

Execution of James P. Casey and Charles Cora, by the vigilance committee of San Francisco on May 22, 1856. (*Library of Congress*)

Marshal William Richardson confronted Cora and Ryan and demanded that the couple leave because Ryan's presence was an affront to his wife. The men encountered each other again a couple of days later, a quarrel erupted, and Cora pulled out a gun and fatally shot Richardson.

Unfortunately for Cora, James King of William used Cora's case to fuel the *Bulletin*'s polemics against the Democrats. The apparently murderous Italian Catholic gambler and his brazen mistress came to symbolize all the vice and crime and corruption in the city, on the streets and in the municipal government, and the failure of one jury to convict him seemingly exposed the complete inadequacy of the entire judicial system. King encouraged women to write to his newspaper, and many agreed with King's argument that prostitution and political corruption were inextricably linked. A correspondent calling herself "Femina" railed: "These evil and shameless women squander by the thousands their ill-gotten gains to fee corrupt lawyers, to screen the *criminal*, whose hands are reeking with blood, from the award of justice, to uphold the *gambling politicians*, who in return fill their hands with plunder derived from, or stolen from, our public offices of trust. . . . You can compel these women to leave our city; will you not do it?" (Jolly 2003).

Letter writers like Femina demanded the inclusion of sexual politics in the vigilantes' program of moral and municipal reform. But antivigilante writers also claimed the gendered moral high ground, such as a letter entitled "A True Woman's Plea for the Frail Portion of Her Sex" (ibid., p. 7). For a few months, as both pro- and antivigilante forces attempted to bolster the legitimacy of their positions by claiming the support of "the ladies," some of the women of San Francisco contributed publicly to the discussion and debate of the reasons and solutions for the city's political and social ills. But Thomas King, who took over his dead brother's newspaper, showed little interest in printing women's letters on any subject, and soon they virtually disappeared from the pages of the *Bulletin*. Moreover, the vigilantes had already shifted their focus from moral evils, such as prostitution, to political corruption, symbolized by a false-bottomed ballot box they claimed to have found in a basement—a "marvelously convenient discovery," as skeptics have pointed out (Senkewicz 1985, p. 119).

Most interpreters, even those who uncritically accepted the vigilantes' crime and corruption justifications for the events, have acknowledged the political power struggle at their center. John Nugent, editor of the *San Francisco Herald*, supported the 1851 vigilantes but condemned the 1856 movement. He described the vigilantes as a "mercantile junta" and warned that the committee's ultimate goal was "[t]he resignation of the county and state officers, and the election of the prominent members of the vigilance committee to the offices thus rendered vacant" (ibid., p. 179). Nugent's prediction was only slightly inaccurate: the executive committee attempted to remain in the background and fielded a slate of candidates under the banner of what it called the "People's Party." They were victorious, and the vigilantes and their supporters took political control of the city and county for the next decade. The 1856 San Francisco vigilance committee had waged an anti-Irish, anti-Catholic, antidemocratic campaign that pitted the upper classes against the lower classes, but from the vigilantes' perspective, the "best," the "leading" men of the city, had merely assumed their natural positions in the rightful scheme of things (Brown 1975; Johnson 1981). Similar men, with identical convictions, organized, led, and supported deadly vigilante movements throughout the West for decades. "Government by the people *en masse* is the acme of absurdity," sneered Thomas Dimsdale, British author of *The Vigilantes of Montana*, his 1866 celebration of one of the most ruthless extralegal killing sprees in U.S. history (Dimsdale 1866, p. 39).

As in California, the Montana vigilantes struggled for control of a key mining district, and there were several direct links between the San Francisco and Montana movements. Paris Pfouts, "president," or "chief," of the Virginia City vigilantes, lived in San Francisco during the "Revolution of 1856" and greatly admired William T. Coleman, president of the San Francisco vigilance committee. According to a member of the executive committee, Adriel B. Davis, a clerk from California administered the vigilante oath: "The question arose as to how we could organize and this man from California suggested he had the oath, and told us what the particulars were and how the committee was organized in California" (Callaway 1982, p. 43). Davis and the man who captained the vigilantes' death squad, James Williams, as well as other members of the executive committee, had previously resided in Denver, where a vigilance committee modeled on that of San Francisco hanged a number of men (precisely how many remains unclear) in 1859 and 1860 (ibid.; Leonard 2002, pp. 23–24).

During the winter of 1863–1864, the merchants, professionals, and tradesmen who composed the leadership of the Montana vigilantes claimed to have discovered the existence of a vast criminal conspiracy, a gang of "road agents" or robbers, led by none other than William Henry Plummer, the popular, hard-working sheriff of Bannack, the first boomtown of Montana's gold rush. They extracted the first "confession" about this bloodthirsty band of desperados from a man named "Long John" Franck through torture, repeatedly hoisting him with a rope around his neck until they found his agonized answers satisfactory. The vigilantes took Franck along to lead them to the outlaw "shebangs," or hideouts, he claimed were in the area, but they could not seem to locate them, or Alex Carter, an alleged murderer they were seeking. The vigilantes did find two men at the Rattlesnake Ranch, Erastus "Red" Yeager and George Brown. Under interrogation both men denied being members of any outlaw gang, but later Yeager panicked and offered to identify all of the "bloodthirsty villains" (Mather and Boswell 1991a). Hoping for mercy, Yeager furnished a list of about two dozen names, but the vigilantes hanged both men from cottonwood trees shortly afterward.

A few days later, Williams sent a party to Bannack to lynch the accused criminal mastermind of the gang, Sheriff Henry Plummer, and his two deputy accomplices. The lawmen protested that at least they had a right to a trial, but a vigilante informed them that their only trial waited at the end of a rope. Soon all three men dangled from a gallows that Plummer and his lawmen had recently erected to legally hang someone else. In Virginia City, the vigilantes marched five men to an unfinished building in town and hanged them, one by one, from its central beam. A vigilante death squad scoured the frozen countryside for the rest of the men named in the list.

They encountered no resistance from the supposedly all-powerful gang of road agents but easily picked their victims off in ones and twos—surprising them at home, in bed, many of them crippled with frostbitten hands and feet; one was snowblind, and another badly wounded man was drawn to his place of execution on a sled. A middle-aged double amputee died for commenting that the vigilantes had hanged some of the wrong men in Bannack (Mather and Boswell 1991b).

As in San Francisco, the vigilantes claimed that the good citizens of Bannack and Virginia City were so terrorized by a recent crime wave that they had been forced to take the law into their own hands. The vigilantes and their supporters later insisted that Plummer's gang perpetrated numerous thefts, robberies, and murders. However, according to the contemporary sources, there had been just four major crimes in the area during the final months of 1863—two homicides, a stage coach robbery, and the attempted robbery of a freight caravan by two inept bandits, one of whom was described as trembling from head to foot during the botched holdup. Instead of the vigilantes' simplistic narrative of good citizens versus bad men, "the contest was not so much about highway robbery as about supremacy at the mining settlements" (Mather and Boswell 1991c).

The gold rush began in what is now Montana in July 1862, at Grasshopper Creek, and by the end of the summer the population of nearby Bannack was already 500. In May 1863, prospectors found gold at Alder Gulch. Thousands of miners from all over the West headed for the new fields, including many who had followed the shifting mining frontier from California to Oregon to what is now Idaho. Often called "other-siders," these adventurers from the West frequently encountered determined attempts to turn them back as they crossed the Bitterroot Mountains by the goldseekers flowing north out of Colorado and west from the Midwest and Northeast. "Other-siders" constituted more than 75 percent of the vigilantes' twenty-one victims (Mather and Boswell 1991). In addition to attempts to dominate the new mines, the vigilantes also waged a battle for political, social, cultural, and moral control of the region. Langford, Dimsdale, Pfouts, Davis, and the other merchants and professionals who traveled to the camps considered themselves far superior to the "roughs," the workingmen who gambled, drank, whored, and brawled in the saloons, dance-halls, brothels, and road ranches. Yet, as Langford acknowledged, all classes of men participated in the raucous entertainments. Despite the elites' pretensions to loftier purposes, they had all "stampeded" toward the Montana gold fields with the same boundless greed and ambition as their lesser brethren.

Some historians have emphasized the clashes between Democrats, like Plummer and some of the other victims, and Republicans such as Sidney Edgerton, newly appointed chief justice of Idaho Territory and the future governor of Montana Territory; Wilbur F. Sanders, his New York–born nephew and future senator; and miner and banker Nathaniel Langford. It is clear from their own literature that the vigilantes viewed their victims' politics as significant; according to Langford, "Most of the gamblers and roughs . . . for the most part sympathized with the Confederates" (Langford 1890a). Yet there is no compelling evidence that Plummer was a Confederate sympathizer or "Secessionist" just because he was a Democrat—he was born in Maine and spent his adult life in the West. It served the vigilantes' purpose to link their local political rivals with the national struggle between the Union and Confederacy because it strengthened their constant claims that "the roughs" had attempted to take over and rule the entire mining region (Langford 1890b).

The vigilantes' tales of Plummer's powerful band of road agents echoed similar legends about secret outlaw gangs told everywhere on the mining frontier, from Colorado to California to Idaho. They also fit squarely within the long U.S. tradition of mythical criminal conspiracies by irredeemably bad men who conspired not just to rob the good citizens of their property and lives but also to overthrow their societies. However, there was no credible evidence of the existence of this vast, sophisticated network of criminals, nor any proof that the recent robberies had any connection with one another. The amateurish bandits who tried to hold up the Moody-Forbes freight caravan, one of them trembling like a leaf and both of them shot in the failed attempt, displayed none of the fierce competence one would expect of members of "the most perfectly organized and best appointed band of desperadoes ever known on the continent" (Mather and Boswell 1991d). Without such a monstrous threat to justify the vigilantes' bloody reign of terror, the inescapable conclusion would be that the only highly organized gang of ruthless killers stalking its prey across the frozen white land during the winter of 1863–1864 was the vigilance committee itself.

Certainly the "crippled loners" targeted by the Montana vigilantes that winter bore little resemblance to the bold and hardy young outlaws that were being forged in the flames of guerrilla warfare in the border West (Mather and Boswell 1991c). The violent war between the North and the South was mirrored in the West for decades, as local groups battled each other and often resisted state authority, as well. The Civil War also furnished many of the bandits and bad men of the 1860s and 1870s with their introduction to theft, pillage, and murder. In May 1863, fifteen-year-old Jesse Woodson James (1847–1882) burned with a need for vengeance after Unionist militiamen raided his mother's farm near Centerville, Missouri, demanding information about a local band of Confederate bushwhackers, including older brother Alexander Franklin "Frank" James. According to the legends, the brutal events of that day drove Jesse down the path of outlawry, and, in April 1864, Jesse became a bushwhacker, too, part of a gang that murdered Unionists in the area, looting and destroying homes and businesses. As one historian noted, his "introduction to warfare [was] not as a gladiator in battle against a tyrannous foe, but as a member of a death squad, picking off neighbors one by one" (Stiles 2002, p. 103).

He continued his education in terrorism when he and Frank joined the band of William "Bloody Bill" Anderson, "the most dangerous guerrilla organization in Missouri" (ibid., p. 112). The war finally ended on April 9, 1865, and the bushwhackers surrendered, but their victims had not forgotten their deeds. Murders and feuds continued and intensified as a political struggle developed between the Radicals, who urged a complete purge of Confederates from all government offices, and the Conservatives and Rebels.

The chaos and violence prompted some of the guerrillas to re-emerge and regroup. During the winter of 1865–1866, Jesse and Frank reunited with several of their bushwhacker companions. Their first target, on February 13, 1866, was the Clay County Savings Association in Liberty, Missouri, owned by the town's most prominent merchant, Radical Edward M. Samuel, and located just a few miles from the farm of their mother, Zerelda Samuel.

During the James and Younger gang's exceptionally lengthy outlaw career between 1866 and 1876, Jesse's admirers, particularly newspaper editor John Edwards, deliberately linked him with Confederate resistance to Reconstruction. Jesse, an inveterate attention-seeker, wrote long letters to the newspapers and claimed that he and his completely innocent friends were being persecuted by the authorities because of political animosities born of wartime hatreds. After operatives from the famed Pinkerton Detective Agency bungled a raid on the Samuel farm on the night of January 25, 1874, resulting in the amputation of Zerelda's arm and the death of her youngest son, Archie, Edwards seized upon the opportunity to build sympathy for the James brothers as heroes of the Lost Cause. Jesse reveled in this role and always linked his postwar banditry with his partisan hatreds. Jesse also viewed the First National Bank in Northfield, Minnesota, as a political symbol because of its connection with the Reconstruction governor of Mississippi, Republican Adelbert Ames (ibid., p. 307).

The James and Younger brothers rode together for the last time on September 7, 1876, as all of Jesse's obsessive narcissistic scheming, his visions of himself as the last great Confederate hero, fell to ruins in a hail of gunfire, and the citizens' fierce resistance forced the outlaws to make a desperate retreat from Northfield. The gang split up, and a posse soon captured the Youngers; they were swiftly tried and sentenced to prison. Frank and Jesse eventually made their way south to safer ground. But with the end of Reconstruction in 1876, the political resentments that furnished Jesse with an ostensibly noble cause and a reservoir of support among former Rebels became largely irrelevant: "In a very real sense, the Civil War had been refought in the years since Appomattox—and the Confederates had won" (ibid., p. 350). Missouri repudiated its 1865 constitution, and prominent Rebels took control of the legislature. The old glamour was wearing off Jesse's romantic partisan image, as well; even Edwards stopped responding to Jesse's communications. Jesse pulled off his last two train holdups in July and September of 1881. But the gang members began to turn against each other, until only Charley Ford was left, and he was scheming with his brother Bob to kill Jesse for the $10,000 reward. They finally accomplished their goal in April, when Bob shot James in the back of the head—and, inadvertently, they also ensured Jesse's place among the pantheon of American outlaws. The James Gang's successors, such as the Daltons and Bill Doolin, drew on strong local networks of kinfolk, friends, and sympathizers, but never tapped into such deep reservoirs of political partisanship among the wider population.

While many of the myths portrayed Jesse James as a romantic "social bandit," a Robin Hood character stealing from the rich to give to the poor, "political bandits" might be a more accurate term for the James and Younger gang. British historian Eric Hobshawm defined social bandits as "peasant

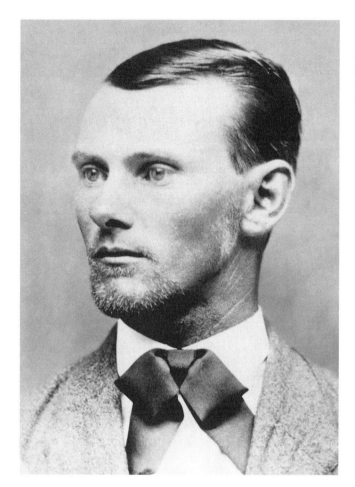

Jesse James (1847–1882) was one of the most famous and notorious outlaws of the American West. (*Library of Congress*)

outlaws whom the lord and state regard as criminals, but who remain within peasant society, and are considered by their people as heroes, as champions, avengers, fighters for justice, perhaps even leaders of liberation, and in any case as men to be admired, helped, and supported (Hobshawm 1969, p. 17). However the James and Younger families and most of their bushwhacker companions were not unsophisticated subsistence farmers (Stiles 2002; White 1981). As middle-class slave owners prior to the Civil War, they had participated fully in the thriving market economy of the region. Jesse James and other American political bandits were not peasant traditionalists resisting capitalism and industrialization. They were modern men resentful of political and social changes that destroyed their own access to land, resources, participation in the market economy, and political power, particularly as the result of conquest and war.

The narratives of the California bandit called Joaquín Murrieta bear many striking resemblances to tales about the James brothers. Stories passed down through generations of Murrietas in Sonora, Mexico, explain that the Murrieta brothers, Joaquín and Jesús, like the James brothers, were sons of *pobladores*—pioneers. As the James's ancestors and parents had migrated from England and Scotland to Ireland, then to Virginia, next to Kentucky, and finally to Missouri, the Murrietas had been moving toward Mexico's northern frontier for generations. According to family lore: "By the time they settled in southern Sonora . . . the Murrietas engaged regularly in three activities—digging gold, raising stock, and fighting Indians" (Johnson 2000, p. 29). Experienced miners from Sonora were among the first to arrive in the California gold fields after the discovery at Sutter's Mill in 1848. Joaquín and his wife, Rosa Felíz de Murrieta, followed them in 1849. Unlike many immigrant groups, Mexican women often traveled with their husbands to the diggings; this contrasts with Robert James's decision to leave his wife, Zerelda, and family behind in Missouri when he trekked out to California in 1850, where he died a few months later.

Like Robert James and the people from around the world who poured into what had so recently been Mexican territory, the Murrietas migrated to California to pursue ambitions of wealth and success in frontier industries such as mining and ranching. However, Anglos forced the Murrietas to abandon rich mining claims and turn to rounding up wild horses and selling them in Mexico. Then, like the James family during the Civil War, the Murrietas became victims of violence. American thugs raped Rosa, lynched Jesús, and flogged Joaquín. In January 1853, newspapers began to report that mounted bandits led by at least one man named Joaquín were attacking and sometimes killing people in Calaveras and Mariposa counties and robbing them of gold and horses. Some historians have speculated that Murrieta's gang killed as many as twenty-eight Chinese and thirteen Anglos.

A plaque in the small Sonoran town traditionally known as Murrieta's birthplace states that he "fought in California against the North American forces" and that they "called him a bandit and killer" but that the Californios knew him simply as "El Patrio," which in English means "the native" (Griswold del Castillo 1999, p. 108). This version, then, takes Murrieta's criminality beyond simple banditry and even personal vengeance into a political realm in which he, like Jesse James, took up arms to defend his country and then continued his campaign against the enemy after the war was lost. Historians have identified as many as four or five men named Joaquín as members of Murrieta's band. Joaquín Valenzuela may have been a former guerrilla fighter in the U.S.-Mexican War who rejected the peace treaty and continued to fight the U.S. forces in Mexico. Valenzuela and some of his guerrilla comrades fled to California and eventually joined Murrieta's band, "bringing with them their slogan of defiance, 'All or nothing,' as well as the notion that the U.S.-Mexican War had never ended," just as the James brothers and their bushwhacker comrades refused to accept the defeat of the Confederacy (ibid., p. 113).

While Joaquín Murrieta may not have been a real person, his story presents a composite of the many injustices suffered by the Californios and Mexicanos at the hands of the Anglo conquerors and the various forms of their fierce resistance. Folklore and Chicano literature have celebrated Murrieta as a social bandit, a Robin Hood figure, although there are no tales of the bandits sharing their plunder with the poor. Like the James and Younger brothers, Murrieta and his men were not unsophisticated peasants seeking to preserve a traditional agrarian society; they initially had the same goals and aspirations for success in a modern market economy as their American rivals. Viewing themselves as economically, politically, and socially dispossessed, the Joaquíns and their followers turned to brigandage and terrorism and disproportionately targeted members of a small and vulnerable ethnic group, the Chinese. Murrieta represents the type of cruel and terrifying bandit that Hobshawm called "the avenger," while Jesse James more closely resembled the "quasi-bandit" type that Hobshawm called the "expropriator," a figure who adopts the methods and rhetoric of social banditry to justify robbery for the sake of a political or terrorist cause (Hobshawm 1969, pp. 62, 64, 110–111; Stiles 2002, pp. 391–392).

Other legendary Western figures, such as Henry McCarty (1859–1881), also known as "William H. Bonney" and "Billy the Kid," played pivotal roles in local battles over economic resources and political power as part of what historian Richard Maxwell Brown called the "Western Civil War of Incorporation" (Brown 1991, pp. 44–45). Between 1860 and 1910, "conservative forces consolidated authority in the West in the interest of property, law, and order," provoking resistance by various groups (ibid., p. 40). Indians battled confinement on reservations, people of Mexican descent struggled against the loss of their land and livelihoods, and the miners, loggers, and laborers of the "wageworkers' frontier" resisted the brutal imperatives of unregulated industrial capitalism with strikes and other forms of collective action. McCarty worked for brief periods at typical frontier jobs—cowhand, farmhand, short order cook, store clerk—but, according to one rancher, in 1877 "he got to running with a gang of rustlers" in Arizona (Nolan 1998, p. 51). He then shot a man named Frank Cahill in a dance hall, stole the swiftest horse he could find, and rode toward Lincoln County, New Mexico.

In November 1876, the small town of Lincoln had become the unlikely site of a titanic struggle between rival capitalists, when John H. Tunstall, the son of a British merchant, and lawyer Alexander McSween opened a store to compete with the only major mercantile firm in the area, L. G. Murphy & Co, known as "The House," and schemed to wrest away its monopoly on government beef contracts. The owners of the House, Murphy and James Dolan, retaliated with various legal maneuvers, and as the hostilities between the two factions deepened in January 1878, Tunstall and McSween hired a number of men, including McCarty, to work as both cowhands and gunfighters at Tunstall's Rio Feliz ranch. But Tunstall's hired guns failed to protect him the following month, when a sheriff's posse consisting of several House employees and some notorious outlaws caught up with him on the road to Lincoln. Tunstall's party scattered for cover, and Tunstall was cut off, trapped in a patch of timber, and shot to death. His murder ignited a series of gun battles, sieges, and assassinations that became known as the Lincoln County War, as McCarty allegedly vowed vengeance on "every son-of-a-bitch who helped kill John if it's the last thing I do" (Horan 1954, p. 59).

McCarty and about a dozen men formed a vigilante group called the "Regulators." Like the Regulators of Massac County, Illinois, or the San Francisco vigilantes, the Lincoln County Regulators argued that virtually the

William H. Bonney, aka "Billy the Kid," western outlaw (1859–1881). (*Circer, Hayward, ed.,* Dictionary of American Portraits, *1967*)

entire local legal system was controlled by the criminals, and so they had no choice but to take matters into their own hands. The Regulators swore a binding vigilante oath and formally organized as a posse to serve arrest warrants issued by the justice of the peace. The Regulators thus claimed the mantle of crime control and the moral, if not legal, high ground. After the Regulators assassinated the sheriff and several other men, however, whatever legitimacy they had possessed as law-restoring vigilantes rapidly eroded. Their enemies described the Regulators as a "mob," invoking images of lawlessness and unchecked vengeance. When McCarty faced execution for murder several years later, *Newman's Semi-Weekly* (Las Cruces) urged that the citizens permit the law to take its course and to avoid "mob rule," particularly since the "Kid himself has been the most terrible exponent of that law in Southern New Mexico" (Nolan 1998, pp. 322–323, n. 12). But McCarty escaped from his jail cell in April 1881, only to die a few months later at Fort Sumner, asking, "Quién es? Quién es?" as a shadowy figure in a darkened room opened fire. Outlaw, vigilante, victim—the ambiguities of McCarty's role in one of the most dramatic conflicts of Western incorporation only enhanced his legend.

Like the Lincoln County War, other "wars" over land, resources, and local politics raged throughout the West and Southwest during the final decades of the nineteenth century. The "Colfax County War" broke out in northern New Mexico in 1875 when the European speculators who had purchased the nearly 2-million-acre Maxwell Land Grant tried to remove the "squatters" who had settled on the land over the previous thirty years. As in the Lincoln County troubles, the Grant owners, supported by the corrupt Santa Fe Ring, used legal maneuvers to harass the settlers. The mysterious murder of minister Franklin J. Tolby, a local leader and prominent critic of the Grant owners' policies, led to the rise of the defiant settlers' "Colfax County Ring," who vowed "No quarter now for the foreign land thieves and their hired assassins" ("Legends of America" 2003–2005). Some fifteen years later, mounted and masked *nuevo mexicano* vigilantes called Las Gorras Blancas ("the White Caps") began a two-year campaign of intimidation, violence, and fence destruction in San Miguel County aimed at large landowners who attempted to restrict public access to grazing, water, and timber resources traditionally regarded by local inhabitants as communal property (Rosenbaum 1981). Similar fence-cutting movements swept across parts of Texas from the 1870s to the 1890s. One of the most notorious episodes of vigilante violence in Western history, the 1889 lynching of Ellen Watson and Jim Averell, constituted a preliminary skirmish in the Johnson County War that broke out between the cattle barons and the small ranchers and homesteaders of Wyoming in 1892.

Ellen L. Watson

Like other ambitious homesteaders throughout the West, Ellen L. Watson and her husband, Jim Averell, took up claims to several parcels of land along Horse Creek and the Sweetwater River in southeastern Wyoming during the late 1880s. In the grass-rich but frequently rain-scarce expanses of the Northern Plains and prairies, access to rivers, streams, and springs was crucial for stockmen and farmers, and by the mid-1870s, hundreds of private ditches carried water away from streams and creeks, leading to many disputes and a number of laws clarifying water use and rights over the next decade. Averell and Watson became entangled in several conflicts over water rights and irrigation ditches with powerful local cattlemen, particularly neighbor Albert J. Bothwell. Averell had further provoked the cattle barons' wrath with his letters to the *Casper Weekly Mail*, protesting the fraudulent claims of the "land grabbers" and arguing that the irrigation laws inhibited the settlement and improvement of the region by the "bona fide settler" (Hufsmith 1993, pp. 170–171). It seems certain that his outlook and beliefs were shared by neighboring homesteader and aspiring rancher, his wife, Ellen L. Watson.

Watson, like Averell, was born in Canada, but she was some ten years younger, born around 1861. As the oldest of eleven children, she probably performed a great deal of the work on her family's farm, furnishing her with the knowledge, experience, and confidence to later claim her own homestead. The Watsons later moved to Kansas, where she married William Pickle in 1879. However, she separated from Pickle two years later, alleging physical abuse, and by the mid-1880s worked in a hotel in Rawlins, Wyoming, as a cook and housemaid, where she met Averell (Meschter 1996; Leigh 1992; Hufsmith 1993). In fact, the first documentary evidence of Watson's arrival in Wyoming is an application by Ellen Liddy Andrews and James Averell for a marriage license, dated May 11, 1886. Watson probably used a false name in the application because the couple wished to evade the rules of the Homestead Act. Married women could not claim land in their own name; thus, Watson had to appear "single" in the eyes of the law until she could "prove up" her claim—take full legal possession of her land. While this clearly was illegal, it should be compared to the big ranchers' practice of using their cowboys as proxies to make preemption claims in order to acquire many thousands of acres of public lands fraudulently.

By 1889, the Wyoming cattle industry was finally shaking off the disastrous losses of the brutal winter of 1886–1887, when hundreds of thousands of cattle on the badly overgrazed open range perished from lack of shelter and food as blizzards swept the Northern Plains and temperatures fell as low as –68° Fahrenheit. The cattlemen who managed to avoid bankruptcy realized "that irrigating foliage to produce winter feed would now have to be a critical part of a successful cattle business. Such a revelation generated a much keener interest in water rights and land patents among cattlemen . . . and claim statements took on a more urgent and serious importance" (Cooper 2004, p. 16). According to the *Casper Weekly Mail* of August 30, one of Watson's employees, John DeCorey, recalled that "Bothwell often came to see [Watson] and tried to buy her land from her, but she refused to sell it to him." In April 1889, after the Carbon County Brand Commission had rejected her proposed brand, Watson purchased John Crowder's LU brand. Now she held a legal land claim that she would surely "prove up" in a few years and owned the nucleus of a large cattle operation and a brand of her own. One historian has speculated that "the vision of a woman pounding on the doors of the Wyoming Stock Growers Association demanding admittance as an equal was simply too much to be tolerated" (Meschter 1996, p. 162).

Five of the six men who rode out to Watson's ranch on that Saturday afternoon in 1889 were members of the WSGA. As the ranchers' buggy rolled up in front of Watson's house, John Durbin jumped out, took down a section of her pasture fence, and drove her cattle onto the open range. Bothwell ordered Watson to climb into the buggy, and she finally complied after he threatened to rope and drag her if she continued to resist. The party then headed toward Averell's ranch and forced him at gunpoint to join Watson in the carriage. The ranchers took their captives to the river, followed a short time later by one of Averell's friends, cowboy Frank Buchanan. Buchanan moved as close as he dared to the scene and saw Watson trying frantically to dodge the noose in Earnest McLean's hands as Bothwell urged Averell to jump off the ledge below. Averell's friend pulled out his pistol and fired on the lynchers, but they drove him back with their rifles. Watson and Averell died slow, cruel deaths from strangulation and struggled wildly for long moments, clawing and kicking, because their amateur executioners had failed to bind their arms and legs.

The lynchers immediately began spreading a series of lies and character assassinations through Ed Towse of the *Cheyenne Daily Leader*, stories that were picked up by the national press and enshrined in Western mythology forever afterward. Towse's well-oiled imagination transformed hardworking homesteader Ellen L. Watson into a perverted, bold, and masculine figure called "Cattle Kate." In his first article, dated July 23, 1889, he claimed that "[she] was the equal of any man on the range. . . . [S]he was a dare devil in the saddle, handy with a six shooter, and an adept with the lariat and branding iron. . . . [S]he was a holy terror . . . [who] rode straddle" on a "vicious broncho [*sic*]." A few months later, on October 15, 1889, the *Leader* reprinted an article from the *Salt Lake Tribune* in which an unidentified man from Carbon County declared "that woman was a terror—a real unsexed terror."

By that time, it was clear that her killers would never be brought to justice. Several witnesses identified all the lynchers at the coroners' inquest, but when the grand jury got the case in October 1889, those witnesses had all died or disappeared, and no indictments were ever brought against the killers. Bothwell and Durbin sold Watson's legally purchased and branded cattle and pocketed the proceeds. And in a final miscarriage of justice, the lynchers' victims, Watson and Averell, would live on in the national historical memory as rustlers and rogues.

The real Ellen Watson bore little resemblance to the newspapers' caricature of the "unsexed," bronco-busting, pistol-packing Cattle Kate, but some Western women did become "authentic" bandits. Annie Byers Richey, known as "Queen Anne," became the first woman ever legally convicted of cattle rustling in Wyoming in 1919 (Pence 1982). After her appeals ran out and she was preparing to enter prison, however, she was mysteriously poisoned in 1922. Belle Starr became notorious in north Texas and the Indian Territory for her multiple marriages to Indian and mixed-race men, rumored participation in a torture-robbery, and for sheltering outlaws at her home even before she was tried and convicted of horse theft in "Hanging Judge" Isaac Parker's Fort Smith courtroom in 1882 (Shirley 1982; Riley 1999). Nevada cattle rustler Susan Raper, however, won three acquittals in her trials for grand larceny in 1870, largely because of the male jurors' reluctance to believe that a woman possessed the ability to run a gang of stock thieves or plot a jewel heist. Raper successfully manipulated these nineteenth-century stereotypes of "true womanhood" throughout her long criminal career (Lara 1996; Sprenger-Farley 1996). What is perhaps more surprising is how those stereotypes have persisted into the modern literature, with few attempts to investigate the subject beyond the same half-dozen or so "outlaw women" limned repeatedly in both popular and historical accounts of the Wild West—usually Starr, "Cattle Kate," Martha "Calamity Jane" Canary, "Cattle Annie and Little Britches," and Pearl Hart.

Many others have been largely forgotten, such as Richey, Raper, or Cora Hubbard, breathlessly dubbed "the second Belle Starr" by one local newspaper after she and two male accomplices robbed a Missouri bank in 1897. Following her arrest, Hubbard defiantly insisted to a Joplin reporter that she was "not a damn bit afraid" during the holdup and that she regretted only that she could not rob "the whole damn town" (Wood 2004). *The Tecumseh*

Ellen Watson and the Johnson County War

The lynching of Ellen Watson and Jim Averell in July, 1889, constituted one of the first battles in the conflict between the small ranchers and homesteaders and the cattle barons of Wyoming in 1892 that became known as the "Johnson County War." During the 1880s, Ellen L. Watson and her husband, Jim Averell, claimed several homesteads along Horse Creek and the Sweetwater River in southeastern Wyoming. Access to springs, creeks, and rivers was essential for stockmen and farmers in the grass-rich but frequently rain-scarce expanses of the Northern Plains and prairies. Hundreds of private ditches carried water away from streams and creeks by the mid-1870s, resulting in numerous local conflicts and new legislation that attempted to simplify and regulate water use and rights over the following decade. Averell and Watson became embroiled in a number of disputes over water rights and irrigation ditches with powerful local cattlemen, particularly their neighbor Albert J. Bothwell. Averell's letters to the *Casper Weekly Mail*, protesting the fraudulent claims of the "land grabbers" and arguing that the irrigation laws inhibited the settlement and improvement of the region by the "bona fide settler" (Hufsmith 1993, pp. 170–171) had further roused the cattle barons' ire. His wife, the neighboring homesteader and aspiring rancher Ellen L. Watson, surely shared his opinions.

Like Averell, Watson was born in Canada sometime around 1861. As the oldest of eleven children, it is likely that she performed a great deal of the work on her family's farm, furnishing her with the knowledge, experience, and confidence to later claim her own homestead. Her family later moved to Kansas, where she met and married William Pickle in 1879. However, she separated from Pickle two years later and by the mid-1880s worked in a hotel in Rawlins, Wyoming, as a cook and housemaid, where she met Averell (Meschter 1996, pp. 29–30; Leigh 1992, pp. 49–56; Hufsmith 1993, pp. 39, 54–55).

Ellen L. Watson, accused of cattle rustling and hanged by a group of vigilantes in Wyoming in 1889. (*Wyoming State Archives, Department of State Parks and Cultural Resources*)

The first documentary evidence of Watson's arrival in Wyoming is an application of May 11, 1886, for a marriage license by Ellen Liddy Andrews and James Averell. Because the couple was attempting to circumvent the rules of the Homestead Act, Watson used a false name in the application. The Act prohibited married women from claiming homesteads in their own names, so Watson was required to appear "single" in the eyes of the law until she could "prove up" her claim—take full legal possession of her land. Watson and Averell's ruse was obviously illegal; however, it should be compared to the big ranchers' practice of using their cowboys as proxies to make preemption claims in order to acquire fraudulently many thousands of acres of public land.

After the disastrous losses of the terrible winter of 1886–1887, when blizzards swept the

Northern Plains and temperatures fell as low as –68° Fahrenheit, killing hundreds of thousands of cattle on the badly overgrazed open range, the Wyoming cattle industry had finally begun to recover by 1889. The cattlemen who hung on and escaped bankruptcy began to understand "that irrigating foliage to produce winter feed would now have to be a critical part of a successful cattle business. Such a revelation generated a much keener interest in water rights and land patents among cattlemen . . . and claim statements took on a more urgent and serious importance" (Cooper 2004, p. 16). Neighboring rancher "Bothwell often came [to Watson's ranch] to see her and tried to buy her land from her, but she refused to sell it to him" (*Casper Weekly Mail*, August 30, 1889), according to one of Watson's employees, John DeCorey. Defying the Carbon County Brand Commission's rejection of her own proposed brand, Watson purchased John Crowder's LU brand in April, 1889. Watson now possessed a land claim that she would certainly "prove up" in a few years, the beginnings of a large cattle operation, and a brand of her own. "The vision of a woman pounding on the doors of the Wyoming Stock Growers Association [WSGA] demanding admittance as an equal was simply too much to be tolerated," according to one historian (Meschter 1996, p. 162).

On the Saturday afternoon of July 2, 1889, five of the six men who suddenly appeared at Watson's ranch were members of the WSGA (ibid., p. 3). Jumping out of a buggy in front of Watson's house, John Durbin tore down part of her pasture fence and drove her cattle onto the open range. Commanded to climb into the buggy, Watson refused until Bothwell threatened to rope and drag her if she failed to comply. The ranchers then drove towards Averell's ranch, met him on the road, and persuaded him, at gunpoint, to join his wife in the buggy. As the ranchers took their captives to the river, one of Averell's friends, cowboy Frank Buchanan, followed and tried to approach the scene. He witnessed Watson's desperate attempts to dodge the noose in Earnest McLean's hands, while Bothwell demanded that Averell jump off the ledge below. Buchanan fired on the lynchers with his pistol, but they drove him back with their rifles. Because their killers had not bothered to bind their arms and legs, Watson and Averell frantically struggled for long, cruel moments, clawing and kicking, before they finally died of strangulation.

Immediately after the lynchings, Ed Towse of the *Cheyenne Daily Leader* began spreading the killers' lies and character assassinations of their victims, stories that were picked up by the national press and became part of Western mythology forever afterward. Hardworking homesteader Ellen L. Watson was transformed by Towse's cynical prose into a bold, masculine, and degenerate figure called "Cattle Kate." He claimed in his first article of July 23, 1889, that Watson "was the equal of any man on the range. . . . [S]he was a dare devil in the saddle, handy with a six shooter, and adept with the lariat and branding iron. . . . [S]he was a holy terror . . . [who] rode straddle" on a "vicious broncho [*sic*]" (*Cheyenne Daily Leader*, July 23, 1889). The *Leader* reprinted an article from the *Salt Lake Tribune* in which an unidentified man from Carbon County declared "that woman was a terror—a real unsexed terror" a couple of months later (*Cheyenne Daily Leader*, October 15, 1889).

By October, it was clear that her murderers would escape justice. Although a number of witnesses positively identified all the lynchers at the coroners' inquest, they had all died or disappeared by the time the grand jury got the case in October 1889. No indictments were ever brought against the killers. Two of those

(continued on following page)

Ellen Watson and the Johnson County War (continued)

murderers, Bothwell and Durbin, sold Watson's legally purchased and branded cattle and simply stole the returns. Perhaps the greatest injustice to their victims, however, has been their enduring reputations in Western history as rustlers and rogues who somehow deserved their terrible ends.

References and Further Reading

Cooper, Craig O. "A History of Water Law, Water Rights, and Water Development in Wyoming, 1868–2002." Laramie, Wyoming Water Development Commission and State Engineer's Office, 2004. Available online: http://wwdc.state.wy.us/history/Wyoming%20Water%20Law%20History.pdf (accessed August 22, 2005).

Hufsmith, George W. *The Wyoming Lynching of Cattle Kate, 1889.* Glendo, WY: High Plains Press, 1993.

Leigh, Sharon. "Ella Watson: Rustler or Homesteader?" *Annals of Wyoming* 64, nos. 3–4: (1992), 49–56.

Meschter, Daniel Y. *Sweetwater Sunset: A History of the Lynching of James Averell and Ella Watson near Independence Rock, Wyoming, on July 20, 1889.* Wenatchee, WA: D. Y. Meschter, 1996.

Republican of October 7, 1898, described another young woman, Dora Cox, as the "central figure in a number of other sensational performances" in Oklahoma following her arrest for horse theft in 1898. Indeed, Oklahoma newspapers positively buzzed with reports of "female outlaws" during the 1890s. Many of these young women—like Hubbard, Cox, and the teenaged Jennie "Little Britches" Stevens—attracted even greater press and public attention because they bobbed their hair, wore men's clothing, and carried guns. Cross-dressing desperado Flora Quick Mundis also used the name "Tom King"; however, on July 18, 1893, *The Guthrie Daily News* acidly dismissed her as "the imitation cowboy and horse thief" (see also Vance 1945). Unless they repented and reformed of their sinful ways, like Stevens and Pearl Hart, press accounts usually depicted these women outlaws as unattractive and unwomanly, and very little is known about most of them.

Women who performed more conventional roles as accomplices and helpmeets to male outlaws have often been deeply romanticized. "The Rose of the Cimarron" supposedly carried bullets to her lover during an 1893 Oklahoma gun battle with lawmen and escaped with him on her horse after he was wounded. Her name appears to have been Rose Dunn, but some sources sentimentally claim to withhold her true identity in order "to protect her character and family influence" (Hunter and Rose 1951, p. 44). A soulful photograph of a beautiful and refined woman usually identified as Etta Place, Harry "Sundance Kid" Longabaugh's lover, has been extensively reproduced in virtually every account of the Rocky Mountain bank and train-robbing gang known as "The Wild Bunch." However, her real name, which may have been Ethel, is a matter of debate, and several women associated with members of the Wild Bunch may have used the alias "Etta Place" at different times. Ethel accompanied Longabaugh and Robert Leroy "Butch Cassidy" Parker when they fled the United States in 1901 for the mining and ranching frontiers of Argentina, Chile, and Bolivia, and she participated in at least one bank robbery in Argentina in 1905. She may have returned to the United

States around 1908, while Longabaugh and Parker committed several hold-ups of mine and railroad construction payrolls in Bolivia, then apparently died in a shootout with a military and police posse near San Vicente (Meadows and Buck 1997). Ethel's subsequent fate remains a mystery.

The old ways of outlawry were changing. During the first decades of the twentieth century, swift horses and rural stage coach holdups gave way to fast cars and robberies of mail trucks. Local, state, and national governments modernized and strengthened law enforcement agencies, and their abilities to track and capture criminals improved with the development of new technologies, particularly the telephone. More Americans lived in urban than rural areas by 1920, and public and press attention shifted to violent organized crime in the industrial cities of the East. As women moved into the workforce, gained the right to vote, shortened their skirts and their hair, Victorian stereotypes about women and crime began to change as well.

By 1934 revisions in federal law made women who aided and abetted fugitives liable as criminal accomplices, and women outlaws played a crucial role in the federal government's expansion of its domestic law enforcement activities (Potter 1995, p. 3). J. Edgar Hoover's "G-Man" would not have been nearly so successful in captivating the public imagination "without the menacing figure of the lawless gun woman," such as Bonnie Parker or Kate "Ma" Barker, to act "as a foil against which the FBI could assert the necessity of the G-Man" (Strunk 2003, p. 5). The professional G-Man also replaced the good citizen as the ultimate law enforcer, and vigilante posses faded away. The most notorious outlaws often achieved spots on the FBI's "Ten Most Wanted" list and fought gun battles with federal agents instead of U.S. marshals, county sheriffs, or elite state police forces such as the Texas Rangers. As Northeastern and Midwestern cities became associated with the violent mayhem of organized crime, the mounted outlaw gangs of the nineteenth-century rural American West and their vigilante pursuers were idealized in new forms of mass media such as films, radio programs, and comic books. Their legends abide in the twenty-first century, on tens of thousands of websites across the nation and around the world.

References and Further Reading

Abrahams, Ray. *Vigilant Citizens: Vigilantism and the State.* Cambridge, UK: Polity Press, 1998.

Brown, Richard Maxwell. *Strain of Violence: Historical Studies of American Violence and Vigilantism.* Oxford: Oxford University Press, 1975.

Brown, Richard Maxwell. *No Duty to Retreat: Violence and Values in American History and Society.* New York: Oxford University Press, 1991.

Brundage, W. Fitzhugh. *Lynching in the New South: Georgia and Virginia, 1880–1930.* Urbana: University of Illinois Press, 1993.

Callaway, Llewellyn L. *Montana's Righteous Hangmen: The Vigilantes in Action.* Norman: University of Oklahoma Press, 1982.

Cooper, Craig O. Wyoming Water Development Commission and State Engineer's Office. "A History of Water Law, Water Rights, and Water Development in Wyoming, 1868–2002," 2004. http://wwdc.state.wy.us/history/Wyoming%20Water%20Law%20History.pdf (accessed March 15, 2006).

Dimsdale, Thomas J. *The Vigilantes of Montana or Popular Justice in the Rocky Mountains* [1977]. Norman: University of Oklahoma Press, 1866.

Etcheson, Nicole. "Good Men and Notorious Rogues: Vigilantism in Massac County, Illinois, 1846–1850." In M. Bellesiles, ed., *Lethal Imagination: Violence and Brutality in American History.* New York: New York University Press, 1999, 149–169.

Griswold del Castillo, Richard. "Joaquín Murrieta: The Many Lives of a Legend." In R. W. Etulain and G. Riley, eds., *With Badges & Bullets: Lawmen & Outlaws in the Old West.* Golden, CO: Fulcrum Publishing, 1999.

Hobshawm, Eric. *Bandits* [1969]. New York: Pantheon Books, 1981.

Horan, James D., and Paul Sann. *Pictorial History of the Wild West.* New York: Crown Publishers, 1954.

Hufsmith, George W. *The Wyoming Lynching of Cattle Kate, 1889.* Glendo, WY: High Plains Press, 1993. Averell's letter to the *Casper Weekly Mail* is quoted on pp. 170–171. Hufsmith claims that after Watson left Pickle, she worked in a hotel in Nebraska and from 1884 to 1886 as a cook and housemaid at Rawlins House, the best hotel in Rawlins, Wyoming (pp. 39, 54–55).

Hunter, J. Marvin, and Noah H. Rose. *The Album of Gunfighters.* N.p., 1951. Bandera, TX: Rose.

Johnson, David. "The Moral Authority of Popular Justice in the Far West." *American Quarterly* 33, no. 5 (1981): 558–586.

Johnson, Susan Lee. *Roaring Camp: The Social World of the California Gold Rush.* New York: W. W. Norton & Company, 2000.

Jolly, Michelle. 2003. "Sex, Vigilantism, and San Francisco in 1856." *Common-Place* 3, no. 4. http://www.common-place.org/vol–03/no–04/san-francisco/ (accessed March 15, 2006).

Langford, Nathaniel Pitt. *Vigilante Days and Ways: The Pioneers of the Rockies, the Makers and Making of Montana, Idaho, Oregon, Washington, and Wyoming.* Boston: J. G. Cupples Co., 1890a. http://www.umwestern.edu/Academics/library/libroth/MHD/vigilantes/LANGFORD/cover.html (accessed March 15, 2006). Quote from Chapter XII, "Pinkham and Patterson," http://www.umwestern.edu/Academics/library/libroth/MHD/vigilantes/LANGFORD/chapters/chap12.html (accessed March 15, 2006).

Langford, Nathaniel Pitt. 1890b. *Vigilante Days and Ways.* "Chapter XX, A Masonic Funeral," http://www.umwestern.edu/Academics/library/libroth/MHD/vigilantes/LANGFORD/chapters/chap20.html (accessed March 15, 2006).

Lara, Kandi. "Susan Raper: Elko County's First Female Cattle Rustler." *Quarterly—Northeastern Nevada Historical Society* 96, no. 2 (1996): 56–63.

"Legends of America." 2003–2005. "The Maxwell Land Grant" http://www.legendsofamerica.com/HC-Maxwell4.html (accessed March 15, 2006).

Leigh, Sharon. "Ella Watson: Rustler or Homesteader?" *Annals of Wyoming* 64, nos. 3–4 (1992): 49–56.

Leonard, Stephen J. *Lynching in Colorado, 1859–1919.* Boulder: University Press of Colorado, 2002.

Lotchin, Roger W. *San Francisco, 1846–1856: From Hamlet to City.* New York: Oxford University Press, 1974.

Mather, R. E., and F. E. Boswell. *Vigilante Victims*, 1991a. http://www.umwestern.edu/Academics/library/libroth/MHD/vigilantes/VV/cover.html (accessed March 15, 2006). Yeager admitted carrying a note for George Brown to Alex Carter, but claimed that he was just doing what any courteous traveler commonly did at the time. George Brown freely acknowledged writing a note warning Carter that the vigilantes meant to kill him, but insisted that doing so was no crime. "The First Two Hangings," http://www.umwestern.edu/Academics/library/libroth/MHD/vigilantes/VV/first2.html (accessed March 15, 2006).

Mather, R. E., and F. E. Boswell. *Vigilante Victims*. "The Joint Hangings of the Virginia City Five," 1991b. http://www.umwestern.edu/Academics/library/libroth/MHD/vigilantes/VV/joint5.html and "Pursuit of More Suspects" http://www.umwestern.edu/Academics/library/libroth/MHD/vigilantes/VV/pursuit.html (accessed March 15, 2006).

Mather, R. E., and F. E. Boswell. *Vigilante Victims*. "Twenty-One Questions," 1991c. http://www.umwestern.edu/Academics/library/libroth/MHD/vigilantes/VV/21quest.html (accessed March 15, 2006).

Meadows, Anne, and Daniel Buck. "The Last Days of Butch & Sundance." *Wild West* 9, no. 5 (1997): 36–43.

Meschter, Daniel Y. *Sweetwater Sunset: A History of the Lynching of James Averell and Ella Watson Near Independence Rock, Wyoming on July 20, 1889.* Wenatchee, WA: D.Y. Meschter, 1996.

Nolan, Frederick W. *The West of Billy the Kid.* Norman: University of Oklahoma Press, 1998.

Pence, Mary Lou. "Petticoat Rustler." *American History Illustrated* 17, no. 4 (1982): 52–57.

Potter, Claire Bond. "'I'll Go the Limit and Then Some': Gun Molls, Desire, and Danger in the 1930s." *Feminist Studies* 21, no. 1 (1995): 41–66.

Ricards, Sherman L., and George M. Blackburn. "The Sydney Ducks: A Demographic Analysis." In E. H. Monkkonen, ed., *The Frontier*. Westport-London: Meckler 1991, 309–320. The first Australians arrived in 1849, and approximately 11,000 had migrated to California by May 1851.

Riley, Glenda. "Belle Starr." In R. W. Etulain and G. Riley, eds., *With Badges & Bullets: Lawmen & Outlaws in the Old West.* Golden, CO: Fulcrum Publishing, 1999, 139–158.

Ring, Eugene. *Sketch of a Three Years Travell in South America, California and Mexico.* From "A Timeline of San Francisco History," 1849a. http://www.zpub.com/sf/history/sfh2.html (accessed March 15, 2006).

Ring, Eugene. From "Eugene Ring: The Voyage to California, Part 3," 1849b. http://www.mtdemocrat.com/columist/ring092898.shtml (accessed March 15, 2006).

Rosenbaum, Robert J. *Mexicano Resistance in the Southwest: "The Sacred Right of Self-Preservation."* Austin: University of Texas Press, 1981, 99–124.

Senkewicz, Robert M. *Vigilantes in Gold Rush San Francisco.* Stanford: Stanford University Press, 1985. According to Senkewicz, p. 156, as a young man James King began calling himself James King of William because his father's name was William, and he desired to distinguish himself from all the other James Kings in his hometown.

Shirley, Glen. *Belle Starr and Her Times: The Literature, the Facts, and the Legends.* Norman: University of Oklahoma Press, 1982.

Soulé, Frank, and John H. Gihon. *The Annals of San Francisco.* San Francisco Genealogy, "Part Third, The Hounds," 1855. http://www.sfgenealogy.com/sf/history/hbann3–1.htm (accessed March 15, 2006).

Sprenger-Farley, Terri. "The Saga of Susie Raper." *Quarterly—Northeastern Nevada Historical Society* 96, no. 2 (1996): 63–67.

Stiles, T. J. *Jesse James: Last Rebel of the Civil War.* New York: Alfred A. Knopf, 2002.

Strunk, Mary. "'The Girl behind the Man behind the Gun': Woman Outlaws, Public Memory, and the Rise and Fall of Hoover's FBI." Ph.D. diss., University of Minnesota, 2003.

Vance, Randolph. *Wildcats in Petticoats: A Garland of Female Desperadoes.* Girard, KS: Haldeman-Julius Publications, 1945, 10–12. A detailed but improbable account of Flora Quick Mundis, "one of the strangest women outlaws that ever rode the west."

White, Richard. "Outlaw Gangs of the Middle Border: American Social Bandits." *Western Historical Quarterly* 12, no. 4 (1981): 387–408.

Wister, Owen. *The Virginian, A Horseman of the Plains.* New York: Grosset and Dunlap, 1902.

Wood, Larry. "Cora Hubbard: 'The Second Belle Starr.'" *Wild West* 17 (2004): 12–15. http://www.historynet.com/we/blcorahubbard/ (accessed March 15, 2006).

Artists and Boosters | 13

Flannery Burke

Anyone attempting to catalog the entirety of Western visual culture immediately encounters the challenge of finding coherency among visual representations of the American West. Such images run the gamut from
colonial New Mexico's Spanish religious saint figures to eighteenth-century
Spanish explorers' sketches of California flora and fauna to nineteenth-
century Plains Indians' hide calendars to Robert Smithson's 1970 earthwork
"Spiral Jetty" in Utah's Great Salt Lake. Despite the variety and richness
of Western visual culture, only two museums east of the Mississippi hold
substantial collections of what is commonly termed "Western art," and
those interested in Western art must generally go west to see it. Nonetheless, defined broadly, Western art is as comprehensive and as reflective of
American history and culture as any that is commonly associated with the
United States. The challenge in understanding and historicizing Western art,
or the broader category of Western visual culture, is not in finding sufficient variety and analytical challenge in what it comprises but in narrowing
one's lens such as to catch Western visual culture's most prominent features.
Addressing artists and boosters, particularly those of the nineteenth century,
provides such a focus.

A focus on artists and boosters of the nineteenth century immediately
brings into view a coherent development of Western images and promotion from the paintings and photographs produced by artists accompanying
exploratory expeditions to the visions of plenty that boosters sold to those far
from the American West. As the writer Wallace Stegner has warned, however, "[T]he western culture and western character with which it is easiest
to identify exist largely in the West of make-believe, where they can be kept
simple" (Stegner, as quoted in Sandweiss 1996, p. 672). Tracing a traditional
trajectory of Western visual cultural and promotion can too easily illustrate
and magnify the "West of make-believe." Indeed, such a trajectory can
exclude much of what makes the West fascinating. The images produced by

explorers, painters, and boosters often froze in time the land and people of the American West. Indians vanished. National parks and their most prominent natural features remained sublime and unchanged. Farms forever produced bountiful harvests in the center of America's heartland. While Indians entered the modern world alongside others in the American West, while national parks began to battle the impact of increasing numbers of visitors, and while farms faced the ecological pressures of market production, the nation's image of the West remained largely static. The West changed over time, but we rarely look for those changes in Western art.

The following history of artists and boosters in the American West follows a traditional trajectory, but bear in mind that the West created by these artists and boosters was a creation only. Images, like words, tell only part of the story and carry with them the biases and inclinations of their times. Many of the images produced in the late nineteenth century helped to fix in the popular imagination the notion that the West was stranded in time—forever a place of battling Indians and cavalry, haunting landscapes, and pioneer farmers. As a result, such images are not transparent windows into the past. They often tell us more about what people wanted to see in the American West than they do what people actually saw. Artists and boosters were the creators of such images. They contributed significantly to the formation of the West of make-believe. Tracing that story shows us the history of a place that never existed.

And yet, the make-believe West had profound effects on the real West. The sketches and paintings produced by artists accompanying exploratory expeditions helped shape the ebb and flow of federal interest in the American West. Painters' sublime images of the West's lofty peaks led to the formation of the nation's first national parks. Boosters' glowing depictions of lush and fertile farmland led farmers to leave their homes and settle on dusty, treeless plains. Many non-Native Americans today continue to expect Indians to wear feathers and express shock when they encounter Native people using modern accoutrements. Suburban developers meanwhile capitalize on views of distant mountains. While the West of make-believe may not be real, its material effects are far too profound to ignore. Studying artists and boosters, then, requires us to keep in mind a seeming paradox. Artists and boosters created a place that never existed, and yet, that imaginary place had profound consequences for those who lived and live in the real American West.

Expedition Artists

Early-nineteenth-century U.S. government expeditions to and beyond the western borders of the United States demanded much of their artists. Artists were expected to convey the vastness of the spaces that they encountered and to render scientifically accurate representations of the land and its plants and animals, as well as to create telling portraits of the Native people who lived in the area. The expeditions themselves often served multiple diplomatic, military, and exploratory functions simultaneously. And the journeys were onerous. Bitter winter temperatures, the fetid, disease-friendly environments of winter camps and summer river travel, and the work of moving across unfamiliar territory made for numerous challenges and obstacles for the committed artist.

Consider the experiences of Samuel Seymour, an English-born engraver and painter, and Titian Peale, the son of Charles Wilson Peale, whose Philadelphia museum housed many of the specimens from the Lewis and Clark Expedition and played a central role in the nation's early intense interest in natural history. Both men were members of the expedition of Major Stephen Long in 1819, Seymour as the first artist named to a government expedition and Peale as a naturalist. Although originally military in intent, Long's expedition became one more of scientific discovery and diplomatic interest when it stalled in Council Bluffs in the winter of 1919. Long backtracked to Washington, D.C., for new orders and returned to lead his group across the prairie westward to the Rocky Mountains and then south along the Front Range. Long's southernmost goal was the Red River, then the southern boundary of Louisiana, but the expedition erred and marked the boundary of the Canadian River instead. Seymour's responsibilities included producing portraits of "distinguished Indians," and "groups of savages engaged in celebrating their festivals or sitting in council," as well as images of especially grand and beautiful landscapes. Peale, as a naturalist, was expected to document the insect, animal, and plant life of the regions through which they journeyed (Goetzmann and Goetzmann 1986, p. 9).

Both men produced images that became definitive for many Eastern Americans when envisioning the West. Seymour returned with 150 sketches and Peale with 122. Both artists converted their drawings to watercolors, and Seymour also produced engravings. Although only six of Seymour's images appeared in the official report of the expedition, his watercolor *Distant View of the Rocky Mountains* did serve, as an engraving, as the frontispiece of the expedition account. The engraving provided images of both buffalo and Native peoples, as well as the sense of vast space where the Plains meet the Rockies. It became the first image that many Americans had of the Western Plains and the Rocky Mountains.

Perhaps more significant than the images of Seymour's included in the report is an image that was not. Long followed the example of a previous expedition leader, Zebulon Pike, when he referred to the area between the 100th meridian and the Rocky Mountains as the "Great American Desert." Because a central goal of Long's expedition was to assess the suitability of the Great Plains for settlement, his chosen moniker was an influential one. Both Pike and Long believed the area to be poorly suited for white farmers but ideal as a future home for Indians. Seymour painted an image of a thunderstorm over the area, but, significantly, this image was not included in the expedition report. Long's and Pike's name for the region that they explored would influence federal government Indian policy for years to come, as well as general opinions of the area. Not until the 1860s did railroads and boosters begin to encourage white settlement with images of fertile plains and the specious scientific theory that "rain follows the plow."

While Seymour's images helped to establish the view that the Far West was inhospitable to white settlement, Peale's images began to influence

Engraving of *Distant View of the Rocky Mountains*, by English-born engraver and painter Samuel Seymour. (*Library of Congress*)

white Americans' views of Native Americans. Indeed, because of his father's museum, far more of Peale's images found a public audience and survived to the present day than did Seymour's. Peale produced a number of sketches, drawings, and watercolors of the wildlife that populated the Great Plains, including muskrats and fox as well as bison. Later in life, he produced drawings and paintings that combined several of the figures he had first rendered, including an image of an Indian man shooting a buffalo with a bow and arrow. The image is now so iconic that most people in the world can envision it without difficulty. According to historians William H. and William N. Goetzmann, once the image was made into a lithograph for Thomas Doughty's *Cabinet of Natural History and American Rural Sports,* it became one of the most widely distributed views of the Far West in the 1830s (ibid., p. 14).

Of course, the influence of expedition art and artists did not end with Seymour and Peale. Artists accompanied expeditions throughout the nineteenth century, particularly after the U.S. victory in its war with Mexico led U.S. leaders to add vast quantities of land to the nation. In 1848, Richard, Edward, and Benjamin Kern, brothers from Philadelphia, accompanied John C. Frémont on an expedition to scout a route along the 35th parallel for a railroad to the Pacific Ocean. And in 1853, seven different expeditions charted routes for a transcontinental railroad. Twelve artists accompanied these reconnaissance expeditions, and they produced a wealth of visual information about Western lands while also creating heroic and adventurous reputations for themselves. Those reputations would prove to be the most lasting of their contributions. None of the expeditions were able to convince a pre–Civil War Congress, torn by sectionalism, of a preferred railroad route.

Indeed, expedition artists were rarely as influential as one might suspect, given that theirs were the first views that most white Americans had of the western half of the continent. The work of artists like Seymour, Peale, and the Kern brothers continues to inform historical assessments of the times and places that artists documented. Nonetheless, white Americans unfamiliar with Western places were far more likely to encounter and to respond to touring shows of Indian portraits, the vivid depictions of boosters, the lure of so-called free land, and the imperialistic drive of many U.S. leaders. Art for the sake of scientific documentation would play a comparatively small role in the national iconography of the American West.

Artists and National Parks

Artists would be far more influential in their images of the places that were to become the nation's first national parks. Yellowstone and Yosemite both owe their status as national parks in part to the images produced by artists and photographers. Unlike the artists who accompanied earlier exploratory and military expeditions, those artists that produced the most widely disseminated views of Yellowstone and Yosemite were concerned more with the artistic merit and less with the scientific accuracy of the drawings and paintings that they produced. Even the photographers who ventured into the Rocky Mountains and the Sierra Nevada Mountains placed a high premium on producing aesthetically appealing images. As a result, the work of artists and photographers played a vital role in teaching white Americans how to think about the West.

These lessons were not confined to the importance of preserving natural spaces. Native peoples are hardly visible in many of the works that depict the areas that became Yosemite and Yellowstone national parks. Their virtual absence from visual representations of the regions made the decision to exclude Native access to the parks an even easier one for federal government officials. To this day, the work of Albert Bierstadt, Carleton Watkins, William Henry Jackson, and Thomas Moran shape the national image of the West's landscape. Their images justify for many Americans the claim that the United States was a land destined for greatness and the erroneous belief that Native people have vanished from the landscape. Perhaps most significantly, their paintings and photographs lend credence to the common opinion that Yosemite and Yellowstone are places of sublime beauty where Americans can experience an almost sacred communion with nature.

Although technically the nation's second national park, Yosemite preceded Yellowstone into the national imagination, in part because of the work of Carleton Watkins. Unlike many of the places visited by earlier expedition artists, Yosemite was already a tourist attraction by 1870. Its relative proximity to San Francisco made it popular among visitors who were eager to see such a geological wonder for themselves. Watkins's photographs, along with those of his rival, Eadward Muybridge, inspired many of these early visitors. A former teamster and carpenter, Watkins had been drawn to Sacramento by the economic ferment accompanying the Gold Rush. In 1853 he moved to San Francisco and fortuitously substituted for an absent employee at a photography studio. He established his own studio and first

photographed Yosemite in 1861. Watkins carried two cameras: a stereo camera, which produced two very similar images that, when viewed through a
mechanism called a stereoscope, created a three-dimensional image, and
his more innovative choice, a mammoth-plate camera. The latter camera
required enormous glass plates, 18 by 22 inches, which helped him to produce the images of grandeur and scale that the Yosemite landscape inspired.
Although Watkins's images were massive, they were also intensely precise,
conveying the geological texture of Yosemite's valley and peaks. His earlier
work as a photographer, during which he made pictures to document land
and mining claims, may have provided him with the necessary training to
catch the finer grain of Yosemite's beauty. Whatever the source of his inspiration, Watkins's photographs were widely influential. Many middle-class
Americans collected stereographs in the late nineteenth century, and photographers often issued their work in sets or volumes for purchase. Senator
John Conness owned a set of Watkins's prints, and Conness set the stage for
the Yosemite Act of 1864, which protected Yosemite from commercial and
industrial development (Sandweiss 2002, p. 183).

Watkins's work also inspired a young painter from Germany, Albert
Bierstadt, to seek his own Western views. Bierstadt saw Watkins's work at
an exhibition at the Goupil Gallery in New York City in 1862. Bierstadt had
already honed his landscape painting skills while working in the Alps and on
an 1859 U.S. expedition to survey an overland trail to California. Bierstadt
volunteered for the expedition, and, as a result, he was not working under
orders to produce topographically or naturally precise images. He chose
instead to work in a far more impressionistic style. He made no complete
paintings on the trip, and instead used drawings, stereo photographs, and
notes on color to inform his work on his return. He left the expedition early
and worked his impressions into an enormous painting of the Wind River
range: *The Rocky Mountains—Lander's Peak*, which he completed in 1863.

For his first monumental work, Bierstadt had chosen the same massive scale as Watkins. *The Rocky Mountains* measured 73½ inches by 120¾
inches. Where Watkins had relied on contrast and composition to convey the
overwhelming nature of the Yosemite landscape, however, Bierstadt chose
imaginative juxtaposition. Jagged, snow-covered peaks reach into the clouds
as they dwarf a group of Indians and their camp. Most of the humans fall
into shadows, but the painting is ultimately redemptive. Sunlight illuminates
a waterfall in the center of the painting, suggesting a sublime encounter
between man and nature. Audiences delighted in *The Rocky Mountains*. Many
saw it at the 1864 New York Sanitary Fair, where it hung opposite another
painting of massive scale, Frederick Church's *The Heart of the Andes*. Although
the two paintings were similar in size and in their use of luminous light,
Bierstadt's painting won the favor of most viewers because it confirmed and
stimulated Americans' faith in the heroic nature of their nation's landscape.
Bierstadt was quick to capitalize on his new status as a blockbuster painter.
To add to his growing reputation, he began developing paintings from images
he had in mind from an 1863 trip he had made to Yosemite.

Throughout the 1860s and 1870s, Bierstadt continued to paint in the
style that had made him such a star at the 1864 fair. In painting after painting

of Yosemite Valley and other Western places, Bierstadt showed tumultuous clouds mixed with glowing light and still pools beneath towering peaks. His work would prove enormously popular with Eastern audiences, and Bierstadt was ultimately able to open a gallery and studio in San Francisco with his profits. Bierstadt's images were often composites that suggested more of the grandeur that Americans wanted to see in their national landscape and less of the local specifics of the places Bierstadt painted. Nonetheless, the paintings became iconic and were probably as influential as Watkins's photographs in executive and congressional decisions to set Yosemite aside from development (Goetzmann and Goetzmann 1986, pp. 166–167).

A pair of artists similarly immortalized the area that would become Yellowstone National Park. William Henry Jackson and Thomas Moran accompanied an 1871 expedition to Yellowstone led by Ferdinand V. Hayden, the head of the U.S. Geological and Geographical Survey of the Territories. Jackson, a photographer, had already accompanied Hayden on an earlier geological expedition and had also documented the building of the Union Pacific Railroad. Moran, in contrast, was a "perfect Greenhorn" by his own admission. Born in England, he had apprenticed to a Philadelphia engraver but was intent on painting romantic scenes, particularly those of the American landscape. Although not the official engraver on Hayden's expedition, he formed a fast friendship with Jackson, and the two documented Yellowstone in tandem, framing views together. While Jackson provided crisp and to-scale images of the geysers and canyons, Moran ensured a sense of the area's color and its otherworldly geological features (ibid., p. 174).

It is important to recognize the extent to which Moran and Jackson were employees of Hayden's expedition. As such, their images were part of the arguments that Hayden used to justify his work. Moran's paintings and Jackson's photographs were visual evidence for Hayden's contention that Yellowstone was a part of a consumable Western landscape. According to Hayden, where the areas of the West did not provide minerals or land for settlement, it did provide landscapes of divine beauty, meant for Americans' enjoyment. Such areas, in Hayden's view, were worthy of preservation and required active protection from the United States. Moran and Jackson supported this position with their images. In fact, the two artists published their work in tandem with Hayden's descriptions of the expedition. Moran published a series of watercolors as chromolithographs along with a description of Hayden's findings. Jackson, who had worked longer with Hayden, published his photographs in volumes with captions drawn from the language of Hayden's reports. Seen independently of any narrative, viewers may have come to their own conclusions regarding the meaning and importance of the images. In tandem with Hayden's words, however, viewers were more likely to absorb a specific message: these were areas of sublime beauty and worthy of preservation.

The message of Jackson's and Moran's images persevere to the present day. As the historian Martha Sandweiss has argued, Jackson's photographs led "the reader from sight to sight, laying out Yellowstone as a series of consumable vistas, an approach still echoed in the park's carefully plotted roads, vehicle turnouts, and photographic viewing points" (Sandweiss 2002,

p. 198). Jackson and Moran had created an American playground. Their images taught readers where to go to appreciate the land and how to see it once they arrived. Their work led to the formation of Yellowstone National Park and a particular type of landscape preservation. But their paintings and photographs also narrowed the vision of Americans looking at their own landscape. Today, middle-class families planning vacations rarely decide to spend several days driving through America's prairies in order to appreciate scenic beauty. Similarly, the nation's wetlands and swamps do not often illuminate advertising campaigns. And visitors to the nation's deserts have more often been looking for signs of extraterrestrial life than they have communion with nature. Recent admissions to the National Park System—Death Valley in 1994 and Colorado's Great Sand Dunes in 2004—show the slow rate at which Americans have come to appreciate landscapes different from those that appeared in late-nineteenth-century art. In short, after the work of Jackson, Moran, and other artists was raised to iconic status, certain American landscapes came to have great meaning and importance to the nation, while others—those that had not had the benefit of dramatic artistic representation—received little attention and, subsequently, little care.

Images of Native Americans

A by-product of Moran's and Jackson's close working relationship with Hayden was the virtual exclusion of images of Native people from the paintings and photographs each man produced of Yellowstone. Although evidence existed that Shoshone and Mountain Crow used trails through the region and hunted and gathered in the area that would become park land, a popular myth prevailed that Indians feared the geysers. Jackson himself took pictures of nomadic groups near the area, but his images of Yellowstone generally showed a landscape without humans. Jackson did photograph Indian people and the ruins of ancient Native settlements. He even published a catalogue of his own and others' photographs of Native people, but those images appeared separately from his images of landscapes. That the land he had photographed was a peopled land would not have been clear to most viewers. Jackson himself subscribed to the belief that the Indians were vanishing. He wrote that Indians were "fast passing away or conforming to the habits of civilization" (Jackson, as quoted in ibid., p. 204). His words echoed those of many previous artists of the nineteenth century, particularly those of George Catlin.

Catlin was born in Wilkes Barre, Pennsylvania, in 1796. Although mostly self-trained, the art education that he did receive he gathered at the Pennsylvania Academy in Philadelphia, when Peale's Museum was at its height. It was outside the museum that Catlin encountered a delegation of Native Americans en route to Washington, D.C. He recalled later that it was in that moment that he resolved to make a record of Native life, thereby "lending a hand to a dying nation, who have no historians or biographers of their own to portray with fidelity their native looks and history" (Catlin, as quoted in Goetzmann and Goetzmann 1986, p. 17). That Native people did have means of tracking their history and heritage escaped Catlin. He preferred instead to see himself as a recorder of a vanishing race.

Although Catlin's motivation was condescending, his commitment to his project and to the Indians whom he encountered was tremendous. Like expedition artists, Catlin endured treks over vast stretches of countryside, weathered unfamiliar climates, and engaged in complicated cultural exchanges with Native Americans. All the while, he was enormously productive. In the course of his career, he painted more than 325 portraits and 200 scenes of Indian life. His work includes portraits of Mandan, Crow, Assiniboine, Gros Ventre, Blackfoot, Cheyenne, Oglala, and Dakota men and women, as well as depictions of buffalo hunts, religious ceremonies, and Western landscapes. His inspiration may have rested on a flawed premise, but his work has proven invaluable. Indeed, his images continue to provide data for Native Americans researching their own past and for historians, ethnographers, and anthropologists of all races interested in the customs and clothing of American Indians in the 1830s.

In 1830, Catlin moved to St. Louis, a common meeting ground for Europeans, Americans, and different Native tribes. There, he concluded that he would have to go still farther West to find Native people less touched by European and American culture. Although he did find more remote groups, by 1832, when he left St. Louis to head up the Missouri, most Native people had connections to Europeans and white Americans via trade, diplomacy, and religious and social exchanges. In fact, Catlin's most productive time would be at Fort Union, which the American Fur Company ran as both a military fort and a trading post. Catlin returned to the West again in 1835, when he accompanied an ill-fated military expedition under Colonel Henry Leavenworth to the Southern Plains. Leavenworth and many of his men died of cholera, and Catlin feared for his own life enough to teach an assistant basic painting techniques. His near-death experience did not deter him from heading West again in 1839, however, this time to a quarry where Sioux removed stone for pipe-making. Catlin returned home with a sample, and the stone now bears his name: catlinite. In between Western sojourns, Catlin painted Indians who had journeyed east, and he lobbied against the removal of the Cherokees from their Native lands in the South. By the close of the decade, Catlin had seen much of the Southern and Northern Plains, as well as the West's major river trading routes. Throughout his journeys, he had recorded images of the Native people that he had met.

By 1840, Catlin began to feel the economic pressures of his unorthodox career. He had already begun a gallery of his portraits of Native people, comprising approximately 500 paintings, in 1839. To capitalize on his work, he began a tour of his Indian Gallery and took it to London and across Europe. The tour included the paintings themselves, artifacts that Catlin had collected from various Native groups, and sometimes even Native people or members of Catlin's family dressed in Native garb. The gallery was a popular success, but Catlin never seemed to manage his funds well; also, he was plagued by bad luck. He invested heavily in a colonization scheme in Texas that failed abysmally. And in 1848, after several months spent working for King Louis-Philippe at the Louvre, Catlin was left unpaid when the king and

Portrait of Ee-Ha-A-Duck-Chee-A, or He Who Ties His Hair Before, a Crow chief. Published in George Catlin's *North American Indians: Being Letters and Notes on their Manners, Customs, and Conditions, Written During Eight Years' Travel Amongst the Wildest Tribes of Indians in North America, 1832–1839.* (*Hulton-Deutsch Collection/Corbis*)

his family fled Paris during the 1848 revolution. Over the next decade Catlin frequently petitioned Congress to buy his works, but because of lobbying pressure from Catlin's detractors and sectional conflict, Congress consistently refused. Eventually, Catlin was forced to sell his collection to Joseph Harrison, a locomotive manufacturer, who let the gallery languish in his boiler factory. Years later Catlin began reproducing the collection from memory, but he was still unsuccessful in convincing Congress to purchase his work. He died in 1872 without the federal government's ever acknowledging his contribution to the artistic and ethnographic record.

Ironically, his work is now perhaps the most comprehensive collection the government holds. When fire destroyed much of the Smithsonian's collection in 1865, the paintings of John Mix Stanley, who had completed a collection of 154 paintings of Indian peoples and who harbored aspirations similar to those of Catlin, were hanging in the museum awaiting congressional action on purchase. The destruction of all but five of Stanley's paintings left Catlin's collection, still in the hands of the Harrisons, unrivaled. In 1879 the Smithsonian finally purchased Catlin's collection from Harrison's heir. Catlin had finally secured his goal, but he was not present to see the success of his work (Catlin, Gurney, and Dippie 2002).

Throughout his career, Catlin had stressed that his motivating force was his conviction that Native people would disappear. He strove to preserve what he saw as authentic Indian life, believing that Indian cultures would vanish altogether. In his first published work he imagined "the certain approach of this overwhelming system which will inevitably march on and prosper . . . the luckless savage will turn back his swollen eyes on the illimitable hunting-grounds from which he has fled; and there contemplate . . . their splendid desolation . . . all this is certain . . . and if he could rise from his grave and speak or would speak from the life some half century from this, they would proclaim my prophecy true and fulfilled" (Catlin, as quoted in Goetzmann and Goetzmann 1986, pp. 34–35). Catlin had never been a good forecaster. A half-century later, Native people were still present. Nonetheless, Catlin's legacy contributed to the trend of white artists like Jackson decrying what they perceived as the Indians' inevitable decline.

Into the twentieth century, white American artists continued to lament the vanishing of Native people. Indeed, Catlin's most obvious successor in the photography genre was Edward Curtis, a photographer of the first decades of the twentieth century. Curtis eliminated signs of modernity, like clocks, from his photographs of Native people, and often asked Indians to pose in tepees and costumes manufactured abroad. His images, often distant views of Native people at sunset, fed the common misperception that Indians were on the brink of extinction. Catlin's belief, well preserved in his paintings of Native people, had endured and even matured in a whole new medium: photography. Meanwhile, Native people themselves were leaving their own artistic record, a record suggesting that they had no intention of disappearing.

Images by Native Americans

Because Catlin so eagerly imagined an encounter with a Native person several decades from the time of his work, it is interesting to speculate how he would respond to a modern Native-American artist, Zig Jackson, a photographer enrolled in the Mandan, Hidatsa, and Arikara tribes. Zig Jackson's photographs, unlike those of Curtis and William Henry Jackson, stress Native people's modernity while they comment on the continued desire of white Americans to see Native people as exotic creatures from the past. His series "Indian Photographing Tourist Photographing Indian" pokes fun at a long tradition of the production of images of Indians for tourist consumption. Such images became particularly popular in the early twentieth century, when Curtis was producing his photographs. Painters in Taos, New Mexico,

Maria Martinez

Maria Martinez, a potter and a member of San Ildefonso Pueblo, is one of the best known women artists of the turn of the century. Probably only the painter Georgia O'Keeffe surpasses her in popularity. Like O'Keeffe's painting, Martinez's pottery has come to symbolize the Southwest for people throughout the United States and the world. While O'Keeffe broke into a traditionally male sphere with her painting, however, Martinez worked in a medium that Pueblo people traditionally reserved for women: pottery. Nonetheless, through her success and her guidance of others, Martinez extended pottery making to her entire community. Martinez also differed substantially from O'Keeffe in that she faced unique demands because she was an American Indian. Like the work of Cheyenne artist Buffalo Meat, Martinez's pottery represented both modern and traditional influences. Nonetheless, she struggled in her art and in her life to remind patrons and purchasers of her work that she was not a figure from an earlier, simpler time. As the work of Zig Jackson demonstrates, American Indians have for years battled the impression that they are not modern people. Martinez's pottery is a part of that contest.

Although Martinez herself does not appear to have used her art to boost New Mexico or the Southwest, there is no question that her art served such a function. The popularity of Martinez's work brought many visitors to the Southwest, and she may have owed her first foray into her distinctive style in part to one of New Mexico's most intrepid boosters, Edgar Lee Hewett. Given the dual role of her work as aesthetically pleasing expression and as an iconic image of the Southwest, one can ask if her pottery blurred the line between art and boosterism. Such a question forces us to ask how independent artists were of market and popular and social pressures. When we see Western art, are we seeing the artists' visions or what artists believed the public wanted to see and buy?

Martinez was born sometime in the late 1880s and lived for almost 100 years. She learned pottery making from her Aunt Nicolasa. Martinez attended Catholic boarding school in Santa Fe and considered becoming a schoolteacher. Instead, she married a man named Julian Martinez who farmed and worked part-time at an archaeological dig and as a janitor in Santa Fe. In 1904 the Martinezes were invited to participate in the Louisiana Purchase Exposition in St. Louis, where they shared their traditional dances, songs, and pottery making techniques. At the time, such presentations from Pueblo Indians were seen more as a sign of American Indians' distance from the assumed advances of civilization than they were as a sign of the Indians' artistic ability. That opinion was soon to change, however. According to some researchers, a few years later, Edgar L. Hewett, a self-trained archaeologist and promoter of Santa Fe, New Mexico, asked the Martinezes to reproduce pottery like that he had found in one of his archaeological digs. The pottery that the Martinezes created was enormously successfully among Hewett's peers, largely because it was seen as "authentic" and "traditional." The Martinezes shared their techniques and success with many of their neighbors at San Ildefonso. By the 1930s, Maria Martinez's name was known worldwide. The signature black-on-black style that she and her husband had created had become emblematic of New Mexico and the Southwest, and pottery rivaled agriculture as the greatest source of wealth at San Ildefonso Pueblo.

There is no question that pottery became an art form that helped to promote the Southwest. Hewett was one of the most involved organizers of the New Mexico display at the 1915 Panama-California Exposition in San Diego. His promotion of the region followed closely on the heels of the completion of the Atchison, Topeka, and Santa Fe Railroad's route to California in the 1880s. Pueblo people had previously sold to

Potter Maria Martinez (ca.1881–1980), San Ildefonso Pueblo, New Mexico, ca. 1940. (*Horace Bristol/Corbis*)

traders, but now they could sell directly to tourists at stops along the railroad once the road was complete. Tourists collected and continue to collect Pueblo Indian pottery as a reminder of their visit to a presumably more authentic and traditional locale. If tourists did not purchase pottery to remember their visit, chances are that they saw the work of white advertisers and painters who often chose native craftspeople as their subject. Pottery had become one of the ways that the region lured visitors.

Did the Martinezes intend to spark a craze for Southwestern pottery? As an economically depressed region far from industrial centers,

San Ildefonso Pueblo certainly benefited from the income that pottery could bring. Nonetheless, the Martinezes struggled with the demands of their purchasers. Even the origin of San Ildefonso's famous black-on-black style suggests the extent to which the Martinezes had to balance the demands of their market. According to one account, Julian put too much manure on the fire used to finish the pots, rendering them completely black. The Martinezes considered the batch ruined and put them away. When a trader pressed for work, how-

(continued on following page)

Maria Martinez (continued)

ever, Julian Martinez explained that they had rare pots, but they were more expensive. The trader bought the "ruined" black pottery and sold it quickly. He asked for more. The pottery's style was not "traditional," yet it succeeded in the market that prized just that quality. In later years, the Martinezes would argue over using electric kilns and other techniques that might lead buyers to question the "authenticity" of their work. They owed their success, however, to a recent innovation in their work and to the "modern" developments of the railroad and the tourist market. Were the Martinezes modern or traditional artists? Did they follow their inner muse or the demands of their buyers?

The aesthetic value of their work, their commitment to their communities, and their own self-promotion would suggest that they were both modern and traditional and that they followed both their own aesthetic demands and those of the market. Perhaps most significantly, their success along with their frustration at being labeled "traditional" suggests that we need to ask different questions if we are to understand how artists understood their own work (Jacobs 1999, pp. 172–178). There is no question that Maria Martinez's pottery changed the landscape of San Ildefonso Pueblo and the Southwest more broadly. It most certainly played a role in how non-Indians perceived American Indian people.

Reference and Further Reading

Jacobs, Margaret D. *Engendered Encounters: Feminism and Pueblo Cultures, 1879–1934.* Lincoln: University of Nebraska Press, 1999.

produced a similar body of work, prompting an ever-increasing number of visitors to northern New Mexico. If tourists did not see Taos painters' images before heading to New Mexico, it is likely that they saw them on the train. The Atchison, Topeka, and Santa Fe rail lines used images of Southwestern landscapes and Native people to prompt more tourist travel. Today, Zig Jackson responds to the artists of Taos as well as to Curtis, William Henry Jackson, and even Catlin, in his work.

His images, which juxtapose modern tourists taking photographs of modern Indians, often in a combination of modern and traditional dress, adds a Native perspective to a long and complicated past of white images of Native people. Native people are present in Jackson's photographs. They are also actively addressing one of their most persistent modern annoyances: tourists who want them to look as though they are trapped in time. Catlin's legacy is obviously a strong one. Jackson feels compelled to counter it with new images of his own. In place of the vanishing American, Jackson's photographs show how Native American tradition can persevere into the present day, even in the face of tourists' misconceptions. His images are statements of both Indian perseverance and Indian modernity.

Nineteenth-century Native American artists also produced art that reflected both Native perseverance and Native adaptation to contemporary events. Perhaps the best example of such work is ledger art. In the late nineteenth century, as buffalo populations declined and Plains Indian groups began to lose their military campaigns against the U.S. federal government,

Native artists switched from using buffalo hides to using account ledgers as their canvas. The account ledgers were themselves an indication of changing times for Native people. Usually, Plains Indians acquired the books through trade with white Americans or through capture following a military victory. At the same time, Native artists began using colored pencils and sometimes water colors in lieu of traditional paints. The very acquisition of new materials showed an adjustment to changes in Native life.

Ledger art itself demonstrates that Plains Indian people used images to represent and to comment on their contemporary circumstances. The art work reflects the continuation of Indian artistic tradition. Viewers could determine the importance of the various figures portrayed by size and level of detail, conventions that had characterized hide paintings as well. At the same time, the art showed the changing lives of Native people. Plains Indian combatants recorded their military exploits while they were imprisoned at Fort Marion in Florida, following their capture by U.S. federal troops. Later, when Plains Indian children were sent to boarding schools, where Native languages were not permitted, they created pieces in ledgers to communicate. Ledger art was a product of both continued tradition and changing circumstances (Plains Indian Ledger Art Digital Publishing Project).

Artists themselves lived lives in flux. The artist Buffalo Meat, whose Cheyenne name was Oweotoh, began making ledger art when he was imprisoned at Fort Marion. His work often reflected nostalgia for the trading and hunting that had marked Cheyenne life before the Cheyennes' confinement to reservations. Nonetheless, Buffalo Meat himself lived a life of change. He later worked as a policeman on his reservation and served as a delegate to Washington, D.C. Even his nostalgic art work showed a sense of the changing world of the Cheyenne. His 1876 piece *Going in to Trade* shows a group of Cheyenne on horseback carrying stacks of hides. One might see the scene as entirely traditional, but for two figures who carry brightly colored umbrellas. Buffalo Meat lamented the passing of one way of life, but, unlike Catlin's imagined Indian, he did not weep and then disappear. Like Zig Jackson's photographs today, his art and his choices in his life's work showed a continual engagement with the present (Amon Carter Museum).

Emergence of a National Western Art

Ledger art, however, rarely received the kind of attention that paintings, drawings, and photographs produced by white artists did. As a result, Native art produced in the nineteenth century was far less likely to shape popular opinion in the way that Catlin's paintings or William Henry Jackson's photographs had done. Such was the case with the work of Amos Bad Heart Buffalo. In the early twentieth century, he created his series chronicling the famous Battle of the Little Big Horn, based on memories from Lakota warriors who had participated in the battle itself. His images show the confusion of war, with soldiers and warriors running afoot and on horseback in all directions. Death is at every turn. In his drawings there is no famous last stand, and Custer is not at the center of activity. Amos Bad Heart Buffalo's work, however, hardly entered the national pantheon of images of Custer (Limerick and White 1994, pp. 40–42).

Instead, most Americans chose to embrace the story told in Cassily Adams's and Otto Becker's *Custer's Last Fight.* Painted by Adams in 1896, more than 200,000 copies of the image were distributed as a lithograph by the Anheuser-Busch Brewing Company in succeeding years. Pub patrons were likely to see the image above the bar of their favorite watering holes for years to come (Goetzmann and Goetzmann 1986, p. 225). Based more on the iconic role that Custer and the battle had come to play in white Americans' visions of themselves, the lithograph showed a sunlit Custer repelling an Indian foe while more warriors bear down on him. Cavalrymen fall to the ground, many at the hands of their scalping victors. Given its extensive distribution, its public display, and its resonance with white Americans' perception of their history, the lithograph was likely responsible, in part, for the common misperception that the battle was an Indian ambush of white soldiers rather than a cavalry attack on a well-positioned Indian camp.

Alongside the work of artists who chronicled the Plains Indian Wars, such misperceptions shaped film and television representations of Native Americans for years to come and even influenced American history textbooks. Although Custer's fight was a loss, his tragic demise and his elevation as a popular national hero in the years that followed complemented the kind of art that had become emblematic of the Plains Indian Wars. The many images that white artists produced of the Battle of the Little Big Horn were unique in that most American artists of the Plains Wars chose to portray cavalrymen as heroes, always facing death, but never encountering it. Frederic Remington was the best known of these artists, and he prided himself on the accuracy of his work. One of Remington's favorite views was to show a cavalry charge coming straight at the viewer. Images of Custer dying were an exception to the rule of the cavalry hero, but they were also consistent with how white Americans had chosen to see the U.S. army. The story of the Plains Indian Wars that entered school books, Western film screenplays, and radio and television broadcasts was one of brave cavalry heroes triumphing over savage foes. Custer's loss fulfilled the narrative role of tragic counterpoint in an otherwise victorious story.

The emergence of Custer as a national icon was not the result of the visual arts alone. The showman Buffalo Bill and his Wild West Show, innumerable dime novels, and, later, in the twentieth century, radio, television, and film images helped to solidify the narratives that Americans told themselves about the West. This dynamic element to cultural representations is what gives them much of their power. Photographs, school books, paintings, drawings, advertisements, newspaper articles, and fiction produced a national conversation about the meaning and the importance of the West. Within this national conversation emerged some stock sets: the vast expanse of the prairie, the sunlit granite mountain, and the desert mesa at sunset. Stock characters like the noble cavalryman, the lone cowboy, the savage warrior, and the vanishing Indian came to populate these sets and to enact a national drama of predestined American victory.

These were not mere stories. The images that artists produced shaped national policy, school curriculums, and the very land of those areas deemed beautiful enough to warrant preservation. Combined with the words of government reports, expedition artists allowed federal policy-makers to see distant land and determine its suitability for white settlement. In tandem with the lobbying and expedition findings of explorers, the photographs and paintings of Yosemite and Yellowstone led lawmakers to set those areas aside from development. Even today some of the parks' caretakers see the land through the eyes of Watkins and Bierstadt, Jackson, and Moran. They, in turn, shape the parks' roadways and trails to reflect the expectations that visitors have built from viewing photographs and paintings from the past. Catlin's traveling portrait gallery and inspiration of subsequent artists led many Americans to conclude that the defeat and even erasure of Native people was inevitable. Such a conclusion seemed to be reinforced by a subsequent generation of artists and their depictions of military campaigns on the Great Plains. When assessing who was and who was not American and what was and what was not an American place, Americans, and even world audiences, turned to the paintings, drawings, and photographs that artists had produced when depicting the American West.

Alternatives to the narrative produced in such images existed. Native artists showed themselves changing and persevering. Even expedition artists and popular artists produced the occasional image that challenged viewers to see the West differently—as a place of hard labor, rapid environmental change, and even urban development. The existence of these alternative images suggests the existence of alternative narratives and, thus, alternative outcomes. If art has the power to change what governments do and what people think, then such images invite us to look for different images and to speculate what impact they could have had if they had garnered a wider or more influential audience. Art demands that we seek out those paintings, photographs, drawings, and sketches that show American Indians in the modern world, the beauty and ugliness of landscapes that were not preserved by national decree, and the less glamorous kinds of work that occupied soldiers, settlers, and cowboys. Although far less common, such images presented a different kind of West and could have provoked different policies, actions, and behavior—differences that could, in turn, have shaped the real American West and its inhabitants.

Boosters

Perhaps one of the most widespread alternatives to the dominant image of wild West heroes and villains that emerged in popular art was the picture of the West produced by boosters. Boosters worked for many different employers, including themselves, and promoted diverse regions as well as a variety of types of employment. Arguably, anyone was a booster who put pen to paper with the intention of encouraging Argonauts to explore California's gold fields, missionaries to convert Native people in the Pacific Northwest, laborers to put their backs at the service of railroad companies, or settlers to pack up their families and belongings to begin a new life in an unsettled, but presumably better, place. Of the many kinds of boosters, those that promoted settlement probably had the most in common with artists who painted the American West. Regional boosters devoted the bulk of their writing to painting pictures of the lands that they promoted. Moreover, like artists, some regional boosters had seen the regions and scenes they described, and some had only imagined what opportunities and treasures might exist to the West of their present location. Regardless of their experience with the land that they described, virtually all regional boosters let imagination be their guide. Like artists, they, too, created a West of make-believe with consequences in the real world. Their make-believe West had a different landscape and different heroes than that of artists, and thus it had different effects on the lives of real westerners.

Railroad companies, chambers of commerce, and land speculators all employed boosters to write and publish brief guides to areas in the American West that sang the praises of the land, the weather, and the economic and political future of the places depicted. With such promises boosters hoped to spur settlement, usually because they themselves had a stake in land sales in the region that they "boosted," but sometimes also because they had genuine faith in the climate and economic prospects of the area they promoted. By the late nineteenth century, publishers had distributed lots of 10,000, 15,000, and sometimes even 20,000 pamphlets at a time and sent them to readers across the Eastern United States and Europe for free, or for only the cost of postage. Whether readers chose to pack up and move to the West or not, the literature that they received from boosters must have shaped how they viewed and imagined the West, just as paintings, photography, and drawings did (Wrobel 2002, p. 2).

The images in regional booster literature did not mirror those of artists who had painted and photographed the West. Unlike the paintings, photographs, wild West shows, and dime novels that taught Americans to see the West as a place of wide-open spaces designed for adventurous exploits and sublime encounters with nature, booster literature more often showed fruitful, pastoral landscapes ripe for development. The West in booster literature was safe. Regardless of whether boosters were describing Oregon in the 1840s, Kansas in the 1870s, or California in the 1880s, the West was a place that was once dangerous but had just recently become an almost Edenic garden. In the boosters' West, the frontier was always on the brink of closing. Native people were noticeably absent from booster literature. For tract writers, the Native inhabitants of the area were a part of the dangerous frontier that had already passed from existence. As historian David Wrobel has noted, the perception of a recently closed frontier "probably served as a catalyst to western settlement by European Americans. Potential settlers were motivated to stake their claims while there were still some frontier lands left" (ibid., p. 26).

If settlers came quickly, the boosters' West promised untold opportunities. Early boosters of Oregon country, for example, worked both to overcome the popular image of Oregon as a wilderness populated by hardy fur trappers and the opinion of apprehensive politicians who believed settlement beyond the Rockies to be unwise. In their writings, boosters of Oregon country promised smooth and easy journeys and fertile lands for those willing to come quickly. Pushed by harsh winters and wet springs in the Midwest, migrants were pulled, in part, by the possibilities that filled boosters' prose.

Later generations felt a similar draw. Boosters promised smooth travels, fertile lands, easy transportation of goods, healthful climates, and all the benefits of civilization from schools to churches to commerce. In general, not even heaven itself could compare to the places created in the pages of boosters' promotional tracts. By the late nineteenth century, the self-named "Inland Empire" of the Pacific Northwest promised newcomers that the area was a "fascinating panorama of picturesque scenery and thriving industry" (Morrissey 1997, p. 140). Describing Minnesota in 1868, one booster wrote: "Perhaps the eye of man never rested on a spot of land better fitted to supply his material wants and meet the necessities of his nature since shut out from the original Eden." The Minnesota promoter apparently had not rested his eyes on Riverside, California, which was, according to one booster, God's "perfect spot," and he evidently had not yet had a chance to enjoy the climate in Lubbock, Texas, which, by 1908, one booster had described as "the *fountain of youth* which men have long sought" (Wrobel 2002, pp. 40–41, 64).

Images, albeit ones very different from those produced by artists at the time, were extraordinarily useful for the ambitious and competitive booster. The visual images that predominated in booster literature were maps, not paintings of lofty peaks or cavalry charges or Indian attacks. Nonetheless, like Bierstadt's paintings of sublime encounters or Seymour's sketches of the Plains, what was included and excluded from boosters' maps mattered substantially for how settlers imagined the West. A sponsoring railroad company would sometimes position their own name on a map strategically, so that it just covered a rival railroad's route. Railroads that did not yet exist often appeared on maps because, as boosters usually explained in smaller print, such images suggested what the area could become in the very near future. Town plans that included churches and schools—both common markers of "civilization" and "progress" for prospective settlers—sometimes showed structures that did not yet exist, but could, like the railroad routes, in the very near future. While seemingly objective, maps were just as subject to bias and interpretation as paintings and photographs. As such, maps could work hand-in-hand with boosters' exaggerated claims to spur settlement (Morrissey 1997, p. 23; Wrobel 2002, pp. 34–35).

By the 1870s, boosters had promoted areas from North Dakota to Nebraska with claims of healthful climates and fertile lands. Such assertions increasingly required some form of scientific theory. How could lands previously labeled "The Great American Desert" suddenly be the paradise for farmers that promotional tracts promised? At least one booster and amateur scientist had the answer. In 1881, Charles Dana Wilber, in his book *The Great Valleys and Prairies of Nebraska and the Northwest*, proposed the idea that God rewards the labor of farmers with rain. Unlike Remington's later images of cavalrymen, Wilber proposed a different hero: the yeoman farmer (Smith 1950, p. 182). The farmer's tool of choice, indeed his divine instrument, was not the gun, but the plow. For Wilber, "the plow was the unerring prophet, the procuring cause, not by any magic or enchantment, not by incantations or offerings, but instead by the sweat of his face toiling with his hands, man can persuade the heavens to yield their treasures of dew and rain upon the land he has chosen for his dwelling. The raindrop never fails to fall and answer to the imploring power or prayer of labor" (Wilber 1881, p. 69). Wilber promised farmers that rainfall would arrive alongside the farmer's labor. Farmers need only bring their plow, their willingness to work, and their faith in the fertile lands of promotional tracts.

Plows alone, however, did not always produce the results that Wilber and other boosters had promised. Although the idea that "rain follows the plow" persisted in some literature into the twentieth century, farmers found that the Western Plains, the Southwest, and California did not always yield the fine weather and fertile fields they expected. Ultimately, farmers came to depend on government policy and irrigation technology as well as their own high hopes when contemplating settlement. Boosters followed suit in their promises. Where climate made claims of perfect farming weather simply impossible, boosters turned instead to the magic of irrigation, which, as boosters regularly noted, had aided farming since the days of ancient Egypt. Boosters less frequently noted the need for major investment and centralized planning for the kinds of irrigation necessary to make the area west of the hundredth meridian bloom.

By the early twentieth century, however, boosters had a partner in the federal government. The Newlands Reclamation Act of 1902 established the Reclamation Bureau in the Department of the Interior. The bureau's irrigation projects made possible the growth of cities like Phoenix and Boise. The Enlarged Homestead Act of 1909 and the Stock Raising Homestead Act of 1916 meanwhile led the General Land Office to take on a decidedly boosterlike tone in its materials distributed to prospective settlers. Along with unusually high rainfalls and high crop prices in the decade following after 1910, the government's efforts led to widespread settlement in areas poorly suited to long-term farming. Rain may not have followed the plow, but that did not stop settlement in areas prone to drought (Wrobel 2002, p. 56).

Given that boosters lured settlers to areas poorly suited for sustainable farming and that they obviously exaggerated the advantages and charms of the areas they promoted, it is easy to dismiss them as rank hucksters. Boosters were sensitive to such accusations, however, and their writings suggest that they did not see themselves in such a light. Early boosters of Oregon country knew that they were arguing against a commonly held opinion that Oregon was too distant for settlement. As a result, many early boosters made clear that they themselves had made the journey. Their description of their own experience made more believable their assertion that they were reliable informants. Indeed, by the early twentieth century, claims to reliability had become a stock feature of the booster genre. Tables of statistics that selectively documented rainfall, educational institutions, and the health of residents further substantiated the credentials of boosters who praised Western lands.

In addition to stressing their own knowledge of the area, boosters also indicated that they had genuine faith in the potential of the areas that they promoted. In their enthusiasm for the future, some boosters simply promised what they believed would eventually exist. And, with the aid of the federal government and large-scale irrigation projects, boosters were sometimes right. Settlers would arrive in an area only to discover that the churches, schools, railroads, farms, and water that they had been led to expect were theirs to create. Despite their disappointment, some newcomers stayed to make the place that they had imagined a reality. To borrow the phrasing of historian David Wrobel, boosters had helped "imagine into being" the places that they promoted (ibid., p. 16).

Imagination did not spur only white settlers. While most popular images show Europeans and European Americans settling in the West, not all boosters targeted white audiences. African Americans in the South heard of Western lands through announcements in churches and circulars passed through family members. Many African-American migrants followed the lead of utopian booster Benjamin "Pap" Singleton and set their sights on Kansas. Singleton had repeatedly run away from slave owners in the South. Age seventy in 1879, he made migration campaigns and independent African-American business ownership his focus following the Civil War. By 1880, Kansas contained 15,000 African Americans, and Singleton claimed responsibility for most of the African-American settlement in the state. At one point he announced that he was "the whole cause of the Kansas migration." But Singleton had not operated in a vacuum. The close of Reconstruction in the South in 1877 had provided some significant push factors. Immediately after the Civil War African Americans encountered difficulty owning their own land in the South, and following the 1878 election, many felt endangered by violent campaigns and legislation designed to restrict them to jobs working for whites at low wages. They joined the exodus from the South, seeking not just fertile farmland but also independent working environments and freedom from persecution. Dubbed "Exodusters," 6,000 blacks moved to Kansas between March and May of 1879, and up to 20,000 may have headed to Kansas and Kansas City, Missouri, in 1879 and 1880. Whites tried, sometimes violently, to stop the exodus, but they were rarely successful. Many of the African-American settlers had been moved by the utopian image of a promised land in the West. Like whites, they did not always find the place that they had been seeking (White 1993, p. 198). African Americans encountered race-based violence and limited opportunities in Kansas as well, but like European Americans, African Americans strove to "imagine into being" the places that they had hoped to find.

In short, like artists, boosters shaped the West in unintended ways. Although boosters promoted a safer, more appealing West, like artists, they also presented a place that differed markedly from the real West. Rain fell, water flowed, church-goers gathered, and children learned in the West of booster literature even while drought reigned and tumbleweeds blew in the actual places that boosters purported to describe. Nonetheless, the enthusiasm and genuine faith of many boosters led newcomers to settle in areas and create the very institutions and infrastructure that boosters had promised would someday exist. Granted, many settlers and boosters eventually had the help of federal money and organization. Without such aid, many of the places that remember their hardy pioneer forebears would not even exist.

Handbill published by Benjamin "Pap" Singleton advertising a campaign for African Americans to migrate to Kansas, 1878. (*Library of Congress*)

Like the artists' West, the boosters' West was a place of make-believe, and yet boosters' fantasies, like those of artists, had determined, in part, who settled the West and how those settlers changed the land they claimed.

As in art, alternatives to the dominant image in booster literature existed. Those Americans familiar with Native people would have wondered at their absence from promotional tracts. One alternative to the West promoted by boosters was a West populated by Native Americans. At the same time, discerning migrants who compared the promotional tracts for many different regions would no doubt have noticed that every region in the West seemed to have perfect weather, ideal farming conditions, and all the benefits of modern civilization. Some may have expressed skepticism about the possibility of such uniformity and made their decisions to migrate without complete faith in the Edenic picture painted by boosters. And, not all boosters promised the same benefits. Kansas was a promised land to Singleton, not just because it offered land for farming but also because it offered a place presumably free from violence and inequity. Had his vision of the West been even more influential, Americans might look at Kansas very differently than they do today. Like the less popular images in Western art, the lesser-known voices of boosters suggest a West that might have been.

Conclusion

The West of make-believe can be a dangerous and confusing place. Well-known places can seem remote, and remote places can seem accessible. Rain falls regularly in the desert, but it is always dry enough to offer clear views to the mountains. Heroes can be so much larger than life that they are said to have won the battles in which they lost their lives. Everyday people do not exist. Every explorer shows undaunted courage; every soldier serves a cause higher than a paycheck; every farmer exhibits the self-possession of the noble pioneer. No one works for wages. There is no debt. Government and factories have been left behind somewhere in the East. Everyone is industrious, but every human mark, from the presence of Native people to the dams and aqueducts of an irrigation project, is quickly forgotten. The West of make believe always has a murky past and the most promising of futures.

Why turn to such a place when assessing history? Historians, after all, prize accuracy and evidence, not the fantasies and exaggerations of a deluded audience and their deceivers. And yet, we ignore the West of make-believe at our peril. The West of make-believe contributed to federal policy that determined the scope of exploration, the preservation of national parks, and the development of arid lands. Daily encounters with non-Native tourists and even some policy-makers bring Native Americans face to face with their shadows in the West of make-believe. In asserting their presence in the real world, Native people insist on their distance from the way many non-Indians imagine them to be. Settlers set their sights on regions within the West of make-believe, but they ultimately made their homes in the real West. The West of make-believe does not exist, and it never did. But it is a place that we must visit if we are to understand why the history of the real West unfolded as it did.

References and Further Reading

Amon Carter Museum, www.cartermuseum.org.

Carey, Ryan. "Building a Better Oregon: Geographic Information and the Production of Space, 1846–1906." Ph.D. diss., University of Texas at Austin, 2003.

Catlin, George, George Gurney, and Brian Dippie. *Catlin and His Indian Gallery.* Washington, DC: Smithsonian American Art Museum, 2002.

Goetzmann, William H., and William N. Goetzmann. *The West of the Imagination.* New York: W. W. Norton and Company, 1986.

Limerick, Patricia, and Richard White. *The Frontier in American Culture.* Berkeley: University of California Press, 1994.

Milner, Clyde A., Carol O'Connor, and Martha Sandweiss. *The Oxford History of the American West.* Oxford: Oxford University Press, 1996.

Morrissey, Katherine G. *Mental Territories: Mapping the Inland Empire.* Ithaca: Cornell University Press, 1997.

Plains Indian Ledger Art Digital Publishing Project, www.plainsledgerart.org.

Sandweiss, Martha. *Print the Legend: Photography and the American West.* New Haven: Yale University Press, 2002.

Smith, Henry Nash. *Virgin Land: The American West as Symbol and Myth.* [1950]. Cambridge: Harvard University Press, 2005.

White, Richard. *"It's Your Misfortune and None of My Own": A New History of the American West.* Norman: University of Oklahoma Press, 1993.

Wilber, Charles Dana. *The Great Valleys and Prairies of Nebraska and the Northwest.* Omaha: Daily Republican Print, 1881.

Wrobel, David. *Promised Lands: Promotion, Memory, and the Creation of the American West.* Lawrence: University Press of Kansas, 2002.

Primary Documents

John Townsend, Narrative of a Journey across the Rocky Mountains to the Columbia River (1839)

John K. Townsend was hired by the American Philosophical Society and the Academy of Natural Sciences in Philadelphia in 1834 to join a wagon train to Oregon in order to collect birds. Many of the bird and mammal specimens he collected on this trip were used by naturalist John James Audubon in his famous and influential wildlife paintings. Townsend published his journal from this and other trips in 1839.

Toward evening, we struck Blackfoot river, a small, sluggish stagnant stream, heading with the waters of a rapid rivulet passed yesterday, which empties into the Bear river. This stream passes in a north-westerly direction through a valley of about six miles in width, covered with quagmires, through which we had great difficulty in making our way. As we approached our encampment, near a small grove of willows, on the margin of the river, a tremendous grizzly bear rushed out upon us. Our horses ran wildly in every direction, snorting with terror, and became nearly unmanageable. Several balls were instantly fired into him, but they only seemed to increase his fury. After spending a moment in rending each wound, (their invariable practice,) he selected the person who happened to be nearest, and darted after him, but before he proceeded far, he was sure to be stopped again by a ball from another quarter. In this way he was driven about amongst us for perhaps fifteen minutes, at times so near some of the horses, that he received several severe kicks from them. One of the pack horses was fairly fastened upon by the terrific claws of the brute, and in the terrified animal's efforts to escape the dreaded gripe, the pack and saddle were broken to pieces and disengaged. One of our mules also lent him a kick in the head while pursuing it up an adjacent hill, which sent him rolling to the bottom. Here he was finally brought to a stand.

The poor animal was so completely surrounded by enemies that he became bewildered. He raised himself upon his hind feet, standing almost erect, his mouth partly open, and from his protruding tongue the blood fell fast in drops. While in this position, he received about six more balls, each of which made him reel. At last, as in complete desperation, he dashed in to the water, and swam several yards with astonishing strength and agility, the guns cracking at him constantly; but he was not to proceed far. Just then, Richardson, who had been absent, rode up, and fixing his deadly aim upon him, fired a ball into the back of his head, which killed him instantly. The strength of four men was required to drag the ferocious brute from the water, and upon examining his body, he was found completely riddled; there did not appear to be four inches of his shaggy person, from the hips upward, that had not received a ball. There must have been at least thirty shots made at him, and probably few missed him; yet such was his tenacity of life, that I have no doubt he would have succeeded in crossing the river, but for the last shot in the brain. He would probably weigh, at the least, six hundred pounds, and was about the height of an ordinary steer. The spread of the foot, laterally, was ten inches, and the claws measured seven inches in length. This animal was remarkably lean; when in good condition, he would, doubtless, much exceed in weight the estimate I have given. Richardson, and two other hunters, in company, killed two in the course of the afternoon, and saw several others.

This evening the roaring of the bulls in the *gang* near us is terrific, and these sounds are mingled with the howling of large packs of wolves, which regularly attend upon them, and the hoarse screaming of hundreds of ravens flying over head. The dreaded grizzly bear is also quite common in this neighborhood; two have just been seen in some bushes near, and they visit our camp almost every night, attracted by the piles of meat which are heaped all around us. The first intimation we have of his approach is a great *grunt* or *snort*, unlike any sound I ever heard, but much more querulous than fierce; then we hear the scraping and tramping of his huge feet, and the snuffing of his nostrils, as the savory scent of the meat is wafted to them. He approaches nearer and nearer, with a stealthy and fearful pace, but just as he is about to accomplish the object of his visit, he suddenly stops short; the snuffing is repeated at long and trembling intervals, and if the slightest motion is then made by one of the party, away goes *"Ephraim,"* like a cowardly burglar as he is, and we hear no more of him that night.

James Mooney, Ghost Dance Movement

From James Mooney, *The Ghost-Dance Religion and the Sioux Outbreak of 1890*; originally published as Part 2 of the *Fourteenth Annual Report of the Bureau of Ethnology to the Secretary of the Smithsonian Institution, 1892–1893* (Washington, DC: Government Printing Office, 1896). Republished, among others, by the University of Chicago Press, 1965).

James Mooney was an anthropologist working for the federal government's Bureau of American Ethnology who was assigned to investigate the Ghost Dance movement in the early 1890s. He collected and published many accounts of the movement and of the Wounded Knee Massacre that white fear of it helped to provoke. The following account is excerpted from the account of an Oglala Sioux named George Sword, who at one point was captain of the Indian police at the

Pine Ridge reservation. His account was translated by another Indian and then transcribed by an Anglo-American.

In the story of ghost dancing, the Oglala heard that the Son of God was truly on earth in the west from their country. This was in the year 1889. The first people knew about the messiah to be on earth were the Shoshoni and Arapaho. So in 1889 Good Thunder with four or five others visited the place where Son of God said to be. These people went their without permission. They said the messiah was there at the place, but he was there to help the Indians and not the whites. Good Thunder, Cloud Horse, Yellow Knife, and Short Bull visited the place again in 1890 and saw the messiah. Their story of visit to the messiah is as follows:

"From the country where the Arapaho and Shoshoni we start in the direction of northwest in train for five nights and arrived at the foot of the Rocky Mountains. Here we saw him and also several tribes of Indians. The people said that the messiah will come at a place a smoke descended from heaven to the place where he was to come. When the smoke disappeared, there was a man of about forty, which was the Son of God. The man said:

"'My grandchildren! I am glad you have come far away to see your relatives. These are your people who have come back from your country. . . . My grandchildren, when you get home, go to farming and send all your children to school. And on way home if you kill any buffalo cut the head, the tail, and the four feet and leave them, and that buffalo will come to live again. When the soldiers of the white people chief want to arrest me, I shall stretch out my arms, which will knock them to nothingness, or, if not that, the earth will open and swallow them in. My father commanded me to visit the Indians on a purpose. I have came to the white people first, but they not good. They killed me, and you can see the marks of my wounds on my feet, my hands, and on my back. My father has given you life—your old life—and you have come to see your friends, but you will not take me home with you at this time. I want you to tell when you get home your people to follow my examples. Any one Indian does not obey me and tries to be on white's side will be covered over by a new land that is to come over this old one. You will, all the people, use the plains and grass I give you. In the spring when the green grass comes, your people who have gone before you will come back, and you shall see your friends then, for you have come to my call.'"

Juan Cortina, "Proclamation to the Mexicans of Texas, 1859"

Born in 1824, just south of the Rio Grande into a prominent ranching family, Juan Cortina soon became a symbol of resistance to Anglo-American racism. After witnessing an Anglo law enforcement official pistol-whipping an employee, in September of 1859 Cortina led an armed force that captured Brownsville, Texas, and inaugurated a guerrilla war that lasted for the next six months. His proclamation, originally published in the Brownsville newspaper, captured Mexican-American anger at Anglo political and economic encroachment.

[U. S. Congress, House, Difficulties on the Southwestern Frontier, 36th Congress; 1st Session, 1860, H. Exec. Doc. 52, pp. 70–82.]

Mexicans! When the State of Texas began to receive the new organization which its sovereignty required as an integrate part of the Union, flocks of vampires, in the guise of men came and scattered themselves in the settlements, without any capital except the corrupt heart and the most perverse intentions. Some, brimful of laws, pledged to us their protection against the attacks of the rest; others assembled in shadowy councils, attempted and excited the robbery and burning of the houses of our relatives on the other side of the river Bravo; while others, to the abusing of our unlimited confidence, when we entrusted them with our titles, which secured the future of our families, refused to return them under false and frivolous pretexts; all, in short, with a smile on their faces, giving the lie to that which their black entrails were meditating. Many of you have been robbed of your property, incarcerated, chased, murdered, and hunted like wild beasts, because your labor was fruitful, and because your industry excited the vile avarice which led them. A voice infernal said, from the bottom of their soul, "Kill them; the greater will be our gain!" Ah! This does not finish the sketch of your situation. It would appear that justice had fled from this world, leaving you to the caprice of your oppressors, who become each day more furious towards you; that, through witnesses and false charges, although the grounds may be insufficient, you may be interred in the penitentiaries, if you are not previously deprived of life by some keeper who covers himself from responsibility by the pretense of your flight. There are to be found criminals covered with frightful crimes, but they appear to have impunity until opportunity furnish them a victim; to these monsters indulgence is shown, because they are not of our race, which is unworthy, as they say, to belong to the human species. But this race, which the Anglo-American, so ostentatious of its own qualities, tries so much to blacken, depreciate, and load with insults, in a spirit of blindness, which goes to the full extent of such things so common on this frontier, does not fear, placed even in the midst of its very faults, those subtle inquisitions which are so frequently made as to its manners, habits, and sentiments; nor that its deeds should be put to the test of examination in the land of reason, of justice, and of honor. This race has never humbled itself before the conqueror, though the reverse has happened, and can be established; for his is not humbled who uses among his fellow-men those courtesies which humanity prescribes; charity being the root whence springs the rule of his actions. But this race, which you see filled with gentleness and inward sweetness, gives now the cry of alarm throughout the entire extent of the land which it occupies, against all the artifice interposed by those who have become chargeable with their division and discord. This race, adorned with the most lovely disposition towards all that is good and useful in the line of progress, omits no act of diligence which might correct its many imperfections, and lifts its grand edifice among the ruins of the past, respecting the ancient traditions and the maxims bequeathed by their ancestors, without being dazzled by brilliant and false appearances, nor crawling to that exaggeration of institution which, like a sublime statue, is offered for their worship and adoration.

Mexicans! Is there no remedy for you? Inviolable laws, yet useless, serve, it is true, certain judges and hypocritical authorities, cemented in evil and injustice, to do whatever suits them, and to satisfy their vile avarice at the cost of your patience and suffering; rising in their frenzy, even to the taking of life, through the treacherous hands of their bailiffs. The wicked way in which many of you have been often-times involved in persecution, accompanied by circumstances making it the more bitter, is now well known; these crimes being hid from society under the shadow of a horrid night, those implacable people, with the haughty spirit which suggests impunity for a life of criminality, have pronounced, doubt ye not, your sentence, which is, with accustomed insensibility, as you have seen, on the point of execution.

Mexicans! My part is taken; the voice of revelation whispers to me that to me is entrusted the work of breaking the chains of your slavery, and that the Lord will enable me, with powerful arm, to fight against our enemies, in compliance with the requirements of that Sovereign Majesty, who, from this day forward, will hold us under His protection. On my part, I am ready to offer myself as a sacrifice for your happiness; and counting upon the means necessary for the discharge of my ministry, you may count upon my cooperation, should no cowardly attempt put an end to my days.

A Trapper Writes to His Sister

In the summer of 1850, St. Louis-born trader Benjamin F. "Frank" Coons led a merchant caravan across southern Texas in order to stock his trading post near present-day El Paso, Texas. On July 16, he paused at the Devils River to write this letter, in which he revealed the vicissitudes of the trader's life. He lamented the toil, described the harsh landscape, pondered over Indian petroglyphs, and dealt with violent men. He also included two allegorical stories—the golden fish and jumping across the river—that expressed his hopes, regrets, and resolve.

Camp on Devils River, Texas, July 16, 1850

My Dearest Little Sister: As I may have an opportunity some of these days to send you a letter I shall proceed to write one that I may not lose the chance when it shall be afforded me. . . .

I last wrote to sister at the first camping at the San Pedro or Devils River and gave her a brief account of the magnificent scenery which one meets with there. After leaving that camp we came next day to the California Springs or as it is called by the Spanish "Piedras pintados" (colored rocks). The water at this camp is confined by low banks of stone; at least half a dozen colors of rock may be seen on all sides, thus giving rise to the name the stream bears. The day following we came only a short distance—the extreme heat of the atmosphere rendering it impossible for us to continue on, however at night we hitched and rolled on twelve miles by daylight reaching the painted caves. This is a very pretty and interesting camp. The cave is a very large one and consists of many rooms running in various directions beneath a large spur of the San Pedro Mts. The sides of the caves are covered with Indian paintings and hieroglyphics, which could one understand them, would no doubt be very entertaining. Some of the paintings are very easily interpreted.

One picture represents a fight between the indians and Mexicans, the latter being designated by their broad brim and hats. Another is a victim tied to a tree and the fiendish crew dancing to the snake dance round the poor prisoner. A third is a squaw building or blowing a fire. There are many other but I could not understand them so shall say nothing of them.

We remained in the caves until 3 p.m. when the whole train moved out. About sundown I was travelling ahead about three miles and as I crossed a high ridge gazed back and as far as the eye could reach might be seen the long line of small white dots—wagons—stretched out on the plain beneath. The view was beautiful, most charming. Night set in and the bright moon was high in the heavens as the sun sank behind San Pedros heights . . . on the train moved . . . over the hills through ravines, across plains bouncing over rocks and again dragging heavily through short stretches of sand. It was nine o'clock the next morning that we reached the second fork of Devils River. Before getting into the river bottom we had to cross some half dozen divides of immense rocks. In making this last four miles some six or eight wagons were broken, but the cattle being tired and nearly dead for thirst, the wagons were left standing in the road and the train moved on. This was a most unfortunate drive and another such would break down the entire train. The poor cattle suffered much from being so tenderfooted. The sharp flint rock soon ruins there hoofs and wherever they go a trail of blood is left behind. I lost in this day and night travel over 40 head of oxen and only because they could not stand up to go on. How shall I get through the remaining parts of this river I know not. Having reached camp and allowed the animals time to rest I started back workmen and teams to bring up the broken wagons—I remained at the second camp at Devel's River five days to repair wagons and recruit my cattle—while here my mind generally was ill at ease though I did all possible to keep from launching out into the sea of melancholy—whose waters are sure to engulph me. I would detail men to attend to all kinds of work and duties early in the morning, and some times I would read, or hunt, or go to the river to fish or take a bath. These fine days are the only days of rest I have had since I landed at Indianola. One evening I lost til near midnight fishing from a large rock. I watched that cork for hours. A bite and a jerk but no fish caught—again and again—until learning the attack and movements of the perch I began to string them up fast. Well, you see, thus it is with us poor spectators through life. We pull and pull and bait and bait and watch and watch—get bite after bite—but all mere nibbles. Once all our bait is gone and with patience well tried we go home in disgust. Again we try our luck and will continue to try—til rod and tackle all are gone and the very rock slips from our feet—letting us fall full into the pond from wherever we seek our game. How often has my cork gone under—My life has been estranged and broken—my rode severely bent—but still, cold and chilled—midst the stones of misfortune and trouble—I sit watching that cork, expecting every moment to see it snatched under and the golden fish of wealth follow the next pull from the water. Why is it that some fish with so much more good fortune than others. I remember when I was a boy I would sit on the same log with Napoleon, my cork within a foot of his, with the same bait on my hook and yet twas he who caught all the fish and why?

Solve me this query if you can. I have studied it long and would grow old would I learn it.

During the past week we had several exciting occurrences in camp. I was sitting in my camp a day or two since eating my dinner—when a man came running in saying, "Oh Mr. Coons there's a man killed down at our corral, do come down and see what we shall do." I hastened to the poor fellow's camp and found a man stretched near the side of a wagon—and close by him a pool of blood. He was a teamster and appeared to be in great pain. A quarrel had ensued between two of the men and during a scuffle that followed one thrust his butcher knife into the breast of the other. Fortunately, the knife entered the right side and only poked about two inches "within," thus rendering favorable the chances of his recovery. I soon cleansed and draped the wound, had the poor fellow carried and put in my tent. The scamp who had used the knife I had tied securely and made fast behind a wagon. The unfortunate man is recovering fast and will in a few days be able to drive his team again. The other is very bold and desperate. I declare he will kill the fellow as soon as I let him loose. This occurrence has given a great deal of trouble in the two men have their friends on the train and places me in an unpleasant situation. However to avoid all trouble I have turned the prisoner over to the Military officers in charge of my escort. The fellow will be tried at El Paso under charges of "intent to kill," and no doubt severely punished.

Emil Bode, "A Dose of Frontier Soldiering"

Reprinted from *A Dose of Frontier Soldiering: The Memoirs of Corporal E. A. Bode, Frontier Regular Infantry, 1877–1882*, edited by Thomas T. Smith by permission of the University of Nebraska Press. ©1994 by the University of Nebraska Press.

Emil A. Bode, born in Hanover in 1856, enlisted in the army in New Orleans in 1877 and served a five-year stint. Like most enlisted men, he was from a humble background, having immigrated to the United States at age thirteen after his parents' death. Although he was in the frontier army and thus in potentially dangerous places, like most Western soldiers he experienced no exchanges of fire with Indians. Instead, he was mostly concerned with the challenges of daily life and survival as an enlisted man stationed at forts in Louisiana, Indian Territory (now Oklahoma), New Mexico, and Texas. Here he relates some of his experience at Fort Sill, Indian Territory, in 1877 and 1878.

Fort Sill, Indian Territory, on the southern extremity of the line of Indian agencies, was first established in 1869 by General Sheridan under the name camp Sheridan. The Kiowa and Comanche Indians had been brought from their wild haunts in Texas and placed there on a reservation with their agency a short distance from the fort. A vigorous but cautious policy had to be followed to accustom them to their present homes. They were well-pleased with their present situation and most of them had farms or herds of cattle from which they derived a comfortable revenue.

American western forts were not, as their name would indicate, fortresses with breastworks in a zig-zag [with] cannons planted behind entrenchments.

Fort Sill, for instance, had a large square parade of 400 to 500 feet with a flagpole in the center. On the north and east sides were neatly constructed officers' quarters, surrounded by an orchard. On the west side were the cavalry quarters with large dining rooms and kitchens adjoining the road, and 300 feet west were the stables [with] a ten foot high wall. On the south side of the square or parade ground was the adjutant's office with two infantry barracks to the right and left. Two hundred feet south were the band quarters, to the east of these were the commissary and further on [was] the quartermaster's storehouses. One hundred feet southwest of the band quarters was the powder magazine, only fifty feet from the latter was the guardhouse, and fifty feet south of this building stood the post bakery.

Directly north of the stables and west of the officers' quarters, in the center of a newly created peach orchard, stood a well-ventilated, nicely constructed hospital overlooking to the north of the valley of Medicine Bluff Creek.

All of these buildings, with the quartermaster stables, comprised the fort proper and were constructed of a blue limestone which was the principal stone of that country. East of the officers' quarters and south of the quartermaster storehouses were the small picket houses constructed of upright logs, isolated shelters of the wives and children of the married soldiers, quartermaster employees, post interpreters, traders, and a church and a schoolhouse.

One-quarter mile northwest of the cavalry stables was the post trader's establishment comprising three or four buildings, one corner of one set apart for the post office with its modern improvement of letter boxes. The post trader was an indispensable evil of the forts. There everything from a collar button to a saddle, and all kinds of hardware and grocery goods could be obtained [by] paying exorbitant prices. Drinks were furnished direct over the bar or through an order signed by an officer of the fort, at the rate of twenty-five cents for one glass of beer and $2.00 a quart for "rot gut" stuff called whiskey.

A stagecoach ran thrice a week to Caddo connecting with the railroad and the rest of civilization, completing a single trip in thirty-six hours.

The municipal power of the fort was vested in one person—the commanding officer, who had as his assistant an adjutant. Next in power to the commanding officer was the "Officer of the Day" selected daily from the officers of the fort, and properly relieved every twenty-four hours by his successor. His duty consisted of quelling any disturbance in the command and seeing that the sanitary rules were properly enforced in the fort and camp. He was always assisted by a sufficient force of guard who were detailed daily and relieved at the same time. The post commissary and quartermaster offices were generally filled from headquarters with either civilian or commissioned appointees belonging to these special branches, as was the post medical staff, ordnance, and telegraph officers. The telegraph office, filled by regular enlisted men or civilians, [was] solely under the surveillance of the signal officer in Washington, and not subject to the orders of the [post] army officers.

The ordnance of every fort was in charge of an ordnance sergeant appointed by the department. The quartermaster at the forts had the power, if permitted by department head-quarters, to select clerks and teamster civilians who in other respect would not be permitted on the reservation fort.

A quartermaster had a wide field for dishonesty placed within his reach. He could (and a great many did so) cheat the government in different ways. There were, for instance, 20,000 lbs of useless corn to be condemned by the commanding officer, where in reality only 5,000 lbs was presented for inspection, the rest of the sacks filled with sawdust or sand. Or some poor government mule died and was examined by the officer, while a day or two later another mule [dies], and if the weather [is] cold, more mules could die in succession, the body of the first mule representing the other absconded animals. These are only two ways, while there were more than a hundred ways to get rich from Uncle Sam's pockets. The medical head and doctor had the same chances as the quartermaster and commissary; as he was generally the post treasurer and in this had charge of the post bakery where an enlisted man could buy an extra loaf of bread for five cents, and a civilian or Indian had to pay ten cents. From a civilian in need of medical treatment the doctor could slide an unobserved bill into his own pocket.

There were the captains of the companies with their share of easy gains. The day on which the commanding officer of a fort examined and condemned serviceless property was always considered a day of rejoicing for all parties concerned, except the superior officer, [who] did his duty and saw personally that the condemned articles were destroyed, in which case he would find a great many bright faces rather disappointed [and] dark. Nevertheless there were always more bright than dark faces. The commanding officer would go to a company, see an old fly of a wall tent, or formerly condemned pieces of tents that were again representing a complete tent, [and] with a superficial glance at the pile, condemn the articles to be destroyed immediately as unfit for further service, remaining until preparations are made to burn the old "tents." Presuming that $500 instead of $5 worth of government property lies in ashes, they are checked as out of existence. A couple of hundred dollars worth of property and tents may [then be] moved by the captain, afterwards represented as his private property. Officers and men could have tents to the value of $40 to $80 and never pay a cent for them.

[There was] an easy way of making a gun or horse. A man for instance deserts a company without taking anything belonging to the government. If he should be caught he might have found in the company records that he stole a horse, saddle, gun, or pistol, for which he would be charged besides desertion. In this case the first sergeant of the company made an affidavit that such and such article was taken when [the man] deserted. There were very few first sergeants who did not make a false affidavit in the five years of [my] service.

Amongst the captains were some great fellows who deserved to be put on ice instead of being in command of troops. There was one captain who stood at attention when speaking to his first sergeant, while the sergeant suited himself about his own position. Another fine specimen of an officer took a lantern when making the rounds of the guard. That same gentleman ridiculed himself by sending reports of his Indian slaughters to certain newspapers, [events] which had never taken place. Most of the company commanders were of a kicking disposition, delighting in aggravating a weak superior in every possible way, and my captain H.A. Theaker, was one of the principal.

Lieutenants were generally good, even second lieutenants, after they lost their West Point ideas. Lieutenant Flipper, the first colored man who passed West Point and was commissioned in the regular army, was assigned for duty with the 10th Cavalry (colored) at Fort Sill. He was at first met with contempt by his brother officers, and his tact kept him away from places where he was not wanted, that is, the officers' homes. But his superior knowledge and good tact soon brought him in close commune with his captain who made him his confidential friend and advisor, and entertained him in his private home. Whenever the Captain got into a scrape his lieutenant was sure to get him out. He also proved his courage in a couple of engagements with horse thieves. While he was apparently enjoying the love of this officer and the respect of the men, his enemies were quietly at work laying snares and traps wherever he went. At last they succeeded. It was later at Fort Davis where Flipper was made acting commissary officer and accused of intentionally defrauding the government by Colonel Shafter. He was found guilty and dismissed from the service.

Torrey L. Austin Oral History

Interview by Jessie L. Embry, June 18, 1976, North Logan, Utah, LDS Polygamy Oral History Project, Charles Redd Center for Western Studies, L. Tom Perry Special Collections and Manuscripts, Harold B. Lee Library, Brigham Young University, Provo, Utah, 1–9. The transcript has been edited for duplication. Some sections have been left out and rearranged.

Torrey Austin grew up on the Mormon frontier in Utah in the 1880s and 1890s. In this interview, conducted in 1976, he recounts some of his childhood memories, including the ways that the outlawing of polygamy affected his family.

Interviewee: Torrey L. Austin
Interviewer: Jessie L. Embry
Date: June 18, 1976
Place: North Logan, Utah
Subject: Life in a polygamous family

E: Brother Austin, tell us about your early family life.

A: I appreciate the opportunity of submitting myself to this interview. What I say here I say freely with no compulsion and no interfering at all.

I was born in the little village or town of Liberty, Bear Lake County, Idaho, December 9, 1882. That makes me at the present time 93 years old. My statement of my birth is a second hand knowledge. I am told I was born in a small log cabin about 16 to 20 that had dirt floors and a dirt roof. It was in the winter. There was a blinding snow storm raging at that particular time. Excitement and expectancy was in the home. My older brothers and sisters had been sent off to the neighbors.

Mary Hymas, the woman who had brought most of the children to that valley at that time, had been summoned. We had no telephone and no doctors. Even the midwife was unschooled. She and my father proceeded to assist my mother in bringing me into the world. There were no anesthetics and no hot water in the house except stove heated and no running water in the house. Although it was a pretty crude birth, I've been able to survive these 93 years.

The next event that I really remember also took place in a blinding snowstorm with five feet of snow on the ground. The family had been spending the day trying to get feed to the stock and wood in the house for the night. We had spent the day out in the blizzard. We were about to retire when a knock came at the door. The only doctor in the valley, C. A. Hoover, who lived in Montpelier ten miles from our place, stood in the doorway. He stated that he was on his way up to the end of Emigration Canyon to visit a sick woman and try to relieve her of some of her suffering. She was a victim of cancer in its last stages. He said, "I need a woman to help me, and I've come to see if Mrs. Austin would go with me there."

This was at night just as we were about to retire. Without any questions, my mother put on my father's fur overcoat and pulled his fur cap down over her ears. She got into that little cutter and went into that blizzard, not knowing whether they'd ever reach their destination five miles away. But she went. Her only assurance that she'd ever get there was her faith in God.

As the years went on, I developed a profound respect and love for my parentage, both Father and Mother. What I say in this little interview I say with all my heart. I believed and I still believe that I was born of goodly parents and neither of them were low-typed people.

E: Tell me about your parents and brothers and sisters.

A: My father was a deputy United States land surveyor and mineral land surveyor. He had to spend the majority of his time out in the field for a good many years. That left the family, the two mothers, to manage the home.

Before I say anything on that I better introduce the fact that I was of a polygamous birth. My father had two wives. They were sisters. They had to take the initiative in most of our family life when I was in my youth. Often times my mother was forced into leaving home and going into hiding to prevent the officers from picking up my father in her home.

Father had built a house which seemed to be a typical house of a polygamous family. There was a central part which was common to both families, and there was a wing on either side for each family. In that house the two families mingled freely together. There was a hall running between the two wings, so the two families mingled freely among themselves. There was no such thing known in our house as half-brothers and half-sisters. It was brothers and sisters. That lasted for about 15 years . . .

There was a good chance for us brothers and sisters, being left without the guidance of their father to develop ill feelings between each other. But of the 21 children in those two families, I have never known of any animosity, any ill feelings to develop among any two of them.

I would say fundamentally that polygamous families can and did live in a peaceful happy life together as it was with our family. I want to say now that I'm not talking about anybody but my own family. My observation all through my early life was that those families who were in the polygamous relationship lived about as other families. There was no difference as I can recall now in the general atmosphere which existed in the family of a polygamous that was different from the monogamous families.

E: Did each wing of the house have its own cooking facilities?

A: Yes, each family had its own. In fact, each family had its own part of the whole life there. We had our own cows to milk; we had our own meals to prepare.

These areas were different but many things were all done together. The attainment of winter firewood and things of that kind were done jointly, but each one knew which part of it was for her. So the two families were independent as far as that goes.

In our village we had only five polygamous families, but in the valley I think as a whole there were about four percent of the marriageable people that were in a polygamous relationship.

E: Did your father have a schedule where he spend so much time with each family?

A: We never knew. We knew, of course, that he had his relationships with both women, but there was no definite schedule for that relationship with either one or the other of his wives. He was away a great deal. We'd never know when he would be home. He might be gone away for a month 100 miles from home at his work.

I want to say this. The marriage of my parents took place with the knowledge and consent of both women. They accepted plural marriage as a divine law to them. They never did say or believe that the same law was to be accepted and lived by all marriageable people. It was a call, an individual call, for each individual to go into that relationship. That was their faith.

E: Did you hear the story about why your father married another wife?

A: That's one thing that I never heard Father tell. He said to me and I think to all of his children, "You have no right to go into that relationship except you are called to do so individually." So I suppose he was called by those over him. A stake president or somebody had called him into that relationship. He always told me, "You have no right to go into it from either a church or a moral force except that you are called by those in authority over you to do so."

E: Why did your father marry his other wife's sister?

A: When Father married his first wife, Alnora, she invited her younger sister Emma to live with them. Emma did for several years. So when Father was to marry in polygamy, he chose my mother Emma. I heard Mother say a number of times that when she married Father, she had married him with the firm belief that she was called to do so.

E: Your mother was the second wife.

A: My mother was the second wife. Now I think maybe that covers that point.

E: Tell me about your mother going into hiding.

A: The condition had arisen in Idaho, and I think that they were about the same in Utah where if a known polygamist was found in the home of the second wife, the illegal wife, he was in trouble with the law. Remember Mother was a legal wife when she married Father because there were no laws against it.

If my father was found in the home of the second wife, that was all the evidence that was needed to send him to the penitentiary and fine him $1000. He didn't have to stand trial; they didn't have to try him at all. Just the fact that he was caught in the home was all the evidence that was needed in the court to send him to the penitentiary.

Because of that and the fight that was on in Idaho against the polygamists, it often caused Mother to go into hiding and to leave her home. Very often she came from our home in Idaho down to Logan, Utah. She stayed a year at a time. She would leave part of her children with the first wife and take maybe one or two of the youngest children with her. When we were left with the first wife, we were treated just as her children, and everybody was happy.

She didn't necessarily have to take anybody. I spent one full year with Mother in Logan. I got the first schooling that I ever had in Logan in the primary grade at the school. Then as things kind of cooled off and there was not very much that the government was doing to force the law, she could go home.

E: Did the marshals ever come to your home?

A: Yes. I recall one time the marshals came to my house when Father was in my mother's home. They knocked on the door and said they wanted to search the house. Father was in the house. We knew it, and Mother knew it. She said, "All right, you might search the home, but where is your search warrant?" He produced one of those made-up search warrants. Mother said, "You can't open that door and come in to this house until you get a search warrant stating what you are searching for. Then you can search the house." He had to go and get a search warrant that was a legal search warrant. By that time Father had time to get into his little room.

When Father built the house, he had a little false room built in the attic right above two windows. It was high enough for a man to stand in. He had a false partition put in that was just like the outer wall as near as he could make it. A marshal could get up in there and see there was a trap door into the attic. He did get up in there. He could put his hand right on that false partition and never know that it was not the outside wall.

I lived in that house for 50 years before I knew that the room was there. After Father left, I tore the old house down. I found the room there. But that is where Father went. The four other polygamists in town often came there. The five of them would get up in that room when they knew the marshal was coming.

E: Did the men know that the marshals were coming?

A: I'm glad you asked that. We had a rather recluse, John Snyder. He was a man who never married who was inclined to be a toper, a heavy drinker. He used to haul block wood from our sawmill to Montpelier and Paris, Idaho, and sell it for firewood. Somehow or other he always was able to find out when the marshals were coming over to that part of the valley. He never failed in coming back. He might be so drunk he didn't know where he was going and his lines were dragging down on the ground. But he'd always make one holler, "The marshals are coming." These four or five polygamists would hurry up and get into that room.

E: Did the Manifesto make a difference in your family?

A: No. Of course, Father went into the polygamous relationship a long time before the Manifesto. After the Manifesto and after the Supreme Court had ruled that the Manifesto was legal, he still continued his relationship with both wives because he considered that he had taken those wives honorably and that as a result he would not abandon either one. I think some of the men in the valley really turned their polygamous wife out, but not very many.

E: Tell me more about your mother and Aunt Nora.

A: My mother died when I was 14 years old. When Mother was gone, Aunt Nora took us in and treated just as if we were her own children.

E: How did the two wives get along?

A: I never new of them ever disagreeing or showing any kind of animosity but once in all my life. That was over a little thing that didn't happen to suit my mother. Three of us, two of Mother's children and one of Aunt Nora's children, were having their picture taken. Not long before Mother had bought me a new hat. Aunt Nora came along and took that hat out of my hand and put it in her boy's hand. That did nettle Mother. [I don't know. I like this story.]

Aunt Nora had daughters almost as old as my mother. The age element did come in there somewhat. Several of Aunt Nora's children were much older and were given the opportunity when Father was gone to dominate over the rest of us. But they didn't want to do it in order to carry out Father's wishes. [And I like this story.]

E: Tell me about church activities.

A: The building that we called the church was a combination of the church and school house. It was a rather large one-roomed building built of adobes. The principal duties of the deacon's quorum [12–14 year-old boys] was to clean that building up on Saturday for church purposes on Sunday.

Most of the people walked to church; there were no cars. If we lived too far away to walk, we could come in a buggy, an old lumber wagon, or on horseback. I have known people from out a distance away coming by horseback with as many as three children on one horse. If we were walking, we would go to that church carrying our shoes in our hands to put on before we entered the building.

After the exercises were over, very often those who lived too far away to go home and then come back to the sacrament meeting were open to an invitation to go out to dinner with some of the people. Very often the people who invited other people to their homes for dinner were some of their bitterest enemies, if they did have any enemies. But we were just raised in that kind of atmosphere. We didn't hold any grudges.

Usually at the end of the regular meeting, my father, who was the bishop there and had been the bishop during all the area's history, would announce a baptismal service to be held in the Austin pasture immediately after meetings. After the meeting was dismissed, that was an invitation for the whole congregation to go down to Austin's pasture and watch the children be baptized.

In the winter it was a peculiar situation. We very often had to cut a hole through the ice to the creek for the baptismal service to be performed. To hear the chattering teeth and see the grimaces on the faces of those little chaps and girls going down into that ice water was a matter of quite a lot of glee to those that were older.

Northern Pacific Railroad Company Authorizing Statute

This 1864 act authorized the creation of the Northern Pacific Railroad, laying out its organization and relation to settlers, Indian peoples, and the federal government. The deep role of the government in creating the company and supporting its endeavors was also characteristic of other railroads. The first seven sections of the Charter follow.

13 Stat., at large 365. The Charter [/] An act granting Lands to aid in the Construction of a Railroad and Telegraph Line from Lake Superior to Puget's Sound, on the Pacific Coast, by the Northern Route. July 2, 1864.

The Charter [/] An act granting Lands to aid in the Construction of a Railroad and Telegraph Line from Lake Superior to Puget's Sound, on the Pacific Coast, by the Northern Route. July 2, 1864. 13 Stat., at large 365.

Be it enacted by the Senate and House of Representatives of the United States of America in Congress assembled, That Richard D. Rice, John A. Poore, Samuel P. Strickland, Samuel C. Fessenden, Charles P. Kimball, Augustine Haines, Edwin R. W. Wiggin, Anson P. Morril, Samuel J. Anderson, of Maine; Willard Sears, I. S. Withington, Josia Perham, James M. Becker, A. W. Banfield, Abiel Abbott, John Newell, Austin L. Rogers, Nathaniel Greene, Jr., Oliver Frost, John A. Bass, John O. Bresbrey, George Shiverick, Edward Tyler, Filander J. Fopristall, Ivory H. Pope of Massachusetts; George Opdyke, Fairley Holmes, John Huggins, Philander Reed, George Briggs, Chauncy Vibbard, John C. Fremont, of New York; Ephraim Marsh, John P. Jackson, Jr., of New Jersey; S. M. Felton, John Toy, O. J. Dickey, B. F. Archer, G. W. Cass, J. Edgar Thompson, John A. Green, of Pennsylvania; T. M. Allyn, Moses W. Wilson, Horace Whittaker, Ira Bliss, of Connecticut; Joseph A. Gilmore, Onslow Stearns, E. P. Emerson, Frederick Smyth, William E. Chandler, of New Hampshire; Cyrus Aldrich, H. M. Rice, John McKusick, H. C. Waite, Stephen Miller, of Minnesota; E. A. Chapin, John Gregory Smith, George Merril, of Vermont; James Y. Smith, William S. Slater, Isaac H. Southwick, Earl P. Mason, of Rhode Island; Seth Fuller, William Kellogg, U. S. Grant, William B. Ogden, William G. Greene, Leonard Sweat, Henry W. Blodgett, Porter Sheldon, of Illinois; J. M. Winchell, Elsworth Cheesbrough, James S.

Emery, of Kansas; Richard F. Perkins, Richard Chenery, Samuel Brannan, George Rowland, Henry Platt, of California; William F. Mercer, James W. Brownley, of Virginia; John H. B. Latrobe, W. Prescott Smith, of Maryland; Greenbury Slack, A. J. Boreman, of West Virginia; Thomas E. Bramlette, Frank Shorin, of Kentucky; John Brough, John A. Bingham, Oran Follett, John Gardner, S. S. L'Hommedieu, Harrison G. Blake, Philo Chamberlin, of Ohio; John A. Duncan, Samuel M. Harrington, of Delaware; Thomas A. Morris, Jesse L. Williams, of Indiana; Samuel L. Case, Henry L. Hall, David H. Jerome, Thomas D. Gilbert, C. A. Trowbridge, of Michigan; Edward H. Broadhead, Alexander Mitchell, Benjamin Ferguson, Levi Sterling, — Marshall, of Wisconsin; J. C. Ainsworth, Orlando Humason, H. W. Corgett, Henry Failling, of Oregon; J. B. S. Todd, M. K. Armstrong, J. Shaw Gregory, J. LeBerge, of Dakota Territory; John Mullen, Anson G. Henry, S. D. Smith, Charles Terry, of Washington Territory; H. W. Starr, Platt Smith, Nixon Denton, William Leighton, B. F. Allen, Reuben Noble, John L. Davies, of Iowa; Willard P. Hall, George R. Smith, H. Gayle King, John C. Sergeant, of Missouri; William H. Wallace, of Idaho Territory; J. H. Lathrop, Henry D. Cooke, H. E. Merrick, of the District of Columbia, and all such other persons who shall or may be associated with them, and their successors, are hereby created and erected into a body corporate and politic, in deed and in law, by the name, style and title of the "Northern Pacific Railroad Company," and by that name shall have perpetual succession, and shall be able to sue and to be sued, plead and be impleaded, defend and be defended, in all courts of law and equity within the United States and may make and have a common seal. And said corporation is hereby authorized and empowered to lay out, locate, construct, furnish, maintain, and enjoy a continuous railroad and telegraph line, with the appurtenances, namely, beginning at a point on Lake Superior, in the state of Minnesota or Wisconsin; thence westerly by the most eligible railroad route, as shall be determined by said company, within the territory of the United States, on a line north of the forty-fifth degree of latitude to some point on Puget's Sound, with a branch, via the valley of the Columbia River, to a point at or near Portland, in the state of Oregon, leaving the main trunk-line at the most suitable place, not more than 300 miles from its western terminus; and is hereby vested with all the powers, privileges, and immunities necessary to carry into effect the purposes of this act as herein set forth.

Section 2. And be it further enacted, That the right of way through the public lands be, and the same is hereby, granted to said "Northern Pacific Railroad Company," its successors and assigns, for the construction of a railroad and telegraph as proposed; and the right, power, and authority is hereby given to said corporation to take from the public lands adjacent to the line of said road, materials of earth, stone, timber, and so forth, or the construction thereof. Said way is granted to said railroad to the extent of two hundred feet in width on each side of said railroad where it may pass through the public domain, including all necessary ground for station buildings, workshops, depots, machine shops, switches, side tracks, turntables and water stations; and the right of way shall be exempt from taxation within the territories of the United States. The United States shall extinguish, as rapidly as may be consistent with public policy and the welfare of the said Indians, the Indian titles to all lands falling under the operation of this act, and acquire in the donation to the [road] named in this bill.

Section 3. And be it further enacted, That there be, and hereby is, granted to the "Northern Pacific Railroad Company," its successors and assigns, for the purpose of aiding in the construction of said railroad and telegraph line to the Pacific Coast, and to secure the safe and speedy transportation of the mails, troops, munitions of war, and public stores over the route of said line of railway, every alternate section of public land, not mineral, designated by odd numbers, to the amount of 20 alternate sections per mile, on each side of said railroad line as said company may adopt, through the territories of the United States, and 10 alternate sections of land per mile on each side of said railroad whenever it passes through any state, and whenever on the line thereof, the United States have full title, not reserved, sold, granted, or otherwise appropriated, and free from pre-emption or other claims or rights at the time the line of said road is definitely fixed, and a plat thereof filed in the office of the commissioner of the general land office; and wherever, prior to said time, any of said section or parts of sections shall have been granted, sold, reserved, occupied by homestead settlers, or pre-empted or otherwise disposed of, other lands shall be selected by said company in lieu thereof, under the direction of the Secretary of the Interior in alternate sections and designated by odd numbers, not more than 10 miles beyond the limits of said alternate sections. Provided, That if said route shall be found upon the line of any other railroad route to aid in the construction of which lands have been heretofore granted by the United States, as far as the routes are upon the same general line, the amount of land heretofore granted shall be deducted from the amount granted by this act: Provided further, That the railroad company receiving the previous grant of land may assign their interest to said "Northern Pacific Railroad Company," or may consolidate, confederate, and associate with said company upon the terms named in the first section of this act: Provided further, That all mineral lands be, and the same are hereby, excluded from the operations of this act, and in lieu thereof a like quantity of unoccupied and unappropriated agricultural lands, in odd numbered sections, nearest to the line of said road may be selected as above provided: And provided further, That the words "mineral," when it occurs in this act, shall not be held to include iron or coal: And provided further, That no money shall be drawn from the Treasury of the United States to aid in the construction of the said "Northern Pacific Railroad."

Section 4. And be it further enacted, That whenever said "Northern Pacific Railroad Company" shall have 25 consecutive miles of any portion of said railroad and telegraph line ready for the service contemplated, the President of the United States shall appoint 3 commissioners to examine the same, and if it shall appear that 25 miles of said road and telegraph line have been completed in good, substantial, and workmanlike manner, as in all other respects required by this act,

The commissioners shall so report to the President of the United Sates and patents of lands as aforesaid, shall be issued to said company, confirming to said company the right and title to said lands, situated opposite to, and coterminous with, said completed section of said road; and, from time to time, whenever 25 additional consecutive miles shall have been constructed, completed and in readiness as aforesaid, and verified by said commissioners to the President of the United States, then patents shall be issued to said company conveying the additional sections of land as aforesaid, and so on as fast as every 25 miles of said road is completed as aforesaid: Provided, That not more than 10 sections of land per mile, as said road shall be completed, shall be conveyed to said company for all that part of said railroad lying east of the western boundary of the State of Minnesota, until the whole of said railroad shall be finished and in good running order, as a first-class railroad from the place of beginning on Lake Superior to the western boundary of Minnesota: Provided also, That lands shall not be granted under the provisions of this act on account of any railroad or part thereof constructed at the date of the passage of this act.

Section 5. And be it further enacted, That said "Northern Pacific Railroad" shall be constructed in a substantial and workmanlike manner, with all the necessary draws, culverts, bridges, viaducts, crossings, turnouts, stations, and watering places, and all other appurtenances, including furniture and rolling stock, equal in all respects to railroads of the first class, when prepared for business, with rails of the best quality, manufactured from American iron. And a uniform gauge shall be established throughout the entire length of the road. And there shall be constructed a telegraph line, of the most substantial and approved description, to be operated along the entire line: Provided, that the said company shall not charge the government higher rates than they do individuals for like transportation and telegraphic service. And it shall be the duty of the Northern Pacific Railroad Company to permit any other railroad which shall be authorized to be built by the United States, or by the legislature of any territory or state in which the same may be situated, to form running connections with it on fair and equitable terms.

Section 6. And be it further enacted, That the President of the United States shall cause the lands to be surveyed for forty miles in width on both sides of the entire line of said road, after the general route shall be fixed, and as fast as may be required by the construction of said railroad; and the odd sections of land hereby granted shall not be liable to sale, or entry, or pre-emption before or after they are surveyed, except by said company as provided in this act; but the provisions of the act of September, eighteen hundred and forty -one, granting pre-emption rights, and the acts amendatory thereof, and of the act entitled "An act to secure homesteads to actual settlers on the public domain," approved May twenty, eighteen hundred and sixty-two, shall be, and the same are hereby extended to all other lands on the line of said road, when surveyed, excepting those hereby granted to said company. And the reserved alternate section shall not be sold by the government at a price less than two dollars and fifty cents per acre when offered for sale.

Section 7. And be it further enacted, That the said "Northern Pacific Railroad Company" be, and is hereby authorized and empowered to enter upon purchase, take and hold any lands or premises that may be necessary and proper for the construction and working of said road, not exceeding in width 200 feet on each side of the line of its railroad, unless a greater width be required for the purpose of excavation or embankment; and also any lands or premises that may be necessary and proper for turnouts, standing places for cars, depots, station houses, or any other structures required in the construction and working of said road. And the said company shall have the right to cut and remove trees and other material that might, by falling, encumber its road-bed, though standing or being more than 200 feet from the line of said road. And in case the owner of such lands or premises and the said company cannot agree as to the value of premises taken, or to be taken, for the use of said road, the value thereof shall be determined by the appraisal of three disinterested commissioners, who may be appointed, upon application of either party, to any Court of Record in and of the territories in which the lands or premises to be taken lie; and said commissioners, in their assessment of damages, shall appraise such premises at what would have been the value thereof if the road had not been build. And upon return into Court of such appraisement, and upon the payment into the same of the estimated value of the premises taken for the use and benefit of the owner thereof, said premises shall be deemed to be taken by said company, which shall thereby acquire full title to the same for the purpose aforesaid. And either party feeling aggrieved at said appraisement may, within 30 days after the same has been returned, file an appeal therefrom, and demand a jury of 12 men to estimate the damage sustained; but such appeal shall not interfere with the rights of said company to enter upon the premises taken, or to do any act necessary and proper in the construction of its road. And said party appealing shall give bonds, with sufficient surety or sureties, for the payment of any cost that may arise upon such appeal; and in case the party appealing does not obtain a verdict, increasing or diminishing, as the case may be, the award of the commissioners, such party shall pay the whole cost incurred by the apellee as well as his own, and the payment into court, for the use of the owner of said premises taken, of a sum equal to that finally awarded, shall be held to rest in said company the title of said land, and of the right to use and occupy the same for the construction, maintenance, and operation of road. And in case any of the lands to be taken, as aforesaid, shall be held by any infant, femme covert, non compos, insane person, or person residing without the territory within which the lands to be taken lie, or persons subjected to any legal disability the court may appoint a guardian for any party under any disqualification, to appear in proper person, who shall give bonds with sufficient surety or sureties, for the proper and faithful execution of his trust, and who may represent in court the person disqualified, as aforesaid, from appealing, when the same proceedings shall be had in reference to the appraisement of the premises to be taken for the use of said company, and with the same effect as has already been described; and the title of the company to the lands taken by virtue of this act shall not be affected or impaired by reason of any failure by any guardian to discharge faithfully his trust. And in case any party shall have a right or claim to any land for a term of years, or any interest therein, in possession, reversion, or remainder, the value of any such estate, less than a fee simple, shall be estimated and determined in the manner herein before set forth. And in case it shall be necessary for the company to enter upon any lands which are unoccupied, and of which there is no apparent owner or claimant, it may proceed to take and use the same for the purpose of said railroad, and may institute proceedings, in manner described, for the purpose of ascertaining the value of, and of acquiring title to, the same; but the judge of the court hearing said suit shall determine the kind of notice to be served on such owner or owners, and he may in its discretion appoint an agent or guardian to represent such owner or owners in case of his or their incapacity or non-appearance. But in case no claimant shall appear within six years from the time of the opening of said road across any land, all claims to damage against said company shall be barred.

A Journalist Describes the Dangers of Work in the Mines

Eliot Lard, *Comstock Mining and Miners* (Washington, DC: U.S. Geological Survey, Government Printing Office, 1883), 217 –222. Republished with introduction and annotations by David F. Myrick (Berkeley, CA: Howell-North, 1959).

Author, historian, and journalist Eliot Lard was hired in 1879 by the U.S. Geological Survey to report on the development of the silver mining industry in the huge deposits known as the Comstock Lode, near Virginia City, Nevada. Lard concerned himself with both the technical aspects of mining exploration and development, as well as the labor conditions and business and labor organizations that made the lucrative operations possible. The following excerpt is taken from his description of those mines.

On the morning of June 15, 1863, a startling crash was heard at the other end of the lode, when half of the Mexican Mine, from the surface to the depth of 225 feet, caved in with an irresistible momentum which bore the ponderous mass of crumbling rock and splintered wood past the limits of the mine into the workings of the Ophir Company. Fifty feet of the fourth gallery or level in the Ophir Mine was at once obliterated, and large portions of the second and third galleries soon gave way before the accumulating pressure. An acre of surface was crushed open as if a blast had exploded beneath; the unsupported roof sunk down; the main shaft on the south line of the Mexican Mine closed up, and part of the engine-house was undermined and destroyed. "The whole mine," wrote an admiring witness, was "a lovely chaos." Caves like this do not occur without a previous warning. A gradual settling of the ground had been going on for a number of days; props were thrown out of place and dull timbers broken; the sharp cracking of overstrained pillars and dull rumbling noises of shifting ground could be plainly heard; still the superintendent remained blind and deaf; weak supports were not braced and sinking roofs were not upheld. At length his underground house came down upon his head and nearly crushed him in its fall. Twenty workmen were in the mine when the roofs of the galleries began to close upon them; headed by the superintendent they rushed toward the incline leading up out of the mine. A mass of crumbling rock fell near them, forcing the air through the drift in a sudden blast, which blew out their candles; the sound of splintering timbers and cracking rock filled their ears. In single file they groped their way up the narrow stairs, crouching and crawling in the darkness through the closing passage which led to the light. After a short but frightful climb they reached the surface and knew what it was to breathe freely, having escaped from an earthmonster's grip far more tenacious than the clutch of the devil-fish. The superintendent scarcely deserved his good fortune. His mine was a wreck and twenty stout men nearly lost their lives through his negligence or incapacity. Under the old Roman Empire, when life and property were guarded as valuable, he would not have escaped judgment, as by the laws of Theodosius and Valentinian those who culpably occasioned loss of life and property by the falling in of a pit or mine were condemned to death, because they had set themselves up as professors of an art they did not understand. In this buoyant, careless-tempered mining district, however, such professors were only laughed at.

Twenty months later another great cave rent the surface of Gold Hill (March 5, 1865), filling the upper levels of the Imperial, Empire, and Eclipse hoisting-works so violently that the engines were thrown out of place. The first level of the Imperial Mine was entirely closed, the supporting timber-frames being crushed like egg-shells, and so great was the concussion of the atmosphere when the vast body of the earth settled, as it did with one might crash, that fragments of rock were thrown more than 300 feet up the Imperial shaft, against the roof of the hoisting-works, with such force that they were instantly powdered and filled the room with a cloud of dust. The shafts of the Eclipse and Empire mines were so warped that the men on the lower levels could not be hoisted out, but made their way to the shaft of the Imperial Company and were then raised to the surface. This was a startling experience, but as the ground had, fortunately, refrained from falling in until the upper levels were exhausted of their ore-contents and no person was killed by its fall, the superintendents agreed in looking upon the cave as a permanent benefit. This cheerful view of the situation was characteristic of the time and place. "Nobody's hurt and who cares," might have been adopted as fitting motto by these happy-go-lucky miners.

Yet the most reckless of them could not always regard these accidents with indifference. When men were crushed and buried under masses of rock and splintered timbers no one could smile. Instant death was here a mercy to the victims. The mangled bodies of men who died like Opie and Sullivan were less piteous to see than the prolonged torture of one like Patrick Price, who was buried alive by a cave in the Chollar-Potosi Mine, October 5, 1867. He was at work near the bottom of an incline when the ground around him suddenly gave way, owing to the insufficient timbering of a lower level, and he was caught and carried down several feet by falling timbers and rocks. The mass above pressed heavily upon him, and he could not move hand or foot, but his head was in some way protected and he was able to call with a strong voice for help. His fellow-miners answered the call, but the walls of the incline were cracking and settling so fast that done dared to venture within twenty feet of the buried man For more than an hour they watched the ground slowly closing above his head, but forced themselves to speak cheeringly that he might not suffer the anguish of despair also. Once they set fire to a ball of oakum saturated with coal-oil and rolled it down toward him. "I see the light," he cried, joyfully. "I am glad you're coming for me, boys!" At this cry a desperate attempt was made to place a rope about his body but in vain. The loose earth was falling about his face, and his voice could scarcely be heard. He had borne his lingering torture bravely, but at length one moaning cry passed his lips. It was his last. In a few moments a great mass of clay, rocks, and timbers slid down upon him and his suffering was ended. It would seem that the recovery of a body, merely to lay it in a shallower grave, was an uncalled-for service to the dead, but miners are very reluctant to leave a corpse in a mine where they are working. Several attempts were, therefore, made at different times to find the body of Price, but without success, until the 27th of May, 1869, when the disfigured remains of the poor miner, half eaten by rats, were uncovered. A simple head-board stands in the Catholic grave-yard to record his death and declare without word the criminal carelessness or ignorance of the men who failed to timber and support a mine-level properly. . . .

While these caves were rending the face of the ground and burying men in the mine-depths, work along the line of the lode was rapidly pushed. American miners may sometimes be reckless, but they have never been accused of being dilatory. As the shafts grew deeper the simple windlass, by which a bucketful of water, rock, or ore was raised to the surface, was replaced by whims turned by horse-power and by small steam-hoisting engines. In 1860 the Ophir Company had first raised ore with steam-power by means of a rope wound round the shaft of their pumping-engine, thus pulling a car filled with rock up the incline which they had sunk on the dip of their ledge; yet, in the spring of 1864, they were working with a large new whim operated by horse-power. One horse turned the whim easily, hoisting a bucket 50 feet with every revolution of the drum. The Sunrise Company in the spring of 1864, were building a whim in place of their former windlass on the score of greater cheapness and rapidity of working. The cost of operating a windlass by two men during three shifts of eight hours each was stated to be $24, while two drivers and two horses would hoist out the same quantity of rock by means of a whim at a total daily expense of $12.

During the first two years of work on the lode only a few companies had the mouths of their shafts covered by buildings, but at the close of 1862 not less than forty companies had erected houses of some sort over their shafts, and twelve, at least, had machinery driven by steam for pumping water or hoisting rock from their mines. Viewed from the mountain summit above the line of the shafts the dingy heaps of rock and sand near the mouth of every pit and tunnel appeared like anti-hills rising imperceptibly from day to day. Some hills were comparatively deserted, but all day long a moving swarm of men, oxen, horses, and mules clustered about the dumps of the chief ore-producing mines, the Ophir, Mexican, California, Gould & Curry, Chollar, Potosi, and the small Gold Hill claims. Here the ore of different grades was assorted, screened, and shoveled into sacks or thrown into carts. Moving trains wound in and out through the surrounding streets, sometimes caught fast for a moment in a confused jam, and then escaping from its meshes with a parting salute of curses and whip-crackings. Below the surface the little army of miners was steadily burrowing its way through the heart of the ledge, cutting a few feet daily with picks and drills, one shift succeeded by another, descending and ascending the shafts in swaying buckets dangling at the end of elastic ropes; or, as in the Ophir Mine, mounting the incline by a steep narrow flight of steps 400 feet in length, bearing flickering candles in a rational torchlight procession.

Margaret Frink, Journal

From Margaret Frink, *Journal* [1897; dates refer to 1850]. Republished in Kenneth Holmes, *Covered Wagon Women: Diaries and Letters from the Western Trails, 1840–1890* (Glendale, CA: Arthur Clark Company, 1983), 60–61, 74–76, 97, 119–120, 138–139, 166–167.

Although Margaret Frink and her husband were significantly wealthier than many white Americans who headed west on the overland trail, her diary is a revealing window onto the challenges and hardship that American pioneer families faced. Frink, like most women on the overland trail, was particularly preoccupied with the difficulty of fulfilling her domestic roles as a wife and cook under the new circumstances of life on the trail.

The wag was packed and we were all ready to start on the twenty-seventh day of March. The wagon was designed expressly for the trip, it being built light, with everything planed for convenience. It was so arranged that when closed up, it could be used as our bedroom. The bottom was divided off into little compartments or cupboards. After putting our provisions, and other baggage, a floor was constructed over all, on which our mattress was laid. We had an India-rubber mattress that could be filled with either air or water, making a very comfortable bed. During the day we could empty the air out, so that it took but little room. We also had a bed and feather pillows. However, until we had crossed the Missouri River, we stopped at hotels and farmhouses every night, and did not use our own bedding. After that, there being no more hotels nor houses, we used it continually all the way to California. . . .

Our outfit for provisions was plenty of hams and bacon, covered with care from the dust, apples, peaches, and preserved fruits of different kinds, rice, coffee, tea, beans, flour, corn-meal, crackers, sea-biscuit, butter, and lard. The canning of fruits had not been invented yet—at least not in the west, so far as we knew.

Learning by letters published in the newspapers, that lumber was worth $400.00 per thousand in California, while it was worth only $3.00 in Indiana, Mr. Frink [her husband] concluded to send the material for a small cottage by the way of Cape Horn. The lumber was purchased and several carpenters were put to work. In six days the whole material was prepared, ready for putting it together. It was then placed on board a flatboat lying in White River, to be ready for the spring rise—as boats could not pass out except at high water. The route was down White River to the Wabash, to the Ohio, to the Mississippi, to New Orleans; thence by sail vessel around Cape Horn to Sacramento, where it arrived the following March, having been just one year on the voyage.

Tuesday, April 23. We got into St. Joseph [Missouri] at 10 o'clock this morning. The whole country around the town is filled with encampments of California emigrants. This is the head of the emigration at the present time. They have gathered here from the far east and south, to fit out and make final preparations for launching out on the great plains, on the other side of the Missouri River. . . .

We still lacked something to complete our stock of supplies; for we had neither pickles, potatoes, nor vinegar. The army of emigration was so numerous that the demand for these and many other articles could only with difficulty be fully supplied. Mr. Frink traveled sixteen miles through the farming country searching for pickled cucumbers.

He was fortunate enough to find a bushel still in the salt, which he bought and brought back with him. This, with some horseradish and one peck of potatoes, was all he could find in the way of vegetables. I prepared these very carefully, and put them up in kegs with apple vinegar; these were to be our principal defense against that dreadful disease, the scurvy, from which the overland emigrants of 1849 had suffered so severely—not only while on the journey, but long after reaching California.

Monday, June 10. It was at this camp [in present-day Wyoming] that we had to leave our cooking stove, which we had found so useful ever since crossing the Missouri. It being light, we had always carried it lashed on the hind end of the wagon. Some careless person, in a hurry, drove his team up too close behind, and the pole of his wagon ran into the stove, smashing and ruining it. After that, we had to cook in the open air. We adopted a plan which was very fashionable on the plains. We would excavate a narrow trench in the ground, a foot deep and three feet long, in which we built the fire. The cooking vessels were set over this, and upon trial we found it a very good substitute for a stove.

Sunday, July 14. If we could have had our own way, this would have been a day of rest in reality, as well as in name; but such it was not to be. Not only the customary duties of camp life, but the weekly laundry, had to be attended to, although the day was excessively warm, the mercury marking one hundred and twenty degrees inside our wagon. The dryness of the air, and the high altitude, made the heat more endurable than it would have been in a moist climate, at a low elevation.

Friday, August 16. It was long before sunrise when we left camp [in present-day Nevada]. Our plan was to travel by easy stages, stopping often to feed and rest our horses. The early morning was cool and pleasant. At six o'clock we halted and rested four hours.

We set forward again at ten o'clock and soon began to realize what might be before us. For many weeks we had been accustomed to see property abandoned and animals dead or dying. But those scenes were here doubled and trebled. Horses, mules, and oxen, suffering from heat, thirst, and starvation, staggered along until they fell and died on every rod of the way. Both sides of the road for miles were lined with dead animals and abandoned wagons. Around them were strewed yokes, chains, harness, guns, tools, bedding, clothing, cooking-utensils, and many other articles, in utter confusion. The owners had left everything, except what provisions they could carry on their backs, and hurried on to save themselves. . . .

As we advanced, the scenes became more dreadful. The heat of the day increased, and the road became heavy with deep sand. The dead animals seemed to become at every step of the way more numerous. They lay so thick on the ground that the carcasses, if placed together, would have reached across many miles of that desert. The stench arising was continuous and terrible.

[Writing in 1897, reflecting on her experiences:]

As the years passed on, the mushroom city of tents and rough board houses [Sacramento] grew, in defiance of fires and floods, to be the capital of the state, and one of its most prosperous, beautiful, and wealthy cities. The modest White River cottage gave way to a larger and more permanent residence. The grounds grew more attractive each year, with the luxuriant shrubbery and flowers that belong to California. The vine and the fig gave their welcome shade to temper the summer warmth. . . . The progress of time only confirmed us more strongly in our choice of a home, and we never had occasion to regret the prolonged hardships of the toilsome journey that had its happy ending for us in this fair land of California.

Reference

Adams, Richard (1864–1921)   Delaware Indian attorney and writer who pushed for Indian political power.

American Federation of Labor (AFL)   A labor union federation founded in 1886. The AFL's emphasis on staying out of partisan politics and organizing native-born, skilled workers avoided cataclysmic confrontations with employers and the government even as it excluded most western workers.

Astor, John Jacob (1763–1848)   A leading American entrepreneur. An immigrant from Germany, he founded the American Fur Company in 1808 and made a fortune off of the Western fur trade that made him the richest person in the United States by the time of his retirement to New York City in the 1830s.

Austin, Stephen F. (1793–1836)   Empresario who contracted with the Mexican government to bring Anglo-American settlers to Texas, then a part of the Mexican state of Coahuila y Tejas. Like most Anglo settlers, Austin ended up opting for independence in 1836, but only after years of trying and in many ways succeeding in being a part of the Mexican nation.

Barcelo, Gertrudis (1800–1852)   New Mexican widow who was able to benefit from the U.S. conquest of the Mexican North through her gambling business, which left her as one of the territory's wealthiest women at her death.

Bear River Massacre (1863)   One of the worst, but least-known, massacres in the history of the American West. Perpetrated during the Civil War by a regiment of California volunteers on a band of Northern Shoshoni near what is now the Utah-Idaho border.

Becknell, William (ca. 1790–1865)   A trader who helped to open up commercial connections between New Mexico and the United States in the early 1820s.

Beckwourth, James (ca. 1800–ca. 1866)   Explorer, trapper, and trader who lived in much of the West before and during its incorporation by the United

States. Of mixed black and white ancestry, Beckwourth accompanied U.S. Army expeditions into the West, lived with Crow, Blackfoot, and Snake peoples, worked for the American Fur Company, ran a saloon in Santa Fe, helped blaze wagon trails to the California gold fields, achieving such fame that he was already the subject of a widely read biography a decade before his death.

Bierstadt, Alfred (1830–1902)   Landscape painter whose images of Yellowstone, the Rockies, and other Western locations communicated a sense of the West's grandeur and enormity to a broad American audience.

Billy the Kid (ca. 1859–1881)   A legendary western outlaw. Born in New York City with the name Henry McCarty, he was a leader of the "Regulators," a vigilante organization in Lincoln County, New Mexico. His violent exploits were widely popularized even before his murder.

Black Kettle (?–1868)   A Southern Cheyenne leader whose efforts to find some kind of accommodation with the influx of Anglo-Americans on the southern Plains ended in tragedy and violence. He narrowly escaped death at the 1864 Sand Creek Massacre and was killed in 1868 by Custer's soldiers on the Cheyenne reservation.

Bracero Program   Joint agreement between the United States and Mexican governments that brought nearly five million Mexican nationals to the United States for short-term agricultural labor between 1942 and 1965.

Brotherhood of North American Indians   American Indian civil rights organization founded in 1911 that sought greater government respect for Indian people's autonomy and greater Indian influence over federal programs concerning Indian peoples.

Buffalo Soldiers   Black soldiers in the U.S. Army. Two cavalry and two infantry regiments composed of African-American enlistees were stationed at various western posts from 1866 to 1900.

Catlin, George (1796–1872)   Influential painter whose extensive depictions of Indian peoples of the West consolidated and popularized the widespread (but erroneous) belief that Indians were doomed to vanish before the onslaught of American civilization.

Central Pacific Railroad   The western portion of the first transcontinental railroad, running from Sacramento, California, east to Utah, where it met the Union Pacific in 1869. The Central Pacific was constructed largely by Chinese laborers.

Chinese Exclusion Act   An 1882 law that ended almost all immigration to the United States until a comprehensive reform in immigration law in 1965.

Chivington, Colonel John M. (1821–1894)   Minister and soldier best-known for leading the Colorado militia's attack on a peaceful band of Southern Cheyenne in 1864.

Chouteau, August Pierre (1749–1829) and **Jean Pierre Chouteau** (1758–1849)   Half-brothers and members of St. Louis' founding family, the

Chouteaus used their connections to fur-trading networks to achieve financial and political prominence after the United States acquired St. Louis in the Louisiana Purchase.

Compromise of 1850   Sectional compromise that addressed the growing crisis over slavery, particularly in the United States' newly-acquired western territories, by admitting California as a free state but passing a fugitive slave act that bolstered the institution of slavery.

Cortina, Juan (1824–1892)   Tejano leader whose 1859 rebellion near Brownsville, Texas, crystallized Mexican-American anger at their treatment by Anglo-Americans in the wake of the U.S. conquest of the southwest.

Cowboys   Mythic figures in estern history, cowboys were also a diverse group of poorly-paid wage laborers whose working life had much in common with other western workers.

Custer, George Armstrong (1839–1876)   Soldier and officer best known for his role in the battle of the Little Bighorn, in which he lead the Seventh Cavalry to complete destruction in an attack on a large village of Plains Indian peoples.

Eastman, Dr. Charles Alexander (1858–1939)   Indian author and civil rights pioneer, Eastman was serving as a government physician on the Pine Ridge Reservation during the Wounded Knee Massacre. Later in his life he founded multiple chapters of the Young Men's Christian Association and helped to found the Boy Scouts of America.

Foreign Miner's Tax   Several laws passed by the California legislature in the early 1850s that kept non-white miners, particularly Mexican and Chinese nationals, from benefiting from the Gold Rush.

Frink, Margaret (?–ca. 1895)   A pioneer woman whose 1850 account of her family's experiences on the overland trail has long been considered a classic of Western history.

Frontier of Inclusion   A frontier in which colonizers plan to include indigenous people in their society, even if on unequal or exploitive terms, as was the case in the Spanish empire in North America.

Frontier of Exclusion   A frontier in which colonizers seek to exclude indigenous people from their society, instead seeking their land above all else. Characterizes most of the English frontier in North America.

Gentlemen's Agreement   1907 agreement between the governments of Japan and the United States to drastically curtail Japanese immigration.

Gold Rush, California   The flood of people into California from across the world following the publicity of the discovery of gold near John Sutter's timber mill on the American River.

Gorras Blancas   Organized resistance movement to outside Anglo encroachment in San Miguel County, New Mexico, that cut fences and burned railroad works from 1889 to 1891.

Guadalupe-Hidalgo, Treaty of The 1848 agreement between the United States and Mexico that ended the U.S.-Mexico War. Mexico ceded its northern portion, including the relinquishment of its claims to Texas, and the United States paid $15 million and promised to protect the rights of the Mexican citizens living within its bounds.

Guerrero, Rosa (1934–) El Paso native who founded and directs the artistic group the Rosa Guerrero International Ballet Folklórico.

Hawk, Black Sparrow (1767–1838) Sac leader who spearheaded resistance to American encroachment in what is now Western Illinois and Iowa. His capture in 1832 made him a national celebrity, and he continues to be a symbol of resistance for many Indian peoples.

Hearst, George (1820–1891) Mining entrepreneur and California senator.

Homestead Act of 1862 Law that provided for public lands in the West to be allocated in 160-acre units to settlers in exchange for $1.25 an acre or five years of residence and improvement.

Horse Re-introduced to the Americas by the Spanish Empire, horses had spread across much of North America by the end of the eighteenth century, enabling the transformation of the Lakota, Comanche, and other Indian peoples into powerful equestrian societies.

Horse Whisperer, The 1998 movie produced by Robert Redford in which a horse trainer helps an injured girl, her horse, and her mother heal themselves and their relationships.

Hudson's Bay Company British trading company originally founded in 1670 whose field of operations included, at its height, the territory between the Rocky Mountains and the Pacific Ocean.

Industrial Workers of the World Radical labor union founded in 1905 by Big Bill Haywood and others. Sought to represent all workers, and, unlike the American Federation of Labor, never accepted the legitimacy of capitalism.

Jackson, Helen Hunt (1830–1885) Novelist and poet whose 1881 book, *A Century of Dishonor,* focused public scrutiny on American Indian policy.

Jackson, William Henry (1843–1942) Photographer whose work focused on the iconic landscapes of the American West.

Jackson, Zig (1957–) Photographer whose work subverts much of classic Western photography by insisting on the presence of Indian peoples—including the Mandan, Hidatsa, and Arikara tribes in which he is enrolled—as active agents in modern American life.

James, Jesse (1847–1882) Famous outlaw whose exploits became the source of legends and folk songs, most of which presented him as a champion of the common man but left unmentioned his undying sympathy for the Confederacy.

Kearney, Dennis (1847–1907) Head of the Workingmen's Party of California and leading advocate in the 1870s of expelling Chinese people from the United States.

King, Charles (1844–1933) Novelist and Army officer whose popular work featured romantic depictions of military life.

Knights of Labor A national labor federation founded in 1869 that spread across the West in the 1880s. Supplanted by the American Federation of Labor by the end of the nineteenth century.

Lewis and Clark Expedition 1804 to 1806 federal expedition led by Meriwether Lewis and William Clark that traveled from St. Louis to the mouth of the Columbia in order to explore the territory acquired by the United States in the 1802 Louisiana Purchase.

Lincoln County War 1878 to 1881 struggle over control of the New Mexico county between two factions, one allied with the large rancher John Chisum and the other with a group of smaller ranchers. The conflict brought Billy the Kid to prominence.

Lisa, Manuel (1772?–1820) Leading fur trader and founder of the Missouri Fur Company. Like many fur traders, Lisa married into an Indian family.

Little Big Horn, Battle of Also known to some northern Plains peoples as "Peji Sla Wakapa," this June 1876 battle pitted Custer's Seventh Cavalry against a vastly larger force of Lakota and Northern Cheyenne. Custer's entire command perished, but the Indian peoples against whom he had fought were soon defeated and confined on reservations.

Long, Stephen (1784–1864) Army major and explorer who led an 1820 expedition that mapped the upper Mississippi and lower Arkansas rivers, during which he labeled the southern Plains the "Great American Desert."

Luhan, Mable Dodge (1879–1962) Writer and leader of Taos arts colony. Drawn from the east by what she perceived as the richer and more authentic existence of Indians, Mabel Dodge married Taos Pueblo Indian Tony Luhan and played a key role in attracting artists, writers, and intellectuals to the Southwest.

Mexican Revolution (1911–1920) Arguably the first major world revolution of the twentieth century, the Mexican Revolution sent as many as one out of every ten Mexicans fleeing into the United States, thereby transforming and revitalizing many Mexican-American communities across the Southwest.

Moran, Thomas (1837–1926) Painter whose depictions of Yellowstone and other western landscapes achieved wide prominence and helped lead the establishment of Yellowstone National Park in 1872.

Mormon Corridor A term used for the areas of Utah settled before 1865 by Mormon pioneers.

Mountain Meadows Massacre   The 1857 killings of 120 members of on overland migrant train in southern Utah by a Mormon militia led by John Lee. The massacre vexed the relations between Mormons and the U.S. government for much of the rest of the century.

Murrieta, Joaquín (ca. 1830–1853 or 1878)   Legendary Mexican-American blamed for thefts and assaults in California's central valley in the early 1850s. California Rangers killed and beheaded two men in 1853, one of them purportedly Murrieta, who in another account returned to his family in his native Sonora.

National Association for the Advancement of Colored People (NAACP) The preeminent African-American civil rights organization, the NAACP was founded in New York City in 1909 and soon boasted many chapters in western states.

National Congress of American Indians (NCAI)   An organization comprised of Indian nations devoted to advancing the collective interests of American Indians, the NCAI was founded in 1944 to resist the federal drive to dissolve reservations and tribal governments.

Northern Pacific Railroad   The railroad line between Minneapolis-St. Paul and Seattle, completed in 1883.

Otero, Miguel (1829–1882)   Leading New Mexico politician and businessman whose land and railroad ventures allowed him to successfully navigate the U.S. takeover of the Southwest.

Peale, Titian (1799–1885)   Painter who focused on depictions of wildlife and natural history. Peale traveled with the 1820 expedition led by Stephen Long.

Rin-Tin-Tin (1916–1932)   German Shepherd star of 1920s films, who appeared in dozens of feature films.

Rose, Edward (?–ca. 1833)   Associate of fur-trade entrepreneur Manuel Lisa who lived extensively with the Crow and Arikara peoples.

Sand Creek Massacre   1864 attack on Southern Cheyenne leader Black Kettle and his band, nearly two hundred of whom were killed by Colorado militia under the command of John Chivington, provoking widespread condemnation even within American society.

Santa Fe Ring   Political machine in territorial New Mexico that brought together Anglo newcomers and elite Hispano families. The "Ring" dominated New Mexico politics for a generation, securing hundreds of thousands of acres and lucrative government contracts for its members.

Santa Fe Trail   The trade route that connected Santa Fe and St. Louis, thereby linking the U.S. and northern Mexican economies. Opened in 1821, the Trail resulted in extensive commercial and personal relationships a generation before the U.S. conquest of the southwest.

Secularization   The disestablishment of Catholic missions in California by the Mexican government between 1834 and 1836, which resulted in the transfer of the missions' extensive and valuable land to elite californios.

Seguin, Juan (1806–1890)   Elite Tejano leader who supported the Texas Revolution (fighting at both the Alamo and San Jacinto), only to be driven from Texas in the 1840s as the independent nation's Anglo majority expelled and dispossessed many of its Mexican-descent inhabitants.

Seton, Earnest Thompson (1860–1946)   Author and naturalist whose work featured romantic portrayals of wild animals, particularly wolves. He was also one of the founders of the Boy Scouts of America.

Shaw, Anna Moore (1898–1975)   Akimel O'odham or Pima writer and cultural activist who used her boarding school education and familiarity with Anglo-American culture to help revive O'odham cultural memory.

Singleton, Benjamin "Pap" (1809–1892)   A leading promoter of African-American migration to the West immediately after Reconstruction, later in life Singleton encouraged African-American migration to Africa.

Smith, Jedediah (1798–1831)   Fur trader and explorer who played a key role in connecting the Pacific Northwest and California to American markets.

Smith, Joseph Jr. (1805–1844)   Founder of the Church of Jesus Christ of Latter-Day Saints, also known as Mormonism. Although Smith's murder in Illinois kept him from seeing the Far West, the religion that he founded shapes the West's culture to this day.

Society of American Indians   American Indian civil rights organization founded in 1911 by Charles Eastman, Carlos Montezuma, and others. SAI served as an important meeting ground for native advocates of treaty rights, citizenship, and the betterment of reservation conditions through the early 1920s.

Standing Bear, Luther (ca. 1868–1939)   Originally named Plenty Kill, Luther Standing Bear was one of the first graduates of the Indian boarding school in Carlisle, Pennsylvania. He used his education and many books to offer severe critiques of federal Indian policy and ultimately rejected the assimilationist philosophy of the boarding schools.

Stanford, Leland (1824–1893)   Railroad magnate and politician who funded Stanford University in 1891 after serving as California governor and senator and helping to create the Central Pacific Railroad.

Starr, Belle (1848–1889)   Outlaw whose role in horse theft and robbery in Missouri, Texas, and Indian Territory earned her the moniker "The Bandit Queen."

Strauss, Levi (1829–1902)   Entrepreneur who seized the opportunity presented by the California Gold rush by selling goods to miners, including the blue jeans that still bear his name.

Tape, Joseph (1852–1935) and **Tape, Mary** (1857–1934)   Chinese immigrants who sued the San Francisco Board of Education in an effort to secure their daughter's admission to a local public school.

Termination   Term used to describe federal Indian policy in 1953, when Congress provided for the eventual elimination of tribal governments, tribally held lands, and government support provided for in treaties, to the mid-1970s, when the government retreated from the policy.

Union Pacific Railroad   The Eastern portion of the first transcontinental railroad, linked to the Central Pacific at Promontory Point, Utah in 1869, and built largely by Irish laborers.

Vásquez, Tiburcio (1835–1875)   California outlaw who achieved notoriety and great respect from many Latinos in California as an image of defiance to Anglo suppression in the 1850s and 1860s.

Watkins, Carleton (1829–1916)   Photographer whose landscape views of Yosemite Valley helped to persuade Congress to preserve it as a park.

Watson, Ella (1861?–1888)   Wyoming homesteader whose conflict with powerful cattle ranchers resulted in her lynching and later depiction as "Cattle Kate," a supposedly perverted and dangerous figure.

Wells Fargo   Western company that began as a California stagecoach service in the 1850s, achieved dominance in western transportation with its purchase of the Overland Mail company, and has endured until the present as a banking and financial services corporation.

Western Federation of Miners   Radical labor union founded in 1893 in Butte, Montana, which played a central role in western labor conflict until it was eclipsed by the Industrial Workers of the World and reconstituted itself as the International Union of Mine, Mill, and Smelter Workers as a part of the American Federation of Labotr.

Winnemucca, Sarah (ca. 1844–1891)   Activist, teacher, and writer who played a crucial role in mediating between Northern Paiutes and the federal government, and in national debates over Indian policy.

Woodruff, Wilford (1807–1898)   Leader of the Church of Jesus Christ of Latter-Day Saints, or Mormons. As head of the Church, in 1890 Woodruff issued the Manifesto ending Mormonism's endorsement of polygamy.

Wounded Knee Massacre   December 29, 1890, killing of hundreds of Lakota by the Seventh Cavalry, which provoked widespread outrage at the time and marked the end of the Ghost Dance religious revitalization.

Young, Brigham (1801–1877)   Mormon leader who became head of the Church of Jesus Christ of Latter-Day Saints with Joseph Smith's murder in 1844. Young orchestrated the Mormon exodus to the Salt Lake Valley and the flourishing of the new religion in the West.

Bibliography

Abrahams, Ray. *Vigilant Citizens: Vigilantism and the State.* Cambridge, UK: Polity Press, 1998.

Acuña, Rodolfo. *Occupied America: A History of Chicanos.* New York: Harper and Row, 1988.

Adams, Kevin. *Caste and Class: Military Life on the Post–Civil War Frontier.* Norman: University of Oklahoma Press, forthcoming.

Adams, Noah. "British Novelist Sells First Book for $6 Million." Nicholas Evans interview, *All Things Considered*, NPR, August 31, 1995.

Alexander, Thomas G. *Mormonism in Transition: A History of the Latter-day Saints.* Urbana: University of Illinois Press, 1986.

Alexander, Thomas G. *Utah: The Right Place.* Layton, UT: Gibbs Smith Publishers, 2003.

Allen, James B., and Glen M. Leonard. *The Story of the Latter-day Saints.* Salt Lake City: Deseret Book, 1992.

Alonzo, Armando C. *Tejano Legacy: Rancheros and Settlers in South Texas, 1734–1900.* Albuquerque: University of New Mexico Press, 1998.

Amon Carter Museum, www.cartermuseum.org.

Anderson, Dean L. "The Flow of European Trade Goods into the Western Great Lakes Region, 1715–1760." In Jennifer H. Brown et al., eds., *The Fur Trade Revisited: Selected Papers of the Sixth North American Fur Trade Conference.* East Lansing: Michigan State University Press, 1994.

Andrews, Richard Allen. "Years of Frustration: William T. Sherman, the Army, and Reform, 1869–1883." Ph.D. diss., Northwestern University, 1968.

Anfinson, John Ogden. "Transitions in the Fur Trade, Continuity in Mandan Economy and Society to 1837." Ph.D. diss., University of Minnesota, Minneapolis-St. Paul, 1987.

Anzaldúa, Gloria. *Borderlands/La Frontera: The New Mestiza.* San Francisco: Spinster/Aunt Lute, 1987.

Arrington, Leonard J. *Brigham Young: American Moses.* New York: Knopf, 1985.

Arrington, Leonard J. *Utah's Audacious Stockman: Charles Redd.* Logan: Utah State University Press, 1995.

Arrington, Leonard, and Davis Bitton. *The Mormon Experience: A History of the Latter-day Saints.* New York: Knopf, 1979.

Atherton, Lewis E. "The Santa Fe Trader as Mercantile Capitalist." *Missouri Historical Review* 77 (1982): 1–12.

Bagley, Will. *Blood of the Prophets: Brigham Young and the Massacre at Mountain Meadows.* Norman: University of Oklahoma Press, 2002.

Bain, David Howard. *Empire Express: Building the First Transcontinental Railroad.* New York: Viking, 1999.

Ball, Durwood. *Army Regulars on the Western Frontier, 1848–1861.* Norman: University of Oklahoma Press, 2001.

Barbour, Barton H. *Fort Union and the Upper Missouri Fur Trade.* Norman: University of Oklahoma Press, 2001.

Bataille, Gretchen M., and Kathleen Mullen Sands. *American Indian Women: Telling Their Lives.* Lincoln: University of Nebraska Press, 1985.

Beller, Jack. "Negro Slaves in Utah." *Utah Historical Quarterly* 2 (October 1929): 122–126.

Berwanger, Eugene H. *The West and Reconstruction.* Chicago: University of Illinois Press, 1981.

Berwanger, Eugene H. "Reconstruction on the Frontier: The Equal Rights Struggle in Colorado, 1865–1867." In Monroe Lee Billington and Roger D. Hardaway, eds., *African Americans on the Western Frontier.* Boulder: University Press of Colorado, 1998.

Betts, Robert B. *In Search of York: The Slave Who Went to the Pacific with Lewis and Clark.* Boulder: Colorado Associated University Press, 1985.

Billington, Monroe Lee, and Roger D. Hardaway, eds. *African Americans on the Western Frontier.* Boulder: University Press of Colorado, 1998.

Billington, Ray Allen. *Westward Expansion: A History of the American Frontier.* 4th ed. New York: Macmillan, 1974.

Bleeg, Joanne Wagner. "Black People in the Territory of Washington." MA thesis, University of Washington, 1970.

Blenkinshop, Willis. "Edward Rose." In LeRoy Hafen, ed., *The Mountain Men and the Fur Trade.* Glendale, CA: Arthur H. Clark Company, 1972.

Bonner, Thomas D., ed. *Life and Adventures of James Beckwourth.* Lincoln: University.

Boyle, Susan Calafate. *Los Capitalistas: Hispano Merchants and the Santa Fe Trade.* Albuquerque: University of New Mexico Press, 1997.

"Brigham Young Said: On Recreation." *Improvement Era* (June 1950): 529.

Bringhurst, Newell G. "Mormons and Slavery: A Closer Look." In Monroe Lee Billington and Roger D. Hardaway, eds., *African Americans on the Western Frontier.* Boulder: University Press of Colorado, 1998.

Brininstool, E. A. *A Trooper with Custer.* Columbus, Ohio. The Hunter-trader-trapper Co., 1926.

Brooks, Juanita. *The Mountain Meadows Massacre* [1962]. Norman: University of Oklahoma Press, 1991.

Brown, Dee. *The Gentle Tamers.* London: Barrie and Jenkins, 1973.

Brown, Richard Maxwell. *Strain of Violence: Historical Studies of American Violence and Vigilantism.* Oxford: Oxford University Press, 1975.

Brown, Richard Maxwell. *No Duty to Retreat: Violence and Values in American History and Society.* New York: Oxford University Press, 1991.

Brundage, W. Fitzhugh. *Lynching in the New South: Georgia and Virginia, 1880–1930.* Urbana: University of Illinois Press, 1993.

Callaway, Llewellyn L. *Montana's Righteous Hangmen: The Vigilantes in Action.* Norman: University of Oklahoma Press, 1982.

Camarillo, Albert. *Chicanos in a Changing Society: From Mexican Pueblos to American Barrios in Santa Barbara and Southern California, 1848–1930.* Cambridge: Harvard University Press, 1979.

Campbell, Randolph B. *An Empire for Slavery: The Peculiar Institution in Texas, 1821–1865.* Baton Rouge: Louisiana State University Press, 1989.

Canfield, Gae Whitney. *Sarah Winnemucca of the Northern Paiut*es. Norman: University of Oklahoma Press, 1983.

Carey, Ryan. "Building a Better Oregon: Geographic Information and the Production of Space, 1846–1906." Ph.D. diss., University of Texas at Austin, 2003.

Carhart, Arthur, and Stanley Paul Young. *The Last Stand of the Pack.* New York: Sears, 1929.

Catlin, George. *Letters and Notes on the Manners, Customs, and Conditions of North American Indians* [1844]. 2 vols. New York: Dover Publications, 1973.

Catlin, George, George Gurney, and Brian Dippie. *Catlin and His Indian Gallery.* Washington, DC: Smithsonian American Art Museum, 2002.

Census Bureau. *Seventh Census of the United States, 1850.* Washington, DC: Robert Armstrong, Public Printer, 1853.

Census Bureau. *Eighth Census of the United States, 1860, Population.* Washington, DC: Government Printing Office, 1864.

Census Bureau. *Twelfth Census of the United States, 1900, Population Part 1.* Washington, DC: U.S. Government Printing Office, 1901.

Census 2000 Brief: The Hispanic Population, According to Census 2000 (http://www.census.gov/prod/2001pubs/c2kbr01–3).

Chan, Sucheng. *This Bittersweet Soil: The Chinese in California Agriculture, 1860–1910.* Berkeley: University of California Press, 1987.

Chan, Sucheng. *Asian Americans: An Interpretive History.* Boston: Twayne Publishers, 1991.

Chávez, John R. *The Lost Land: The Chicano Image of the Southwest.* Albuquerque: University of New Mexico Press, 1984.

Chávez-García, Miroslava. *Negotiating Conquest: Gender and Power in California, 1770s to 1880s.* Tucson: University of Arizona Press, 2004.

Chen, Yong. *Chinese San Francisco, 1850–1943: A Transatlantic Community.* Stanford: Stanford University Press, 2000.

Cheney, Thomas E. *Mormon Songs from the Rocky Mountains: A Compilation of Mormon Folksong.* Austin: University of Texas Press, 1968.

Chinn, Thomas W., ed. *A History of the Chinese in California; A Syllabus.* San Francisco: CHSA, 1969.

Chipman, Donald. *Spanish Texas, 1519–1821.* Austin: University of Texas Press, 1992.

Christiansen, Scott R. *Sagwitch: Shoshone Chieftain, Mormon Elder, 1822–1887.* Logan: Utah State University Press, 1999.

Clash of the Wolves, DVD, directed by Charles A. Logue. In *More Treasures of the American Film Archives, 1894–1931, Program Two, 1925.* San Francisco: National Film Preservation Foundation, 2004.

Clokey, Richard M. *William H. Ashley: Enterprise and Politics in the Trans-Mississippi West.* Norman: University of Oklahoma Press, 1980.

Coffman, Edward. *The Old Army: A Portrait of the American Army in Peacetime, 1784–1898.* New York: Oxford University Press, 1986.

Cole, Olen. *The African American Experience in the Civilian Conservation Corps.* Gainesville: University of Florida Press, 1999.

Coleman, Ronald. "A History of Blacks in Utah, 1825–1910." Ph.D. diss., University of Utah, 1980.

Cooper, Craig O. Wyoming Water Development Commission and State Engineer's Office. "A History of Water Law, Water Rights, and Water Development in Wyoming, 1868–2002," 2004. http://wwdc.state.wy.us/history/Wyoming%20Water%20Law%20History.pdf (accessed March 15, 2006).

Cooper, Jerry. *The Army and Civil Disorder: Federal Military Intervention in Labor Disputes, 1877–1900.* Westport, CT: Greenwood Press, 1980.

Cornford, Daniel. *Workers and Dissent in the Redwood Empire.* Philadelphia, PA: Temple University Press, 1987.

Cornford, Daniel. "'We All Live More Like Brutes than Like Humans': Labor and Capital in the Gold Rush." In James J. Rawls and Richard J. Orsi, eds., *A Golden State: Mining and Economic Development of Gold Rush California.* Berkeley: University of California Press, 1999.

Coy, Jimmie Dean. *Valor: A Gathering of Eagles.* Theodore, AL: Evergreen Press, 2003.

Custer, George A. *My Life on the Plains,* ed. Milo Milton Quaife. Lincoln: University of Nebraska Press, 1966.

Davis, Sarah. "Diary from Missouri to California, 1850." In Kenneth L. Holmes, ed., *Covered Wagon Women: Diaries and Letters from the Western Trails, 1850.* Vol. 2. Lincoln: University of Nebraska Press, 1996.

Debo, Angie. *And Still the Waters Run: The Betrayal of the Five Civilized Tribes.* Princeton: Princeton University Press, 1972.

DeBow, Samuel P., and Edward A. Pitter, eds. *Who's Who in Religious, Fraternal, Social, Civic and Commercial Life on the Pacific Coast.* Seattle, WA: Searchlight Publishing Company, 1927.

De Graaf, Lawrence B. "Race, Sex, and Region: Black Women in the American West, 1850–1920." *Pacific Historical Review* 49 (1980): 285–313.

De Graaf, Lawrence B., Kevin Mulroy, and Quintard Taylor, eds. *Seeking El Dorado: African Americans in California.* Seattle: University of Washington Press, 2001.

De la Teja, Jesús F., ed. *A Revolution Remembered: The Memoirs and Selected Correspondence of Juan N. Seguín.* Austin, TX: State House Press, 1991.

De León, Arnoldo. *Mexican Americans in Texas: A Brief History.* 2d ed. Wheeling, IL: Harlan Davidson, 1993, 1999.

Delo, David. *Peddlers and Post Traders: The Army Sutler on the Frontier.* Salt Lake City: University of Utah Press, 1992.

Deverell, William. *Railroad Crossing: Californians and the Railroad, 1850–1910.* Berkeley: University of California Press, 1994.

Deverell, William. *Whitewashed Adobe: The Rise of Los Angeles and the Remaking of Its Mexican Past.* Berkeley: University of California Press, 2004.

DeVoto, Bernard. *Across the Wide Missouri.* New York: Houghton Mifflin Company, 1947.

DeVoto, Bernard. *The Course of Empire.* Boston: Houghton Mifflin, 1952.

Dimsdale, Thomas J. *The Vigilantes of Montana or Popular Justice in the Rocky Mountains* [1977]. Norman: University of Oklahoma Press, 1866.

Dunwidde, Peter W. "The Nature of the Relationship between the Blackfeet Indians and the Men of the Fur Trade." *Annals of Wyoming* 46 (1974): 123–133.

Durham, Philip, and Everett L. Jones. *The Negro Cowboys.* Lincoln: University of Nebraska Press, 1965.

Eastman, Charles A. (Ohiyesa). *From the Deep Woods to Civilization: Chapters in the Autobiography of an Indian.* Lincoln: University of Nebraska Press, 1977.

Edwards, Malcolm Edwards. "The War of Complexional Distinction: Blacks in Gold Rush California and British Columbia." *California Historical Quarterly* 56, no. 1 (spring 1977), pp. 34–45.

Embry, Jessie L. "'All Things unto Me Are Spiritual': Contrasting Religious and Temporal Leadership Styles in Heber City, Utah." In Jessie L. Embry and Howard A. Christy, eds., *Community Development in the American West: Past and Present Nineteenth and Twentieth Century Frontiers.* Provo, UT: Charles Redd Center for Western Studies, 1985.

Embry, Jessie L. *Mormon Polygamous Families: Life in the Principle.* Salt Lake City: University of Utah Press, 1987.

Embry, Jessie L. *A History of Wasatch County.* Salt Lake City and Heber City: Utah State Historical Society and Wasatch County Commission, 1996.

Embry, Jessie L. *North Logan Town, 1934–1970.* North Logan, UT: North Logan City, 2000.

Enstam, Elizabeth York. "Women and the Law." *Handbook of Texas Online, 1999.* http://www.tsha.utexas.edu/handbook/online/articles/WW/jsw2.html (accessed April 3, 2006).

Etcheson, Nicole. "Good Men and Notorious Rogues: Vigilantism in Massac County, Illinois, 1846–1850." In M. Bellesiles, ed., *Lethal Imagination: Violence and Brutality in American History.* New York: New York University Press, 1999.

Faragher, John Mack. *Women and Men on the Overland Trail.* New Haven, CT: Yale University Press, 1979.

Faragher, Johnny, and Christine Stansell. "Women and Their Families on the Overland Trail to California and Oregon, 1842–1867." *Feminist Studies* 2, nos. 2, 3 (1975): 150–166.

Field, Matthew. *Matt Field on the Santa Fe Trail.* Compiled by Clyde and Mae Reed Porter. Norman: University of Oklahoma Press, 1960.

Foner, Eric. *A Short History of Reconstruction.* New York: Harper and Row Publishers, 1990.

Foos, Paul. *A Short Offhand Killing Affair: Soldiers and Social Conflict during the Mexican-American War.* Chapel Hill: University of North Carolina Press, 2002.

Fowler, Arlen L. *The Black Infantry in the West, 1869–1891.* Norman: University of Oklahoma Press, 1996.

Fox, Richard Wightman. *Archaeology, History, and Custer's Last Battle.* 1993. Norman: University of Oklahoma Press, 1993.

Franklin, John Hope, and Alfred A. Moss. *From Slavery to Freedom: A History of African Americans.* 8th ed. New York: McGraw Hill, 2000.

Franklin, William E. "The Archy Case: The California Supreme Court Refuses to Free a Slave." *Pacific Northwest Historical Review* 32 (May 1963). pp. 137–154.

Fremont, John Charles. "A Report of the Exploring Expedition to Oregon and North Carolina in the Years 1843–44." U.S. 28th Congress, 2d Session, House Document 166, December 2, 1844–March 3, 1845.

Friedan, Betty. *The Feminine Mystique.* New York: W. W. Norton, 1963.

Gibbs, Mifflin W. *Shadow and Light: An Autobiography.* New York: Arno Press and the New York Times, 1868.

Gilman, Rhoda R., ed. *Aspects of the Fur Trade: Selected Papers of the 1965 North American Fur Trade Conference.* St. Paul: Minnesota Historical Society, 1967.

Gilpin, William. *Letters* [1837]. St. Louis: Missouri Historical Society.

Goetzmann, William H. "The Mountain Man as Jacksonian Man." *American Quarterly* 15 (1963): 402–415.

Goetzmann, William H. *Exploration and Empire: The Explorer and the Scientist in the Winning of the American West.* New York: W. W. Norton and Company, 1966.

Goetzmann, William H., and William N. Goetzmann. *The West of the Imagination.* New York: W. W. Norton and Company, 1986.

González, Deena J. *Refusing the Favor: The Spanish-Mexican Women of Santa Fe, 1820–1880.* New York: Oxford University Press, 1999.

González, Juan. *Harvest of Empire: A History of Latinos in America.* New York: Penguin Books, 2000.

Gonzales, Manuel G. *Mexicanos: A History of Mexicans in the United States.* Bloomington: Indiana University Press, 1999.

Grant, U. S. *Personal Memoirs of U. S. Grant.* Lincoln: University of Nebraska Press, 1996.

Greer, Germaine. *The Female Eunuch.* London: MacGibbon and Kee, 1970.

Gregg, Josiah. *Commerce of the Prairies* [1844]. 2 vols. Ann Arbor, MI: University Microfilms, 1966.

Griswold del Castillo, Richard. "Joaquín Murrieta: The Many Lives of a Legend." In R. W. Etulain and G. Riley, eds., *With Badges & Bullets: Lawmen & Outlaws in the Old West.* Golden, CO: Fulcrum Publishing, 1999.

Griswold del Castillo, Richard, and Arnoldo De León. *North to Aztlán: A History of Mexican Americans in the United States.* New York: Twayne Publishers, 1996.

Gutiérrez, David G. *Walls and Mirrors: Mexican Americans, Mexican Immigrants, and the Politics of Ethnicity.* Berkeley: University of California Press, 1995.

Gutiérrez, David G. *Between Two Worlds: Mexican Immigrants in the United States.* Wilmington, DE: Scholarly Resources, 1996.

Gutiérrez, Ramón A. "Unraveling America's Hispanic Past: Internal Stratification and Class Boundaries." *Aztlán* 17 (spring 1986): 79–102.

Haeger, John Denis. *John Jacob Astor: Business and Finance in the Early Republic.* Detroit: Wayne State University Press, 1991.

Haglund, Karl T., and Phillip F. Notarianni. *The Avenues of Salt Lake City.* Salt Lake City: Utah Historical Society, 1980.

Hämäläinen, Pekka. "The Western Comanche Trade Center: Rethinking the Plains Indian Trade System." *Western Historical Quarterly* 29 (1998): 485–513.

Hämäläinen, Pekka. "The Rise and Fall of the Plains Indians Horse Cultures." *Journal of American History* 90 (December 2003): 833–862.

Hayden, Delores. "Biddy Mason's Los Angeles, 1851–1891." *California History* 68, no. 3 (fall 1989), pp. 86–99.

Hayes, Ralph, and Joseph Franklin. *Northwest Black Pioneers: A Centennial Tribute.* Seattle, WA: The Bon Marche Corporate Sponsor, 1994.

Hine, Robert V., and John Mack Faragher. *The American West: A New Interpretive History.* New Haven, CT: Yale University Press, 2000.

Hobshawm, Eric. *Bandits* [1969]. New York: Pantheon Books, 1981.

Horan, James D., and Paul Sann. *Pictorial History of the Wild West.* New York: Crown Publishers, 1954.

Hsu, Madeline. *Dreaming of Gold, Dreaming of Home: Transnationalism and Migration between the United States and South China, 1882–1943.* Stanford: Stanford University Press, 2000.

Hufsmith, George W. *The Wyoming Lynching of Cattle Kate, 1889.* Glendo, WY: High Plains Press, 1993.

Hune, Shirley, and Gail Nomura. *Asian/Pacific Islander American Women: A Historical Anthology.* New York: New York University Press, 2003.

Hunter, J. Marvin, and Noah H. Rose. *The Album of Gunfighters.* N.p., 1959.

Hutton, Paul. *Phil Sheridan and His Army.* 1985. Lincoln: University of Nebraska Press, 1985.

Hyslop, Stephen G. *Bound for Santa Fe: The Road to New Mexico and the American Conquest, 1806–1848.* Norman: University of Oklahoma Press, 2002.

Ichioka, Yuji. *The Issei: The World of the First Generation Japanese Immigrants 1885–1924.* New York: Free Press, 1988.

Igler, David. *Industrial Cowboys: Miller & Lux and the Transformation of the Far West, 1850–1920.* Berkeley: University of California Press, 2001.

Isenberg, Andrew C. "The Market Revolution in the Borderlands: George Champlin Silbey in Missouri and New Mexico, 1808–1826." *Journal of the Early Republic* 21 (2001): 445–466.

Jacobs, Margaret D. *Engendered Encounters: Feminism and Pueblo Cultures, 1879–1934.* Lincoln: University of Nebraska Press, 1999.

James, Ronald M. *The Roar and the Silence: A History of Virginia City and the Comstock Lode.* Reno: University of Nevada Press, 1998.

Jameson, Elizabeth. "Toward a Multicultural History of Women in the Western United States." *Signs* 13, no. 4 (summer 1988): 761–791.

Jameson, Elizabeth, and Susan Armitage, eds. *Writing the Range: Race, Class, and Culture in the Women's West.* Norman: University of Oklahoma Press, 1997.

Jeffrey, Julie Roy. *Frontier Women: The Trans-Mississippi West, 1840–1880.* New York: Hill and Wang, 1979.

Jensen, Joan M. *One Foot on the Rockies: Women and Creativity in the Modern American West.* Albuquerque: University of New Mexico Press, 1995.

Johnson, David. "The Moral Authority of Popular Justice in the Far West." *American Quarterly* 33, no. 5 (1981): 558–586.

Johnson, Susan Lee. "'A Memory Sweet to Soldiers': The Significance of Gender." In Clyde A. Milner II, ed., *A New Significance: Re-envisioning the History of the American West.* New York: Oxford University Press, 1996.

Johnson, Susan Lee. *Roaring Camp: The Social World of the California Gold Rush.* New York: W. W. Norton, 2000.

Jolly, Michelle. 2003. "Sex, Vigilantism, and San Francisco in 1856." *Common-Place* 3, no. 4. http://www.common-place.org/vol–03/no–04/san-francisco/ (accessed March 15, 2006).

Jung, Maureen A. "Capitalism Comes to the Diggings: From Gold Rush Adventure to Corporate Enterprise." In James J. Rawls and Richard J. Orsi, eds., *A Golden State: Mining and Economic Development of Gold Rush California.* Berkeley: University of California Press, 1999.

Kappler, Charles J., ed. *Indian Affairs: Laws and Treaties.* Vol. 2: *Treaties.* Washington, DC: Government Printing Office, 1904.

Katz, William Loren. *Black People Who Made the Old West.* New York: Thomas Y. Cowell Company, 1977.

Katz, William Loren. *The Black West.* New York: Touchstone, 1996.

Kelley, Robin D. G. "We Are Not What We Seem: Rethinking Black Working-Class Opposition in the Jim Crow South." *Journal of American History* (June 1993): 75–112.

Kenner, Charles. *Buffalo Soldiers and Officers of the Ninth Cavalry, 1867–1898: Black and White Together.* Norman: University of Oklahoma Press, 1999.

King, Charles. *Campaigning with Crook, and Stories of Army Life.* 1890.

Langford, Nathaniel Pitt. *Vigilante Days and Ways: The Pioneers of the Rockies, the Makers and Making of Montana, Idaho, Oregon, Washington, and Wyoming.* Boston: J. G. Cupples Co., 1890a. http://www.umwestern.edu/Academics/library/libroth/MHD/vigilantes/LANGFORD/cover.html (accessed March 15, 2006).

Langford, Nathaniel Pitt. 1890b. *Vigilante Days and Ways.* "Chapter XX, A Masonic Funeral," http://www.umwestern.edu/Academics/library/libroth/MHD/vigilantes/LANGFORD/chapters/chap20.html (accessed March 15, 2006).

Lansing, Michael. "Plains Indian Women and Interracial Marriage in the Upper Missouri Trade, 1804–1868." *Western Historical Quarterly* 31 (2000): 413–433.

Lara, Kandi. "Susan Raper: Elko County's First Female Cattle Rustler." *Quarterly—Northeastern Nevada Historical Society* 96, no. 2 (1996): 56–63.

Larsen, Gustive. *The "Americanization" of Utah for Statehood, 1897–1978.* San Marino, CA: Huntington Library, 1971.

Leckie, William H. *Buffalo Soldiers: A Narrative of the Negro Cavalry in the West.* Norman: University of Oklahoma Press, 2003.

Lee, Erika. *At America's Gates: Chinese Immigration during the Exclusion Era, 1882–1943.* Chapel Hill: University of North Carolina Press, 2003.

Lee, Mary Paik. *Quiet Odyssey: A Pioneer Korean Woman in America.* Seattle: University of Washington Press, 1990.

"Legends of America." 2003–2005. "The Maxwell Land Grant" http://www.legendsofamerica.com/HC-Maxwell4.html (accessed March 15, 2006).

Leigh, Sharon. "Ella Watson: Rustler or Homesteader?" *Annals of Wyoming* 64, nos. 3–4 (1992): 49–56.

Leonard, Stephen J. *Lynching in Colorado, 1859–1919.* Boulder: University Press of Colorado, 2002.

Leonard, Zenas. *Narrative of the Adventures of Zenas Leonard* [1839]. Ann Arbor, MI: University Microfilms, 1966.

Limerick, Patricia Nelson. *The Legacy of Conquest: The Unbroken History of the American West.* New York: W. W. Norton, 1987.

Limerick, Patricia Nelson, Clyde A. Milner, II, and Charles E. Rankin, eds. *Trails: Toward a New Western History.* Lawrence: University Press of Kansas, 1991.

Limerick, Patricia, and Richard White. *The Frontier in American Culture.* Berkeley: University of California Press, 1994.

Lotchin, Roger W. *San Francisco, 1846–1856: From Hamlet to City.* New York: Oxford University Press, 1974.

Lyman, Edward Leo. *Political Deliverance: The Mormon Quest for Utah Statehood.* Urbana: University of Illinois Press, 1986.

Mack, Dwayne A. "'May the Work I've Done Speak for Me': African American Civilian Conservation Corps Enrollees in Libby and Troy, Montana, 1933–34." *Western Journal of Black Studies* 27, no. 4 (winter 2003): 236–245.

Madsen, Brigham D. *The Shoshoni Frontier and the Bear River Massacre.* Salt Lake City: University of Utah Press, 1985.

Malone, Michael P. *The Battle for Butte: Mining and Politics on the Northern Frontier, 1864–1906.* Seattle: University of Washington Press, 1981.

Marable, Manning. *Race, Reform, and Rebellion: The Second Reconstruction in Black America, 1945–1990.* Jackson: University Press of Mississippi, 1991.

Mather, R. E., and F. E. Boswell. *Vigilante Victims,* 1991a http://www .umwestern.edu/Academics/library/libroth/MHD/vigilantes/VV/cover.html (accessed March 15, 2006).

Mather, R. E., and F. E. Boswell. *Vigilante Victims.* "The Joint Hangings of the Virginia City Five," 1991b. http://www.umwestern.edu/Academics/library/ libroth/MHD/vigilantes/VV/joint5.html and "Pursuit of More Suspects" http://www.umwestern.edu/Academics/library/libroth/MHD/vigilantes/ VV/pursuit.html (accessed March 15, 2006).

Mather, R. E., and F. E. Boswell. *Vigilante Victims.* "Twenty-One Questions," 1991c. http://www.umwestern.edu/Academics/library/libroth/MHD/vigi lantes/VV/21quest.html (accessed March 15, 2006).

Matsumoto, Valerie. *Farming the Home Place: A Japanese American Community in California, 1919–1982.* Ithaca: Cornell University Press, 1993.

May, Dean L. *Three Frontiers: Family, Land and Society in the American West, 1850–1900.* Cambridge: Cambridge University Press, 1994.

McCunn, Ruthanne Lum. *Thousand Pieces of Gold.* Boston: Beacon Press, 1981.

McCunn, Ruthanne Lum. *Chinese American Portraits: Personal Histories 1828–1988.* Seattle: University of Washington Press, 1988.

Meadows, Anne, and Daniel Buck. "The Last Days of Butch & Sundance." *Wild West* 9, no. 5 (1997): 36–43.

Meier, Matt S., and Feliciano Ribera. *Mexican Americans/American Mexicans: From Conquistadors to Chicanos.* New York: Hill and Wang, 1993.

Meinig, Donald William. "Mormon Culture Region: Strategies and Patterns in the Geography of the American West." *Association of American Geographers* 5 (June 1965): 191–220.

Melmer, David. "Sand Creek Returned to Rightful Owners." *Indian Country Today,* May 6, 2002.

Meschter, Daniel Y. *Sweetwater Sunset: A History of the Lynching of James Averell and Ella Watson Near Independence Rock, Wyoming on July 20, 1889.* Wenatchee, WA: D. Y. Meschter, 1996.

Meyerson, Harvey. *Nature's Army: When Soldiers Fought for Yosemite.* Lawrence: University Press of Kansas, 2001.

Miller, Alfred Jacob. *The West of Alfred Jacob Miller.* Norman: University of Oklahoma Press, 1968.

Miller, Steward Alexander. *Papers* [1843]. Austin: Center for American History, University of Texas at Austin.

Millett, Kate. *Sexual Politics.* Garden City, NY: Doubleday, 1970.

Milner, Clyde A., Carol O'Connor, and Martha Sandweiss. *The Oxford History of the American West.* Oxford: Oxford University Press, 1996.

Montoya, Maria E. *Translating Property: The Maxwell Land Grant and the Conflict over Land in the American West, 1840–1900.* Berkeley: University of California Press, 2002.

Morrison, Samuel Eliot. *The Oxford History of the American People.* New York: Oxford University Press, 1965.

Morrissey, Katherine G. *Mental Territories: Mapping the Inland Empire.* Ithaca, NY: Cornell University Press, 1997.

Mulford, Ami Frank. *Fighting Indians in the Seventh U.S. Cavalry: Custer's Favorite Regiment.* 1972. Fairfield, WA: Ye Galleon Press, 1972.

"Mutual Messages." *Improvement Era* (April 1941): 239.

Myres, Sandra L. *Westering Women and the Frontier Experience, 1800–1915.* Albuquerque: University of New Mexico Press, 1982.

National Association for the Advancement of Colored People, Branch Files, NAACP Spokane, Washington, Manuscript Division, Library of Congress, Washington, D.C.

Nichols, Roger, ed. *Black Hawk's Autobiography.* Ames: Iowa State University Press, 1999.

Nolan, Frederick W. *The West of Billy the Kid.* Norman: University of Oklahoma Press, 1998.

Notarianni, Phillip F., ed. *Carbon County: Eastern Utah's Industrial Island.* Salt Lake City: Utah State Historical Society, 1981.

Oglesby, Richard Edward. *Manuel Lisa and the Opening of the Missouri Fur Trade.* Norman: University of Oklahoma Press, 1963.

Olson, James S., and Raymond Wilson. *Native Americans in the Twentieth Century.* Urbana: University of Illinois Press, 1984.

Oman, Kerry R. "Winter in the Rockies: Winter Quarters of the Mountain Man." *Montana: The Magazine of Western History* 52 (2002): 34–47.

Pai, Margaret K. *Dreams of Two Yi-Min.* Honolulu: University of Hawaii Press, 1989.

Painter, Nell Irvin. *Exodusters: Black Migration to Kansas after Reconstruction.* New York: W. W. Norton and Company, 1992.

Pascoe, Peggy. *Relations of Rescue: The Search for Female Moral Authority in the American West, 1874–1939.* New York: Oxford University Press, 1991.

Peck, Gunther. *Reinventing Free Labor: Padrones and Immigrant Workers in the North American West.* New York: Cambridge University Press, 2000.

Pence, Mary Lou. "Petticoat Rustler." *American History Illustrated* 17, no. 4 (1982): 52–57.

Peyer, Bernd C. *The Tutor'd Mind: Indian Missionary-Writers in Antebellum America.* Amherst: University of Massachusetts Press, 1997.

Phillips, Paul Chrisler. *The Fur Trade.* 2 vols. Norman: University of Oklahoma Press, 1961.

Plains Indian Ledger Art Digital Publishing Project, www.plainsledgerart.org.

Pomeroy, Earl. *The Pacific Slope: A History of California, Oregon, Washington, Idaho, Utah, and Nevada.* New York: Knopf, 1965.

Porter, Kenneth W. "Black Cowboys in the American West." In Monroe Lee Billington and Roger D. Hardaway, eds., *African Americans on the Western Frontier.* Boulder: University Press of Colorado, 1998.

Potter, Claire Bond. "'I'll Go the Limit and Then Some': Gun Molls, Desire, and Danger in the 1930s." *Feminist Studies* 21, no. 1 (1995): 41–66.

Prucha, Francis Paul. *Broadax and Bayonet: The Role of the United States Army in the Development of the Northwest, 1815–1860.* Madison: State Historical Society of Wisconsin, 1953.

Prucha, Francis Paul. *The Sword of the Republic; The United States Army on the Frontier, 1783–1846.* New York: MacMillan, 1968.

Prucha, Francis Paul, ed. *Documents of United States Indian Policy.* 3d ed. Lincoln: University of Nebraska Press, 2000.

Ravage, John W. *Black Pioneers: Images of the Black Experience on the North American Frontier.* Salt Lake City: University of Utah Press, 1997.

Redd, Charles. "As I Remember Him—My Father, L. H. Redd, Jr." *La Sal Reflections: A Redd Family Journal.* La Sal, UT: Charles Redd Foundation, 1984.

Ricards, Sherman L., and George M. Blackburn. "The Sydney Ducks: A Demographic Analysis." In E. H. Monkkonen, ed., *The Frontier.* Westport-London: Meckler, 1991.

Rice, Lawrence D. *The Negro in Texas, 1874–1900.* Baton Rouge: Louisiana State University Press, 1971.

Richards, Daniel B. Hill. *The Hill Family History.* Salt Lake City, UT: Magazine Printing Company, 1927.

Rickey, Don. *Forty Miles a Day on Beans and Hay: The Enlisted Soldier Fighting the Indian Wars 1863.* Norman: University of Oklahoma Press, 1963.

Riley, Glenda. *A Place to Grow: Women in the American West.* Arlington Heights, IL: Harlan Davidson, 1992.

Riley, Glenda. "Belle Starr." In R. W. Etulain and G. Riley, eds., *With Badges & Bullets: Lawmen & Outlaws in the Old West.* Golden, CO: Fulcrum Publishing, 1999.

Ring, Eugene. *Sketch of a Three Years Travell in South America, California and Mexico.* From "A Timeline of San Francisco History," 1849a. http://www.zpub.com/sf/history/sfh2.html (accessed March 15, 2006).

Ring, Eugene. From "Eugene Ring: The Voyage to California, Part 3," 1849b. http://www.mtdemocrat.com/columist/ring092898.shtml (accessed March 15, 2006).

Rohrbough Romero, Mary, Pierrette Hondagneu-Sotelo, and Vilma Ortiz, eds. *Challenging Fronteras: Structuring Latina and Latino Lives in the U.S.* New York: Routledge, 1997.

Ronda, James P. *Astoria and Empire.* Lincoln: University of Nebraska Press, 1990.

Rosenbaum, Robert J. *Mexicano Resistance in the Southwest: The Sacred Right of Self-Preservation.* Austin: University of Texas Press, 1981.

Ruiz, Vicki L. *Cannery Women, Cannery Lives: Mexican Women, Unionization, and the California Food Processing Industry, 1939–1950.* Albuquerque: University of New Mexico Press, 1987.

Ruiz, Vicki L. "Oral History and La Mujer: The Rosa Guerrero Story." In Vicki L. Ruiz and Susan Tiana, eds., *Women on the U.S.-Mexico Border: Responses to Change.* Boston: Allen and Unwin, 1987.

Ruiz, Vicki L. *From out of the Shadows: Mexican Women in Twentieth-Century America.* New York: Oxford University Press, 1999.

Saldívar-Hull, Sonia. *Feminism on the Border: Chicana Gender Politics and Literature.* Berkeley: University of California Press, 2000.

Sánchez, George J. *Becoming Mexican American: Ethnicity, Culture, and Identity in Chicano Los Angeles, 1900–1945.* New York: Oxford University Press, 1993.

Sandweiss, Martha. *Print the Legend: Photography and the American West.* New Haven, CT: Yale University Press, 2002.

Sarris, Greg. *Mabel McKay, Weaving the Dream.* Berkeley: University of California Press, 1994.

Savage, W. Sherman. *Blacks in the West.* Westport, CT: Greenwood Press, 1976.

Savage, W. Sherman. "Slavery in the West." In Monroe Lee Billington and Roger D. Hardaway, eds., *African Americans on the Western Frontier.* Boulder: University Press of Colorado, 1998.

Saxton, Alexander. *The Indispensable Enemy: Labor and the Anti-Chinese Movement in California.* Berkeley: University of California Press, 1971.

Scharff, Virginia. *Twenty Thousand Roads: Women, Movement, and the West.* Berkeley: University of California Press, 2003.

Schitz, Thomas F. "The Gros Ventres and the Upper Missouri Fur Trade, 1806–1835." *Annals of Wyoming* 56 (1984): 21–28.

Schlissel, Lilian. *Women's Diaries of the Westward Journey.* New York: Schocken Books, 1982.

Schmid, Calvin F., Charles E. Nobbe, and Arlene E. Mitchell. *Non-White Races: State of Washington.* Olympia: Washington State Planning and Community Affairs Council, 1968.

Schubert, Frank. *Buffalo Soldiers, the Braves, and the Brass: The Story of Fort Robinson, Nebraska.* Lincoln: University of Nebraska Press, 1995.

Schwantes, Carlos. *Railroad Signatures across the Pacific Northwest.* Seattle: University of Washington Press, 1993.

Schwantes, Carlos A. The *Pacific Northwest: An Interpretive History.* Lincoln: University of Nebraska Press, 1996.

Schwantes, Carlos. *Long Day's Journey: The Steamboat & Stagecoach Era in the Northern West.* Seattle: University of Washington Press, 1999.

Schweikart, Larry, and Lynn Pierson Doti. "From Hard Money to Branch Banking: California Banking in the Gold Rush Economy." In James J. Rawls and Richard J. Orsi, eds., *A Golden State: Mining and Economic Development of Gold Rush California.* Berkeley: University of California Press, 1999.

Scott, Douglas D., P. Willey, and Melissa A. Conner. *They Died with Custer: Soldiers' Bones form the Battle of the Little Bighorn.* Norman: University of Oklahoma Press, 1998.

Senkewicz, Robert M. *Vigilantes in Gold Rush San Francisco.* Stanford: Stanford University Press, 1985.

Seton, Ernest Thompson. *Wild Animals I Have Known* [1898]. Mineola, NY: Dover, 2000.

"Sexual Assault in Indian Country: Confronting Sexual Violence." Enola, PA: National Sexual Violence Resource Center, 2000.

Shah, Nayan. *Contagious Divides: Epidemics and Race in San Francisco's Chinatown.* Berkeley: University of California Press, 2001.

Shaw, Anna Moore. *A Pima Past.* Tucson: University of Arizona Press, 1974.

Sheridan, Thomas E. *Los Tucsonenses: The Mexican Community in Tucson, 1854–1941.* Tucson: University of Arizona Press, 1986.

Shirley, Glen. *Belle Starr and Her Times: The Literature, the Facts, and the Legends.* Norman: University of Oklahoma Press, 1982.

Smith, Andrea. *Conquest: Sexual Violence and American Indian Genocide.* Boston: South End Press, 2005.

Smith, Henry Nash. *Virgin Land: The American West as Symbol and Myth* [1950]. Cambridge: Harvard University Press, 2005.

Smith, Jedediah Strong. *Papers* [1826]. St. Louis: Missouri Historical Society.

Smith, Sherry. *The View from Officers' Row: Army Perceptions of Western Indians.* Tucson: University of Arizona Press, 1990.

Smith, Sherry, ed. *Sagebrush Soldier: Private William Earl Smith's View of the Sioux War of 1876.* 1989. Norman: University of Oklahoma Press, 1989.

Smith, Thomas, ed. *A Dose of Frontier Soldiering: The Memoirs of Corporal E.A. Bode.* Lincoln: University of Nebraska Press, 1994.

Soulé, Frank, and John H. Gihon. *The Annals of San Francisco.* San Francisco Genealogy, "Part Third, The Hounds," 1855. http://www.sfgenealogy.com/sf/history/hbann3–1.htm (accessed March 15, 2006).

Sprenger-Farley, Terri. "The Saga of Susie Raper." *Quarterly—Northeastern Nevada Historical Society* 96, no. 2 (1996): 63–67.

Standing Bear, Luther. *My People the Sioux.* Lincoln: University of Nebraska Press, 1975.

Standing Bear, Luther. *Land of the Spotted Eagle.* Lincoln: University of Nebraska Press, 1978.

Stannard, David E. *American Holocaust: The Conquest of the New World.* New York: Oxford University Press, 1992.

Stiles, T. J. *Jesse James: Last Rebel of the Civil War.* New York: Alfred A. Knopf, 2002.

Strunk, Mary. "'The Girl behind the Man behind the Gun': Woman Outlaws, Public Memory, and the Rise and Fall of Hoover's FBI." Ph.D. diss., University of Minnesota, 2003.

Takaki, Ronald. *Strangers from a Different Shore*: *A History of Asian Americans.* Rev. ed. Boston: Little, Brown and Company, 1998.

Tate, Michael. *The Frontier Army in the Settlement of the West.* Norman: University of Oklahoma Press, 1999.

Taylor, Joseph E. *Making Salmon: An Environmental History of the Northwest Fisheries Crisis.* Seattle: University of Washington Press, 1999.

Taylor, Quintard. "Migration of Blacks and Resulting Discriminatory Practices in Washington State between 1940 and 1950." *Western Journal of Black Studies* (1977). v2 n1 p65–71 Mar 1978.

Taylor, Quintard. *The Forging of a Black Community: Seattle's Central District from 1870 through the Civil Rights Era.* Seattle: University of Washington Press, 1994.

Taylor, Quintard Taylor. *In Search of the Racial Frontier: African Americans in the American West, 1528–1990.* New York: Norton, 1998.

Thompson, Jerry D. *Vaqueros in Blue and Gray.* Austin, TX: Presidial Press, 1977.

Thompson, Jerry D. *Mexican Texans in the Union Army.* El Paso: Texas Western Press, 1986.

Thwaites, Ruben, ed. *Original Journals of the Lewis and Clarks Expedition.* New York: Antiquarian Press, 1959.

Tindall, George Brown, and David E. Shi. *America: A Narrative History.* New York: Norton, 1989.

Unruh, John D., Jr. *The Plains Across: The Overland Emigrants and the Trans-Mississippi West, 1840–60.* Urbana: University of Illinois Press, 1979.

U.S. Senate Committee on Indian Affairs. *Memorial of the Brotherhood of North American Indians*, 62d Cong., 2d sess., S. Doc. 489, 1912.

U.S. Senate Select Committee on Indian Affairs. *Wounded Knee Memorial and Historic Site: Hearings on S. 2869 and H.R. 4660*, 101st Cong., 2d sess., 1990.

Utley, Robert. *Frontiersmen in Blue: The United States Army and the Indian, 1848–1865.* New York: Macmillan, 1967.

Utley, Robert. *Frontier Regulars: The United States Army and the Indian, 1866–1891.* New York: Macmillan, 1973.

Utley, Robert. *Cavalier in Buckskin: George Armstrong Custer and the Western Military Frontier.* Norman: University of Oklahoma Press, 1988.

Utley, Robert M. *A Life Wild and Perilous: Mountain Men and the Paths to the Pacific.* New York: Henry Holt and Company, 1997.

Valerio-Jiménez, Omar S. "Indios Bárbaros, Divorcées, and Flocks of Vampires: Identity and Nation on the Rio Grande, 1749–1894." Ph.D. diss., University of California, Los Angeles, 2001.

Vogt, Evon Z., and Thomas F. O'Dea. "A Comparative Study of the Role of Values in Social Action in Two Southwestern Communities." *American Sociological Review* 18 (December 1953): 645–654.

Walker, Cheryl. *Indian Nation: Native American Literature and Nineteenth-Century Nationalisms.* Durham: Duke University Press, 1997.

Walker, Henry P., ed. "The Reluctant Corporal: The Autobiography of William Bladen Jett." *Journal of Arizona History* 12, no. 1 (1971): 13.

Webb, James Josiah. *Adventures in the Santa Fé Trade, 1844–1847.* Edited by Ralph P. Bieber. Glendale, CA: Arthur H. Clark Company, 1931.

Weber, David J. *New Spain's Far Northern Frontier: Essays on Spain in the American West, 1540–1821.* Dallas, TX: Southern Methodist University Press, 1979.

Weber, David J. *The Mexican Frontier, 1821–1846: The American Southwest under Mexico.* Albuquerque: University of New Mexico Press, 1982.

Weber, David J. *The Spanish Frontier in North America.* New Haven, CT: Yale University Press, 1992.

Welch, James. *Killing Custer: The Battle of the Little Bighorn and the Fate of the Plains Indians.* New York: Penguin Books, 1994.

Welter, Barbara. "The Cult of True Womanhood: 1820–1860." *American Quarterly* 18, no. 2, part 1 (summer 1966): 151–174.

White, Bruce M. "A Skilled Game of Exchange: Ojibway Fur Trade Protocol." *Minnesota History* 50 (1987): 229–240.

White, Bruce M. "The Woman Who Married a Beaver: Trade Patterns and Gender Roles in the Ojibwa Fur Trade." *Ethnohistory* 46 (1999): 109–147.

White, David A., comp. *News of the Plains and Rockies, 1803–1865.* 2 vols. Spokane, WA: Arthur H. Clark Company, 1996.

White, Richard. "Outlaw Gangs of the Middle Border: American Social Bandits." *Western Historical Quarterly* 12, no. 4 (1981): 387–408.

White, Richard. *"It's Your Misfortune and None of My Own": A New History of the American West.* Norman: University of Oklahoma Press, 1993.

White, Richard. "Animals and Enterprise." In Clyde A. Milner II, et al., eds., *The Oxford History of the American West.* New York: Oxford University Press, 1994.

White, Richard. "Information, Markets, and Corruption: Transcontinental Railroads in the Gilded Age." *Journal of American History* 90 (2003): 19–43.

Whitman, Walt. *Collected Poems.* New York: Penguin, 1977.

Wilber, Charles Dana. *The Great Valleys and Prairies of Nebraska and the Northwest.* Omaha, NE: Daily Republican Print, 1881.

Wilson, Pamela. "Confronting the 'Indian Problem': Media Discourses of Race, Ethnicity, Nation, and Empire in 1950s America." In Sasha Torres, ed., *Living Color: Race and Television in the United States.* Durham: Duke University Press, 1998.

Wilson, Paul. Memorandum, Files *re Brown vs. Topeka Board of Education* (1954), 3–4, Kansas Historical Society.

Winnemucca, Sarah. *Life among the Paiutes: Their Wrongs and Claims.* Reno: University of Nevada Press, 1994.

Wister, Owen. *The Virginian, A Horseman of the Plains.* New York: Grosset and Dunlap, 1902.

Wood, Larry. "Cora Hubbard: 'The Second Belle Starr.'" *Wild West* 17 (2004): 12–15. http://www.historynet.com/we/blcorahubbard/ (accessed March 15, 2006).

Woods, Randall B., "Integration, Exclusion, or Segregation? The 'Color Line' in Kansas, 1878–1900." *The Western Historical Quarterly*, Vol. 14, No. 2 (Apr. 1983): 181–198.

Wooster, Robert. *The Military and United States Indian Policy, 1865–1903.* New Haven, CT: Yale University Press, 1988.

Worster, Donald. *An Unsettled Country: Changing Landscapes of the American West.* Albuquerque: University of New Mexico Press, 1993.

Wrobel, David. *Promised Lands: Promotion, Memory, and the Creation of the American West.* Lawrence: University Press of Kansas, 2002.

Wynn, Neil A. *The Afro-American and the Second World War.* New York: Homes and Meier, 1993.

Yung, Judy. *Unbound Feet: A Social History of Chinese Women in San Francisco.* Berkeley: University of California Press, 1995.

Yung, Judy. *Unbound Voices: A Documentary History of Chinese Women in San Francisco.* Berkeley: University of California Press, 1999.

Index